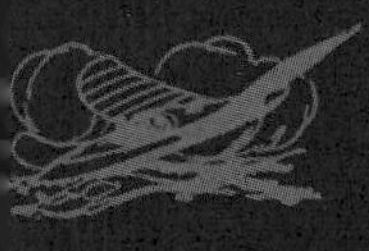

E

ng Bat-Boats:

.) Maginnis Motor,

Hargreaves Motor,

argreaves (Radium
der.

n on the South
ockabout boats,
ation. *Griselda*
racing vans and
n smooth water
The others do
e recommended

ng B. B. *Tarpon*
, 60 ft.; Long-
udder, new this
nom. Maginnis
Pond generator.
nd treble rein-
lfourd rockered
ns, giving maxi-
ft.
held seven feet
d touch.
and family Bats

Hinks's Moderator

¶ Monorail overhead starter for family and private planes up to twenty-five foot over all

Absolutely Safe

Hinks & Co., Birmingham

As worn by Her Majesty's Imperial Expeditionary Forces.

ZERO GRAVITY WELLINGTON BOOTS.

Stay light on your feet even in the swamps of equatorial Venus.
For list of stockists please contact Mordings, Piccadilly, London.

STEAMPOWERED

CARPET TRAVEL

Adventure to Baghdad, oasis of oriental splendour, jewel of the desert and mecca of princes and paupers. Seats up to four.
Air conditioned.
Write for brochure.
Yahya Abdul Al-Drubi,
Outer Zone, London.

MISCELL

WANTS

REQUIRED IMMEDIATELY, FOR East Africa, a thoroughly competent Plane and Dirigible Driver, acquainted with Petrol Radium and Helium motors and generators. Low-level work only, but must understand heavy-weight digs.

MOSSAMEDES TRANSPORT ASSOC.
84 Palestine Buildings, E. C.

MAN WANTED — DIG DRIVER for Southern Alps with Saharan summer trips. High levels, high speed, high wages.

Apply M. STONEY
Hotel San Stefano, Monte Carlo.

FAMILY DIRIGIBLE. A COMPETENT, steady man wanted for slow speed, low level Tangye dirigible. No night work, no sea trips. Must be member of the Church of England, and make himself useful in the garden.

M. R.,
The Rectory, Gray's Barton, Wilts.

COMMERCIAL DIG. CENTRAL and Southern Europe. A smart, active man for a L. M. T. Dig. Night work only. Headquarters London and Cairo. A linguist preferred.

BAGMAN
Charing Cross Hotel, W. C. (urgent.)

FOR SALE — A BARGAIN — SINGLE Plane, narrow-gauge vans, Pinke motor. Restayed this autumn. Hansen air-kit, 38 in. chest, 15½ collar. Can be seen by appointment.

N. 2650. This office.

1s. 6d.; cloth, 2s. 6d. Ready Jan. 15.
ARCTIC AEROPLANINO. Siemens and Galt. Cloth, bds. 8s. 6d.
LAVALLE'S HEART OF THE CYCLONE, with supplementary charts. 4s. 6d.
RIMINGTON'S PITFALLS IN THE AIR, and Table of Comparative Densities. 3s. 6d.
ANGELO'S DESERT IN A DIRIGIBLE. New edition, revised. 5s. 9d.
VAUGHAN'S PLANE RACING IN CALM AND STORM. 2s. 6d.
VAUGHAN'S HINTS TO THE AIR-MATEUR. 1s.
HOFMAN'S LAWS OF LIFT AND VELOCITY. With diagrams, 3s. 6d.
DE VITRE'S THEORY OF SHIFTING BALLAST IN DIRIGIBLES. 2s. 6d.
SANGER'S WEATHERS OF THE WORLD. 4s.
SANGER'S TEMPERATURES AT HIGH ALTITUDES. 4s.
HAWKIN'S FOG AND HOW TO AVOID IT. 3s.
VAN ZUYLAN'S SECONDARY EFFECTS OF THUNDERSTORMS. 4s. 6d.
DAHLGREN'S AIR CURRENTS AND EPIDEMIC DISEASES. 5s. 6d.
REDMAYNE'S DISEASE AND THE BAROMETER. 7s. 6d.
WALTON'S HEALTH RESORTS OF THE GOBI AND SHAMO. 3s. 6d.
WALTON'S THE POLE AND PULMONARY COMPLAINTS. 7s. 6d.
MUTLOW'S HIGH LEVEL BACTERIOLOGY. 7s. 6d.
HALLIWELL'S ILLUMINATED STAR MAP, with clockwork attachment, giving apparent motion of heavens, boxed, complete with clamps for binnacle, 36 inch size, only £2. 2. 0. (Invaluable for night work.) With A.B.C. certificate, £3. 10s. 0d.
Zalinski's Standard Works.
PASSES OF THE HIMALAYAS, 5s.
PASSES OF THE SIERRAS, 5s.
PASSES OF THE ROCKIES, 5s.
PASSES OF THE URALS, 5s.
The four boxed, limp cloth, with charts, 15s.
GRAY'S AIR CURRENTS IN MOUNTAIN GORGES, 7s. 6d.

A. C. BELT & SON, READING

U

VEYO

ng mar
heart with
Numerous
but Lightv
to avoid
Gives a bo
makes him

Sold by
Dealers ac
booklet. N

H
Largest R

SPARES

ACCESSORIES AND SPARES

N WRIGHT & OLDIS

ESTABLISHED 1824

cessories and Spares

-dials automatically
inated face).

eet £2 10 0
rtificate £3 11 0
s toned to
elt-driven
. . £6 8 0
to A.B.C.
any case,
. £3 3 0

ors, pithing-irons,
and mooring ropes,
tions.

um or stamped steel,
single-action detach-
with one motion of
ps.

by size) Nos. 00 to
and fog-bombs in
pal clubs (boxed).
£2 17 6
d) £1 11 6

Spare generators guaranteed to lifting power marked on cover (prices according to power).

Wind-noses for dirigibles — Pegamoid, cane-stiffened, lacquered cane or aluminum and flux for winter work.

Smoke-ring cannon for hail storms, swivel mounted, bow or stern.

Propeller blades: metal, tungsten backed; papier-mache; wire stiffened; ribbed Xylonite (Nickson's patent); all razor-edged (price by pitch and diameter).

Compressed steel bow-screws for winter work.

Fused Ruby or Commercial Mineral Co. bearings and collars. Agate-mounted thrust-blocks up to 4 inch.

Magniac's bow-rudders — (Lavalle's patent grooving).

Wove steel beltings for outboard motors (non-magnetic).

Radium batteries, all powers to 150 h.p. (in pairs).

Helium batteries, all powers to 300 h. p. (tandem).

Stun'sle brakes worked from upper or lower platform.

Direct plunge-brakes worked from lower platform only, loaded silk or fibre, wind-tight.

Catalogues free throughout the Planet

OTHER WORLD'S TAXIDERMY

Serving your taxidermy needs since 1860.
"YOU KILL IT, WE FILL IT"
From Moon Wabbles to Martian Desert Gimps we can mount your galactic hunting trophies.
105 Essex Road, London N.

At Last! As developed by Mr. Herbert George Wells

THE ACME INVISIBILITY TONIIC.

Send S. A. E. for your free sample to
Miss S. J. Wheatley, Bromley Science Laboratories, Kent

STRENGTH OF CHARACTER

Are you plagued by salesmen, panhandlers, or women?
Inflate your strength of character with our mechanical enhancement device and just say "NO, by Jove!"

Send half a crown to
Jay Strongman Esq.,
32 Indianola, the Colonies.

SAFET

Flickers

Hig

"H
F

¶ Ha
res
in price
Pure p
shoulde
Unequa
Our tre
plus ult
Gas-bu
conduc
fitting
ated ta

Hanse

The
chevi
from

Flickers

STEAMPUNK

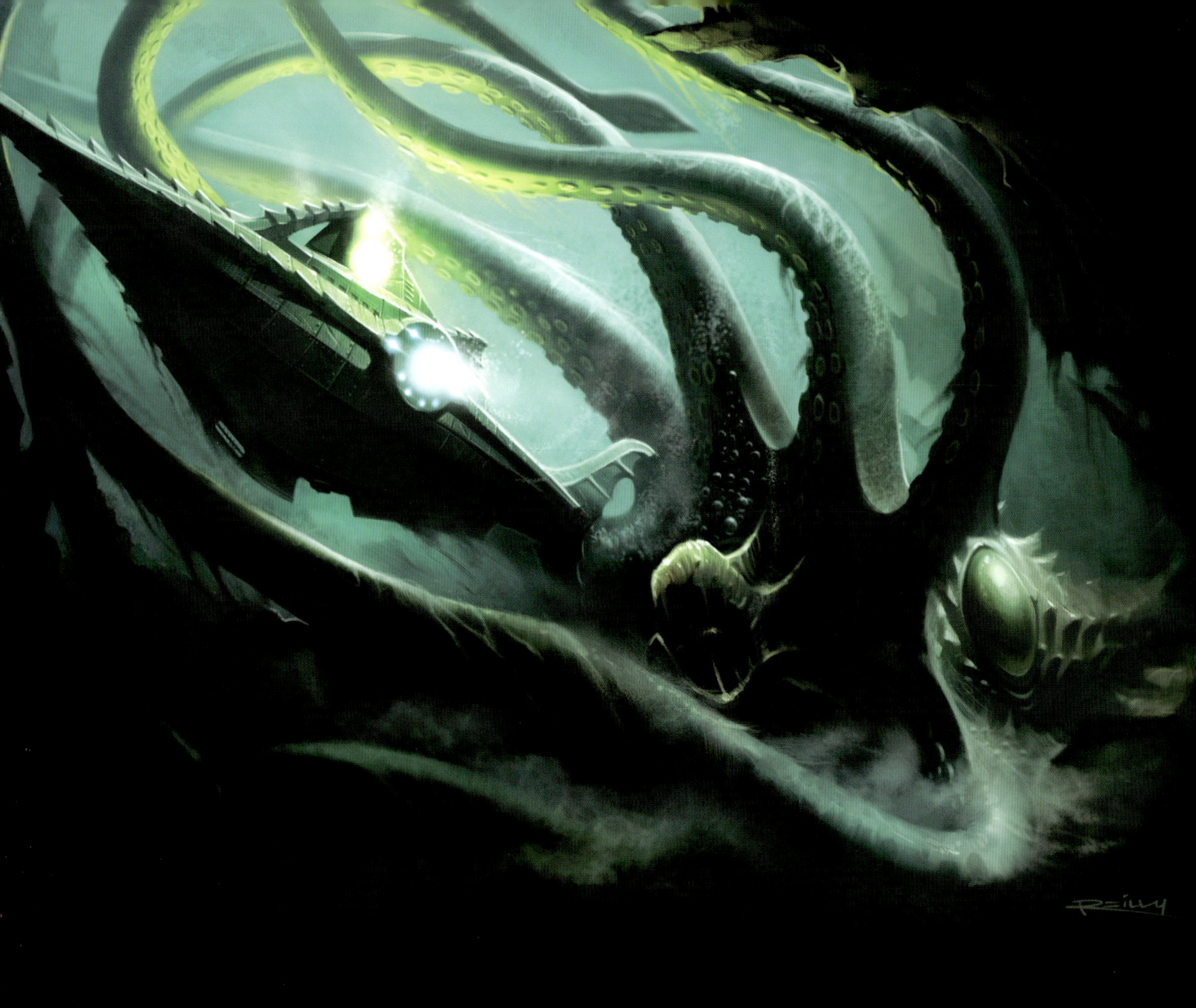

Published in 2011 by Korero Books LLP, 32 Great Sutton Street, London, EC1V 0NB, UK

www.korerobooks.co.uk

ISBN 978-1-907621031

Printed in China

Above: Patrick Reilly, *The Deep*, 2005.

STEAMPUNK

The Art of Victorian Futurism

Jay Strongman

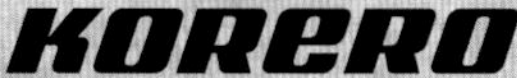

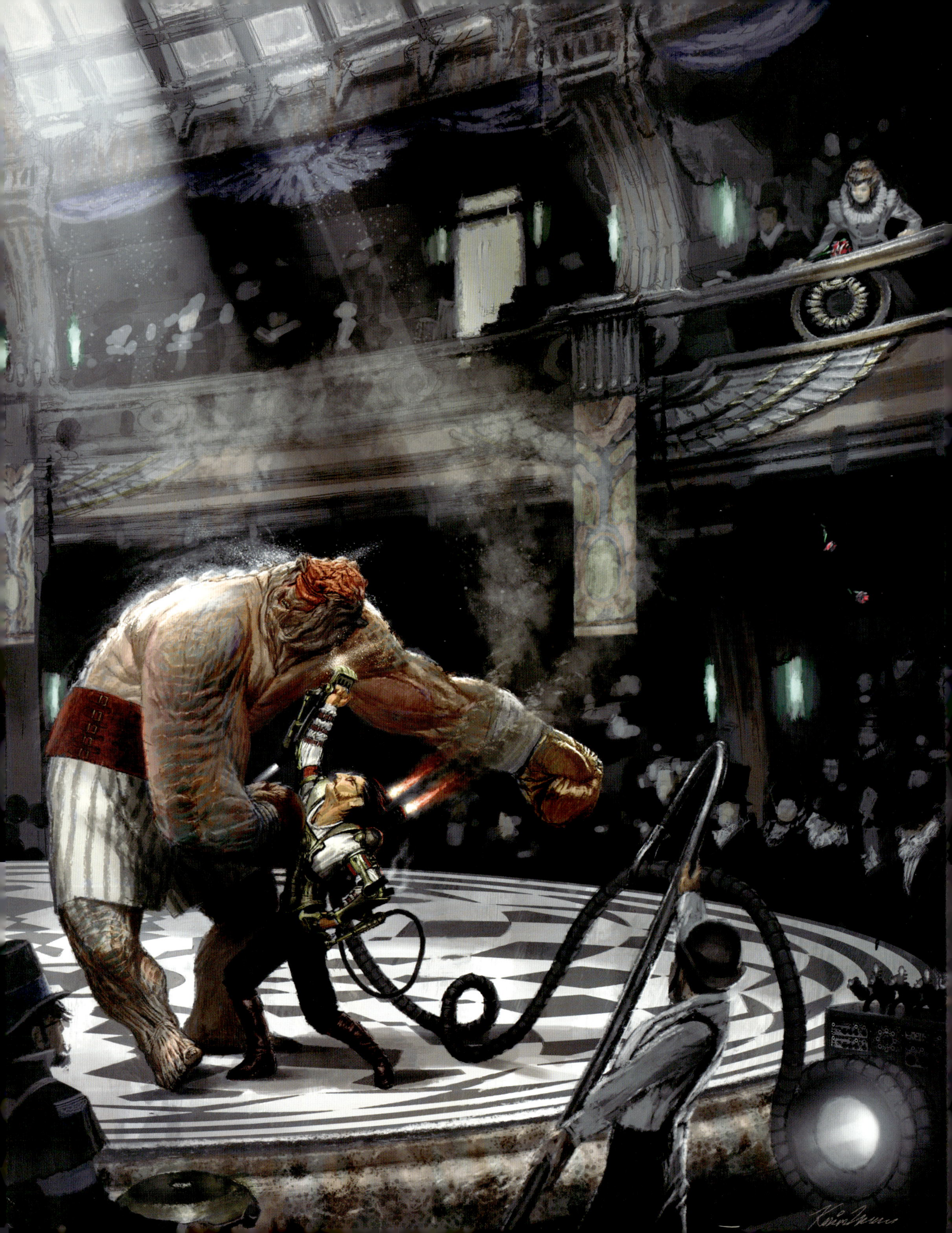

CONTENTS

Left: Kevin Mowrer, *The Fight Against Goliath*, 2010. Pencil and digital.

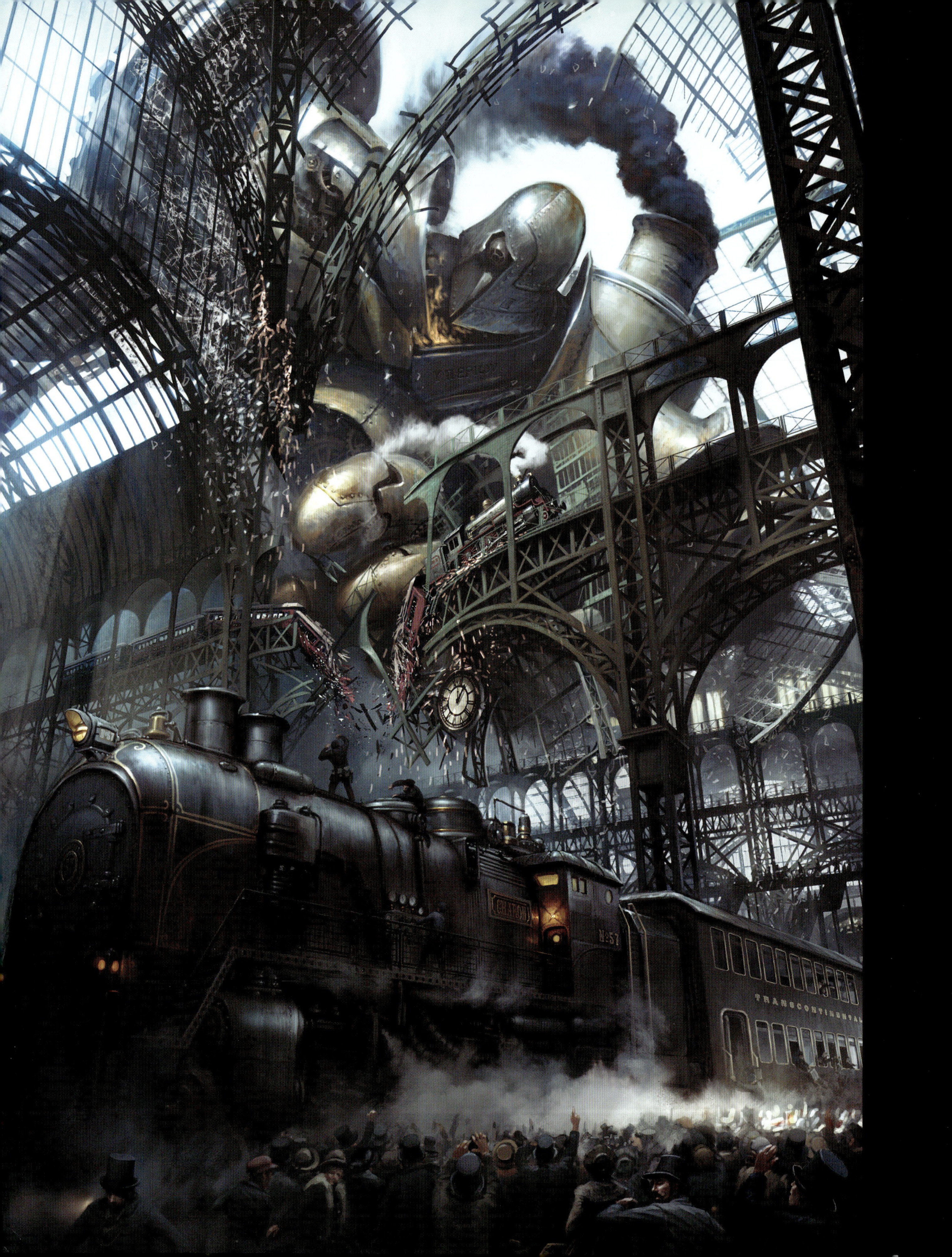
TRANSCONTINENTAL

"Steampunk lives in the reincarnated past of shadows and the forgotten. We behold the mystery of possibility; we seek reminiscence about a more elegant age of adventure that never really was; we liberate the machine from technocracy and re-create her from desire and dreams. Steampunk 'overthrows the factory of consciousness by beautiful entropy'; the living dream of progress that guides us in the exploration of otherwise unknowable territories."

The Gatehouse blog

INTRODUCTION

In just over thirty years, the word 'Steampunk' has gone from being a generic name, used to describe a loosely linked group of Science Fiction novels, to describing a global movement – a movement that now encompasses fashion, design, art, music, literature and more. During that time the label has come to mean different things to different people. For many it's a celebration of Victorian technology and aesthetics, to others it's about a past that almost was and a future that could have been. It's about a fictional place in time and space where Victorian and Edwardian elegance collide with gothic horror and modern science – a sepia-tinted world where *My Fair Lady* meets *The Terminator*. It encompasses the romance of flickering gas lamps, foggy streets bustling with horse-drawn hansom cabs, men dressed in frock coats and top hats, women in bustles and corsets; but it also juxtaposes those images with a world of steam-powered robots and airships, of analogue computers, of time travellers and of parallel universes. It's about recapturing the wonder and excitement of the *fin de siècle* novels of H. G. Wells and the *Voyages Extraordinaires* of Jules Verne, but also about acknowledging the grime, soot, squalor and chaos of the 'dark satanic mills' of the Industrial Revolution.

Like Neo-Victorianism, which preceded and then paralleled it, Steampunk is in some ways a form of escapism – a yearning for a simpler time, a period in which there was little doubt that the future, with technology's help, was going to get better and brighter. With hindsight this was an age of relative innocence when the threat of extinction by nuclear or biological weapons simply did not exist. Indeed, none in the Victorian era would really believe that the world as they knew it could come to a sudden, violent end – a luxury which few of us can now share. There's a yearning too, for a time when the environmental devastation of the 20th Century

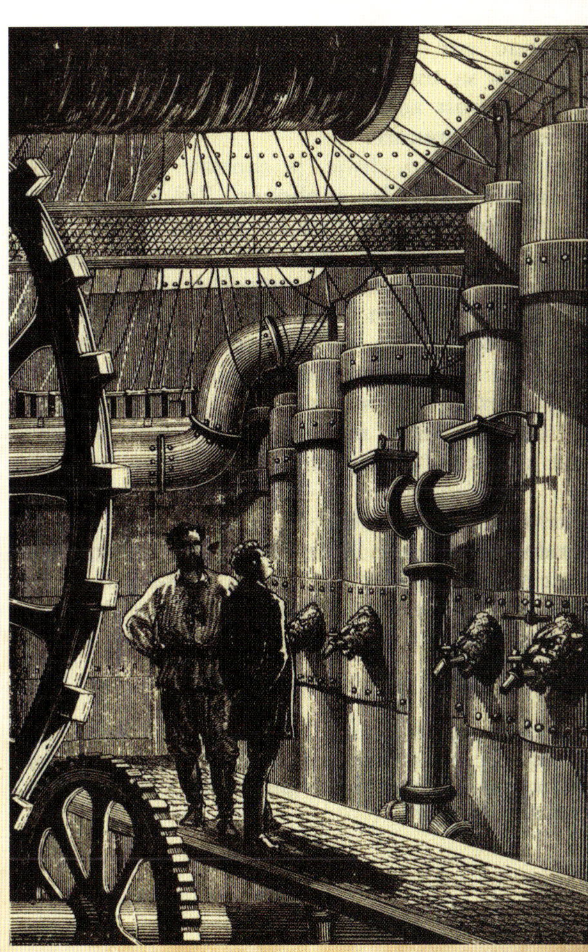

Above: Prof. Aronnax examining the bowels of the Nautilus, from Jules Verne's *20,000 Lieues Sous les Mers*. Illustration by Alphonse de Neuville and Édouard Riou, from the Hetzel edition of 1871.

Left: Marcin Jakubowski, *Titanomachy: Fall of the Hyperion*, 2009. Digital artwork.

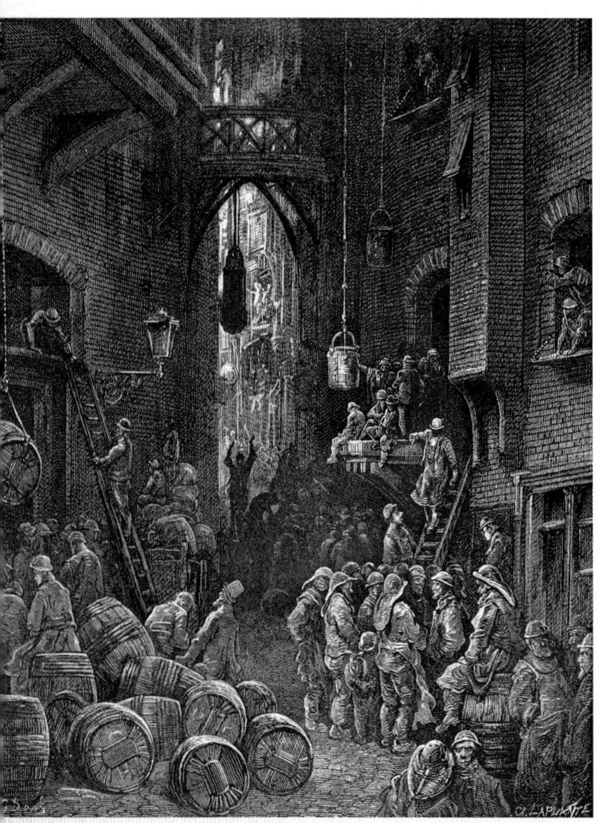

Above: Gustave Doré, *A Riverside Street*, 1872. Illustration for *London, A Pilgrimage,* engraved by Charles Laplante. Doré's gothic view of London, which included searing images of steam engines crossing viaducts over dark and mean back-to-back housing, and threatening narrow alleys lined with steep buildings (as well as magnificent images of gothic masterpieces such as Westminster Abbey), irritated contemporaries, but have provided fertile inspiration for contemporary Steampunk artists, not least Kevin Mowrer.

Right: Kevin Mowrer, *Steampunk Slums of Travaille*, 2011. Mowrer is an artist, writer and designer who has rethought and remodelled the Frankenstein myth, updating it for the 21st Century by drawing inspiration from Steampunk. His ambitious illustrated tale is called *Frahnknshtyne* and was developed via a series of richly detailed blog posts showing the work in progress. The slums of Travaille are the setting for much of the action in the story, where the wealthy and powerful come to find illegal 'entertainment' to "break the monotony of their preternaturally long lives."

hadn't yet occurred, before the mechanised slaughter of two World Wars, the Nazi Holocaust and the organised genocides of Stalin, Mao and Pol Pot. There is also in Steampunk a nostalgic hunger for a period in recent history when much of the world, for the West, was still an unexplored, exotic mystery waiting to be discovered and space travel was just a fanciful dream. But, more significantly, (and this is where we put the 'Steam' into Steampunk) there is also a longing for an age in which machines were awe-inspiring steam-powered engines and magnificent clockwork mechanisms of gleaming brass, polished wood and shining steel – so unlike today's bland boxes of micro-chips, grey plastic and hidden, integrated circuits. One has only to be lucky enough to witness the raw power and grandeur of a restored steam locomotive, belching smoke as it pulls out of a railway station, and compare it with the characterless, box-like utilitarianism of a modern electric suburban train, to see the allure of the steam age.

But, truth be told, it isn't only the relentless changes and technological advances of the Victorian period that makes it so interesting for those looking back from the other side of the 20th Century. The late Victorian era is, in so many ways, tantalisingly similar to our own. The average 21st Century inhabitant of London, New York or Paris would have little problem understanding or being understood by the 1890 inhabitants of those cities (or by the characters of Jules Verne's or H. G. Wells' novels) and would find those societies having many parallels with their own. Just as today society is being changed at a furious pace by modern technology, so too was 19th Century society – as urbanisation and industrialisation fast replaced the slow rural life of previous centuries. In purely materialistic terms too, we of the present would find much to recognize in the 1890s, such as trains, banks, department stores, newspapers, public libraries, street-lighting and electricity. We also have a surfeit of photographs, diaries, novels, textbooks and early film to show us how our Victorian antecedents lived and thought. Anyone reading *Diary Of A Nobody* by George & Weedon Grossmith or Jerome K. Jerome's *Three Men In A Boat* can see how similar the concerns, humour and aspirations of that period are to our own.

But the attraction also lies in the fact that so much is different today from the experiences of our Victorian ancestors. There was no universal suffrage, no television or radio, no air travel, no computers or Internet, no motorways, no surveillance cameras, and no Twitter. Those too, were the days when foreign travel – let alone air travel – for the average man in the street was non-existent unless he was in his nation's armed forces. In fact, the grandeur of the British Empire and its military might is another part of the Steampunk equation. The biggest Empire in human history and the colonial apparatus that maintained its global might holds a deep fascination for a large swathe of the movement. And there is something about the idea of a tiny island nation exporting its language and customs to the far-flung corners of the world that fires the imagination.

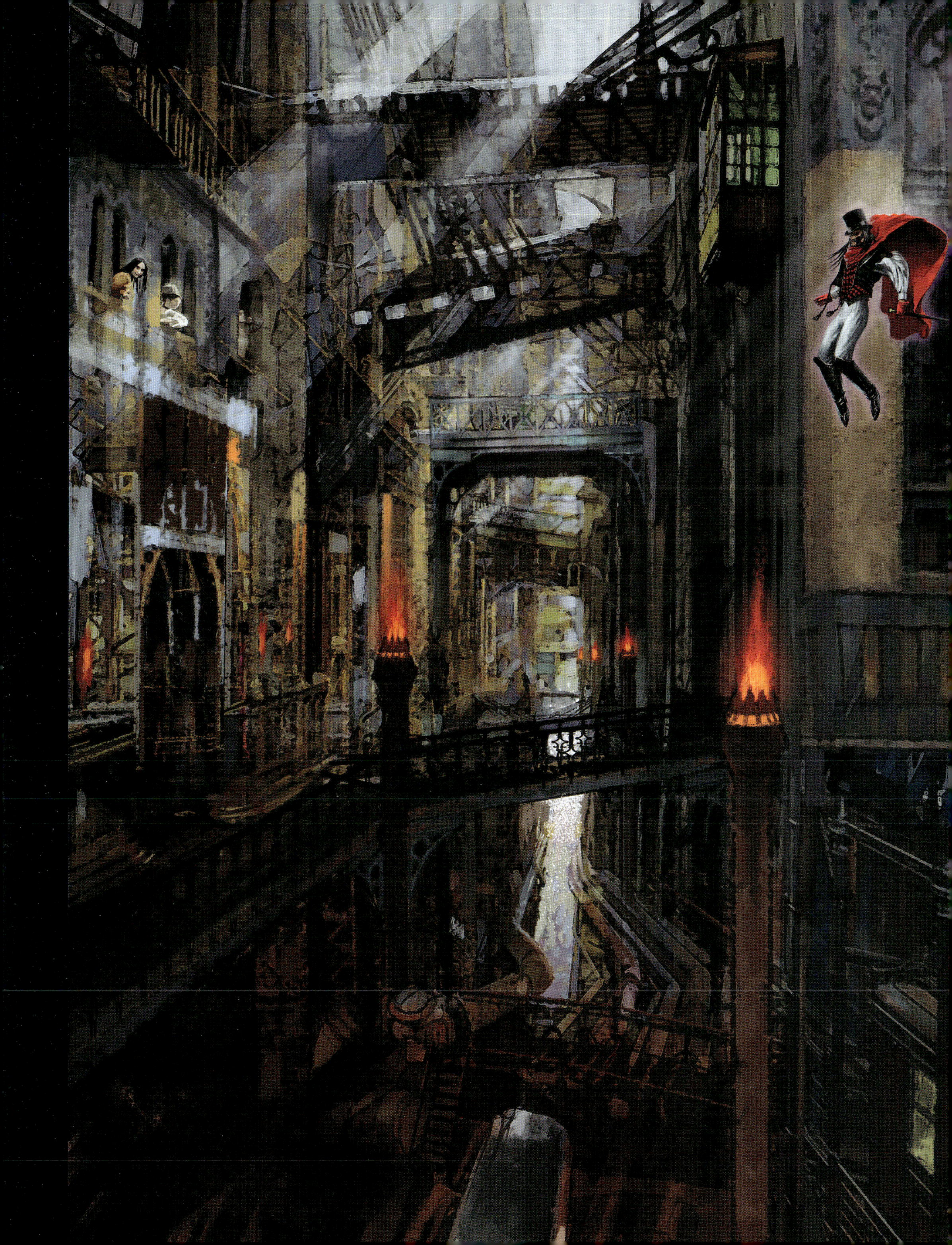

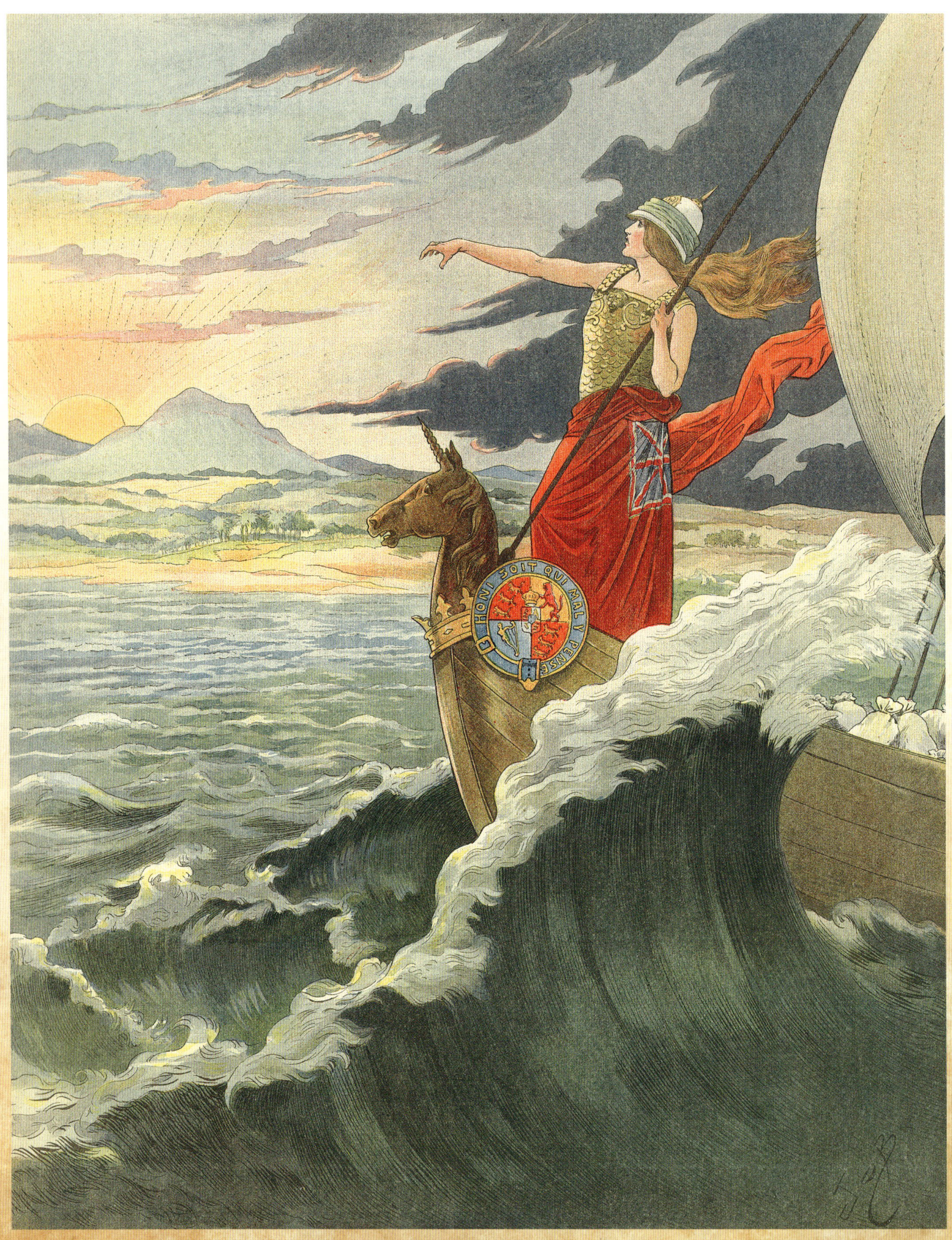
HONI SOIT QUI MAL Y PENSE

More than a few Steampunk novels deal with the 'what-might-have-been' possibilities of the British military possessing fantastic airships and modern weapons of mass destruction, and many Steampunkers enjoy donning the pith helmets and uniforms of Her Majesty's Imperial Britain (albeit often updated with the requisite addition of clockwork prosthetic arms or brass goggles).

But while some find the days of Empire fascinating and accept colonialism and imperialism as facts of life and just the way things were at the time, others are determined to challenge these past assumptions. The thinking is that by confronting the transgressions of the past, we can learn how to change the politics and socio-economics of the present. Others argue that the 'punk' in Steampunk should stand for something and that the movement should follow a more anarchic approach by emphasising Steampunk's rejection of 21st Century consumerism and the bland mass-produced material goods our modern corporate culture bombards us with. This argument ties in to widespread global concerns about sustainability; the fact that this part of the movement is interested in D.I.Y. and recycling is something that has attracted growing attention. By recycling discarded garments and objects, Steampunk fashions and art pieces are an integral part of this process. Steampunk author Gail Carriger catches the mood nicely in this quote from the *Steampunk II (Steampunk Reloaded)* anthology, *"There is a pervading sense of political upheaval and economic chaos right now, a sense that the world is crumbling around us... Steampunk is quietly coping with this impending doom by busily tying itself to the green movement, reusing old parts for new beauty."*

Leaving aside the movement's part in a new green consciousness, what cannot be denied is that Steampunk as an art movement is all about old-fashioned craftsmanship. Many of the artists featured in this book had developed a love of building clockwork mechanisms and machines of beauty (if not functionality) before they'd even heard the term Steampunk. In a world where digital gadgets perform so many tasks, and where people are so disconnected from the technologies they use every day, the idea of actually building things that have visible mechanisms took on a global resonance. Across the world, from Japan to America, from Australia to Europe, craftsmen, artists and tinkerers happily got their hands dirty putting together cogs and gears to recapture the spirit of do-it-yourself that had seemed to be fading from society. Steampunk art was thus uniquely forged in the workshop glow of soldering irons and welding tools, in the idea that people could and should build things for themselves. With the engineers and the D.I.Y. brigade in the vanguard, other forms of art quickly followed – from custom-made items of clothing, to paintings and animation. But the inspiration for all of it is almost always the throbbing, steam-powered heart of Victorian technology and the world it created. Thanks to the great advances achieved over those years, the future, to the Victorian mind, had

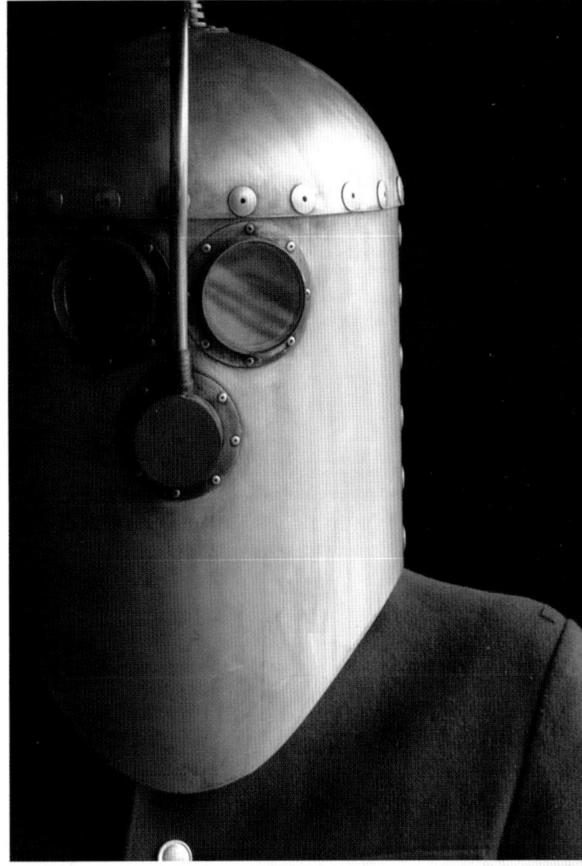

Above: Jeff de Boer, *Steampunk Gasmask*, 2003. Aluminium, brass and steel.

Left: Job (J. Onfray de Brevillé), *Rule Britannia*. Illustration for *Les Chants Nationaux* (circa 1900).

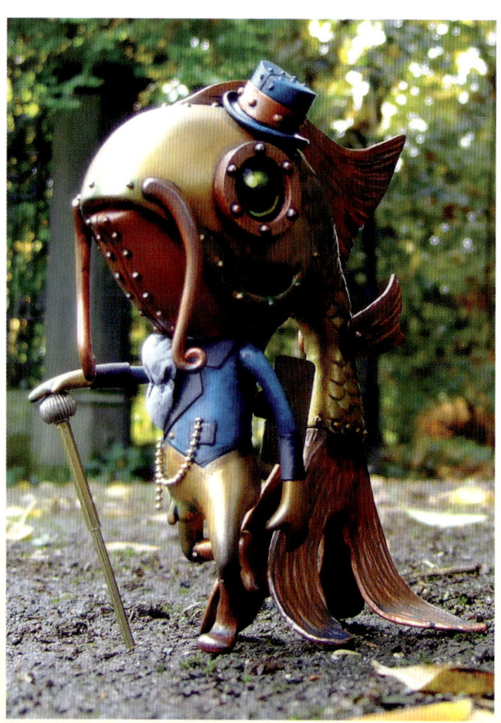

a seemingly infinite number of possibilities opened up to it. Steampunk not only relishes those possibilities, and attempts to capture them in word and art, but also tries to imagine the innovations of our present and our future as if the Victorians themselves were designing and manufacturing them. In essence then, this movement is fuelled by a love of Neo-Victorianism mixed with a healthy dose of 21st Century post-punk attitude and an embracing of the aesthetics of do-it-yourself technology.

So Steampunk may conjure up visions of guys and girls at Comic-Con dressed in Victorian finery and carrying 19th Century styled ray-guns made of polished wood, iron and brass. Others may imagine a solitary craftsman hard at work transforming (or 'modding') his laptop into a period-friendly spectacle of leather and mahogany. Others still will think of the comic books of Alan Moore's *League Of Extraordinary Gentlemen,* or of the dozens of novels that transform the Victorian era into one of battling steam robots and giant airships. The movement includes all those things and many, many more. So, while Steampunk can be about wearing brass goggles, fancy waistcoats, patent leather boots, lace corsets and dreams of steam-powered airships, it is also about the sheer joy of painstakingly building a clockwork mechanism that a Victorian craftsman would have been proud of. And while it can be just about speculating on what might have been, for others it's about taking the 1890s as a starting point for deconstructing and changing the politics and socio-economic realities of the present. But, whatever the reasons, romantics, goths, punks, geeks, fashionistas, artists and engineers have all embraced this fast growing culture: a culture that now stands on the verge of mainstream recognition.

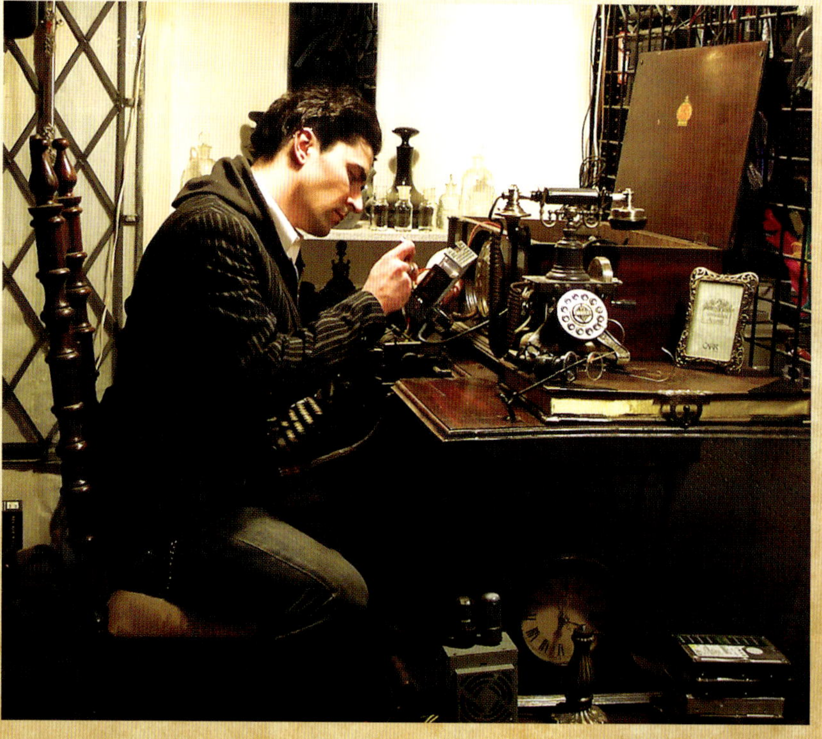

Above: Doktor A, *The Odorous Fish Man: Abhorrent Piscine Denizen of the Deep,* 2009. 6" (15.2 cm) tall. Customised Koibito toy, vinyl, rubber, lead, polymer clay, ABS, and found objects.

Right: Richard 'Doc' Nagy a.k.a. Datamancer. One of the pioneers of Steampunk design, Richard has been 'modding' modern computers for years, turning functional everyday objects into fully functioning works of art. With his motto "I don't just build products, I create heirlooms", Richard creates beautifully crafted keyboards, monitors and laptops that would look at home in a Victorian gentleman's study.

Far Right: Kevin Mowrer, *Gendarme, Inspector Verité.*

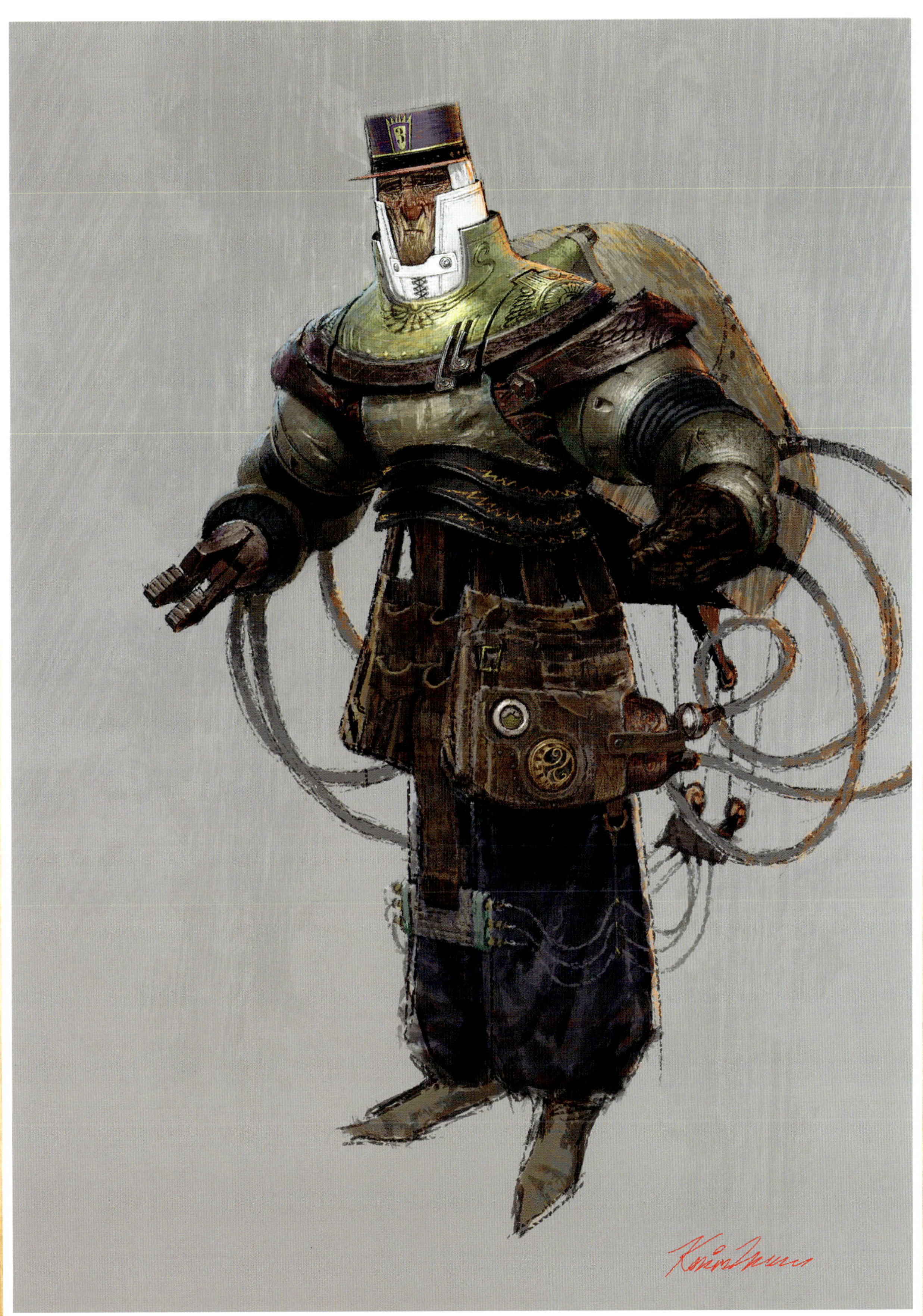

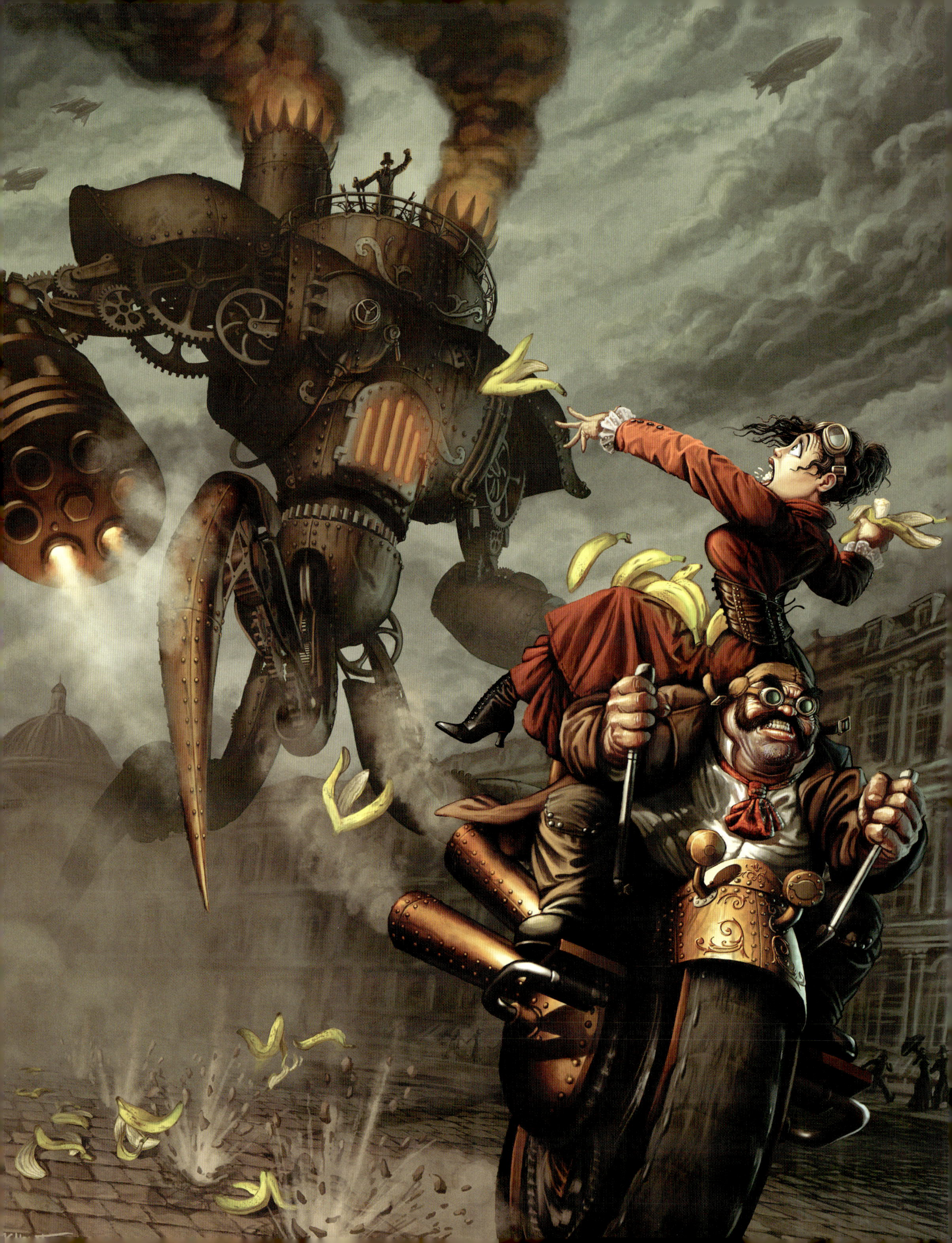

THE RISE OF STEAM

As a contemporary subculture, Steampunk is rare in that it first started life on the printed page, as a literary genre. That genre, an offshoot of Science Fiction, was inspired by a plethora of influences including the gothic horrors of Mary Shelley and Bram Stoker, the works of Edgar Allan Poe, and the novels of H. G. Wells and Jules Verne. It was the rapid industrialisation of Western society, and an accompanying increase in a literate and educated middle class, that led to the unprecedented explosion of novel writing in the latter half of the 19th Century. With the world changing at an ever faster pace as new frontiers were opened up by colonisation and innovation, the boundaries of human imagination were explored by authors excited at the monumental changes they saw happening around them. For a while science and technology were out-running creative imagination but, by the 1880s, that all started to change.

If the last years of the 19th Century saw the blooming of Science Fiction literature as we now know it (called Scientific Romances at the time of their writing), Mary Shelley's *Frankenstein* was the first seed of the genre. Originally published in 1818, *Frankenstein; or, The Modern Prometheus* (to give it its full title) gave the world its first Sci-fi creature and created the blueprint for the 'mad scientist' cliché of modern popular culture.

Although lying firmly in both the Gothic and Romantic novel traditions, *Frankenstein* broke the mould of both, by warning that man's growing scientific knowledge could threaten and ultimately upset the natural order. Shelley's bleak tale of a scientist playing God by creating life (or, more precisely, reanimating it) and then being destroyed by that monster, was a concept that caught the public's imagination at a time of growing unease with the rapid pace of technological innovation. Just a few years before the novel was published there were widespread riots across northern England

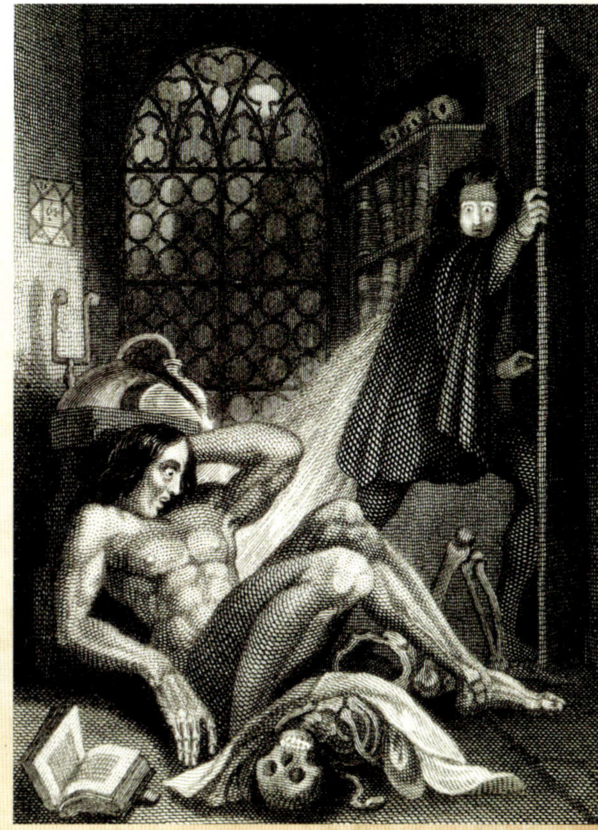

Above: Theodor Von Holst, frontispiece for the 1831 edition of *Frankenstein; or, The Modern Prometheus*.

Left: Michael Dashow, *Escape Plan B*, 2009. Digital artwork, Photoshop and 3DS Max.

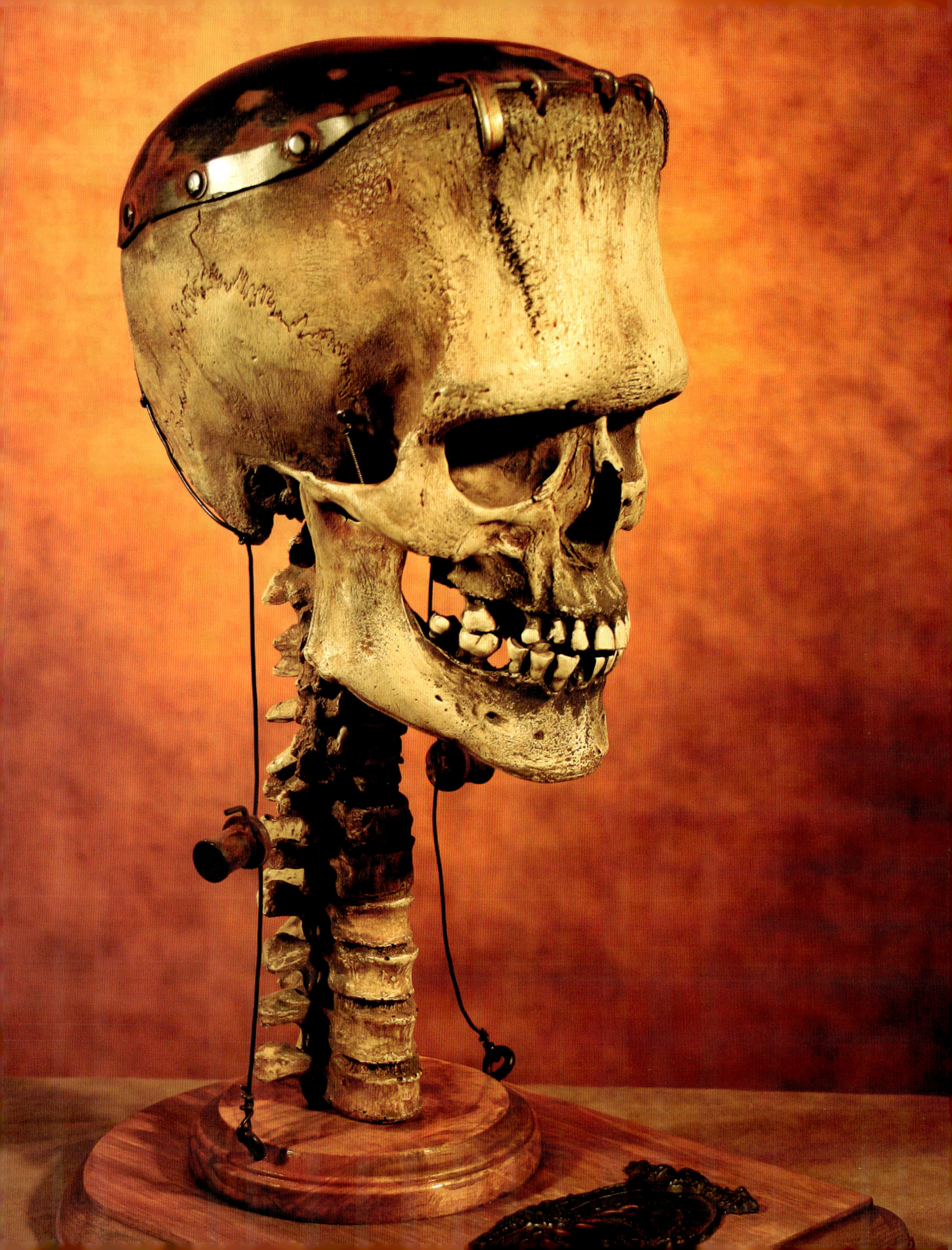

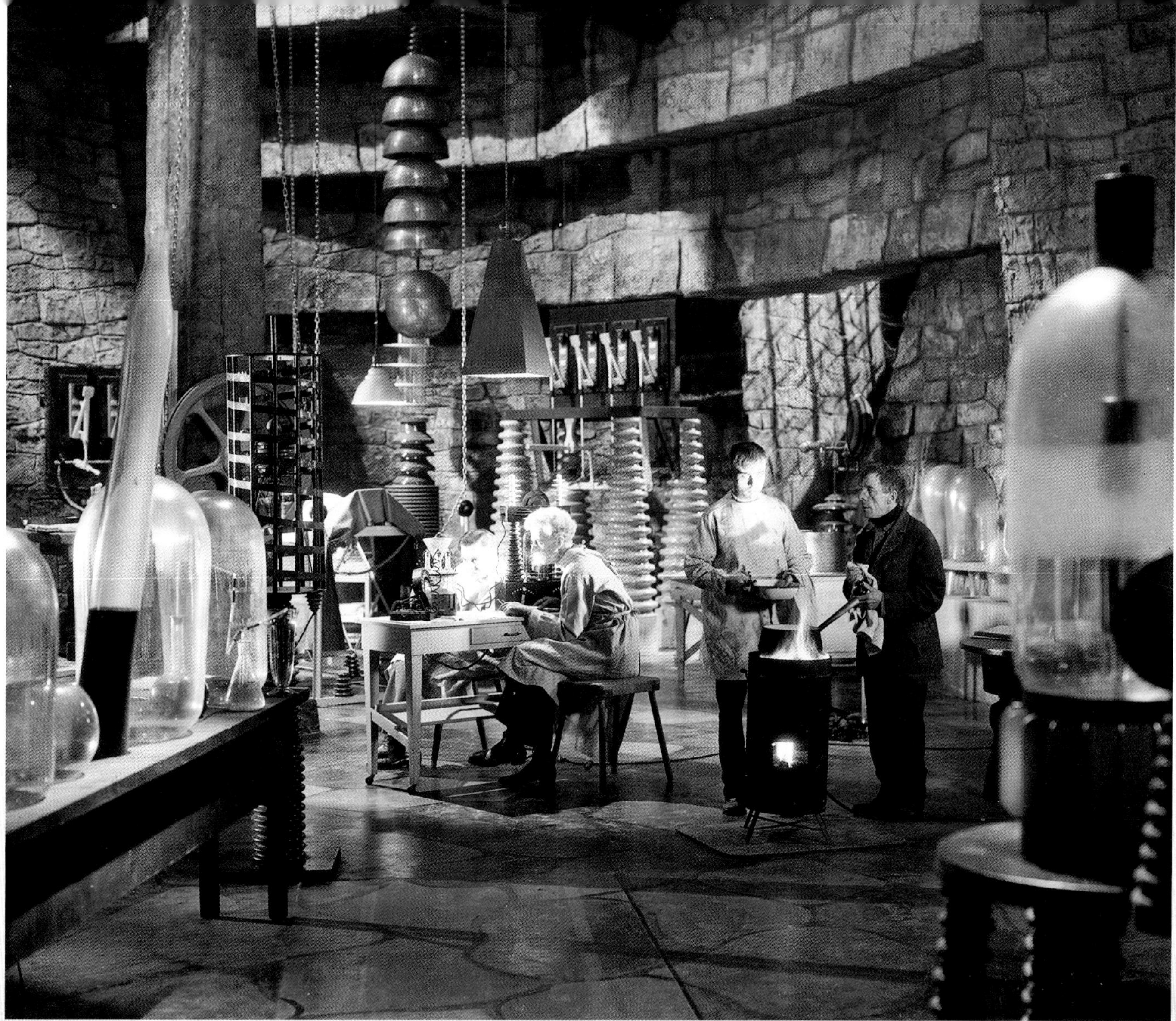

by handloom weavers (called Luddites after their supposed leader, one Ned Ludd) who saw the mechanisation of the textile industry as a threat to their skilled labour. Although the Luddites had failed to halt change (the riots were brutally suppressed in 1812 by the British government), by the time the novel had its third and most popular edition published, in 1831, there were still many who responded to *Frankenstein* as a cautionary tale about the dangers of mechanisation and new technology. The Luddites had smashed mechanised looms in a vain attempt to destroy the man-made 'monsters' making them redundant, while Dr. Frankenstein vainly attempted to destroy his own self-created monster. Indeed, the book has struck such a chord with subsequent generations (thanks mainly to the numerous cinematic adaptations made in the 20th Century) that the expression 'Frankenstein's monster' is often still used to describe any out-of-control scientific experiment.

Although not Steampunk *per se*, *Frankenstein* deservedly has its place in the movement's lexicon and has served as inspiration for both art and

Above: The interior of Dr. Frankenstein's laboratory as seen in the film *Bride of Frankenstein*, in which Dr. Frankenstein and his monster both turn out to be alive, not killed as previously believed. When mad scientist, Dr. Pretorius, kidnaps Dr. Frankenstein's wife, Dr. Frankenstein agrees to help him create a new creature, to be the female companion of the orginal monster. Directed by James Whale in 1935.

Left: Thomas Kuebler, *The Skull of Frankenstein*, 2006. "Discovered amongst several other skeletons in a burned out castle in Darmstadt, Germany this strange skull is all that remains of what is believed to be the creation of Dr. Victor Frankenstein. While somewhat crude in its design, the function of the skull was to enable repeated surgeries as well as to act as a conductor for electricity. A rudimentary iron skull cap is riveted to heavily calcified bone growth and a bulbous forehead. Wired from the skull down to the base, are the two neck electroconductors. Measuring 15 inches from top to base, the skull is the size of that of a large adult male."

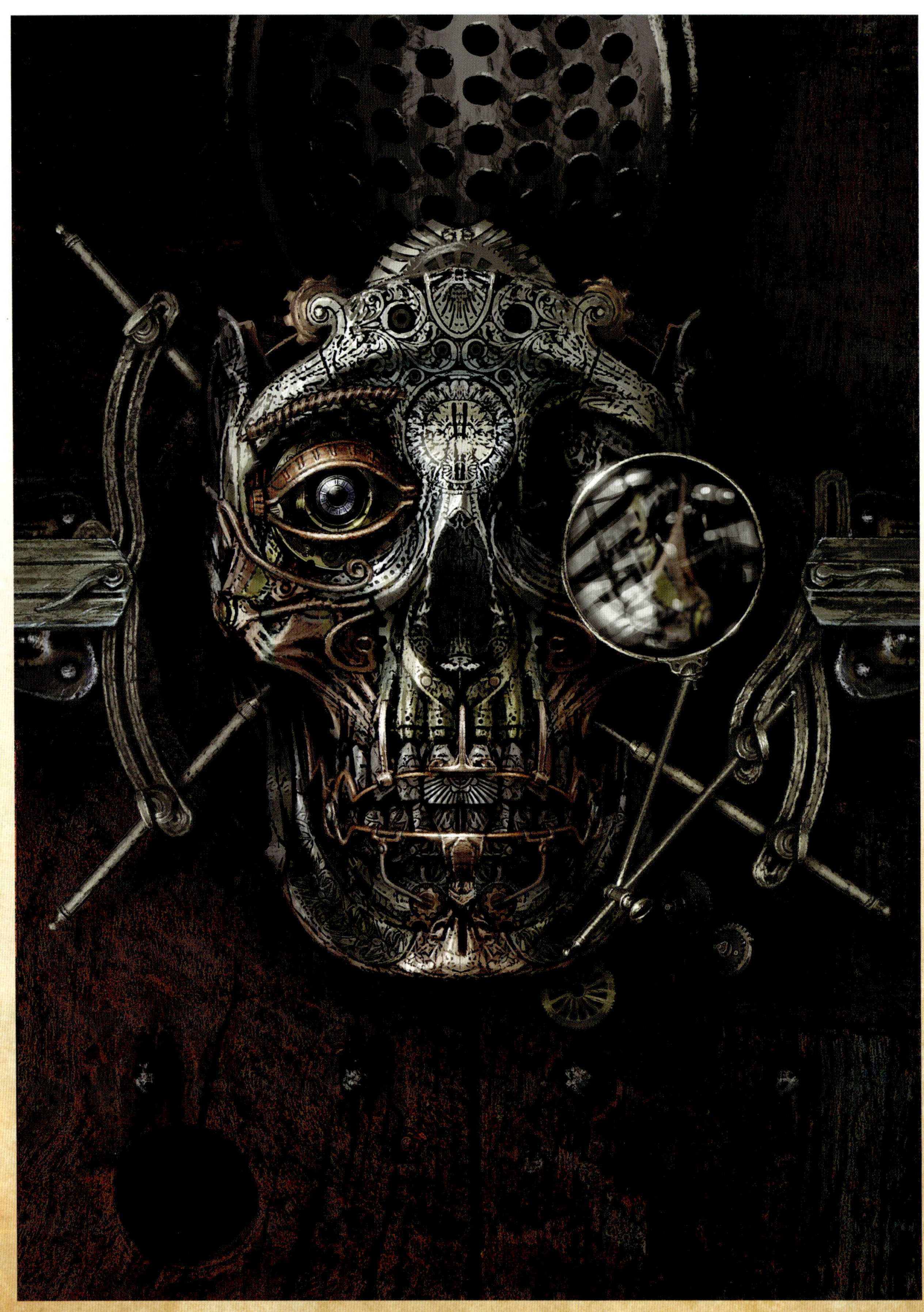

literature over recent years. Two striking works inspired by Shelley's creature are Thomas Scott Kuebler's wonderfully evocative *Skull of Frankenstein* sculpture and Kevin Mowrer's *Frahnknshtyne*. Relating directly to the 1930s movie image of the monster, but looking as though it was created at the time of the original novel, Kuebler's piece manages to capture the gothic horror of Shelley's book, whilst the iron skullcap and electroconductors provide the requisite Steampunk elements. Taking a less conventional look at Frankenstein is artist and writer Kevin Mowrer who is working on an illustrated story that updates and redefines the tale for a 21st Century audience. In doing so, Mowrer has placed his tale firmly in a Steampunk setting as his illustrations show.

Despite the success of Shelley's novel, it took several more decades of fast-paced industrialisation and scientific advancement before the real heyday of Victorian Science Fiction began. And, of course, that heyday was inspired by the sheer magnitude of the transformation that was to sweep Europe and America. The mid to late 19th Century was an age of extraordinary experimentation, when science, industry and technology were driving massive changes in Western society. Innovators, engineers and scientists such as Michael Faraday (magnetic induction and electromagnetic rotary devices), Isambard Kingdom Brunel (bridges and steam ships), Charles Babbage (mechanical computers), Ada Lovelace (writer and arguably the world's first computer programmer), Thomas Edison (the phonograph and the light bulb), Nikola Tesla (electromagnetism) and hundreds of other extraordinary men and a few remarkable women were expanding the boundaries of human knowledge and creating a new world – a world we all now inhabit. This was an era when it seemed that anything might be possible, that mankind's only limit was the human imagination; in addition, the appearance of numerous Science Fiction publications during this period was testament to the way that limit was being pushed.

An early entry into the field and an important component of the Steampunk legacy were the American mass-produced 'dime novels' of the late 19th and early 20th centuries. Aimed mainly at teenage boys, these publications usually featured a young inventor using his wits and his inventions to thwart America's enemies, advance progress and make himself rich. These Edisonades as they are now dubbed (after Thomas Edison) tapped into the growing popular interest in engineering and inventions then sweeping the United States and Europe. The first of the Edisonades was *The Huge Hunter, or The Steam Man Of The Prairies* by Edward S. Ellis (published in 1868); the Steam Man of the title was a steam-powered 'robot' built by a hunch-backed teenager who used it to explore the Wild West, dig up gold and fight 'Injuns'. This simple formula was repeated time and again in subsequent dime novels and the Steam Man has resurfaced in several contemporary US Steampunk short stories and in the guise of the illustrated history of a steam-robot called Boilerplate.

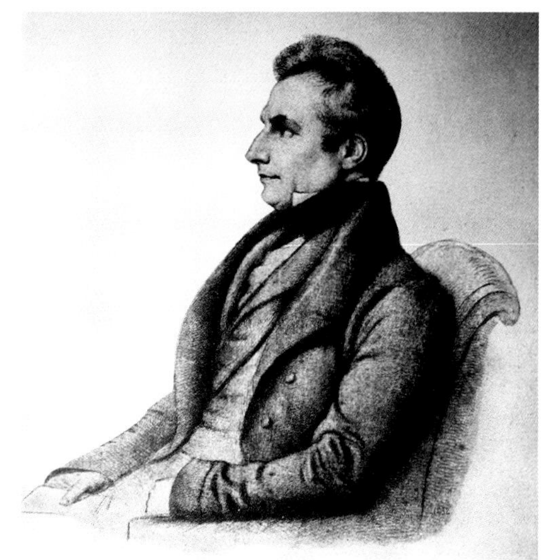

Above: British computing pioneer Charles Babbage (1791-1871). Babbage conceived the idea of an advanced calculating machine to calculate and print mathematical tables in 1812, as he wanted to eliminate all the sources of inaccuracy associated with compiling mathematical tables by hand.

Left: Kevin Mowrer, *Clockwork Skull,* 2010. For Mowrer's *Frahnknshtyne* project: "If sheer artistic application of will and mad obsession alone could bring the device to life, then Doctor Frahnknshtyne's marvelous clockwork-being would have sprung from the table the moment its form was completed. Its hand-crafted beauty and subtlety of construction await only two final elements. The power source, its heart, that will prove to the world that the terrible commerce of Aether can at last come to an end, and a brain that will live forever within this being of perfect craftmanship."

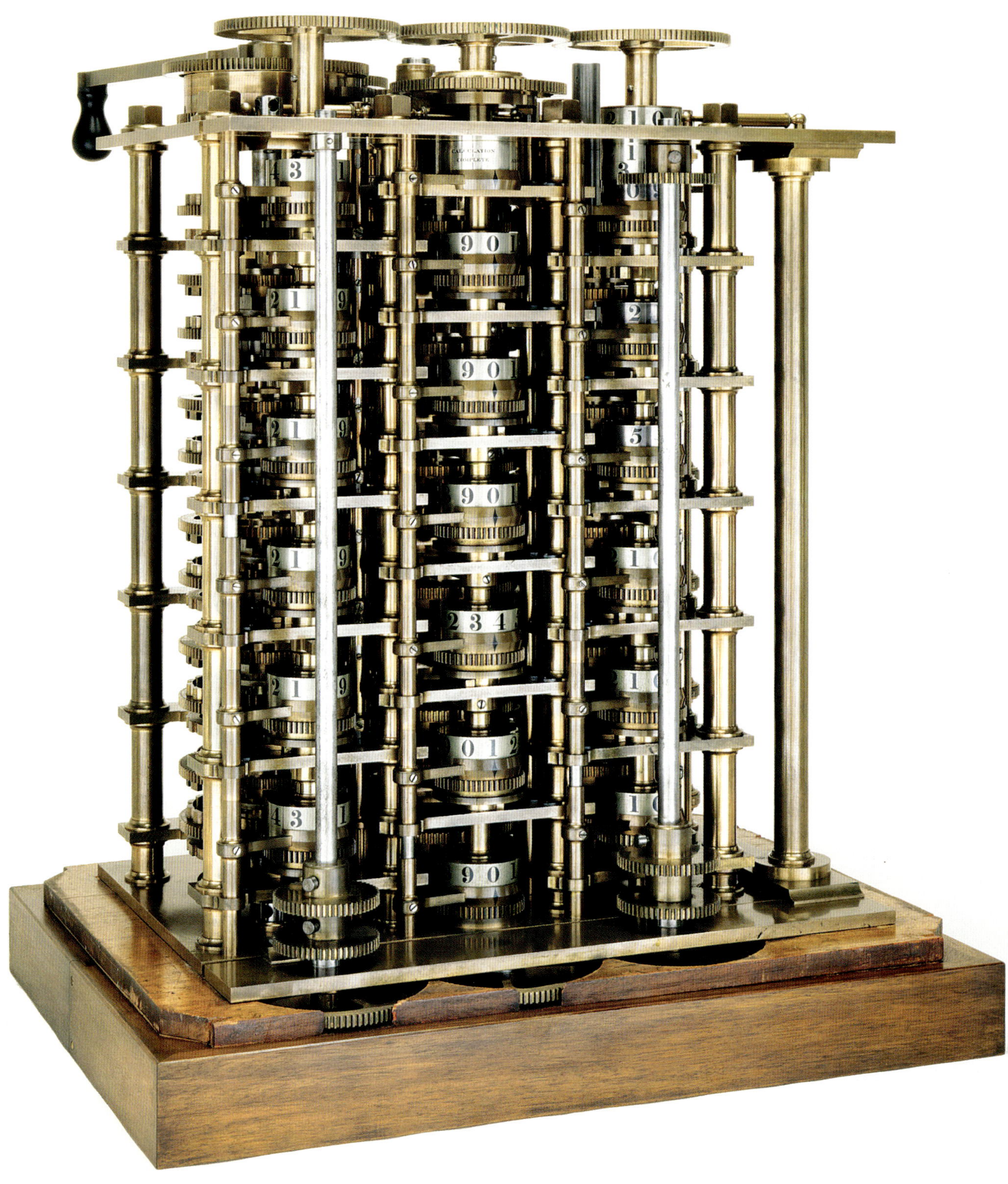

Above: Charles Babbage's *Difference Engine No 1*, 1824-1832. The engine was first conceived in 1824 and assembled in 1832 by Joseph Clement, a skilled toolmaker and draughtsman. It was a decimal digital machine – the value of a number represented by the positions of toothed wheels marked with decimal numbers.

Right: Front cover from an 1880s issue of the *The Huge Hunter; or, The Steam Man Of The Prairies* by Edward S. Ellis. First published in the late 1860s, Ellis' story about a steam-powered robot was so popular with its American boy readership that it was reprinted several times and led to a string of imitators. Later dubbed 'Edisonades' after inventor Thomas Edison, these tales of mechanical men in the Wild West would resurface as inspiration for American Steampunk writers in the 21st Century.

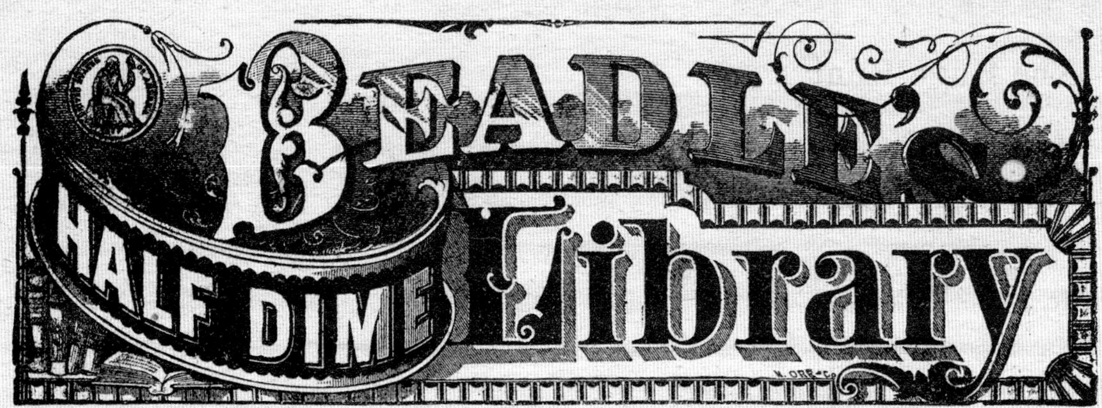

$2.50 a year. Entered at the Post Office at New York, N. Y., at Second Class Mail Rates. Copyrighted in 1882 by BEADLE AND ADAMS. October 3, 1882.

Vol. XI. Single Number. PUBLISHED WEEKLY BY BEADLE AND ADAMS, No. 98 WILLIAM STREET, NEW YORK. Price, 5 Cents. No. 271.

THE HUGE HUNTER; or, THE STEAM MAN OF THE PRAIRIES.

BY EDWARD S. ELLIS.

AUTHOR OF "THE BOY MINERS," "SETH JONES," "BILL BIDDON," ETC., ETC., ETC.

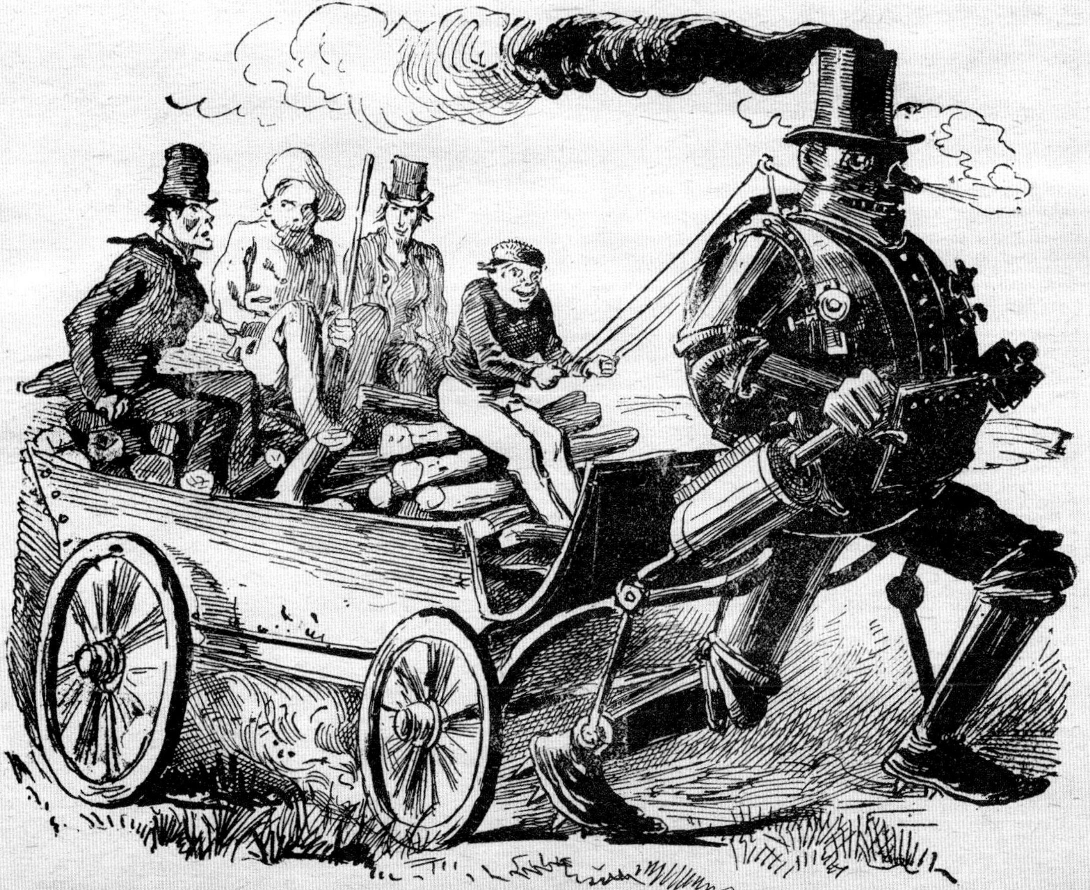

"BEGORRAH, BUT IT'S THE OULD DIVIL, HITCHED TO HIS THROTTIN' WAGING, WID HIS OULD WIFE HOWLDING THE REINS!" EXCLAIMED MICKEY.

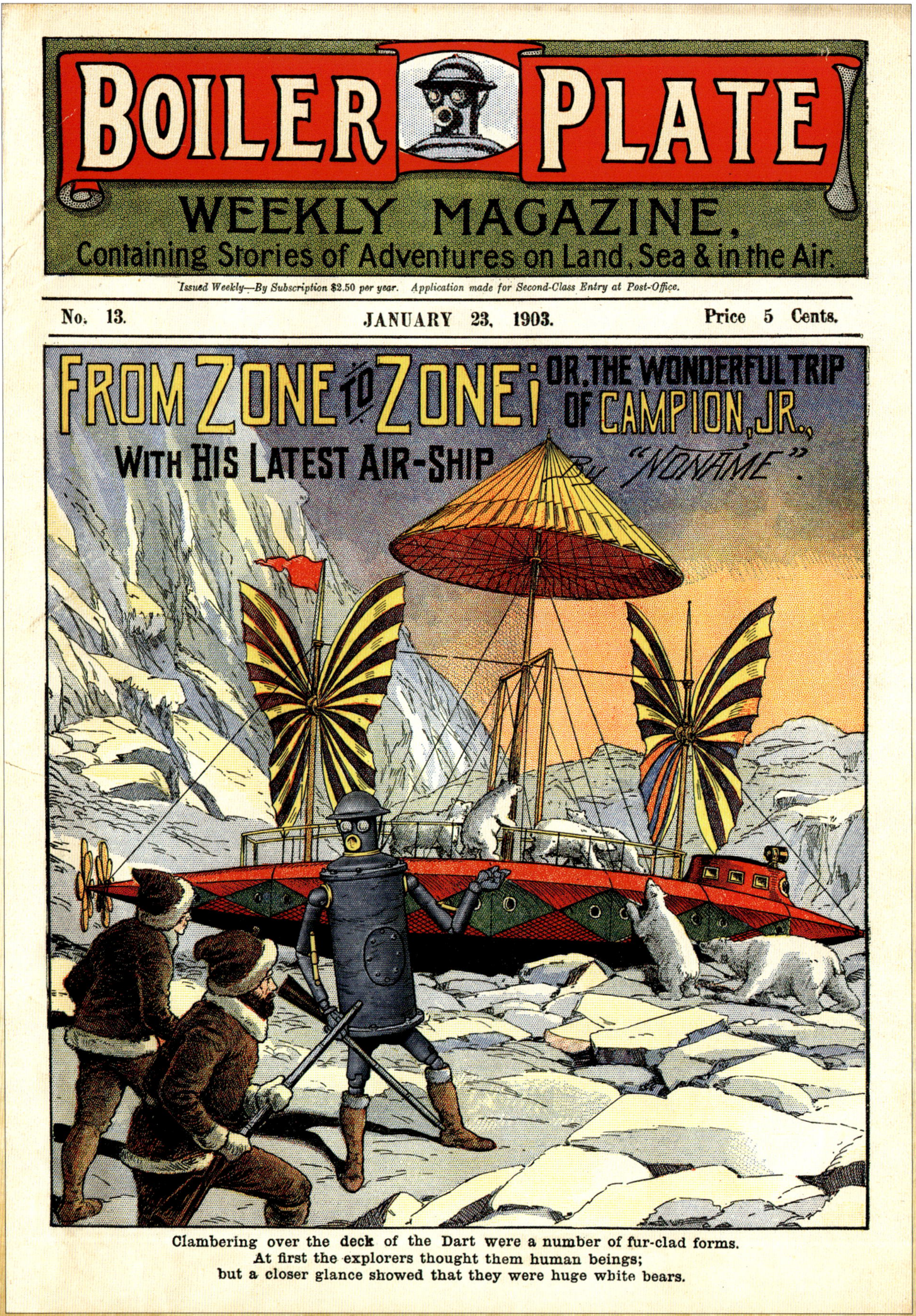

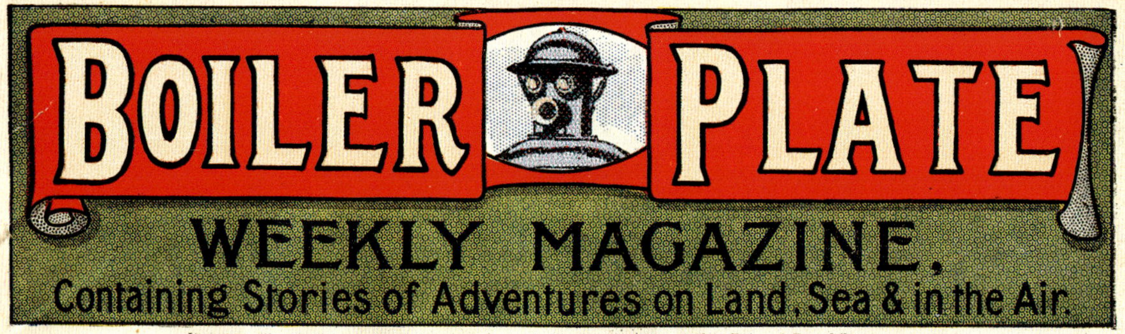

BOILER PLATE

WEEKLY MAGAZINE,

Containing Stories of Adventures on Land, Sea & in the Air.

Issued Weekly—By Subscription $2.50 per year. Application made for Second-Class Entry at Post-Office.

No. 13. JANUARY 23, 1903. Price 5 Cents.

FROM ZONE TO ZONE; OR, THE WONDERFUL TRIP OF CAMPION, JR., WITH HIS LATEST AIR-SHIP

By "NONAME".

Clambering over the deck of the Dart were a number of fur-clad forms.
At first the explorers thought them human beings;
but a closer glance showed that they were huge white bears.

Boilerplate, a fictional robot dubbed 'History's Mechanical Marvel', is the brainchild of artist Paul Guinan, a classic merging of fact and fantasy and was inspired by *The Steam Man Of The Prairies*. Guinan set out, in 2000, to create a graphic novel featuring an imagined mechanical man supposedly unveiled at the Chicago 1893 World's Columbian Exposition. Using a 12 inch articulated model of the robot, Guinan cleverly Photoshopped Boilerplate in a variety of historical settings – alongside Teddy Roosevelt, with Mexican revolutionary Pancho Villa and with the US Army on the Western Front in the First World War – and added a detailed history of Professor Archibald Campion, the man who 'invented' Boilerplate. Posting the photos and Boilerplate's story on his website, Guinan was amazed that so many visitors to his site actually thought that the story was true and the unintentional hoax generated global acclaim for the pioneering robot and his creator. Although the original idea for a Boilerplate graphic novel was shelved, Boilerplate's popularity was such that Guinan and his wife published a lavishly illustrated, coffee-table book in 2009 titled *Boilerplate – History's Mechanical Marvel*. The book covers the adventures of the robot from his invention to his mysterious disappearance in the trenches of France in 1918 and has become a benchmark for Steampunk creations that juxtapose real events and fictional characters.

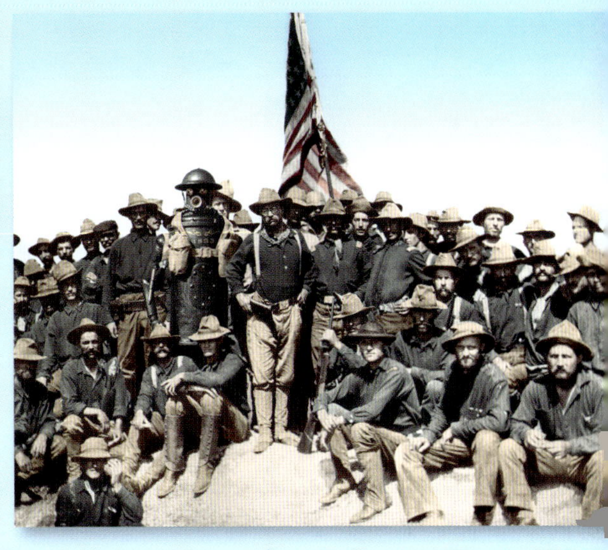

Above: Boilerplate with Teddy Roosevelt's Rough Riders after the robot's first combat mission, Cuba, 1898.

Below: Boilerplate at his first unveiling, at the World's Columbian Exposition, Chicago, 1893.

Left: An issue of *Boilerplate Weekly Magazine*, a dime novel series from 1903.

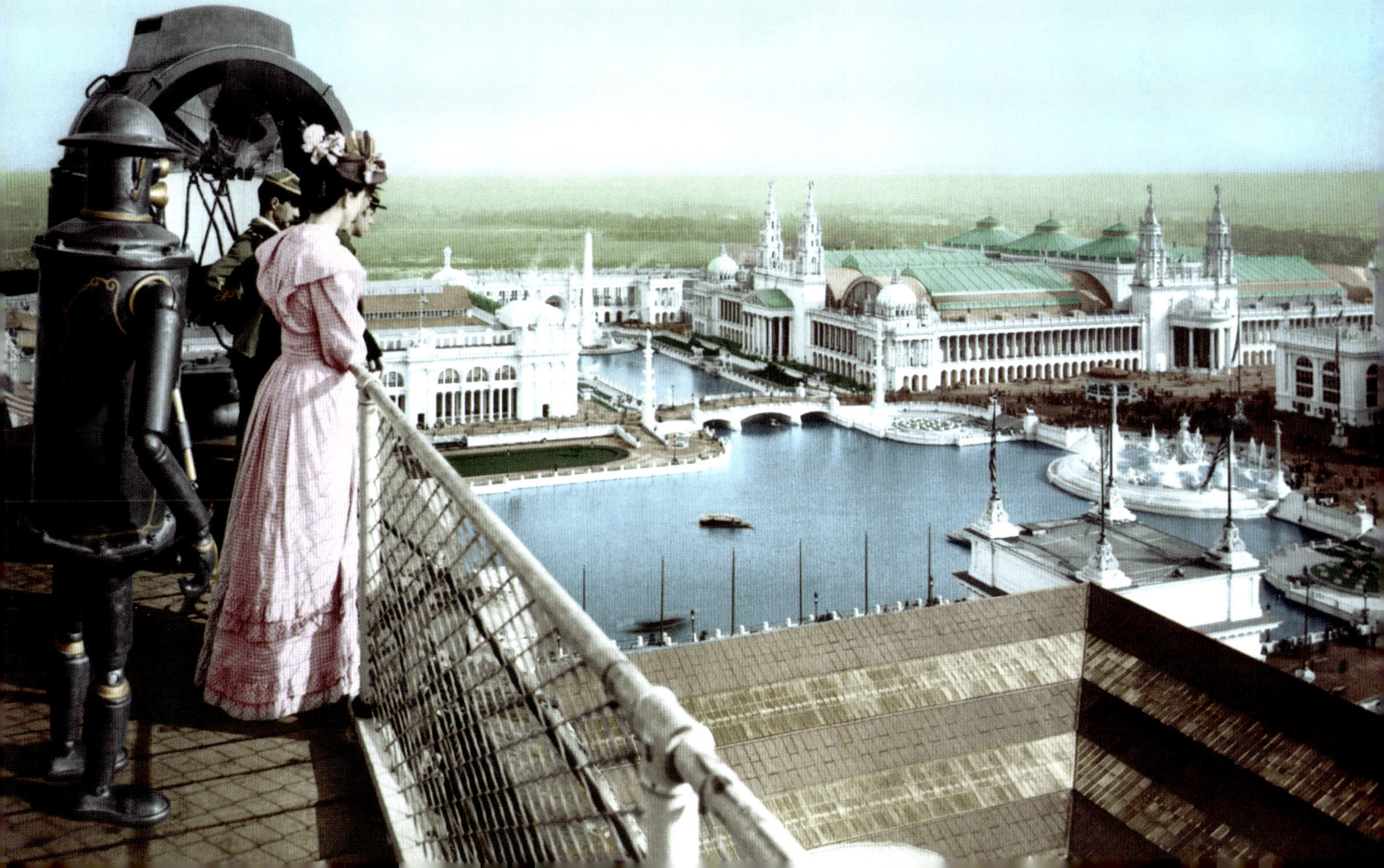

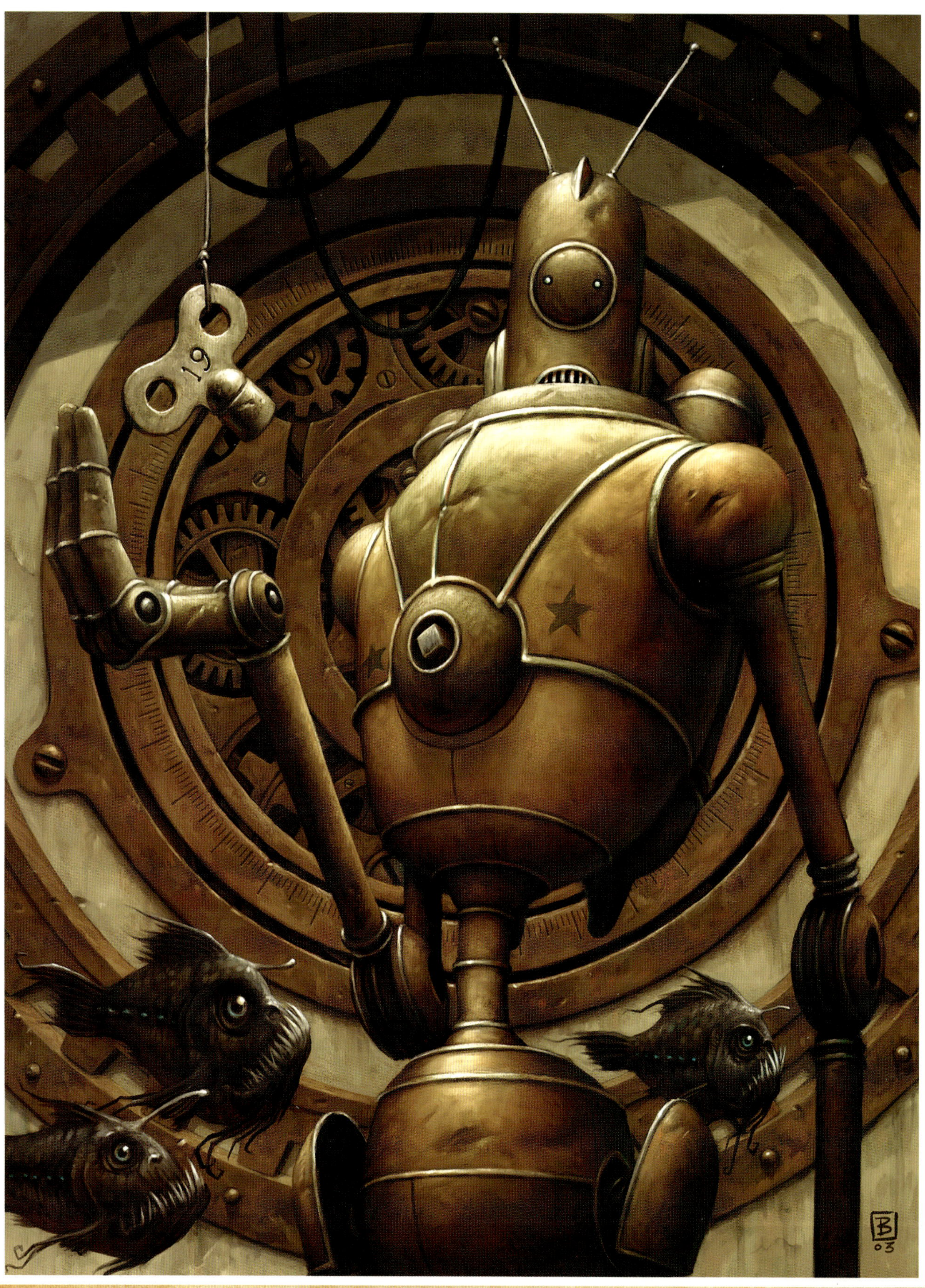
19

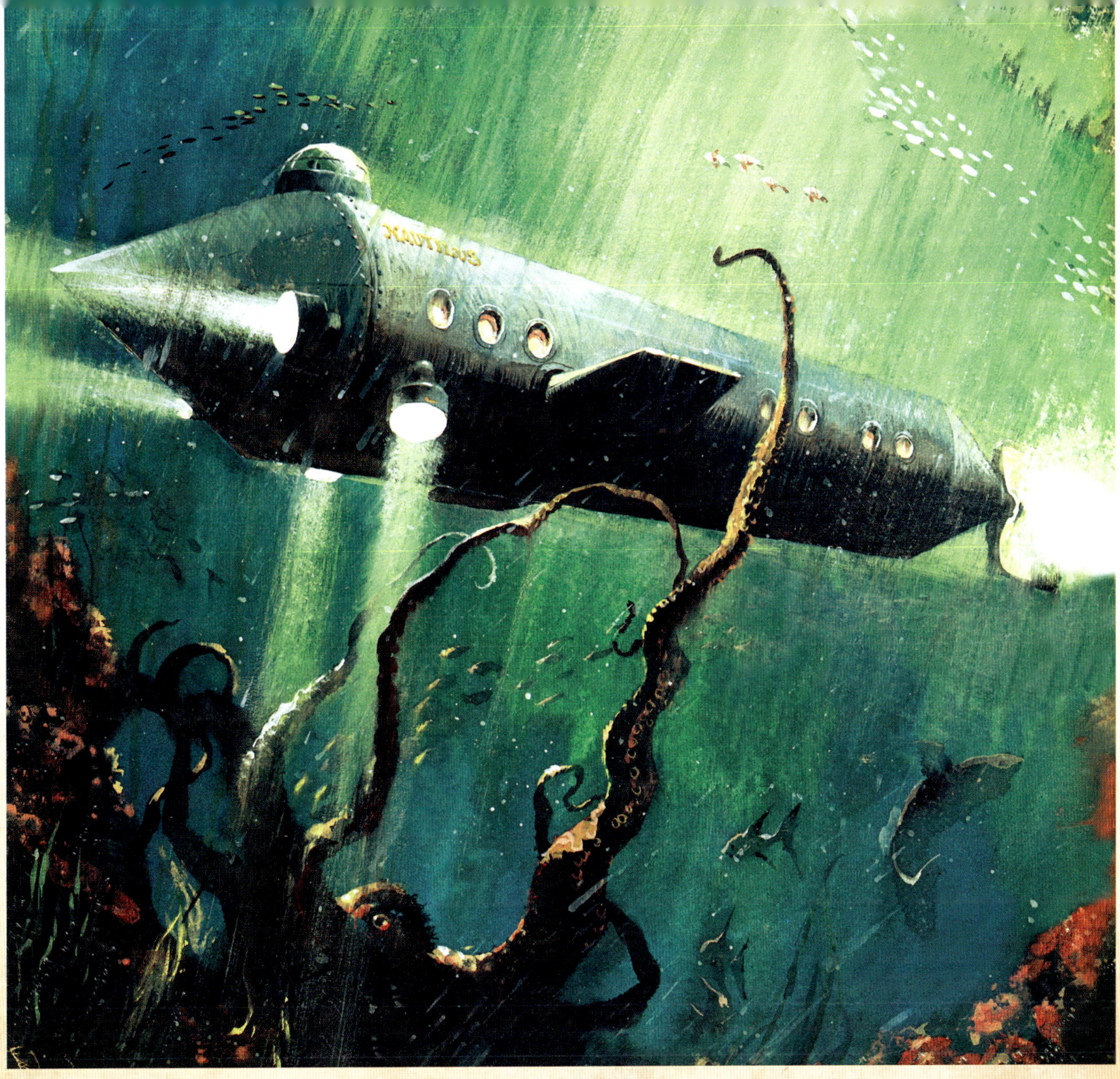

However, it was on the other side of the Atlantic that Steampunk's main inspirations originated. The Frenchman Jules Verne and the Englishman H. G. Wells were the pioneers of modern Science Fiction. They laid the groundwork for almost all the Science Fiction writing that followed. Verne's numerous novels, known under the banner title *Voyages Extraordinaires*, were more on the romantic side of the Scientific Romances than Wells' darker subject matters. But *Journey To The Centre Of The Earth*, *Around The World In Eighty Days*, *20,000 Leagues Under The Sea* and *From The Earth To The Moon* captured the public's imagination with their unprecedented explorations of air, sea and earth. Not only did Verne's *Voyages Extraordinaires* predict such inventions as deep sea submarines, floating cities and spacecraft that splashed down in the ocean on their return from the moon, but he also created such unforgettable characters

Above: The real 'hero' of Jules Verne's *20,000 Leagues Under The Sea* was Captain Nemo's submarine, The Nautilus. The underwater vessel and its prophetic design have inspired generations of Sci-fi fans since the book was first published in 1869.

Left: Brian Despain, *Piscis Ex Machina*.

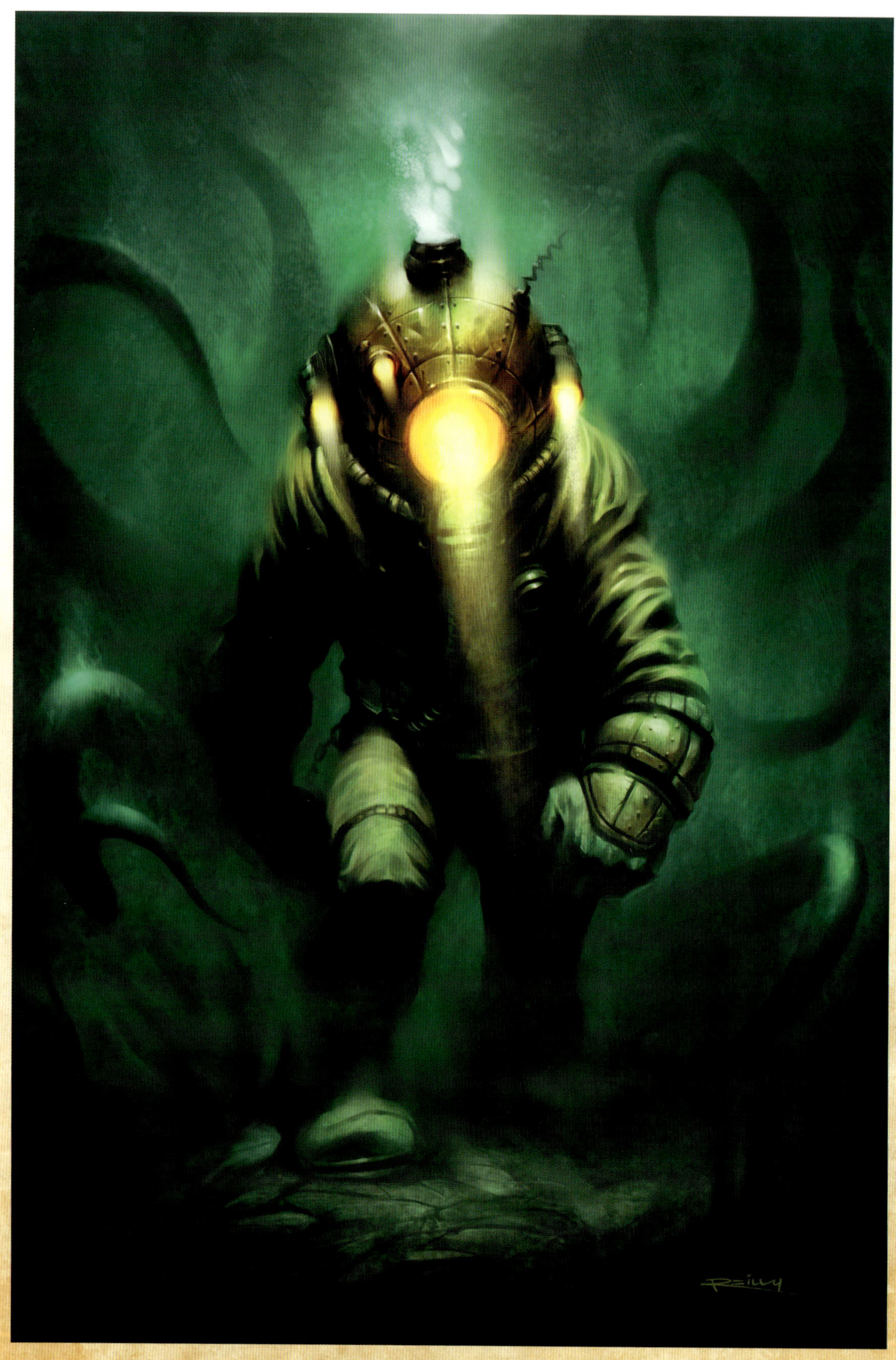

Above: Patrick Reilly, *Into the Depths*, 2007. Digital artwork.

Right: Dennis 'DXTR' Schuster, *The Visionary* (Jules Verne), 2010. Digital artwork.

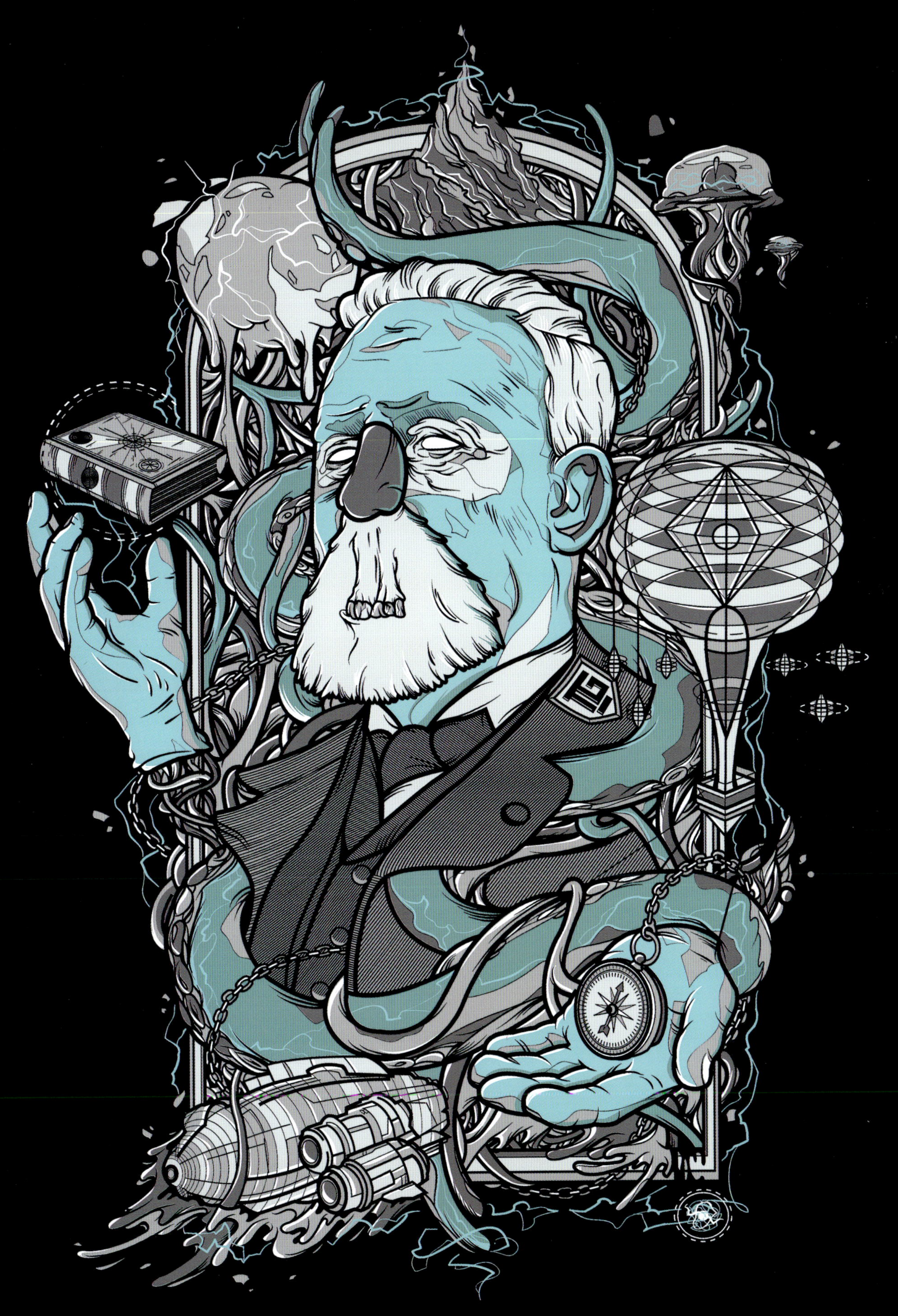

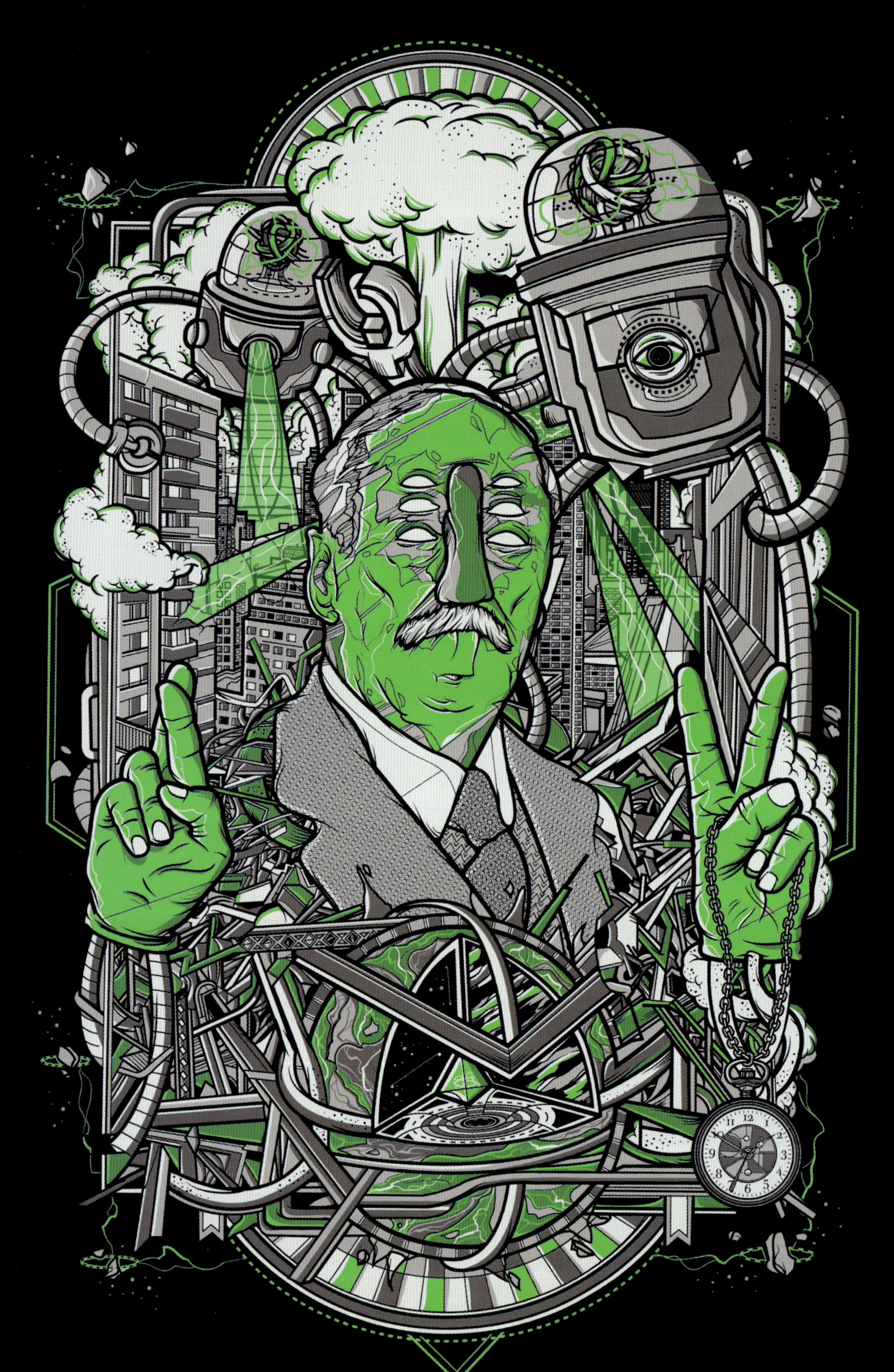

as Phileas Fogg from *Around The World In Eighty Days* and the tormented utopian Captain Nemo in *20,000 Leagues Under The Sea*. From 1864 until his death in 1905, Verne wrote over fifty novels and left behind a body of work that continues to inspire new generations.

Wells' career started somewhat later than Verne's (Wells wasn't born until two years after the publication of *Journey To The Centre Of The Earth*), but his writings had even more influence and popularity than those of the Frenchman's. Single-handedly, Wells not only brought the invading Martians to Earth, took man to the Moon, created a Time Machine and an Invisible Man, but also warned of the consequences of genetic engineering and atomic bombs and predicted mechanized warfare.

Unlike many of his contemporaries, Wells took a rather bleak view of the scientific advances he saw around him and the futures those advances could lead to. In his *The War Of The Worlds* it isn't science or technology that saves mankind from the murderous Martians, but Mother Nature, in the shape of Earth's common or garden bacteria, that destroys the invaders. And in *The Time Machine* he predicted that industrialisation would divide society into two classes and eventually into two almost distinct species –the cannibalistic Morlocks, who dwell below ground and are the descendants of Victorian factory workers, and the Eloi – the offspring of the rich who have regressed into effete, delicate little creatures that still dwell on the surface and live a pampered existence (when not being eaten by the Morlocks). Wells took great delight in juxtaposing the order and straight-laced sensibilities of the late-Victorian era with the chaos caused to that society by the fantastical technologies he dreamt up (from the one man terror of the Invisible Man, to the city-destroying heat rays employed by the Martians in *The War Of The Worlds)*.

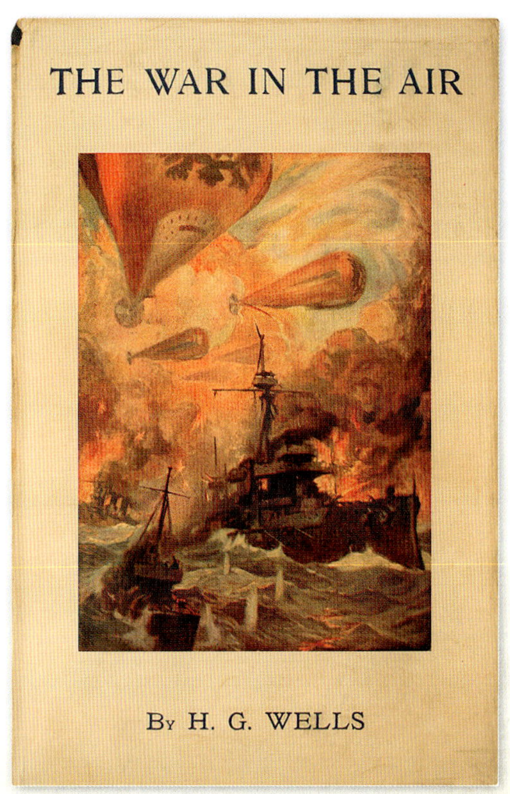

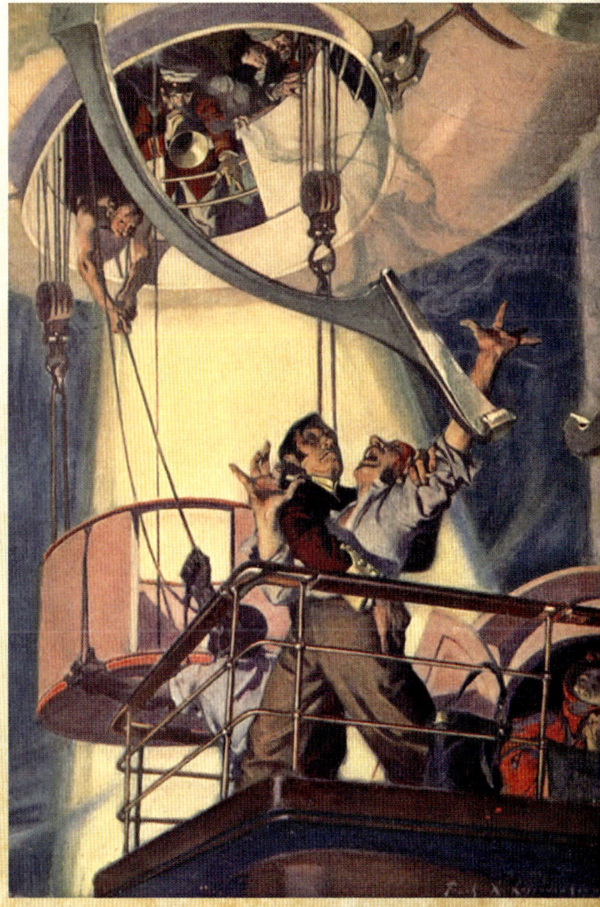

Left: Dennis 'DXTR' Schuster, *The Invader* (H. G. Wells), 2010. Digital artwork.

Above Right: Original dustjacket from H.G. Wells' novel *War In The Air*. First published in 1908 it prophesied not only a devastating world war, but also global economic collapse and an Islamic *jihad*. The book's focus on a war fought mainly with airships and other flying machines was ahead of its time and has made it a favourite with the Steampunk generation. Although not one of Wells' better known novels, its influence can be seen in Michael Moorcock's *The Warlord Of The Air* trilogy and as part of the historical background for Alan Moore and Kevin O'Neill's *The League Of Extraordinary Gentlemen*.

Right: Frank X. Leyendecker, frontispiece for *With The Night Mail* by Rudyard Kipling,, from the 1909 edition. The caption reads: 'A man with a ghastly scarlet head follows, shouting that he must go back and build up his ray.'

First published in 1905, and described as 'A Story of 2000 A.D.', Kipling's short story *With The Night Mail* is a classic of 'forgotten future' fiction. It abounds with what are now Steampunk obsessions: intensely detailed descriptions of aerial technology, control rooms with 'pulsing arrows of some twenty indicators' and heroic characters, including one who develops machine fetishisms because 'war went out of fashion and [he] went out of his mind because he said he couldn't serve his country any more'. Kipling particularly indulges in his descriptions of hi-tech dirigibles: "The three engines are H. T. & T. assisted-vacuo Fleury turbines running from 3000 to the Limit - that is to say, up to the point where the blades make the air 'bell' - cut out a vacuum for themselves precisely as over-driven marine propellers used to do. 162's Limit is low on account of the small size of her nine screws, which though handier than the old colloid Thelussons, 'bell' sooner."

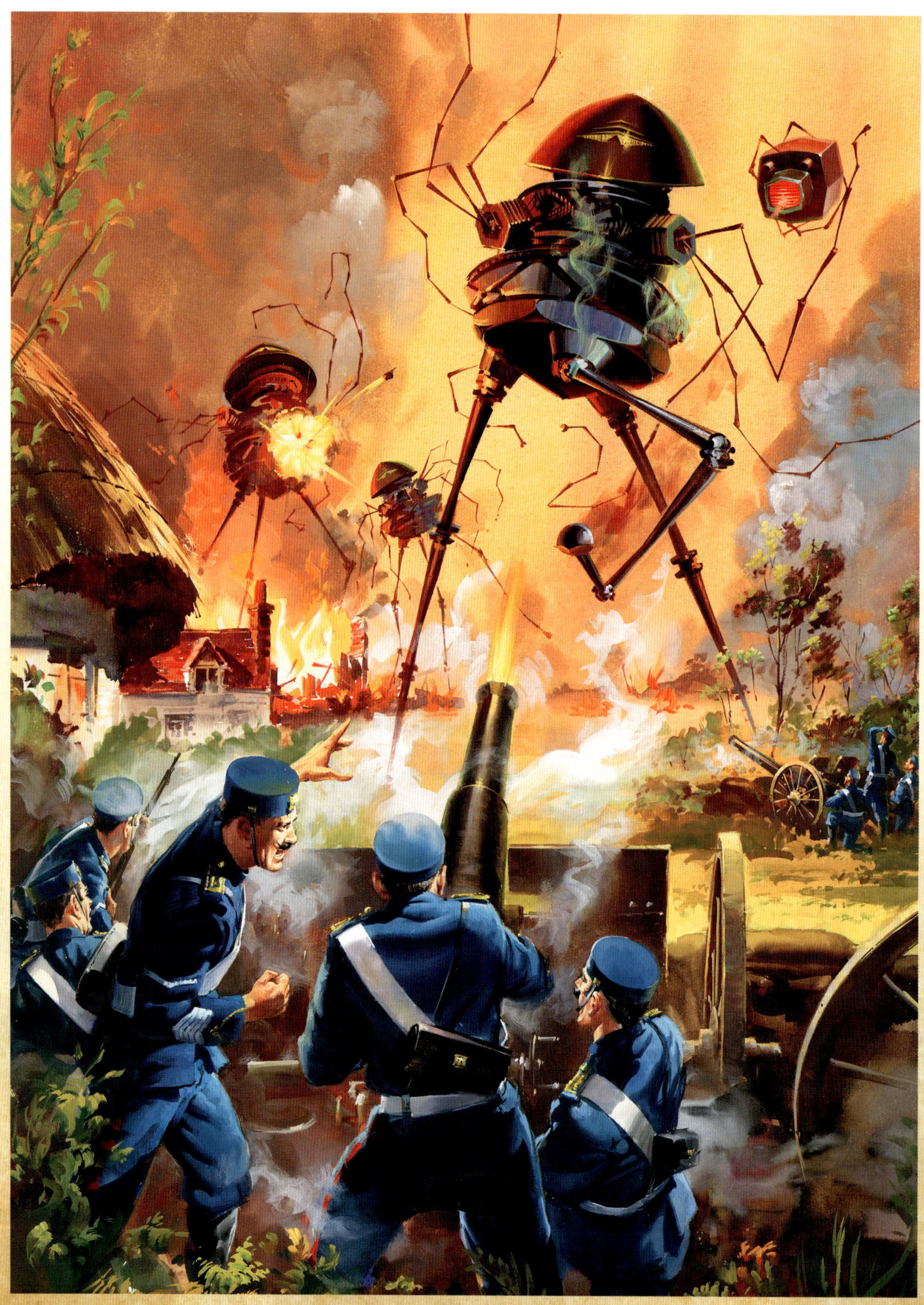

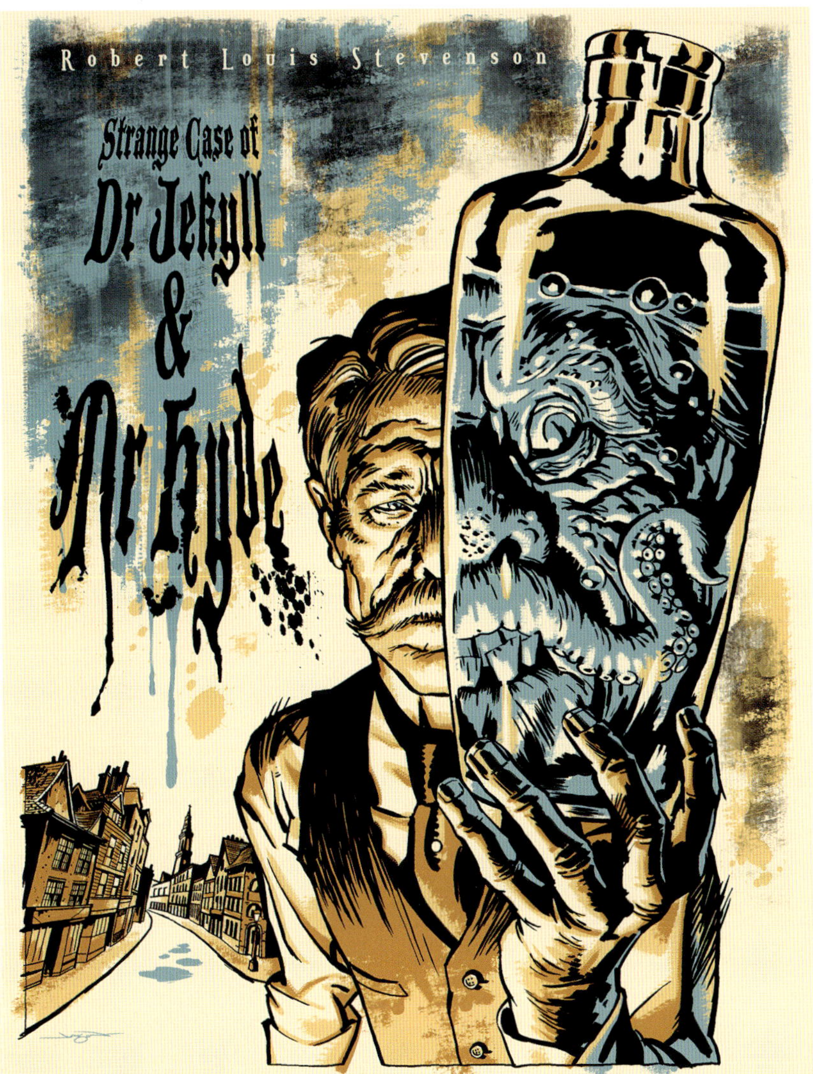

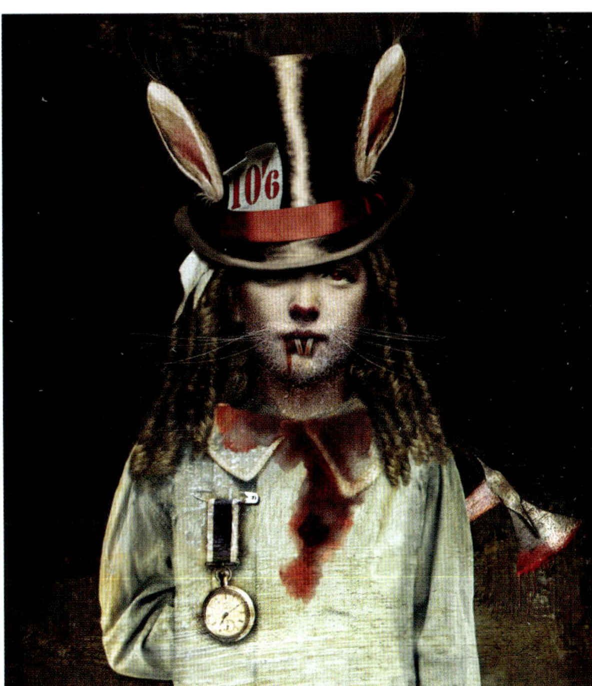

Left: Jason Edmiston, *Strange Case of Dr. Jekyll & Mr Hyde*, 2011. Created for Gallery 1988's group show *Required Reading*. Screenprint.

Above: Stephen Rothwell, *Alice*, 2009.

Far Left: Barrie Linklater, *War of the Worlds*.

The era of Wells' and Verne's most inspired writing was also the golden age of Victorian fantasy, a period which provided numerous works that still resonate in popular culture. From the disturbing *Strange Case Of Dr. Jekyll And Mr. Hyde* by Robert Louis Stevenson and Sir Arthur Conan Doyle's Sherlock Holmes stories, to the relative innocence of Lewis Carroll's *Alice In Wonderland*, a wealth of themes and characters were created – a rich legacy in which Steampunk and Neo-Victorianism have happily revelled. And with the adventure novels of Rudyard Kipling and H. Rider Haggard giving us tales of far-flung empires and lost worlds, the prototypes were provided for contemporary Steampunk stories with their alternative versions of European Imperialism. Indeed, Kipling's 1905 story *With The Night Mail: A Story of 2000 A.D.* features one of the key elements of a current Steampunk obsession – an imagined future in which lighter-than-air machines circle the globe. But it is for the innovative works of Verne and Wells that the *fin de siècle* era is best remembered. With hindsight this was a period of seeming enlightenment and a time of relative peace

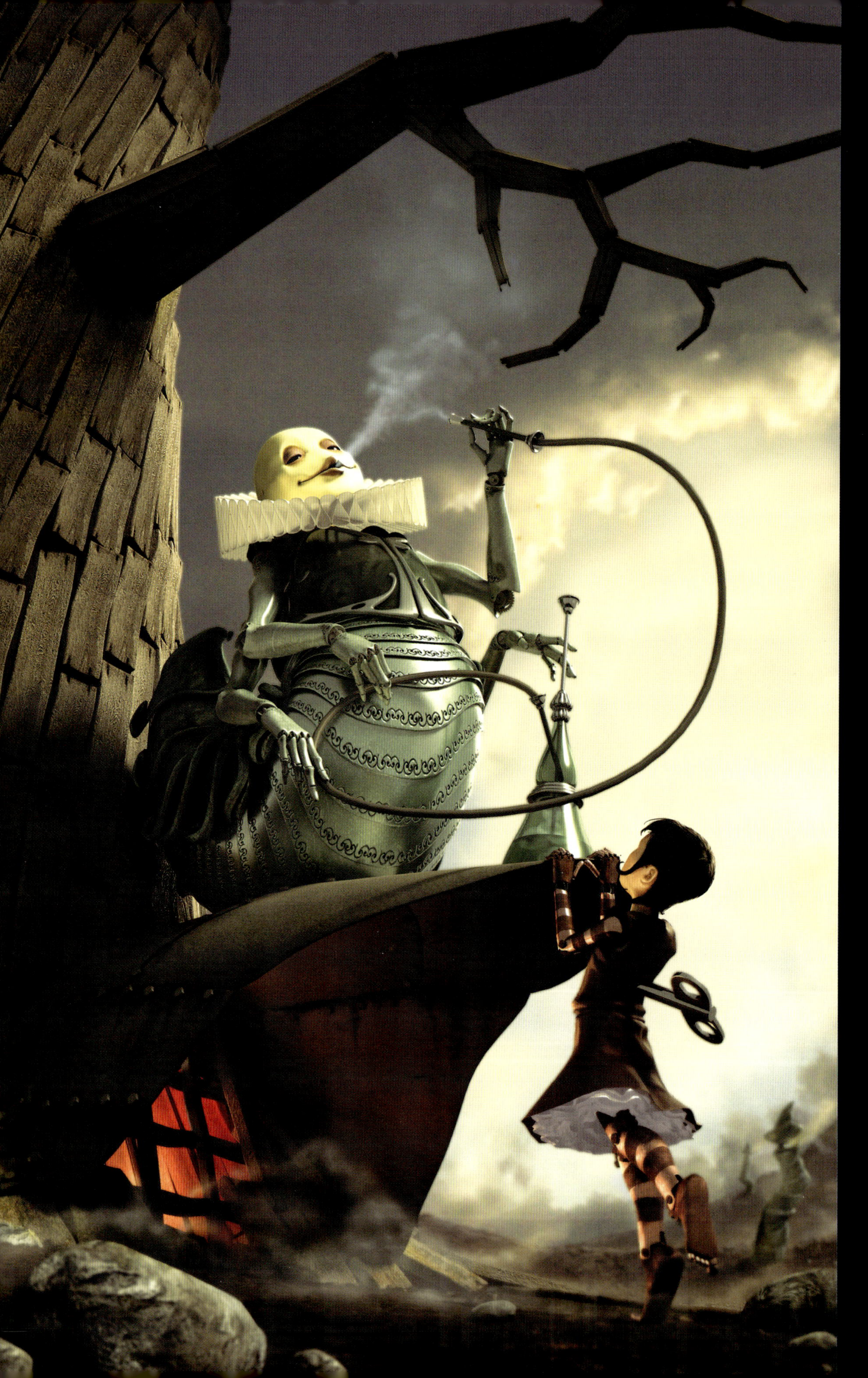

and prosperity compared with what was to come. The age of fantasy and Scientific Romances ended in the bloody carnage of the First World War as the technology that had once inspired the Victorians was used to create machine guns, flame throwers, heavy artillery, Dreadnought battleships, tanks, bomber airships and mustard gas. Next to the brutal realities of the War, and its effects on Western civilisation, the novels of Wells and Verne suddenly seemed naïve and old-fashioned – there's nothing more distant than the recent past.

It was to be over forty years and another horrific World War before their books and the Victorian aesthetic once again had a significant impact on popular culture and public consciousness. The first glimmer of that re-emergence appeared in the strange, claustrophobic gothic novels of Mervyn Peakes's *Gormenghast* trilogy. *Titus Groan* (1946), *Gormenghast* (1950) and *Titus Alone* (1959) were firmly in the gothic fantasy vein and the universe Peake created was steeped in Victorian imagery. However it was Hollywood that really re-introduced the styles and themes of Neo-Victorianism to a mid-Century public. Walt Disney's 1954 adaptation of Jules Verne's *20,000 Leagues Under The Sea*, starring Kirk Douglas and James Mason, gave a whole new generation a chance to discover the wonders that Verne had created. The model of Captain Nemo's Nautilus submarine used in the movie is a prototype of Steampunk fantasy and the very stuff Steampunk dreams are made of – good solid Victorian engineering and elegant design, yet with powers far beyond its time.

A few years later Hollywood put another Verne epic, *Journey To The Centre Of The Earth,* on the silver screen, while behind the Iron Curtain the Czech film, *The Fabulous World of Jules Verne,* used a mixture of animation and real actors to create a masterpiece that looked like the illustrations from Verne's books brought to life. The success of these films led to the movie business then adapting one of Wells' most beloved novels. Released in 1964, *The Time Machine* did a wonderful job of capturing the feel and scope of the original novel and continues to capture imaginations to this day. Hollywood saw that there was money in turn-of-the-century movies and a veritable flood of light-hearted films set in the period appeared around the mid-1960s (*The First Men in the Moon* (1964), *Those Magnificent Men in their Flying Machines* (1965), *The Great Race* (1965) and *Chitty Chitty Bang Bang* (1968), to name but a few).

As for the written word, the beginnings of Steampunk literature itself can be traced back to 1962 and Keith Laumer's novel *Worlds of the Imperium,* which conjured up a series of parallel universes patrolled by an all powerful British Empire. The idea of a past where Queen Victoria's Empire grew more powerful rather than fading away was also picked up in Ronald W. Clark's 1967 novel *Queen Victoria's Bomb*. Clark's novel coincided with an ongoing pop culture rediscovery of Victorian and Edwardian style and sartorial elegance. The British had long had a penchant for the era, a

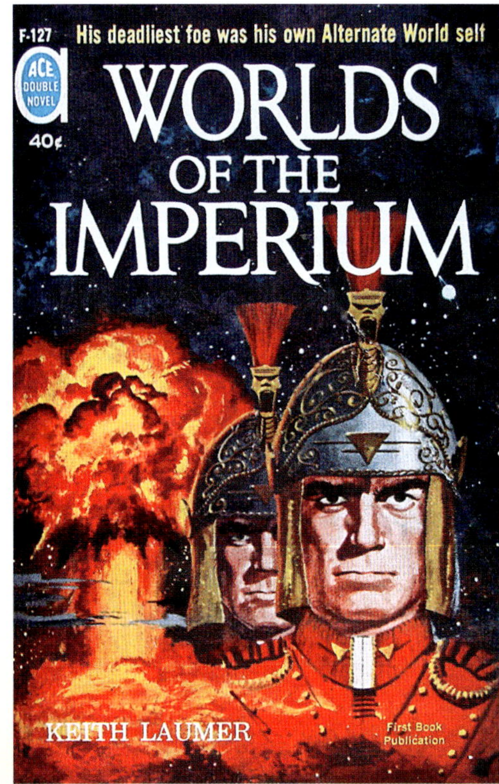

Above: Published by Ace Books in 1962, Keith Laumer's novel *Worlds Of The Imperium* was one of the first in a string of Sci-fi novels that posited an alternative future for the British Empire (a popular Steampunk theme). In Laumer's book the Empire has not only continued to grow on Earth but has also achieved dominion in a parallel universe as well.

Left: Guillaume Dubois, *Alice's Adventures in Steamland.*

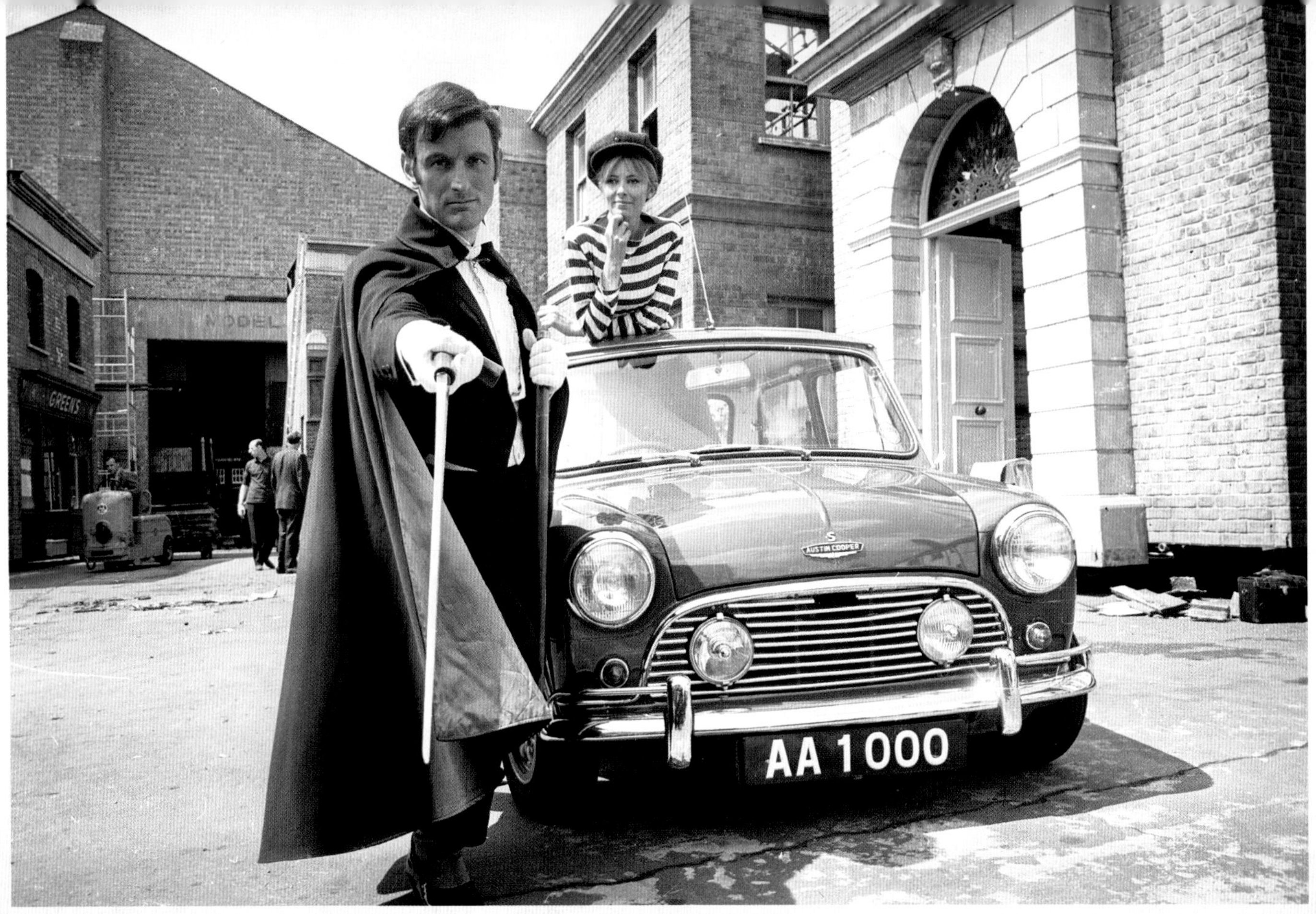

Above: English actor Gerald Harper as Adam Adamant in the 1966 BBC series *Adam Adamant Returns*. The series featured Harper as a swashbuckling Edwardian gentleman who awakes in the Swinging London of 1966 after being frozen in ice since the turn of the century. Befriended by a fashionable Mod chick, played by Juliet Harmer, a bemused Adamant kept his Edwardian panache while gallantly fighting crime in a world of Minis, TV, discotheques and jet planes.

Right: Alastair Fell, *Lady Frances Drake Sets Sail With The Fleet to do Battle With the Armada, 1588*, 2004. A vision of Elizabethan Steampunk: "I imagined a fascist Tudor England, along the lines of Ian McKellen's *Richard III*."

penchant that manifested itself just after the Second World War with the resurgence of Edwardian men's fashion amongst the young upper-classes. Their attempt to recall the heady days of Empire, when Britain still ruled the waves, was quickly adopted and bastardised by aspirational working class youths from South and East London. Completely subverting the posh boys' Imperial nostalgia, the working-class 'Teddy Boys and Girls' ('Ted' shortened from 'Edwardian') made the style their own and thus challenged their perceived place in Britain's class-bound society. This usurpation and subversion of the style of the Edwardian gentlemen is something the more politically minded of today's Steampunks can definitely appreciate.

The dapper Edwardian gentleman was also the inspiration for the suave, bowler-hatted John Steed in the innovative TV detective series *The Avengers,* which ran from 1962 until 1969. Not content with just the Edwardian look, the BBC broadcast a series which took a fictional Edwardian adventurer, frozen in ice in 1902, who is then thawed out in the Swinging London of 1966. *Adamant Lives* had the swashbuckling hero befriend a mini-skirted Mod girl and battle various modern criminals, whilst carrying a sword-stick and living in an Edwardian decorated flat above a multi-storey car park. The growing mid-1960s fascination with that earlier period also manifested itself in the fashion craze of modish youngsters wearing Victorian army tunics – a craze supposedly begun at a London fashion boutique called I Was Lord Kitchener's Valet. Victoriana and flower power seemed to blend

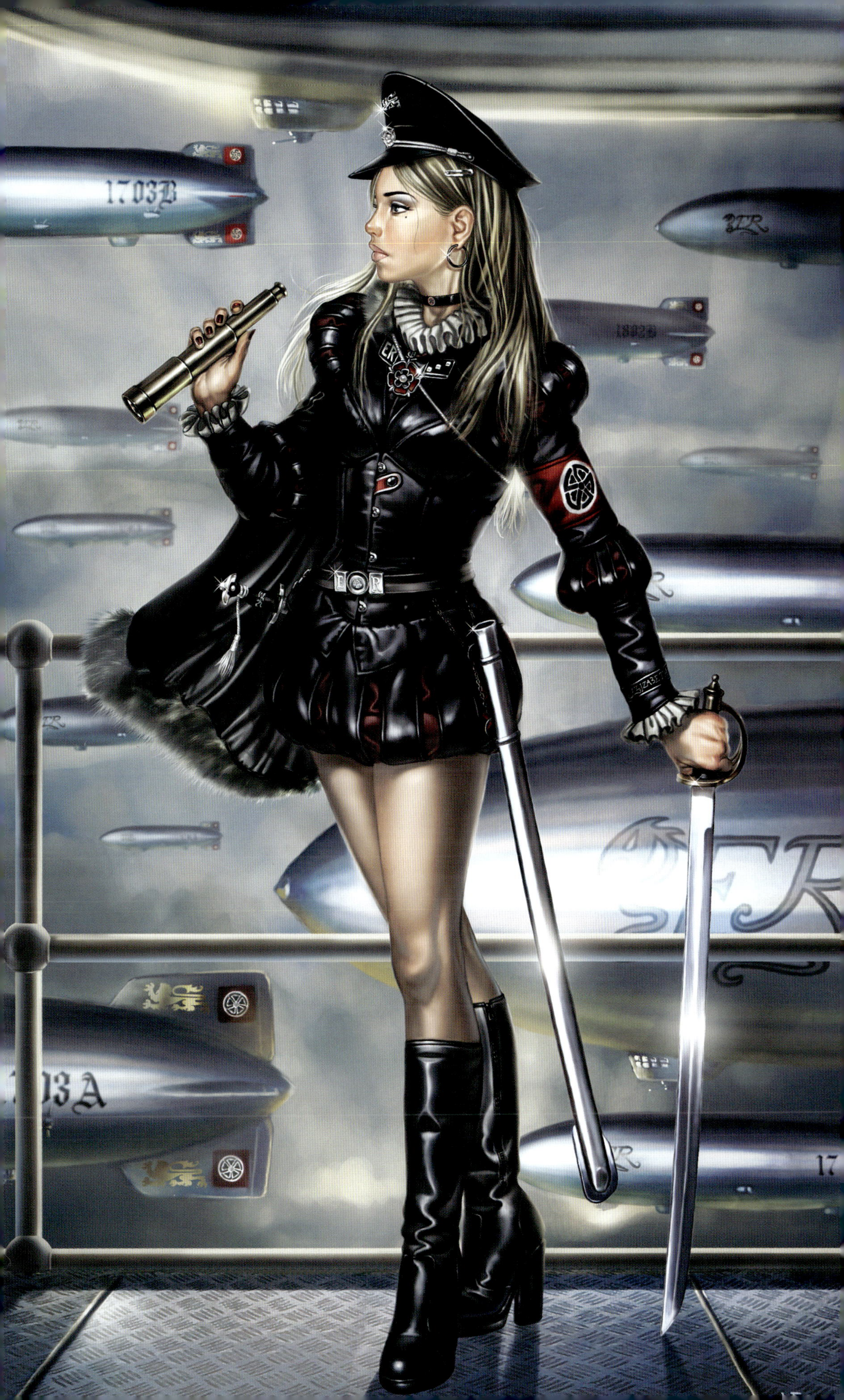
1703B

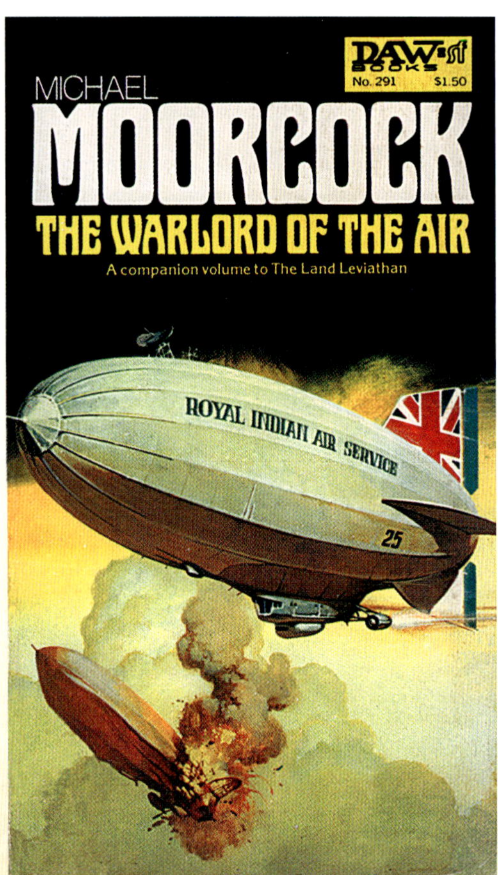

Above: Cover art for the Daw Books paperback edition of *The Warlord of The Air*, 1978.

British Sci-fi writer Michael Moorcock's novel was first published in 1971 and its view of the Victorian era was in keeping with the cynicism and new realities of the 1970s. In *Warlord* Moorcock created an alternative history where the First World War had not happened and the Russian Czar was still on the throne. The same Imperial powers that dominated the Edwardian age (Britain, Russia, Germany, Japan and the USA) continued to rule the world in the '70s and used powerful airships to brutally maintain their global colonies. The book's main character leads an anarchist rebellion against these Imperialist powers that ends in an atomic explosion in Hiroshima. The cover is one of the iconic images of pre-Steampunk Neo-Victorian Science Fiction.

quite happily in the colourful chaos of Swinging London and was adopted by the likes of Jimi Hendrix and the Sgt. Pepper's era Beatles.

But flower power and the innocent days of smoking pot and dressing up as Victorian Hussars didn't last past the end of the decade. After the Manson murders, Altamont and the break-up of the Beatles, the optimism of the Sixties soon mutated into the post-euphoric comedown of the 1970s. And, as the Vietnam War peaked and the global economy tanked, the cultural mood switched to a period of pessimism. That prevailing cultural angst was certainly reflected in the Science Fiction community, both via the written word and on celluloid. It was during this period that one of the most important literary precursors to Steampunk appeared. Michael Moorcock's *A Nomad Of The Time Streams* trilogy began with the 1971 novel *Warlord Of The Air.* Moorcock's trilogy reflected the anti-colonial, anti-American and pro-socialist views then prevalent in Europe, but what made the trilogy also notable from a Steampunk point of view was its pioneering use of steam-powered airships as weapons of war. In 1972 Harry Harrison's novel *A Transatlantic Tunnel Hurrah* also delved into alternate history and imagined a world in which the Americans had lost the War Of Independence and were, decades later, part of an increasingly powerful and aggressive British Empire.

While Moorcock's and Harrison's Victorian-inspired novels were rebellious and anti-establishment in tone, the Sci-fi films of the early 1970s were nihilistic visions of apocalyptic futures, where science had done precious little good and seemingly much harm (H. G. Wells would undoubtedly have approved). A trio of films in 1971 *The Andromeda Strain, The Omega Man* and *A Clockwork Orange* set the trend and *Silent Running* (1972), *Soylent Green* and *Westworld* (1973) and *A Boy And His Dog* (1975) all piled in to portray man's future as either dystopian or post-apocalyptic. A couple of years later and the nihilism prevalent in popular culture seemed complete as the Sex Pistols sang the punk anthem *God Save The Queen* with its sing-a-long 'no future' chorus. Even the relatively upbeat *Star Wars* in 1977 opened with the immortal words: 'A long time ago in a galaxy far far away...'. With the future so effectively written off it was perhaps no wonder that some amongst the Science Fiction community began looking to the previous century for inspiration as the '70s ended. A couple of Hollywood movies of the period dabbled in the Victorian era – H. G. Wells and Jack the Ripper visited San Francisco in the 1979 movie *Time After Time* while Stephen Spielberg gave a nod to Victoriana in the underrated *Young Sherlock Holmes* – but, once again, it was literature which really embraced the revival of Neo-Victorian influence. Taking H. G. Wells' *Time Machine* as his starting point, author K. W. Jeter imagined a past where the Morlocks of the distant future use the Time Machine to invade Victorian London. While it can be argued whether *Morlock Night* is a candidate for one of the first true Steampunk novels, there's

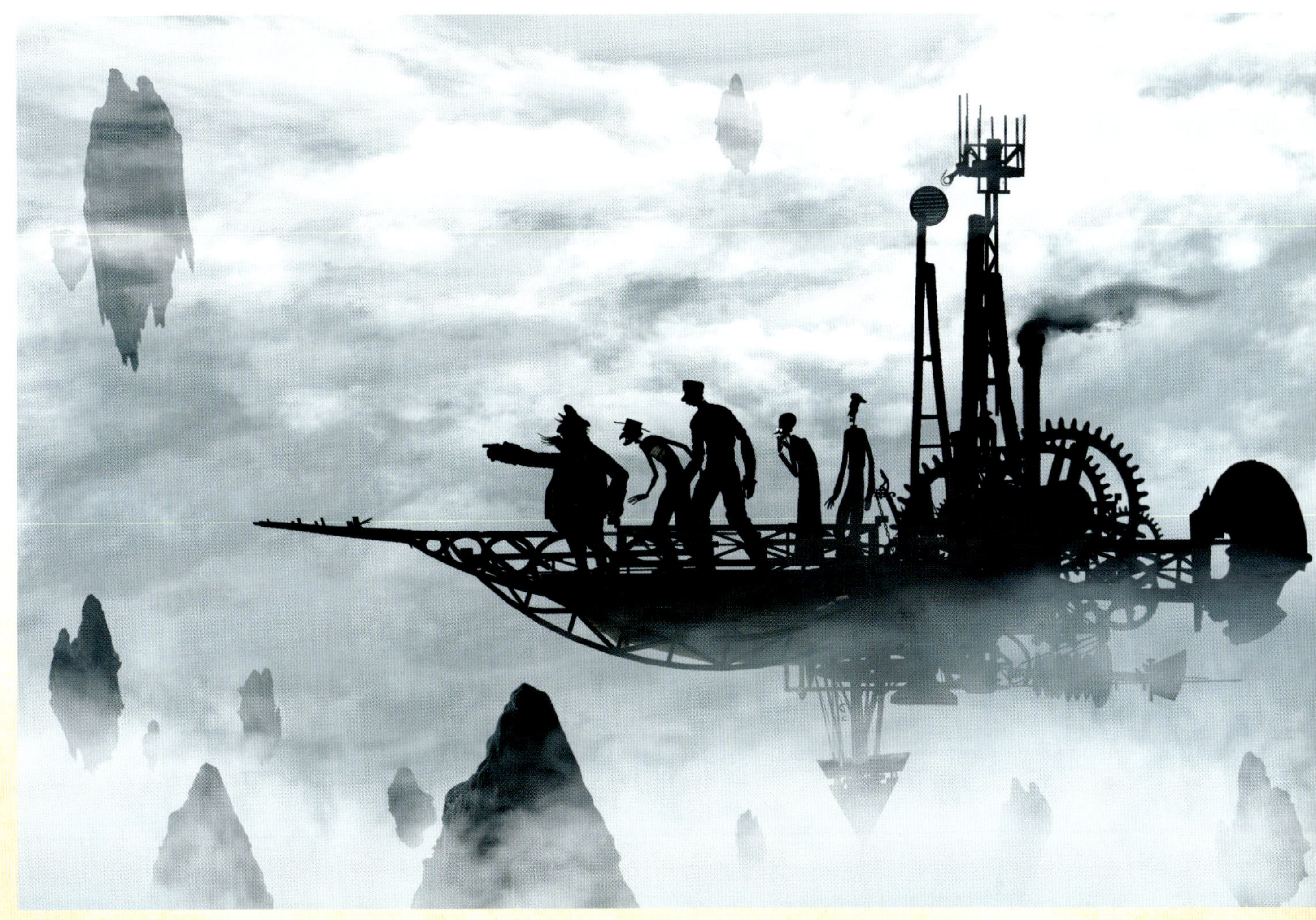

no doubting the fact that Jeter actually coined the word 'Steampunk'. In a letter to the Science Fiction magazine *Locus* in 1987, Jeter, who had just published another proto-Steampunk novel *Infernal Devices,* wrote that he was trying to find a tongue-in-cheek collective term for the Science Fiction of himself, Tim Powers (with *The Anubis Gates* in 1983) and James Blaylock (*Homunculus* in 1986). His letter to *Locus* read, in part... *"Enclosed is a copy of my 1979 novel* Morlock Night... *it's a prime piece of evidence in the great debate as to who in 'the Powers/Blaylock/Jeter fantasy triumvirate' was writing in the 'gonzo-historical manner' first... Personally, I think Victorian fantasies are going to be the next big thing, as long as we can come up with a fitting collective term for Powers, Blaylock and myself. Something based on the appropriate technology of the era; like 'steampunks,' perhaps..."*

So the name was out there but, ironically, the novelists who really put Steampunk on the map were William Gibson and Bruce Sterling, two authors who were most associated with the futuristic genre of Cyberpunk. While Cyberpunk was set in the century to come, Gibson and Sterling embraced the Steampunk concept with their joint work, *The Difference Engine,* and set their epic story in the century past. Published in 1990, it imagined

Above: Poster art for *The Mysterious Geographic Explorations Of Jasper Morello,* 2005.

A classic of Steampunk animation, this Australian film was released in 2005 to great critical acclaim. Beautifully styled, it ticked all the right boxes to make it a great Steampunk movie: a parallel neo-Victorian universe, weird science, steam-powered airships and a morbid, gothic sense of horror. Its use of Indonesian 'wayang kulit' silhouette figures was a clever twist that gave the movie a pan-Pacific flavour and showed that Steampunk is open to non-Western cultural influences.

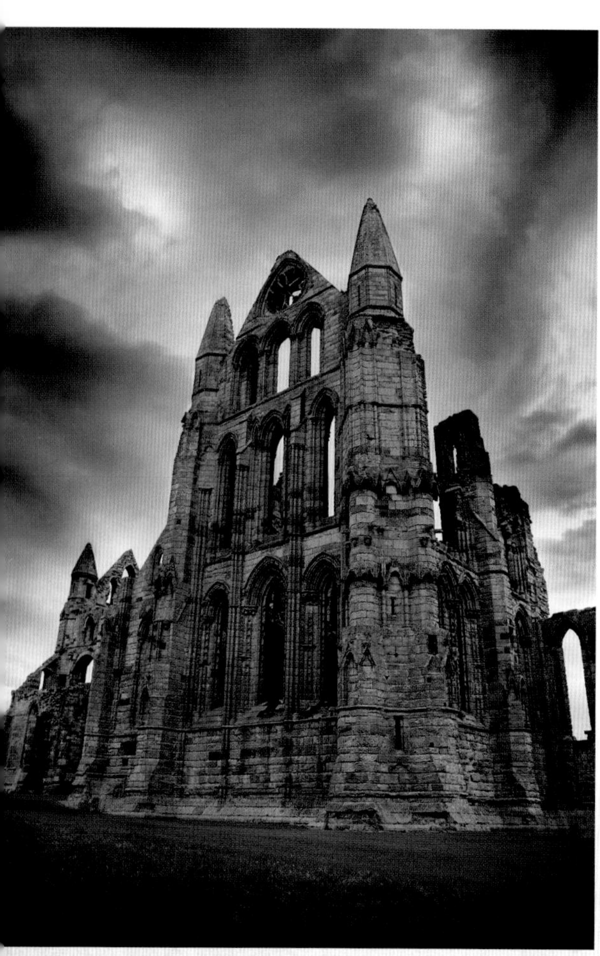

Above: The imposing gothic ruins of Whitby Abbey, North Yorkshire, are set on a headland that projects into the sea. The ruins dominate the town below. Irish author Bram Stoker wrote his famous *Dracula* (first published in 1897) in the fishing town. Whitby Abbey was a setting and part of the inspiration for the novel. The Whitby Gothic Weekend has grown to a twice yearly event with an increasing Steampunk edge.

a violent Dickensian London, where the information age had arrived a hundred years early due to Charles Babbage's successful development of his mechanical computer. The book was a critical and commercial success and the Steampunk genie was well and truly out of the bottle. At around the same time the role-playing game *Space 1889,* created by Frank Chadwick and which had been released in 1988, was gaining popularity with gamers. Set in an alternate Victorian history where, thanks to Thomas Edison, man travels to the other planets on an ether current, the visuals included pith helmeted, red-jacketed Victorian soldiers out to conquer the solar system. A generation which had been influenced by childhood viewings of *Zulu*, *The Time Machine* and *20,000 Leagues Under the Sea* could now indulge their fantasies and enjoy their own alternative Victorian futures. The game's name echoes that of the hit British television show of the '70s *Space 1999*. Paul di Filipo's *The Steampunk Trilogy* in 1995 was the first book to use the term in a title and, from then on, the number of short stories and novels published in the genre grew steadily, rising to something of a crescendo as the first decade of the new century came to an end.

The growth of Steampunk literature was accompanied by a wider fascination with the Victorian and Edwardian eras. This, in turn, drew in new groups. Goths, in particular, were attracted to neo-Victorianism due in part to the 1993 horror film *Bram Stoker's Dracula* starring British actor Gary Oldman. Oldman's stylish portrayal of the younger Dracula in top hat and blue spectacles inspired many Goths to emulate Neo-Victorian fashion. This new influx pushed the fashion boundaries of the movement, allowing for more experimentation and cross-fertilisation of styles. In fact the Goth/Steampunk crossover has become so pronounced that the bi-annual Goth Festival in Whitby, on England's North-East coast (Whitby being one of the locations in which Bram Stoker set his original novel), is often now touted as a Goth and Steampunk festival. As a reaction to an increasingly bland mainstream pop culture the Goth's partial adoption of Steampunk makes sense – the contrast between the current vapid collection of teen vampire movies and TV series (filled with pretty boys and girls who look more like cast members of *Beverly Hills 90210* or *America's Next Top Model* than vampires) and the decadent, frock-coated or corset-clad Victorian blood-suckers couldn't be starker.

On the cusp of the Millennium, everything was in place for Steampunk to go viral and it did so. 1999 saw the release of the landmark film *Wild Wild West,* based on the '60's TV series of the same name. The original series was dubbed 'James Bond on horseback' although 'James Bond on steam locomotive' may have been a more apt definition. Featuring secret service agents, spies, evil scientists, infernal devices and alluring women, the series was typical of the innovative golden age of television. With its heavy dose of Science Fiction themes and the period setting of the late 19th Century, *Wild Wild West* was an obvious precursor to Steampunk and those drawn to

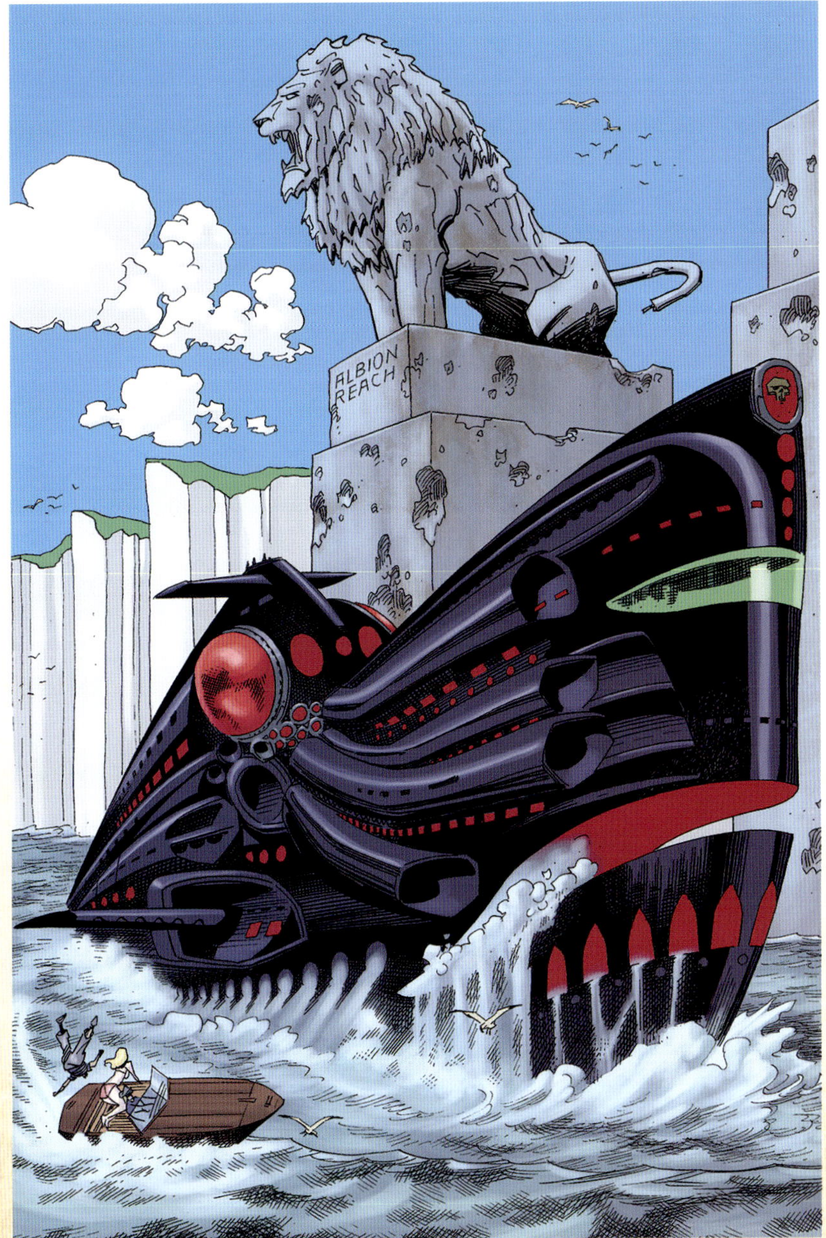

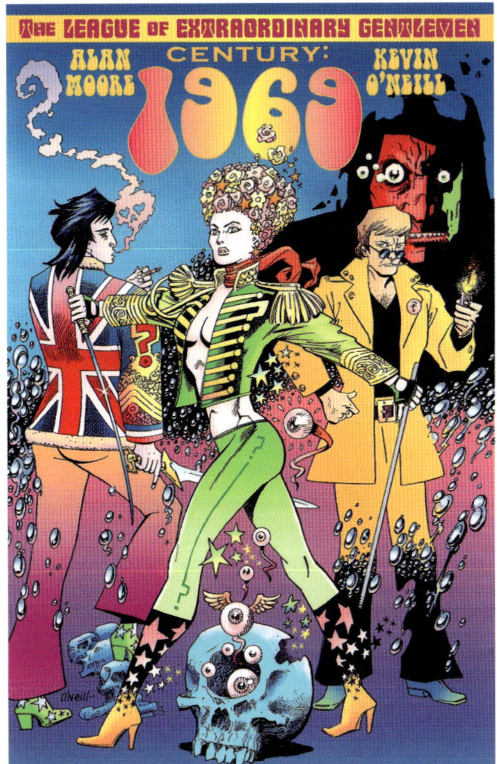

Above: Cover for *Paint It Black* – Chapter 2 of Alan Moore and Kevin O'Neill's *The League Of Extraordinary Gentlemen Volume III: Century*. Published in 2011, this chapter of the long-running *League* story is set in the psychedelic, swinging London of 1969 and features a free rock concert, East End gangsters and a host of other relevant counter-culture and pop-culture references. ©Alan Moore and Kevin O'Neill.

Left: A constant in the *League* series, Nemo's Nautilus surfaces off the white cliffs of Dover in *Paint It Black*. Jules Verne would be intrigued to see his creation still inspiring artists and writers one hundred and fifty years after its first appearance in print. ©Alan Moore and Kevin O'Neill.

the Steampunk banner eagerly awaited the film version. Sadly, the movie left something to be desired – one of those remakes of a TV series which should never have been made – but the fact it was made at all showed that Steampunk had infiltrated Hollywood. Hollywood's flirtation with Steampunk and Victoriana has carried on to include *The Illusionist* and *The Prestige,* both from 2006, and Guy Ritchie's *Sherlock Holmes* in 2009.

A far more important boost to the new movement's popularity came not from a novel or a film but from the comic book series *The League Of Extraordinary Gentlemen,* created by writer Alan Moore and artist Kevin O'Neill. Moore had made his name in the mid-'80s by creating the revolutionary *Watchmen* series for D.C. Comics and his name alone ensured that *The League* would be noticed. Taking various Victorian fictional

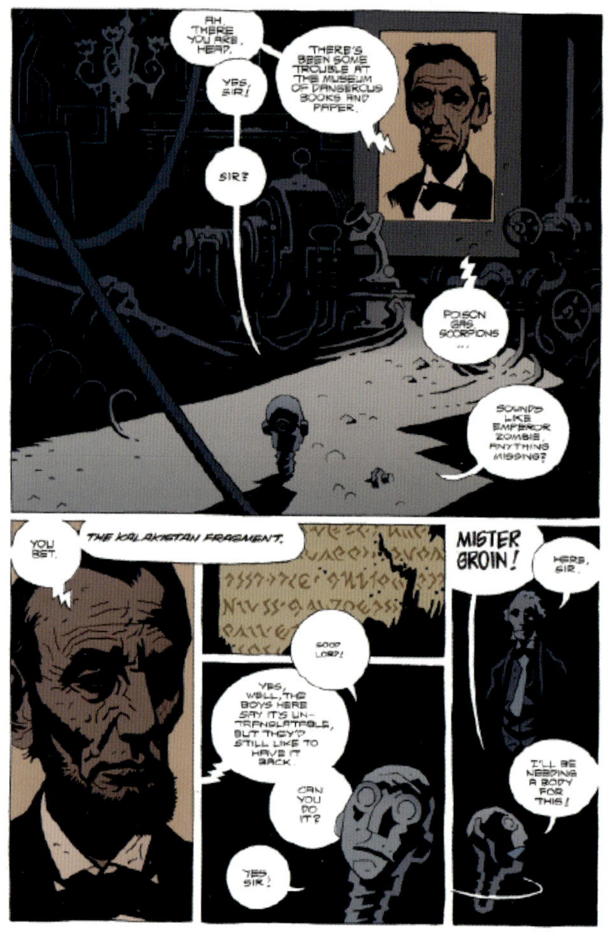

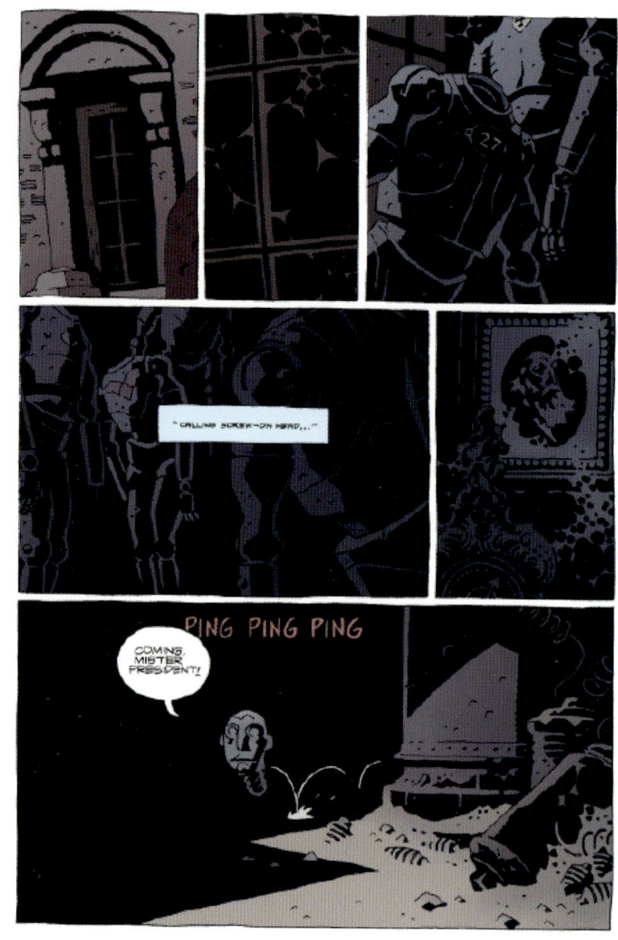

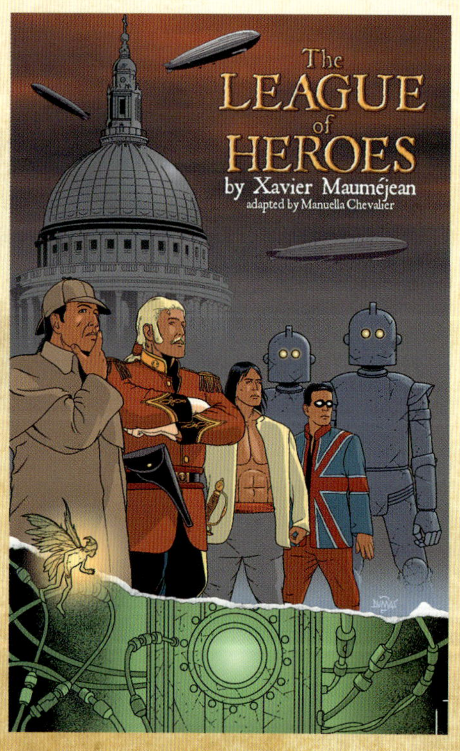

characters, including Mini Harker from *Dracula*, Captain Nemo from *20,000 Leagues Under the Sea* and explorer Allan Quatermain from *King Solomon's Mines*, Moore threw them all together in a kind of Victorian superhero secret service. Adding knowing nods to other icons of British fiction such as James Bond, Dr. Jekyll and Mr. Hyde and Sherlock Holmes, *The League* was a freewheeling, colourful, multi-layered mash-up of Victorian fantasy, gothic horror, modern ultra-violence and Science Fiction. Tongue-in-cheek, cynical and spanning three comic series and a graphic novel, *The League* was a huge success and duly prompted a disappointing film release in 2003. With the Internet connecting people as never before, the word on *The League* and Steampunk spread fast. As Cory Goss, editor of the excellent *Voyages Extraordinaires* website wrote in his online history of Steampunk: *"The League also came at the exact right time... This critical mass of Retro-Victorianism coincided with the real emergence of the Internet into popular consciousness. The Internet, with its plethora of message boards, websites and e-mail groups, enabled Steampunk to coalesce from its varied strands by allowing individuals from all walks of life and fandom to find common ground in what was ultimately a shared love of retro-Victorian scientific fantasies, whatever their form."*

Another comic book that attained cult status was Mike Mignola's *The Amazing Screw-On Head* which was published in 2002 by Dark Horse Comics and was made into a TV pilot in 2006. The Amazing Screw-On Head is a special agent robot working for President Lincoln, whose head can attach to different bodies as and when they are needed. The mix of robotics, vampires and the Lincoln-era setting made the comic an instant Steampunk classic.

Meanwhile, Steampunk's growing global reach was demonstrated by the production of Japanese animated films such as *Steam Boy*, *Castle In The Sky* and *Howl's Moving Castle,* all of which featured steam-powered airships and western fashions from the 19th Century. In turn, Japanese youth culture also embraced Neo-Victorianism via Cosplay (Cosplay being the trend for dressing up in costumes as fictional characters or ideas from comic books, films or Science Fiction). Paralleling the growing trend of Western youth dressing in Steampunk fashion, teenage Japanese girls adopted the Lolita style. Lolita style is Victorianism with a twist – bonnets, lace and Victorian maids' costumes, but usually with very short skirts and more than a hint of Goth make-up. Despite the name, part of the attraction of Lolita is to look cute and girly but not sexually threatening. Like many in the global Steampunk movement the Lolita girls and their boyfriends seem to be yearning for an age of elegance and politeness, both of which are missing from the crassness and blatant sexuality of modern life. In fact, it was through fashion that some of the first Steampunk art and design made its initial appearance. Mechanised clockwork prosthetic arms, gas masks and brass goggles (for the crews of steam-powered airships), cogwheel jewellery and other sartorial additions were created by inspired D.I.Y. designers and fashionistas. In the absence of commercially available accessories, Steampunks got busy and made their own, using their imaginations and inspiration gleaned from the Victorian and Edwardian past.

Concurrent with these developments, other aspects of craftsmanship came to the fore of the movement. Designers and 'tinkerers' like Jake Van Slatt, founder of the innovative Steampunk Workshop website, and Richard 'Doc' Nagy (Datamancer) began 'modding' (remodifying) the keyboards and monitors of modern computers and turning them into objects that were Neo-Victorian in appearance. This was achieved by the painstaking and skillful addition of period-friendly and appropriate materials such as brass fittings, varnished wooden panels and leather inlays. Keyboards were taken to pieces and then re-assembled key by key into something that would not have looked out of place in H. G. Wells' study. The overall effect was both strangely familiar yet confusing, and the transformation was from the purely functional to the elegantly crafted. It is hard not to compare the detail and elegance of the 'modded' version and the plain, just-out-of-the-box blandness of the originals and not come to the conclusion that the Steampunk version is the more visually interesting and more

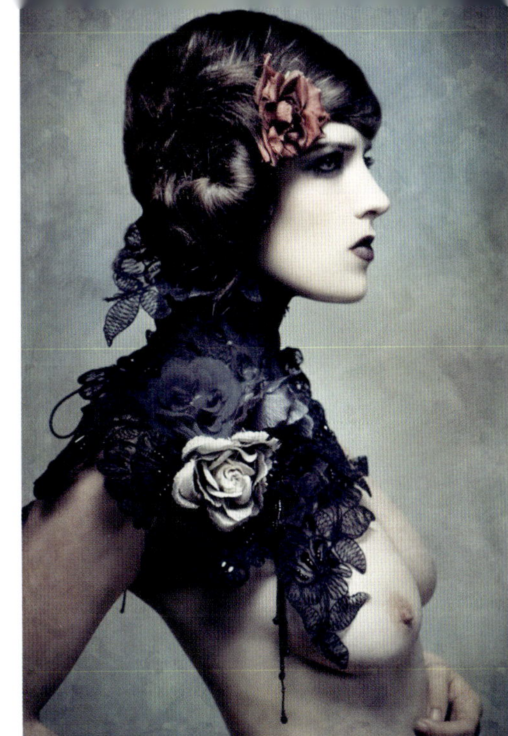

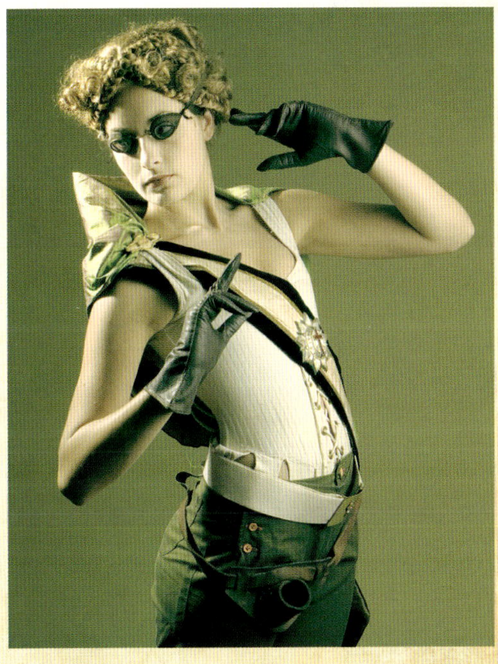

Top: Chad Ward, *Victorian Blue*, 2008. Photography.

Above: Kate O'Brien, *Dystopian Superhero*, 2008. Digital artwork. Steampunk style happily cross-fertilised with elements of Cosplay and fashion.

Left, Top: Two pages from *The Amazing Screw-on Head*, the comic book by Mike Mignola, 2002.

Left, Bottom: Patrick Dumas, Cover art for *League Of Heroes* by Xavier Maumejean, 2005.
Originally published in France in 2003 as *La Ligue Des Heroes*, the comic features Phileas Fogg, Sherlock Holmes, Lord Greystoke and others, protecting the Empire of Albion from the villainy of Peter Pan.

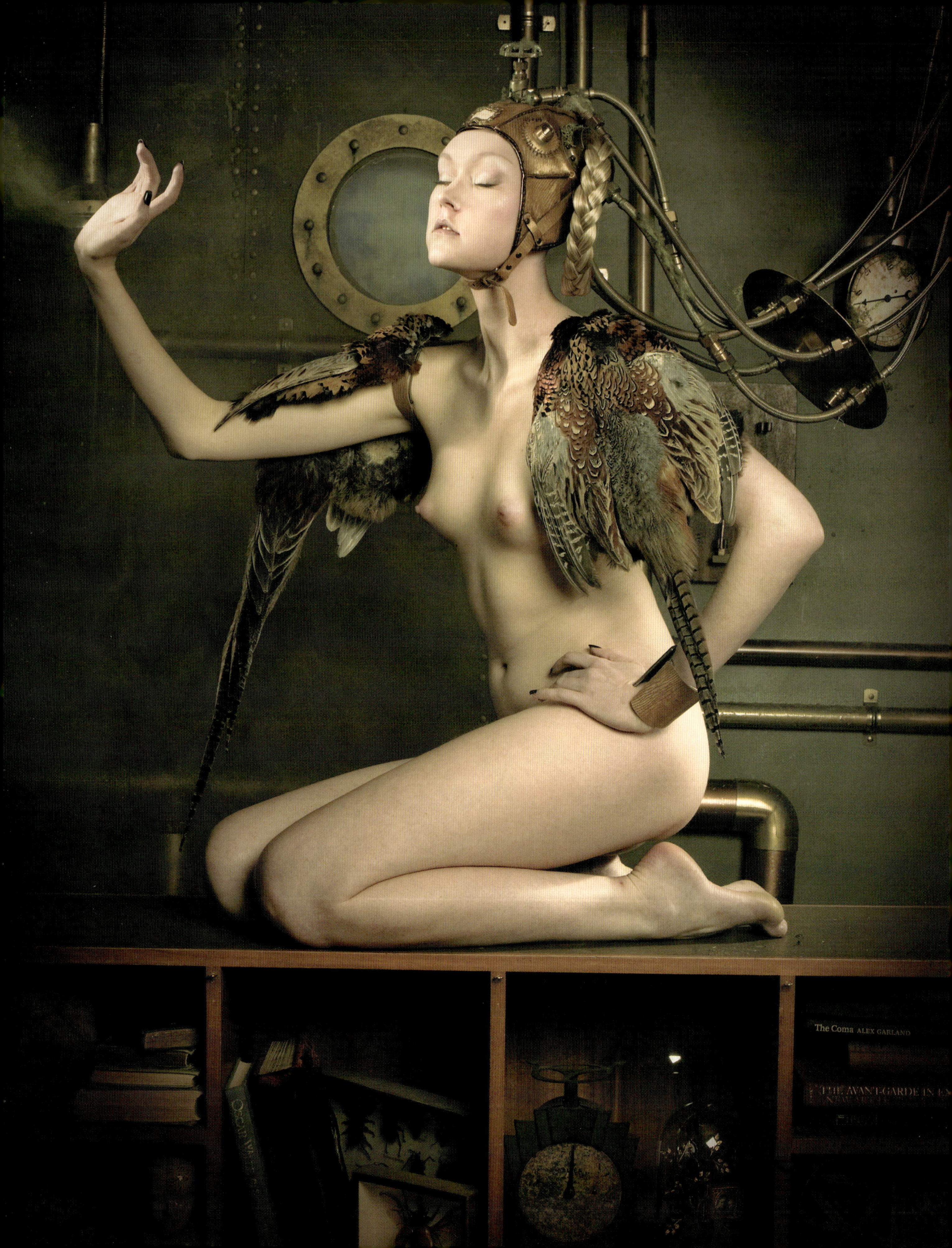
The Coma ALEX GARLAND
THE AVANT-GARDE IN

aesthetically pleasing. Crafting these machines and sculptures by hand also suggests an implicit rejection of modern, passive consumerism. Writer Matthew Crawford, in his recent best-selling book *The Case for Working With Your Hands,* touches on the need and desire amongst men to be able to make and repair things. This all ties in with Steampunk's love of D.I.Y. and mechanical things and its distaste for computerized gadgets and equipment that is increasingly hard to understand and impossible to repair.

Simultaneously, other artists were also busy creating sculptures and non-functional machines that looked as though they had been constructed in the early 1900s rather than a century later. Amongst these works were amazing insects constructed from brass and steel, sleek steam-powered motorbikes, elegant ray-guns that seemed capable of discharging lethal beams of energy, Victorian space-helmets and animal-like robots. To these new craftsmen and craftswomen it didn't matter if the machine they created actually did anything; for them, and those who admired their work, it was all in the construction and beauty of the finished object. But while many of these designs were deliberately non-functional, there were also those who rejoiced in producing clockwork mechanisms such as watches and clocks that not only looked the part but that worked as well. Although the creation of Steampunk art and objects had been almost the last piece of the movement to fall into place, the artists made up for lost time with a vengeance. The last five years have seen an explosion of creativity that shows no signs of abating. Artists, who had been quietly working on their own for years, found out there was a name for what they were doing and their artworks started to be exhibited not just on Steampunk websites, but at various Steampunk gatherings and art exhibitions.

The first major exhibition of Steampunk art objects was held at the Museum of The History of Science, in Oxford, England from October 2009 through to February 2010 and featured eighteen Steampunk artists from around the globe. Curated by New York designer Art Donovan and attended by over 80,000 people, the exhibition was a resounding success and showed that the nascent art and design of the movement was to be taken seriously. A few opening phrases from the broadsheet that accompanied the exhibition almost read like a manifesto for Steampunk creativity: *"In imagining a Victorian future that has not come to pass, Steampunk artists cast an oblique light on the present. But their unrealised 'futures' are more celebratory than commentary. Steampunk revels in the ingenuity and absurdity of mechanism and the unqualified pleasure of making."*

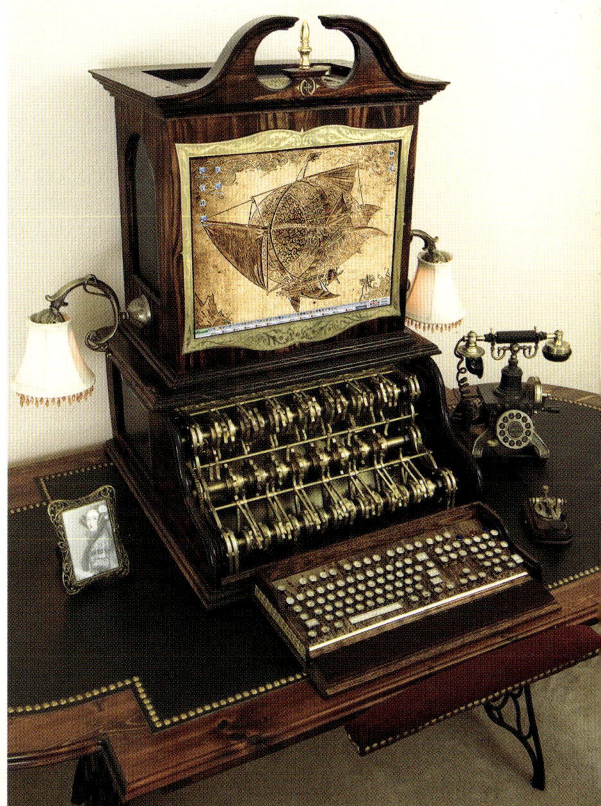

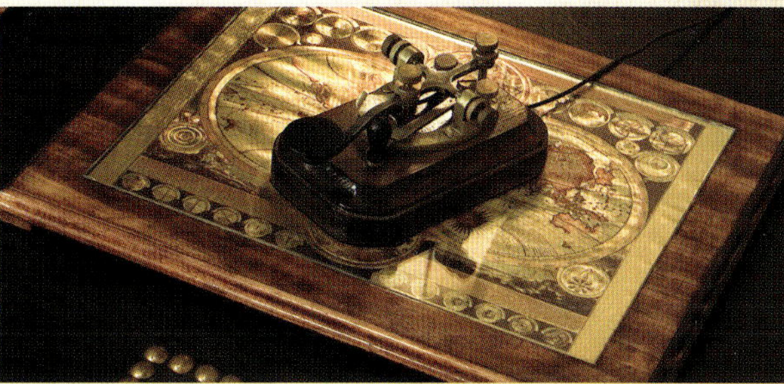

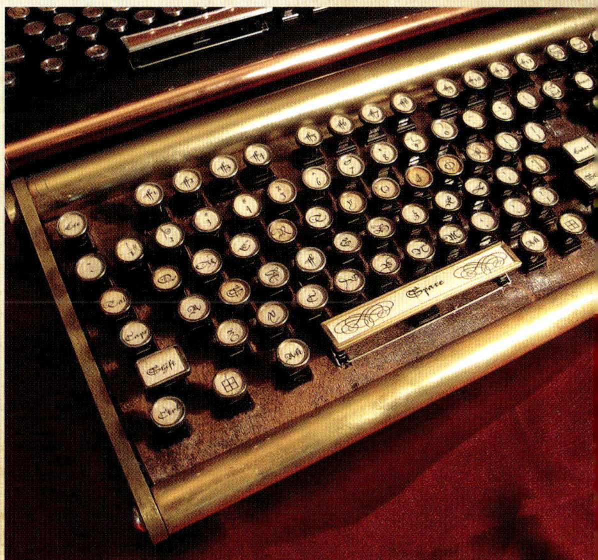

Left: Kate O'Brien, *Vessel*, 2010. Digital artwork.

Right, Top, Middle and Bottom: Richard 'Doc' Nagy, a.k.a. Datamancer, *The Clacker*. Complete PC suite featuring 'Sojourner' keyboard, mouse, mouse pad, speakers and LCD screen. The PC features a spinning brass mechanical display, reminiscent of Charles Babbage's Difference Engine. The name of the work is a reference to the Steampunk novel *The Difference Engine* by William Gibson and Bruce Sterling.

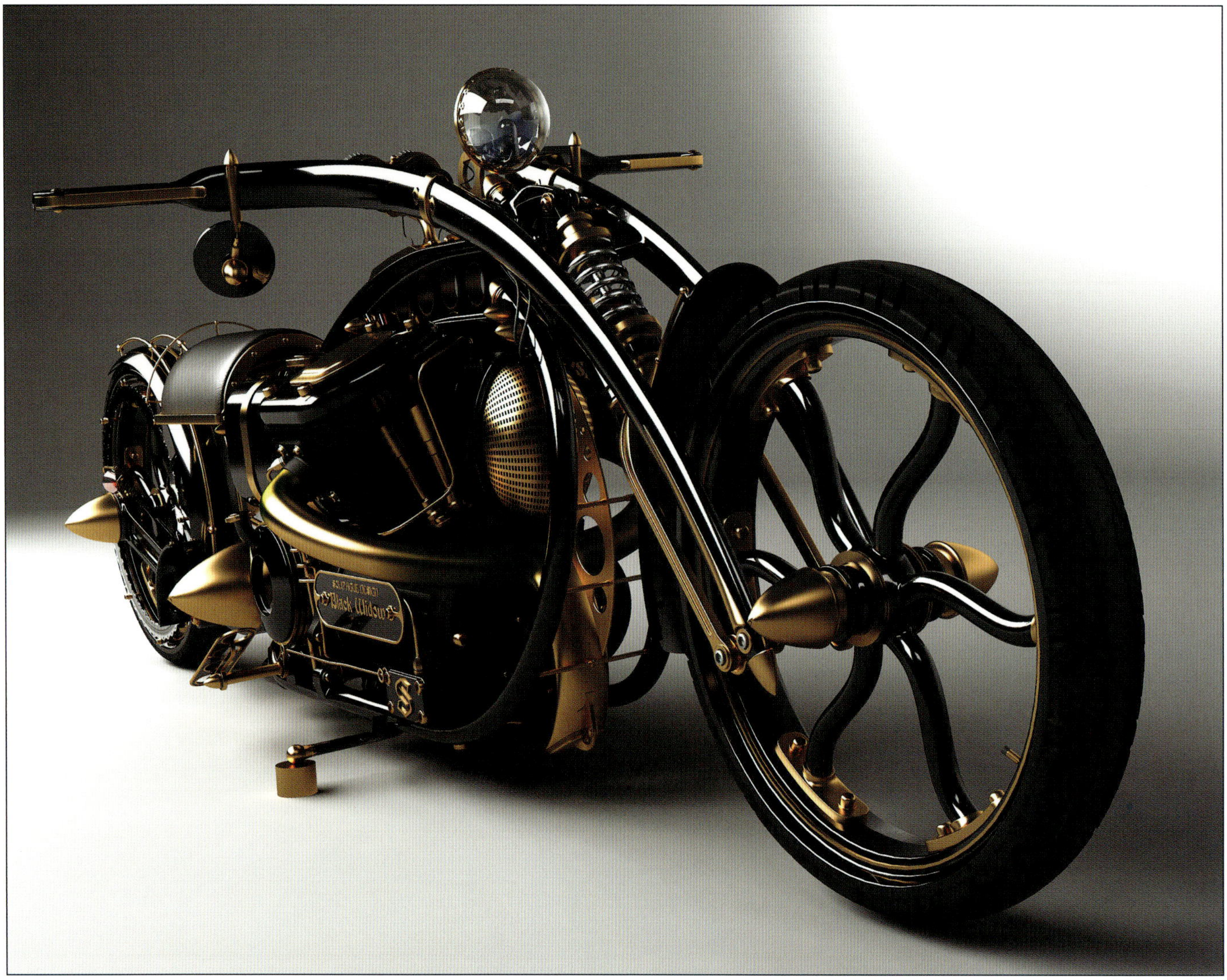

Above and Below: *The Black Widow*. Designed in 3D Max, Russian designer Mikhail Smolyanov's Steampunk chopper is a beguiling mix of high tech and vintage styling. The bike has the requisite amount of brass fittings and period detail to make it a true Steampunk machine, even though it only exists as a design.

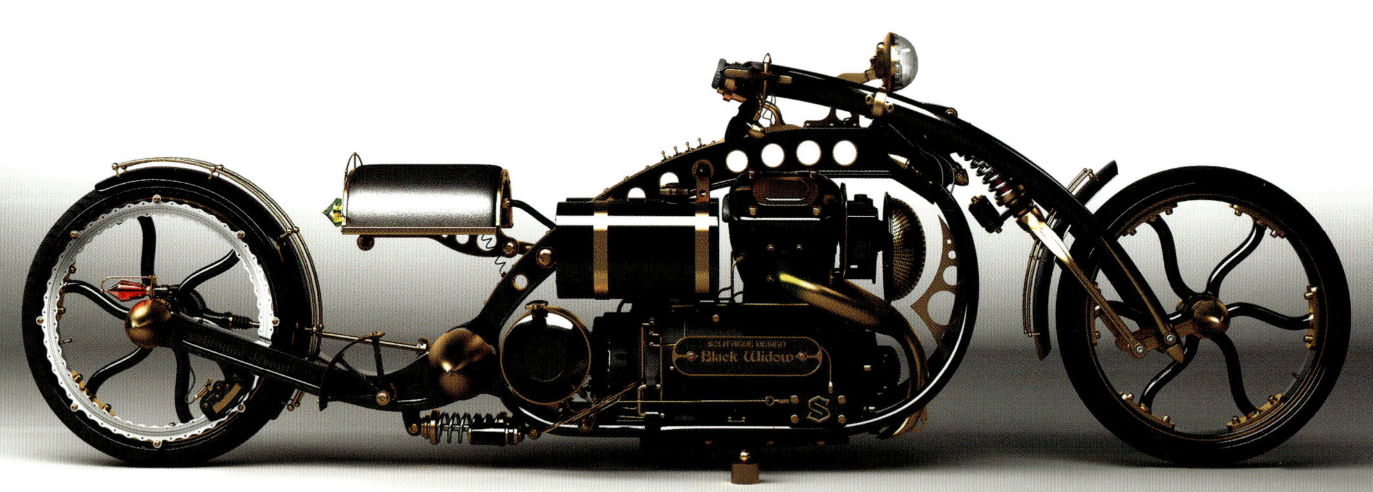

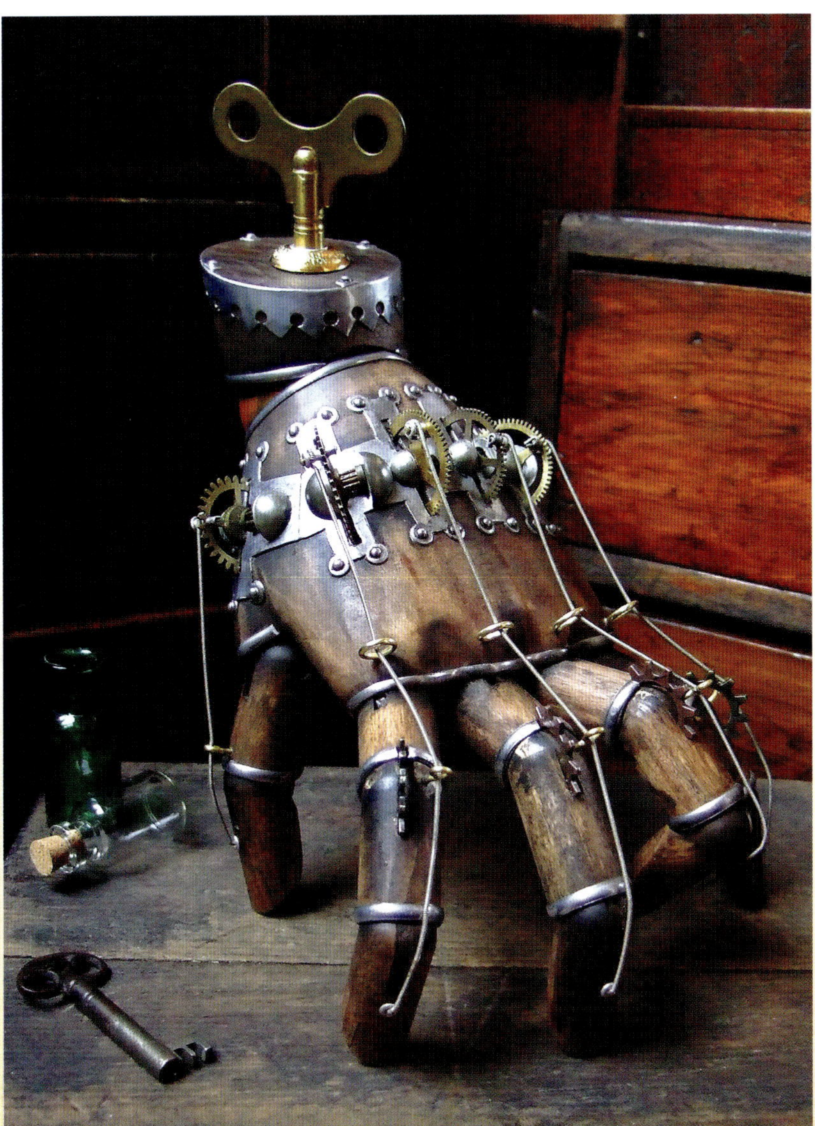

Left: Doktor A, *Thing*, 2010. Rubberwood, lead, brass, copper, steel and found objects. A Steampunk version of the creepy hand monster from the cult TV series *The Addams Family*.

Below: Weyers and Borms design team, *Stereophone*. An amusing take on the idea of a Steampunk hi-fi system.

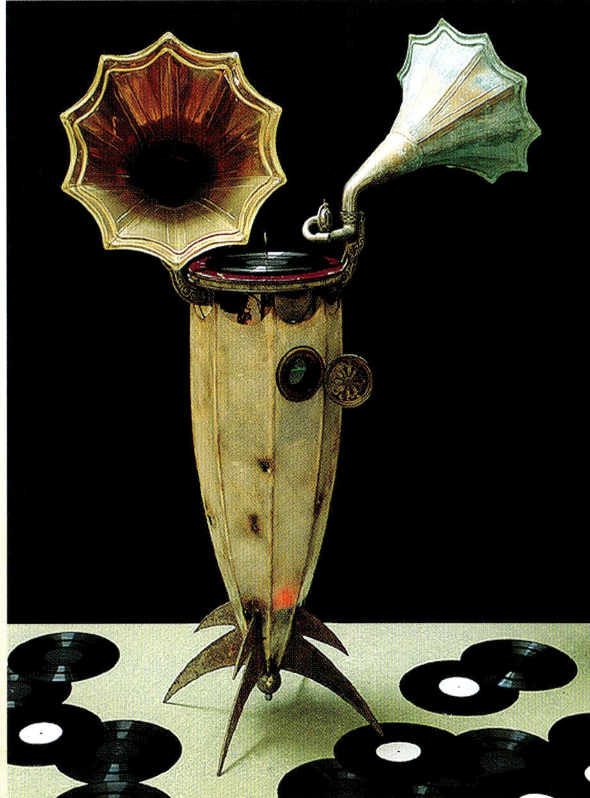

Since Oxford, more and more artists have either embraced Steampunk or produced work that fits the Steampunk aesthetic. Illustrations, paintings and photomontages have expanded the genre from its mechanical beginnings and new themes have moved the subject matter away from a purely Eurocentric core. There has also been a cross-over with the art of Dieselpunk that is focused on the stylings, design and popular culture of the years from 1920 to 1945 including Art Deco, film noir, lounge crooners and big band music. The photomontages of Sam Van Olffen, for instance, seamlessly blend Steam and Diesel punk and it's hard to tell where one genre ends and the other begins. The main linking factor between Diesel and Steam though is a love of pre-digital technology, something that is evident in the growing public appreciation of machines as art works. This appreciation has been encouraged by a series of major art projects that have managed to engage the general public's imagination by blurring the line between fact and fantasy.

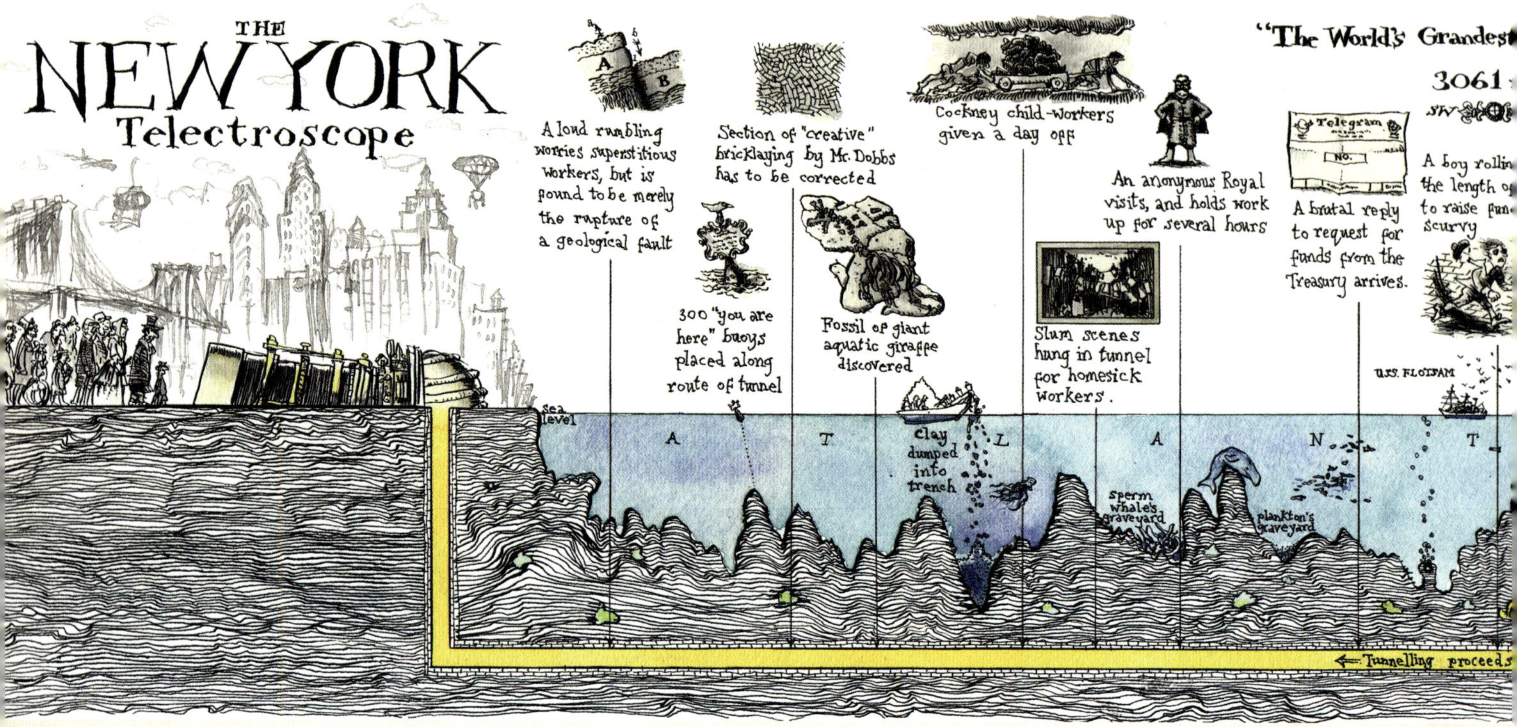

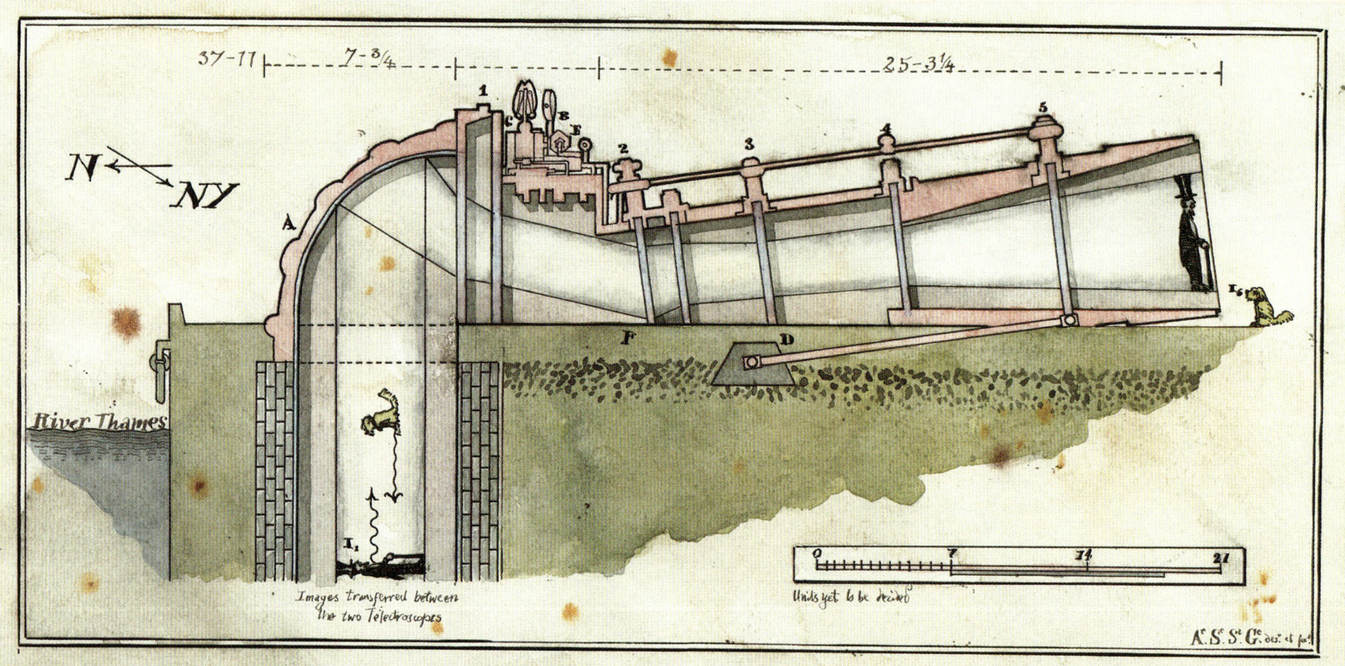

Above: One of Alexander Stanhope St. George's original plans showing the telectroscope's complex series of lenses, with dog watching man, watching dog. Illustration by Felix Bennett.

The Telectroscope was a 2008 art installation erected on both sides of the Atlantic to create the fantasy of a rediscovered Victorian tunnel connecting New York to London. With two giant brass telescopic lenses, that looked like machines from a Verne novel, built near Brooklyn Bridge in New York and Tower Bridge in London, fascinated passers-by could wave to their counterparts across the Atlantic. Supposedly built by Alexander Stanhope St. George during Queen Victoria's reign, the tunnel and its inventor were actually the creations of modern artist Paul St. George. The

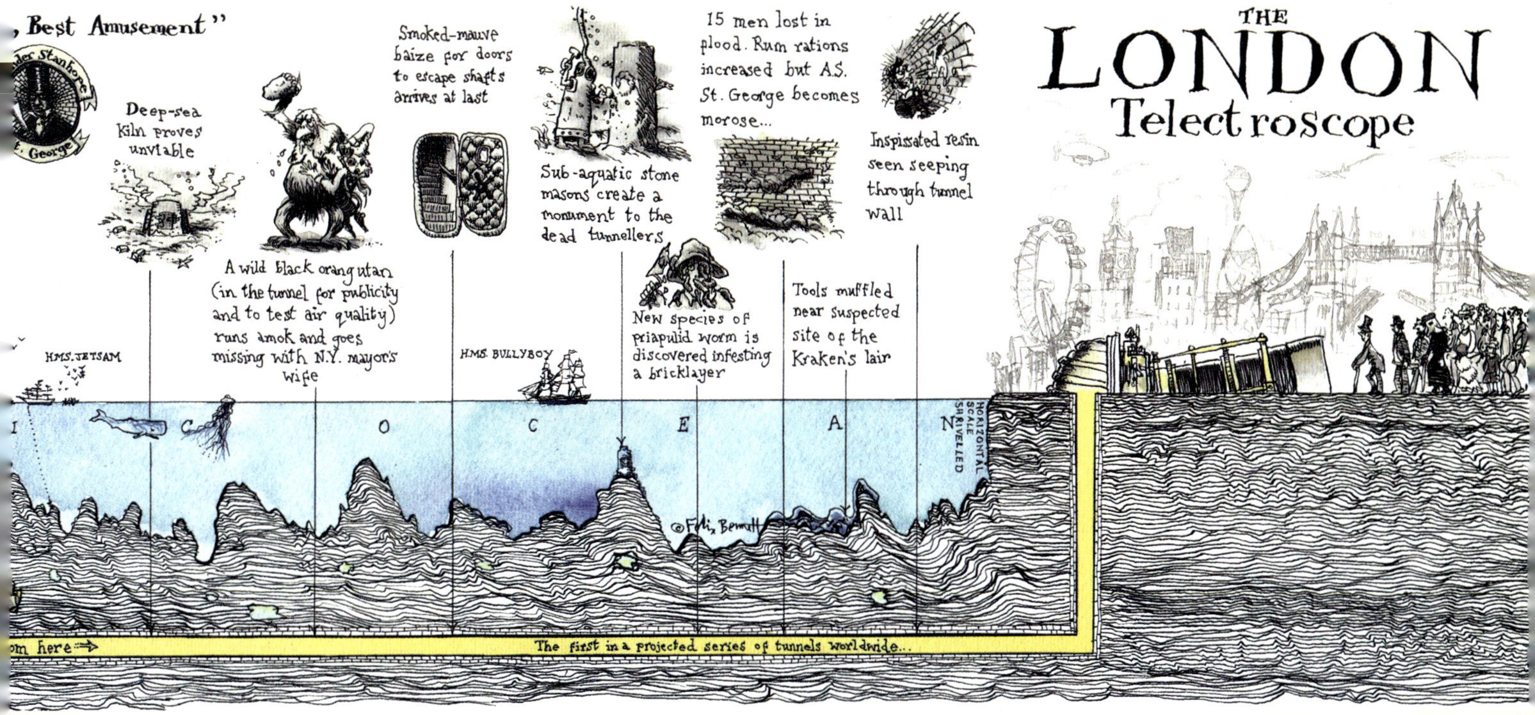

, Best Amusement"

Deep-sea Kiln proves unviable

Smoked-mauve baize for doors to escape shafts arrives at last

15 men lost in flood. Rum rations increased but A.S. St. George becomes morose...

Inspissated resin seen seeping through tunnel wall

Sub-aquatic stone masons create a monument to the dead tunnellers

A wild black orangutan (in the tunnel for publicity and to test air quality) runs amok and goes missing with N.Y. mayor's wife

HMS JETSAM

HMS BULLYBOY

New species of priapulid worm is discovered infesting a bricklayer

Tools muffled near suspected site of the Kraken's lair

O C E A N

HORIZONTAL SCALE SHRIVELLED

om here →

The first in a projected series of tunnels worldwide...

THE LONDON Telectroscope

media and the public didn't care that the two cities were really linked by modern state-of-the-art video technology and everyone seemed happy to go along with the Victorian fantasy so cleverly presented to them. A more permanent example of bringing Steampunk to life is the *Les Machines De L'île Nantes* art project in Nantes, Brittany, France, the birthplace of Jules Verne. Created by François Delarozière and Pierre Orefice, the project is inspired by the mechanical ideas and fantasies of Verne and is built on the site of the former Nantes shipyards. This homage to the city's industrial past and the imagined worlds of Verne's stories features an on-site workshop and giant brass and iron sculptures, including a mechanised thirty-foot-high elephant.

Whatever the fine line between genres, the growing community of artists, designers, engineers, stylists, former Goths, Cyberpunks, and Neo-Victorians, that made up Steampunk, weren't just content with developing fashion and art. Taking musical elements from music hall, folk and goth, amongst other sources, Steampunks started making their own music. In some ways this was a matter of cultural supply and demand. Important though the Internet was to the dissemination of ideas, conventions where people could meet fellow devotees were an important step in the movement's growth. Events Like SalonCon (the first, in 2006), Steamcon in Seattle (launched in 2008) and the UK's White Mischief, proved influential.

As Steampunk and Neo-Victorian conventions started to appear, it made sense for musical entertainment to be provided for the convention-goers. SalonCon, over its three year run (2006 - 2009) run, featured entertainment by Goth solo artist Voltaire and the band Abney Park. Since then groups like Abney Park, Vernian Process

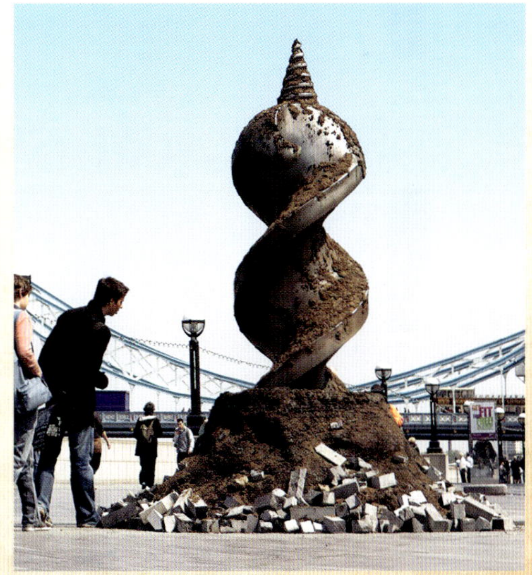

Top: Timeline describing some of the dramatic events which occurred during the construction of the telectrospcope tunnel (horizontal scale reduced). Illustration by Felix Bennett.

Above: The drill bit finally reaching the surface on the south side of Tower Bridge, London, in 2008. Photo by Matthew Andrews.

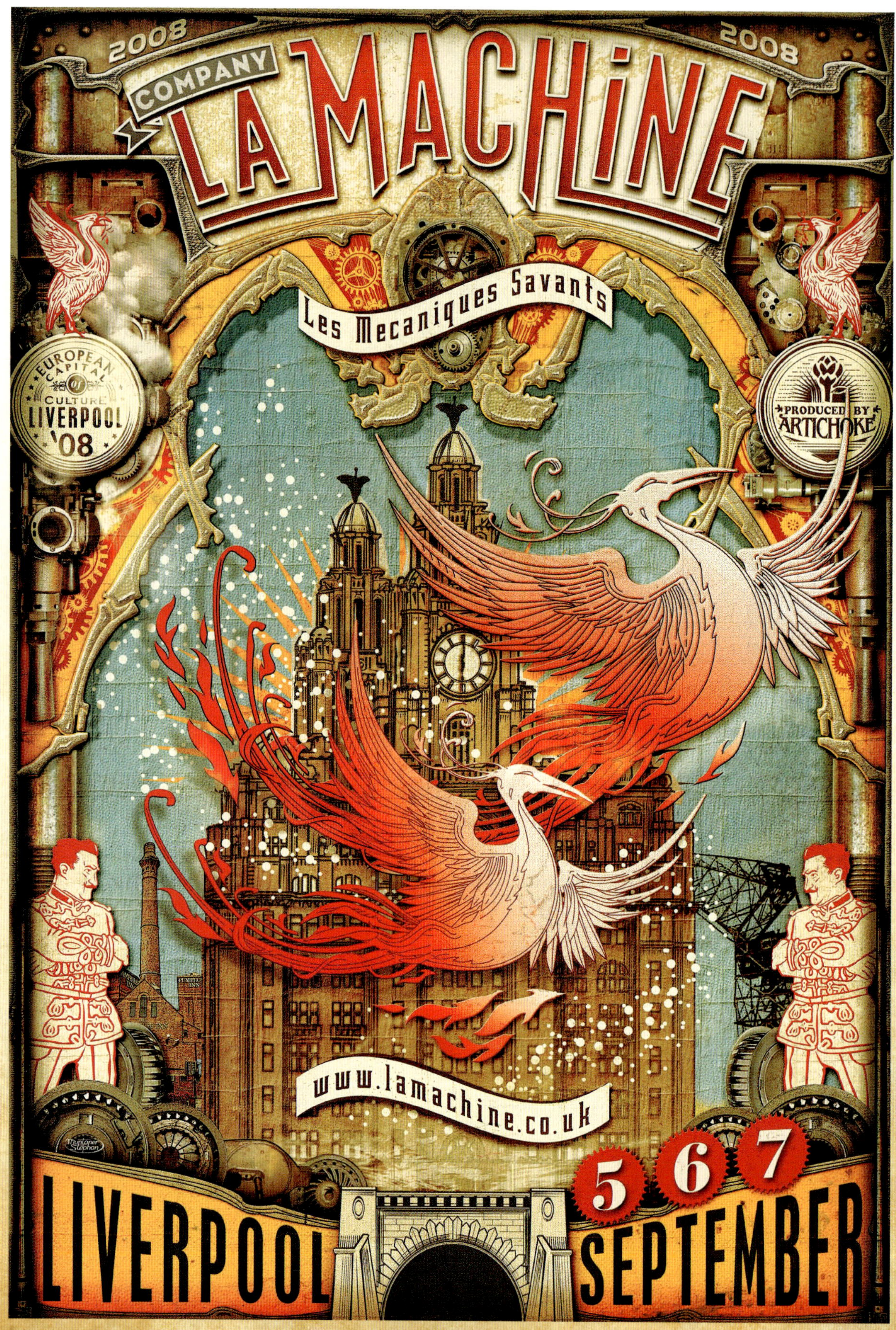
2008
2008
COMPANY
LA MACHINE
Les Mecaniques Savants
EUROPEAN CAPITAL OF CULTURE
LIVERPOOL '08
PRODUCED BY ARTICHOKE
www.lamachine.co.uk
5 6 7
LIVERPOOL
SEPTEMBER

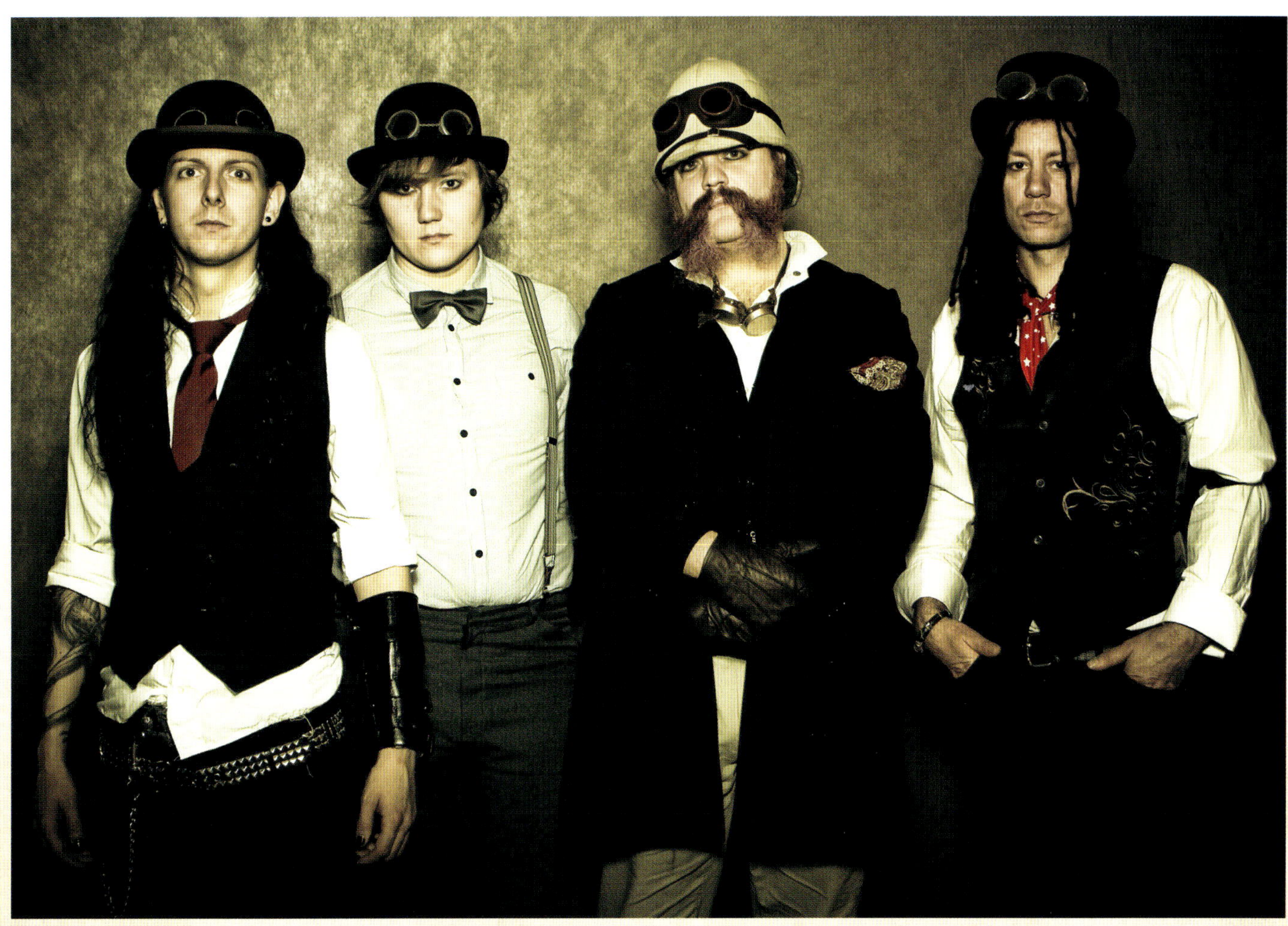

and other sympathetic acts have provided the live musical entertainment at the growing number of Steampunk conventions. Dressed in the appropriate fashions, playing period-friendly or 'modded' instruments and singing of airships and dark Victorian secrets, the bands attracted followings not just from the Steampunk community but also from others who find the mainstream music scene less-than-inspiring. New bands quickly followed the pioneers and the likes of The Men That Will Not Be Blamed For Nothing, The Cog Is Dead, Clockwork Dolls, Dr. Steel and The Clockwork Quartet are all contributing to a musical genre that is as diverse as its numerous influences. Like Steampunk itself there is no exact definition of what constitutes Steampunk music (Cockney Rebel's 1973 song *Sebastian,* with its Faginesque vocals and haunting violins, could be seen as proto-Steampunk), but that is part of its appeal and allows it to keep developing and experimenting.

Music, literature, fashion, art and design: Steampunk has come a long way from its early beginnings as a few books on Victorian futures that never were. The incredible thing about the art in the pages that follow is that it was almost all produced in the last few years. It seems ironic that a movement that celebrates the aesthetics of a past century should also

Above: The Men That Will Not Be Blamed For Nothing at the inaugural World Steam Expo in Dearborn, Michigan in 2010. Photo by Lex Machina.

Left: To celebrate Liverpool's 2008 status as European Capital of Culture, the French artistic/engineering collaboration known as La Machine (co-founder François Delarozière is also one of the partners behind the *Les Machines De L'ile* mechanical project in Nantes) exhibited a giant, 50-foot-high, mechanised spider in the city. Dubbed 'La Princesse' by her creators, the spider was placed in a 'nest' on a building by the railway station, before then making its way through the city centre as huge crowds watched in amazement.

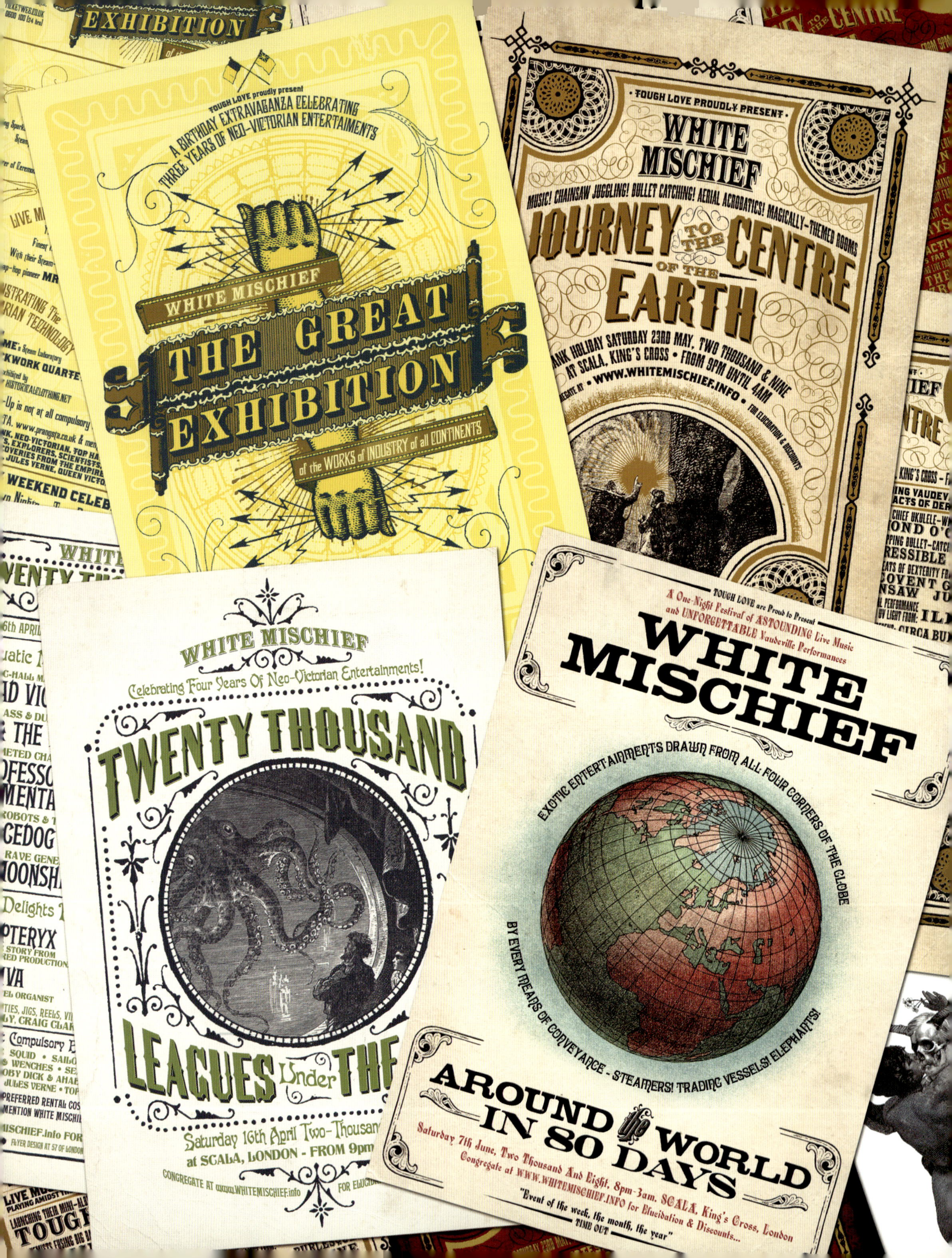

TOUGH LOVE proudly present
A BIRTHDAY EXTRAVAGANZA CELEBRATING THREE YEARS OF NEO-VICTORIAN ENTERTAINMENTS
WHITE MISCHIEF
THE GREAT EXHIBITION
of the WORKS of INDUSTRY of all CONTINENTS
TOUGH LOVE PROUDLY PRESENT
WHITE MISCHIEF
MUSIC! CHAINSAW JUGGLING! BULLET CATCHING! AERIAL ACROBATICS! MAGICALLY-THEMED ROOMS
JOURNEY TO THE CENTRE OF THE EARTH
AT SCALA, KING'S CROSS • FROM 9PM UNTIL 4AM
WWW.WHITEMISCHIEF.INFO
WHITE MISCHIEF
Celebrating Four Years Of Neo-Victorian Entertainments!
TWENTY THOUSAND LEAGUES Under THE
Saturday 16th April Two-Thousand
at SCALA, LONDON - FROM 9pm
CONGREGATE AT www.WHITEMISCHIEF.info
TOUGH LOVE are Proud to Present
A One-Night Festival of ASTOUNDING Live Music and UNFORGETTABLE Vaudeville Performances
WHITE MISCHIEF
EXOTIC ENTERTAINMENTS DRAWN FROM ALL FOUR CORNERS OF THE GLOBE
BY EVERY MEANS OF CONVEYANCE - STEAMERS! TRADING VESSELS! ELEPHANTS!
AROUND the WORLD IN 80 DAYS
Saturday 7th June, Two Thousand And Eight, 8pm-3am. SCALA, King's Cross, London
Congregate at WWW.WHITEMISCHIEF.INFO for Elucidation & Discounts...
"Event of the week, the month, the year"
TIME OUT

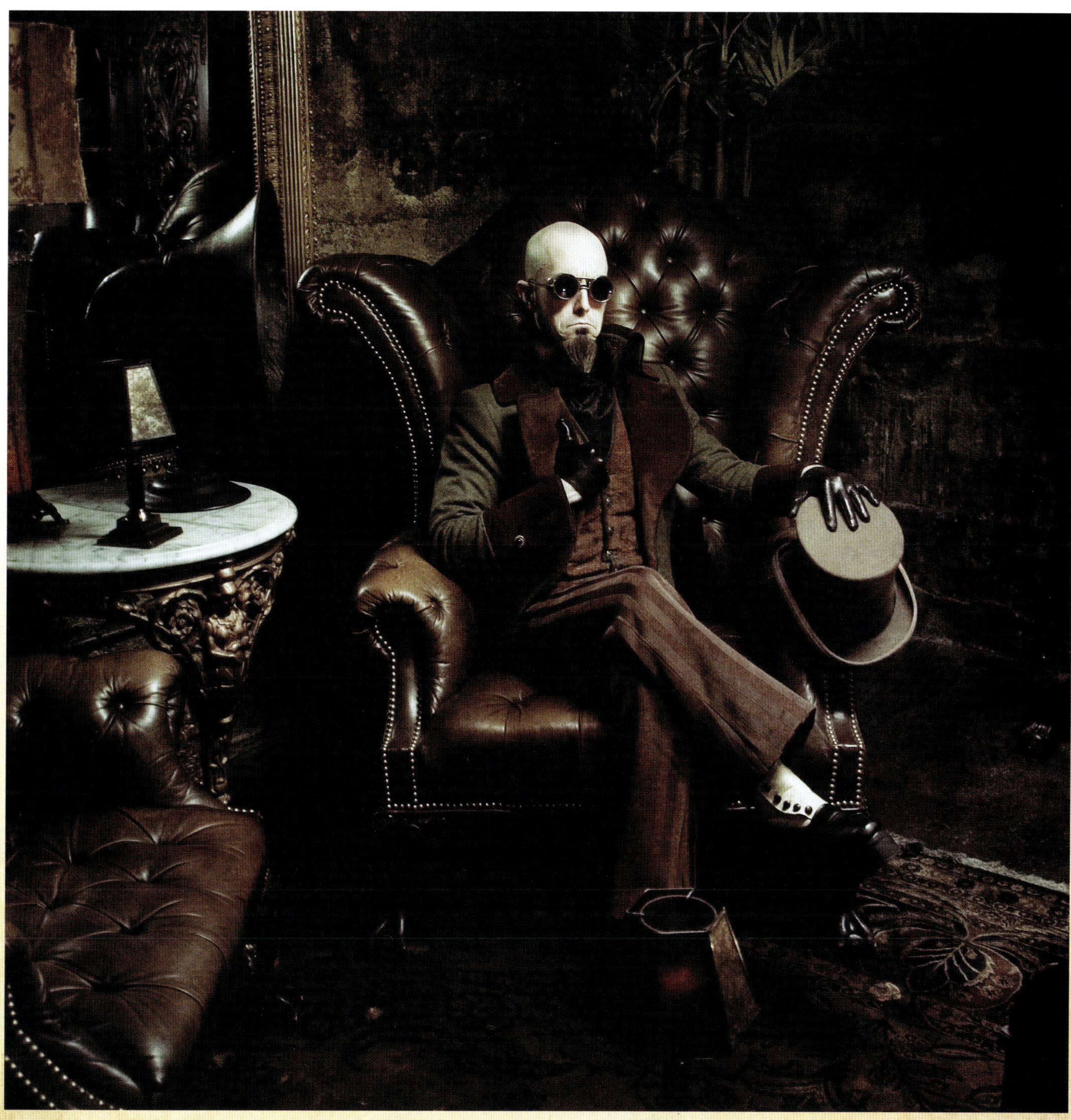

seem so contemporary – but that is what Steampunk is, and Steampunk art is one of the few, genuinely new art genres of the 21st Century. In collecting together the work of the artists featured in these pages, we have endeavoured to present a variety of the styles and artistic media that fall under the Steampunk banner. Our aim has not been to define the undefinable but to present a snapshot of a vital, organic movement that is driven by both reality and fantasy, by what is, what was and what could have been.

Above: Doctor Steel is a singer songwriter who has been involved in the Goth, Rivethead and Steampunk scenes. Mixing hip hop, opera, folk and other eclectic musical genres, Doctor Steel performs in the persona of a mad scientist bent on world conquest. Photograph by Chad Ward, 2008.

Left: Flyer artwork by Steve Mitchell of 57design. Founded in 2007 by tribal pop band Tough Love, White Mischief parties are held in London and other cities in the UK on a regular basis. The events have attracted an increasingly large Steampunk contingent. The themes of the parties have included Jules Verne's *Journey To The Centre Of The Earth*, *Around The World In 80 Days* and *20,000 Leagues Under The Sea.*

TOM BANWELL

Born in Oakland, California in 1948, Tom was fascinated by hats as a child and became an avid collector. A self-taught artist, he dabbled in a variety of media (including leather) before running a business designing and making men's Western leather hats. Then, aged 57, he became seriously ill, and began to re-evaluate his life, realising that he wanted to return to art. He began once more creating in leather, connected with other leatherworkers and, with his wife, opened a shop selling leather masks. Whilst surfing Etsy.com, he came across the term 'Steampunk' and discovered a world "where my sort of creativity would perfectly fit." In 2008 he found a gas mask at a yard sale, recreated it in leather and resin, and his first Steampunk item was born. Now fully recovered, he hasn't looked back; Tom's work was part of the Steampunk exhibition at Oxford University, has been used on TV (*The Cape*, *Smallville*, *Gossip Girls*) and in the movies *After The Fall* and *New Year's Eve*.

Below Left: *Dr. Beulenpest*. "Dressed in his finest for a night out on the town, wearing a Steampunk version of the classic plague doctor mask. Made of leather and cold-cast aluminium, the mask is held together with hand-stitched waxed thread and domed rivets."

Below Right: *The Sentinel*. "He appears in full dress, with a ceremonial antique sword. His headwear consists of three parts. The leather helmet has a cold-cast aluminium front plate (with the Gryphon Interplanetary Aeroship Expedition logo of gryphons rampant in relief), a central headlamp and a metal auditory amplifier. The back of the helmet features a series of luminiferous aether collecting devices. The Defender gas mask has two distinct eyepieces and a pair of Anemone gas canisters. The gorget completes the ensemble."

Right: *The Captain of the Gryphon Airship*. "The Captain strikes a pose wearing a moulded leather helmet, with goggles and horsehair and an Excursionist respirator. He is holding a Raughnold Model 81 raygun."

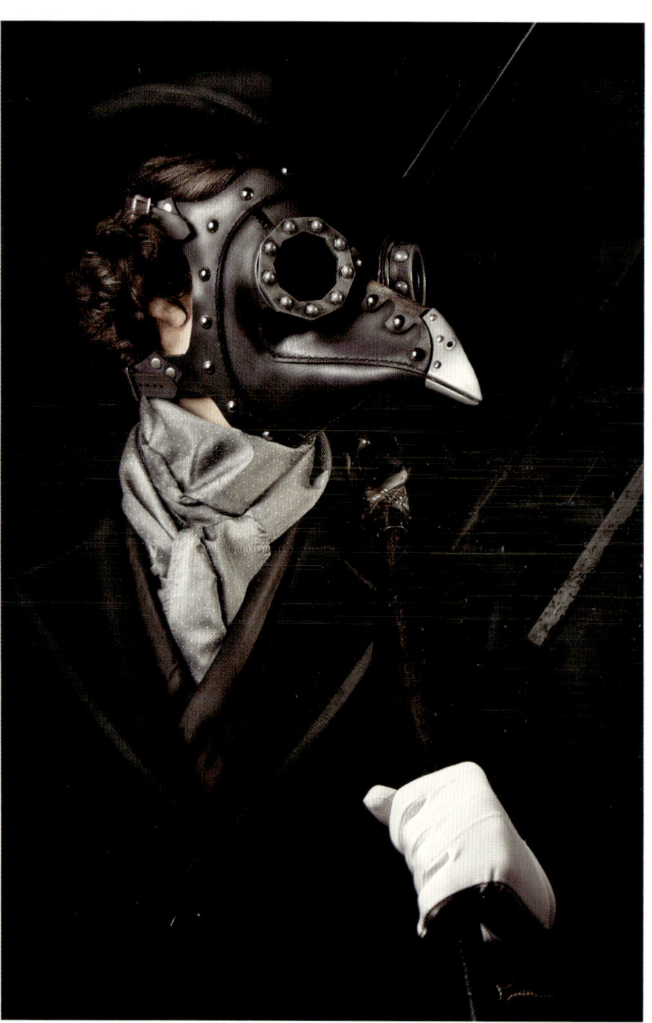

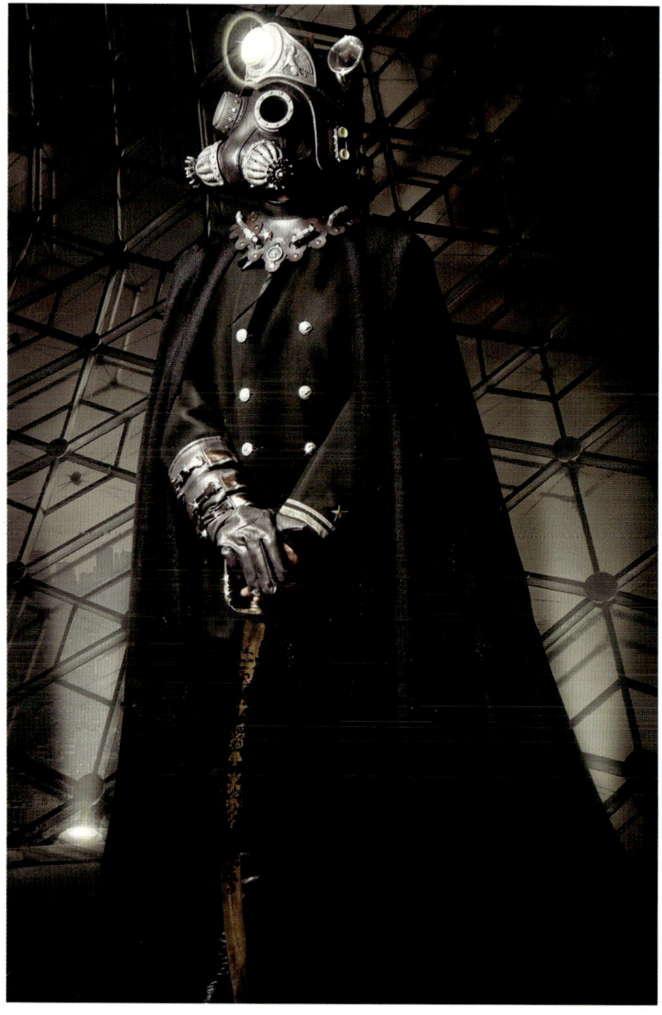

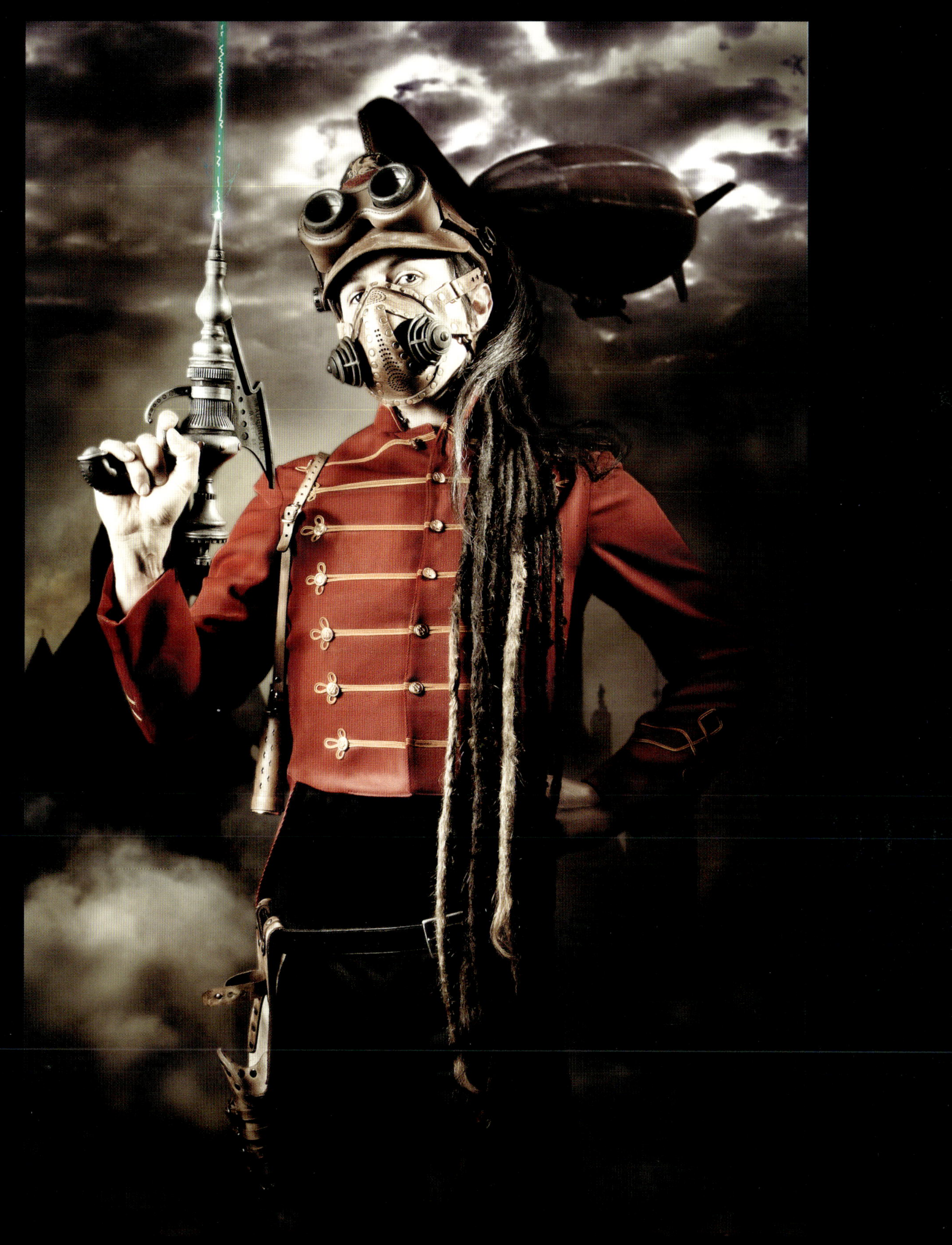

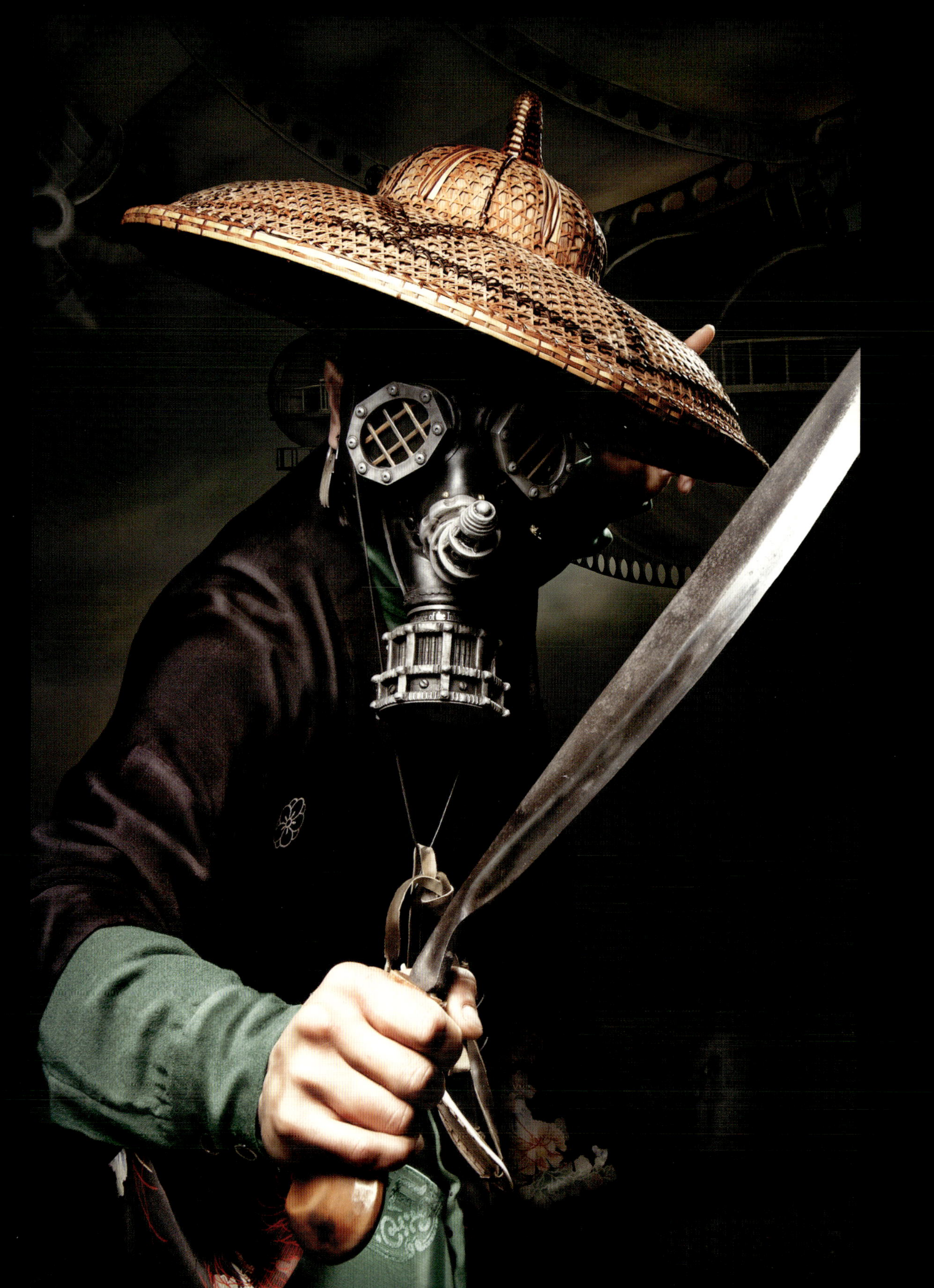

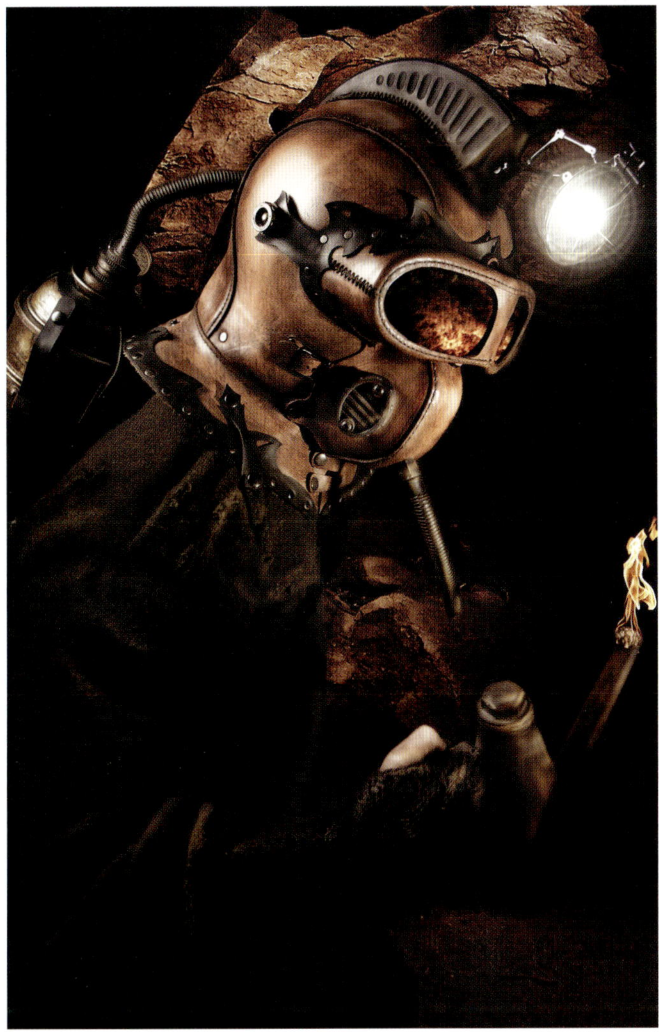

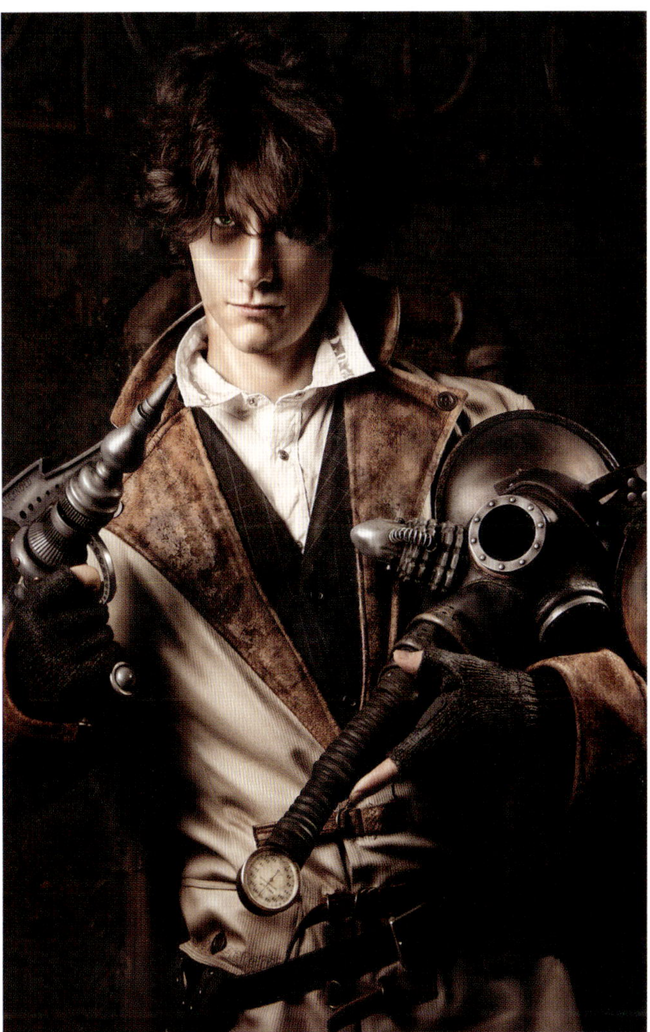

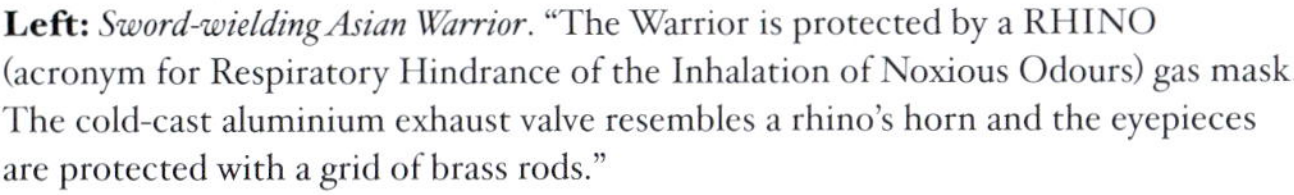

Left: *Sword-wielding Asian Warrior*. "The Warrior is protected by a RHINO (acronym for Respiratory Hindrance of the Inhalation of Noxious Odours) gas mask. The cold-cast aluminium exhaust valve resembles a rhino's horn and the eyepieces are protected with a grid of brass rods."

Above Left: *The Underground Explorer.* "He gazes in wonder at the sights revealed by his headlamp and oil lamp. The backpack tank holds septoxygen, a dense liquid form of the life-giving element, made breathable by catalysts within the mask's snout-like face piece. Both the goggles and respirator are removable."

Above Right: *Intrepid Hero*. "Our hero poses proudly holding an Olifant gas mask and a Raughnold Model 81. The Olifant is a later edition of the Pachydermos gas mask, with an improved set of gas canisters and a neoprene hose in place of leather."

Right: *Pachydermos Gas Mask*: close-up. "This mask bears an uncanny resemblance to an elephant. It is made mostly of hand-stitched leather with cold-cast aluminium canisters and removable copper auditory receivers."

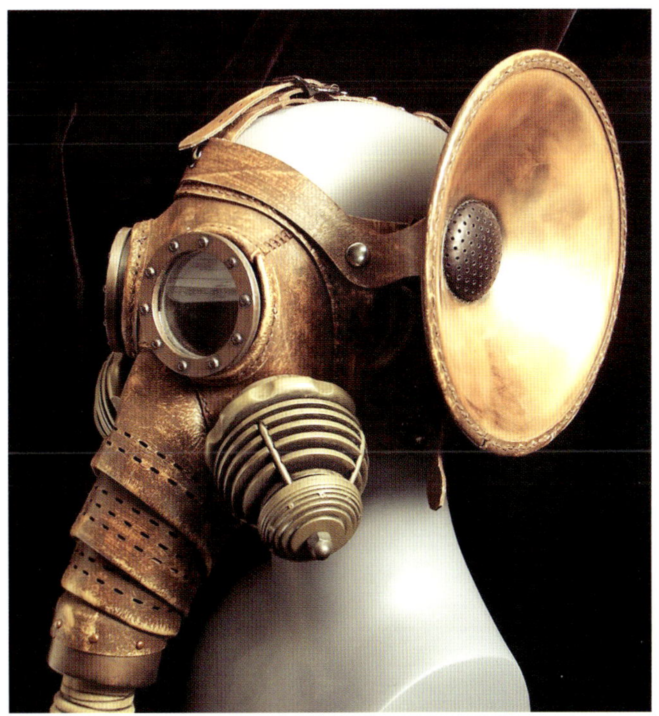

WAYNE MARTIN BELGER

Wayne Martin Belger hails from Pasadena, CA, the son of "very understanding middle-class Catholic parents." He remembers being intrigued by Latin Mass when he was five: "Not knowing Latin, the magic language, magic practices, magic altars and ritual were things with which I communicated visually." The powerful spiritual resonance of his work is no accident: "as the priest is in direct communion with his subject, Jesus, using his tools of gold and silver, and blood and body, so I create my tools of aluminium and titanium, and blood and body, to be in a direct relationship with my subjects." Wayne's chosen medium is the pinhole camera, so there is no intercession of lenses, no chips converting light to binary code; the air surrounding his subjects is in direct contact with the emulsion on the film. "My cameras are there as a sacred bridge, to witness and to be a tool of the horrors of creation and the beauty of decay, presented by the authors: light and time."

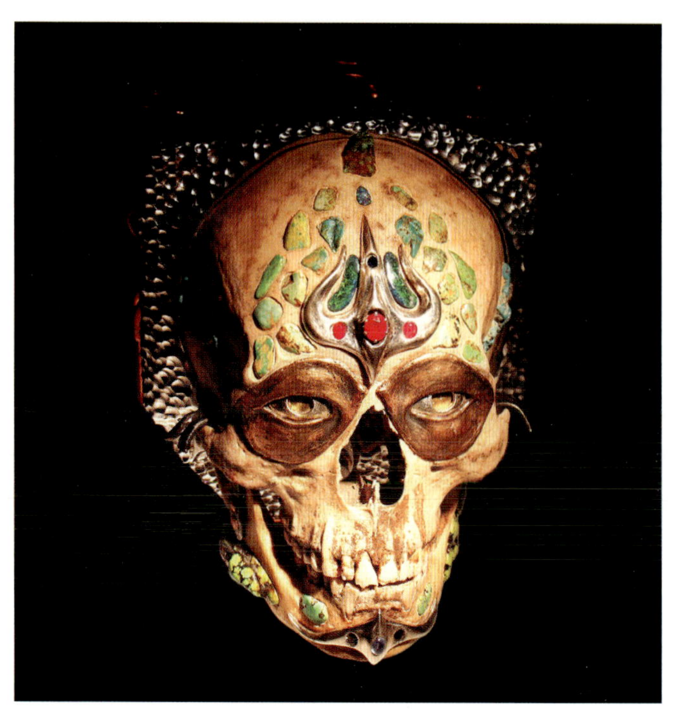

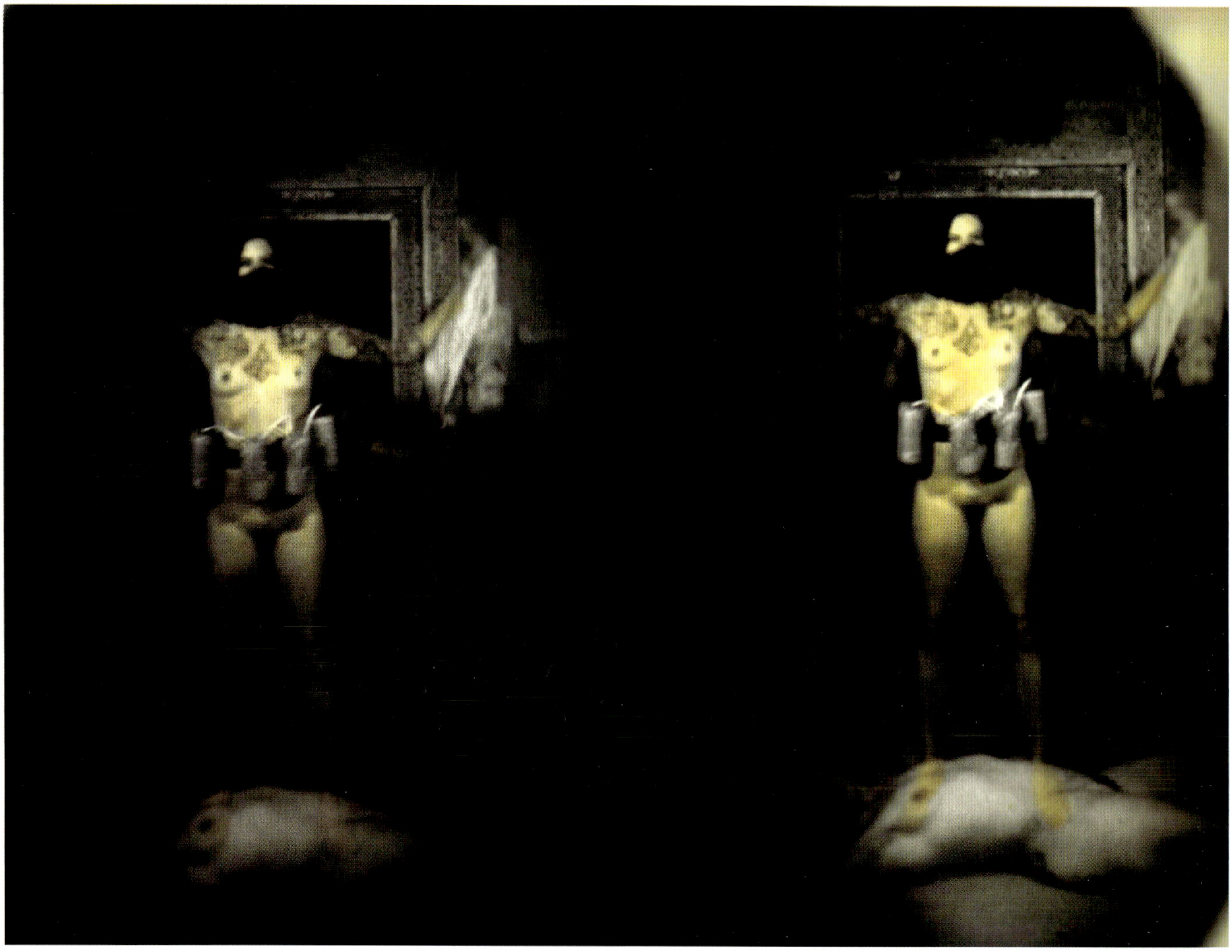

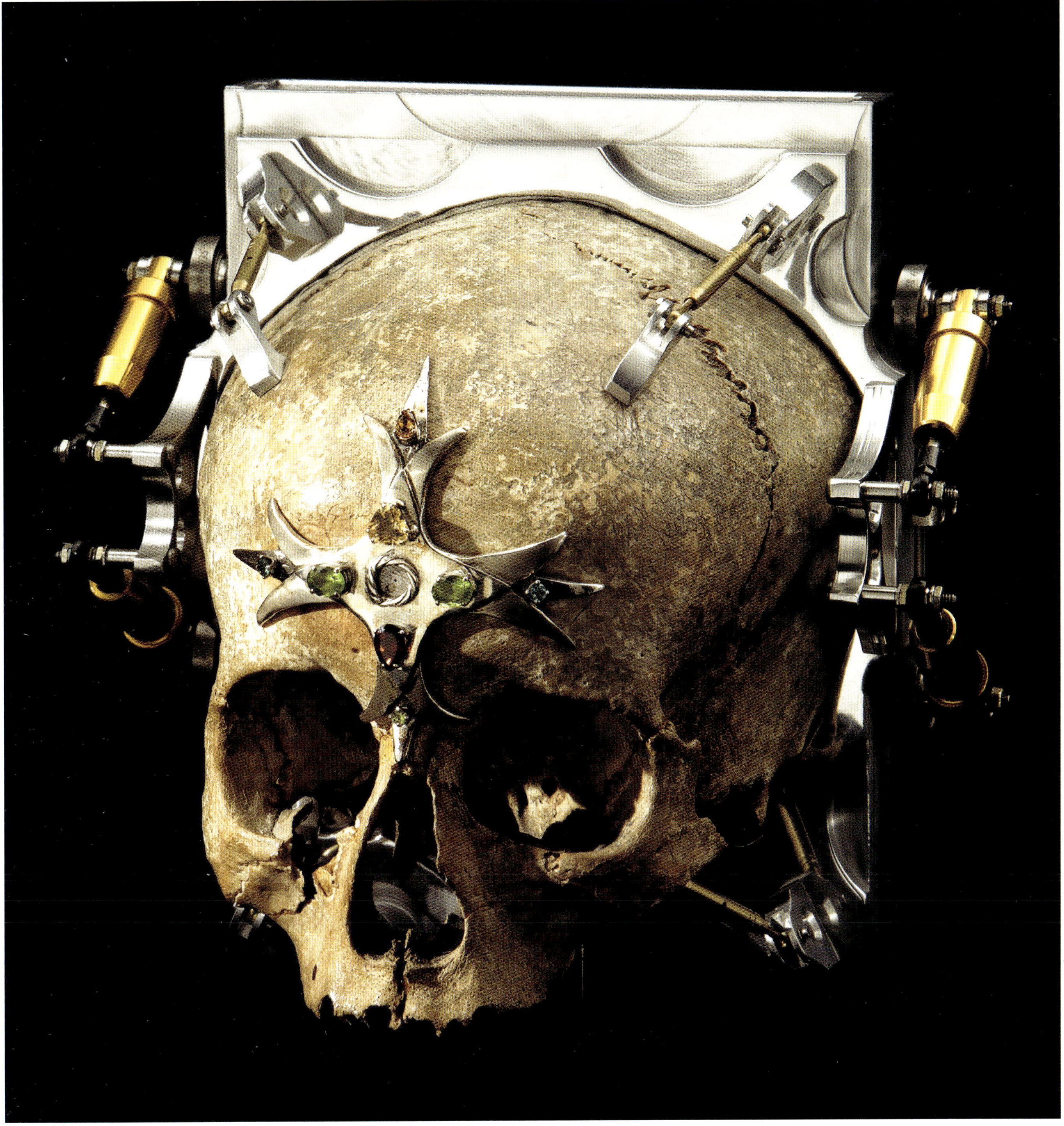

Above: *Third Eye,* 2004.
Functional camera; light and time enters through the 'third eye', exposing the film in the middle of the skull.
Aluminium, titanium, brass, silver, gemstones, 150-year old human skull. 12" x 30"; (30.5 cm x 76.2 cm).

Above Left: *Yama*.
Functional camera. Aluminium, titanium, copper, brass, steel, silver, 999.9% pure gold, turquoise,
four sapphires, three rubies, seven opals, human skull.

Left: *Kali,* 2006.
Toned silver gelatin print from the camera Yama; subject painted with prickly pear black tea.
6" x 2.5" x 6" ; (15 cm x 6.5 cm x 15 cm).

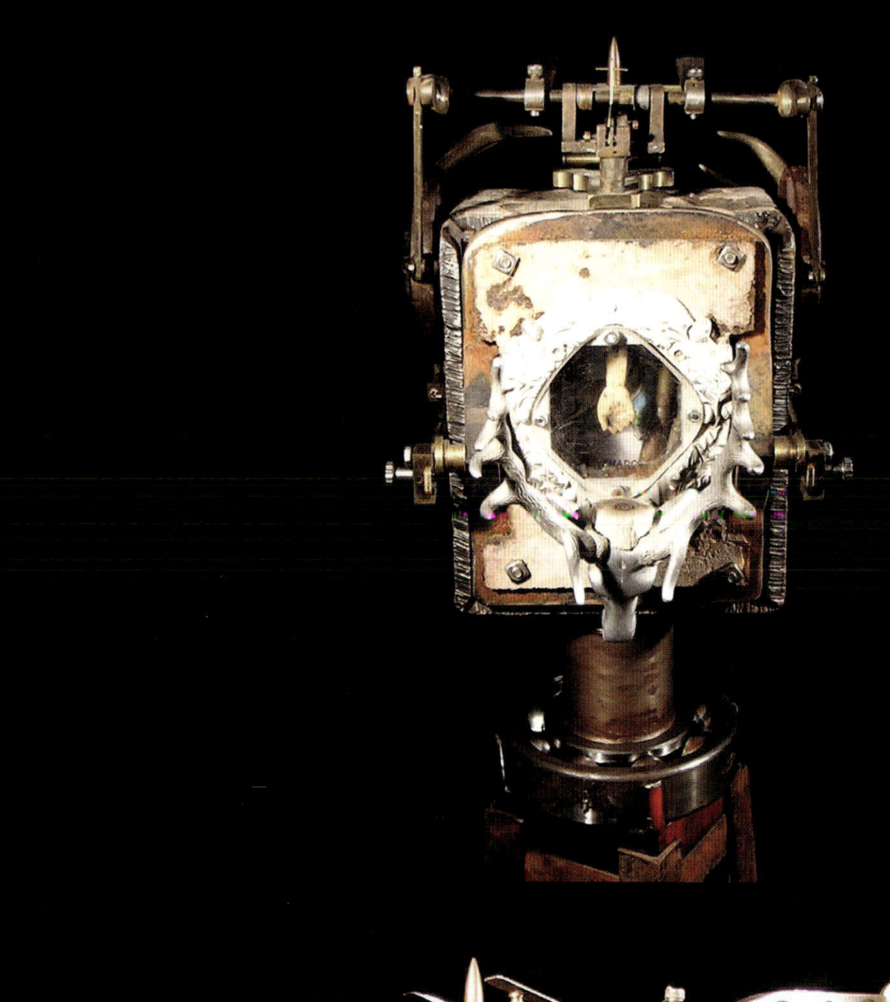

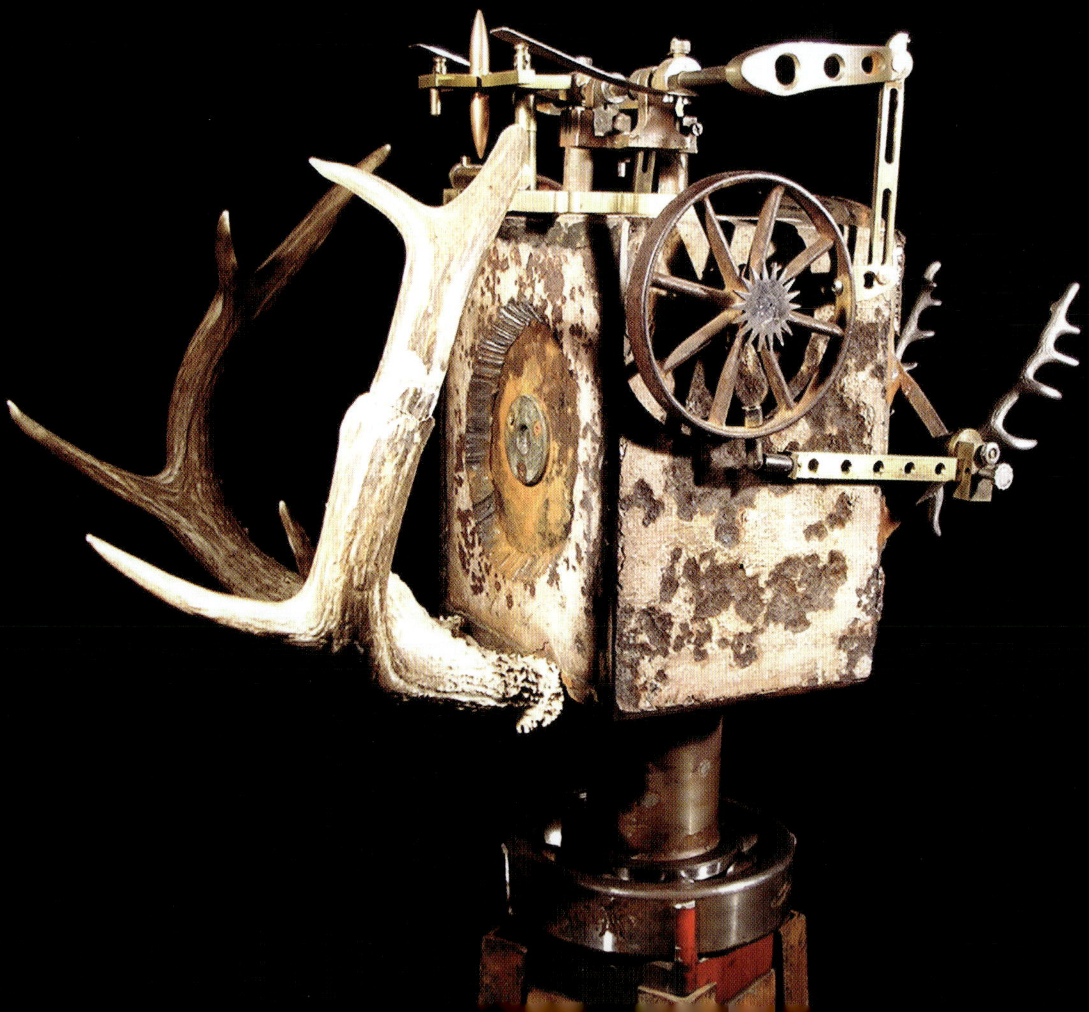

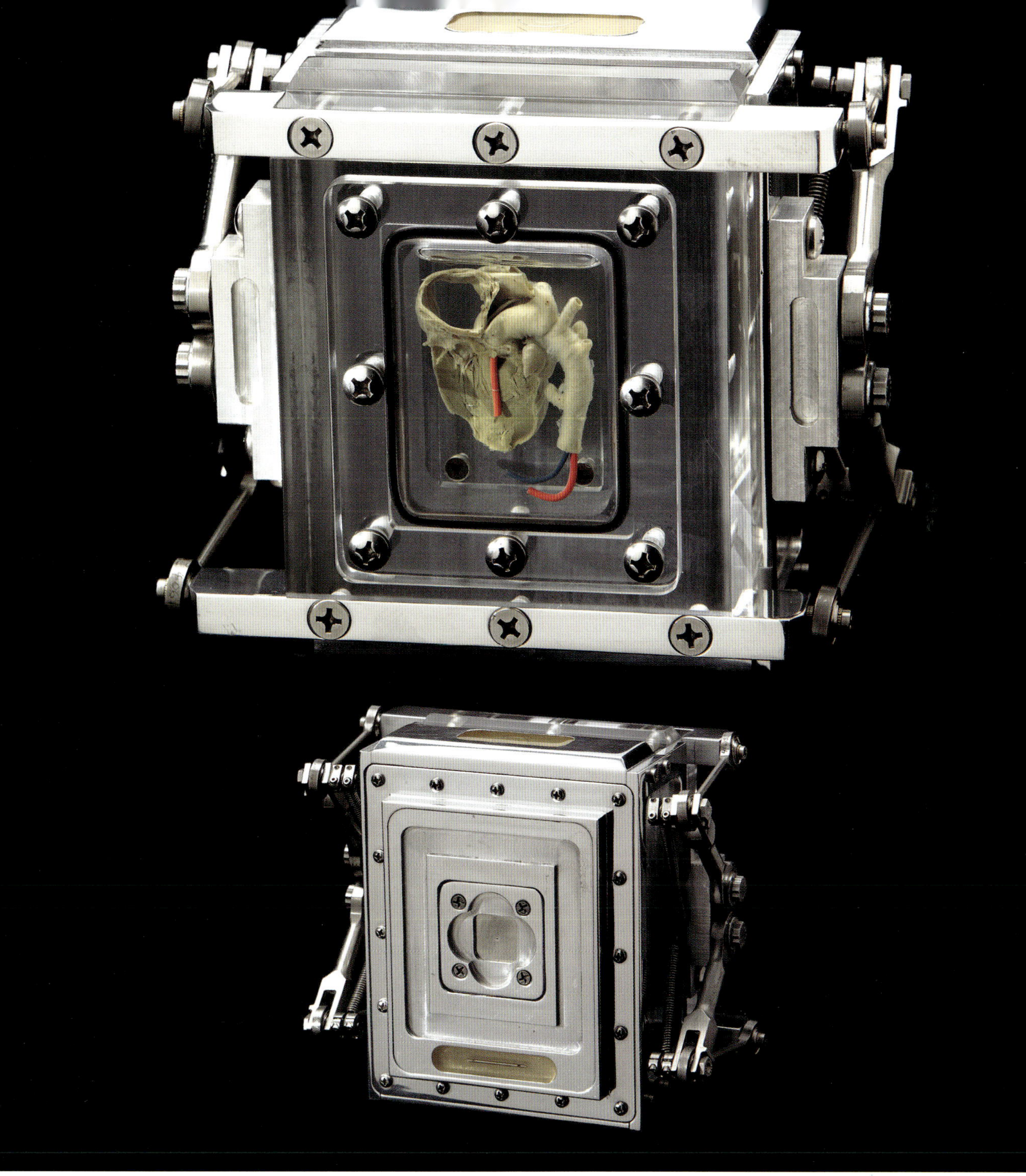

Above: *Heart Camera,* 2004.
Functional camera; designed by Wayne to take photos of soon-to-be pregnant mothers, and as a way of exploring his relationship with his twin brother, who died at birth. Aluminium, titanium, acrylic, formaldehyde, infant heart. 10" x 24"; (25.4 cm x 61 cm).

Left: *Deer Camera,* 2007.
Functional camera; designed to photograph the core ritual of the hunt and man's arrogant separation from nature. Steel plate (found in the desert near Mexico), brass (from 19th Century scales and bullet shells), aluminium, deer antlers and ivory (from an 18th Century figure of Christ). 84" x 72 x 48"; (213.4 cm x 182.9 cm x 121.9 cm).

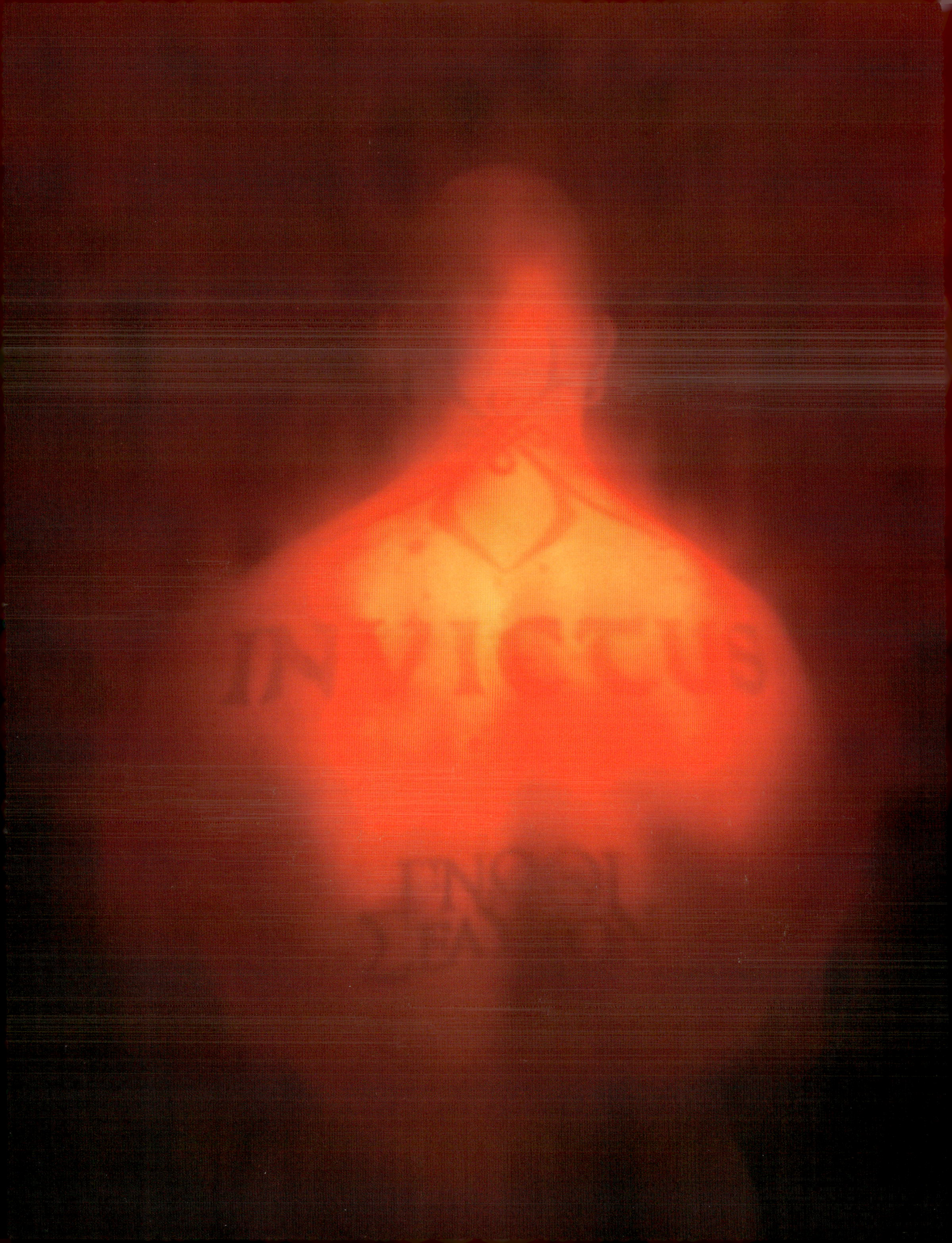

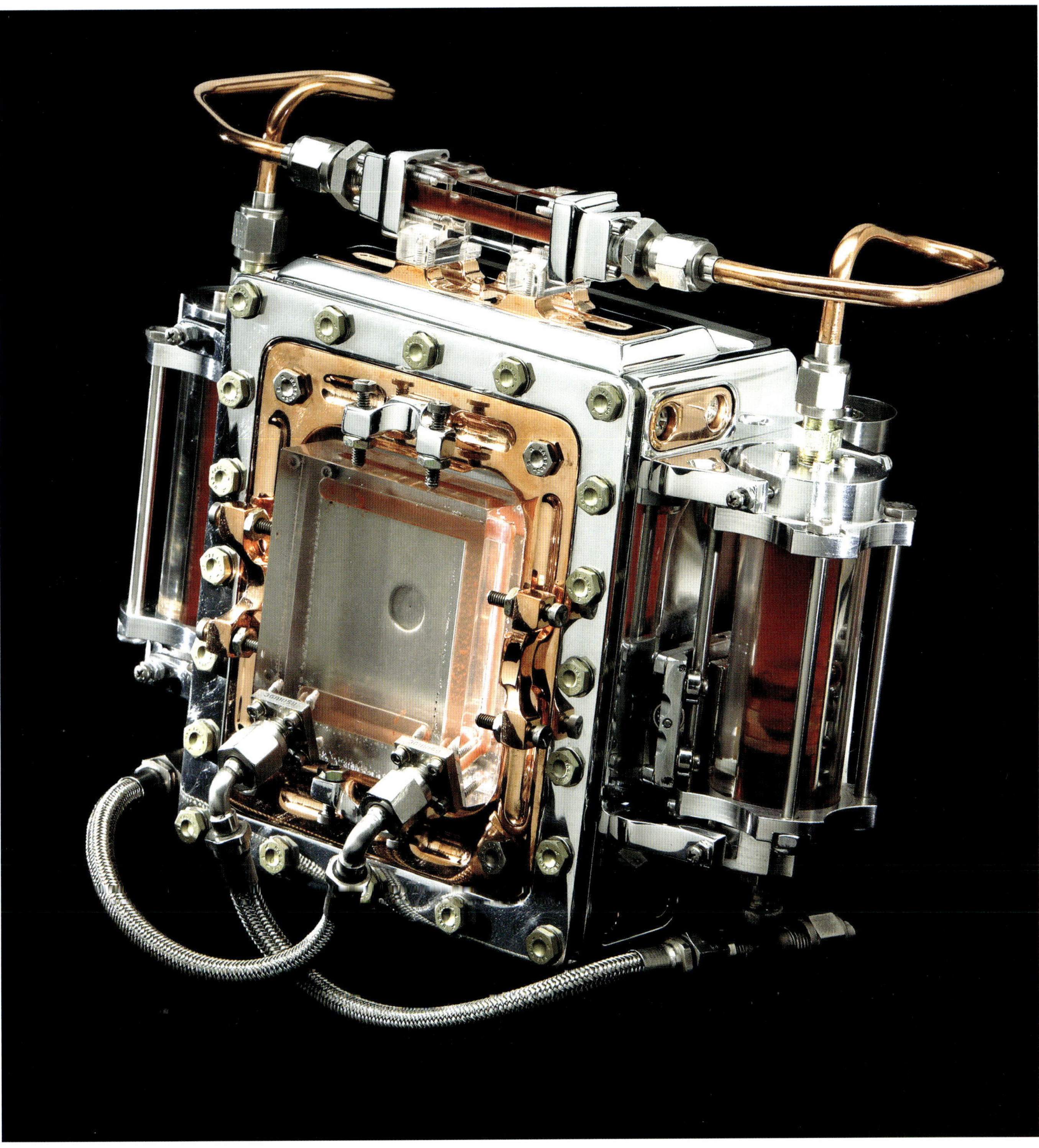

Above: *Untouchable (HIV)*, 2006.
Functional camera; the blood pumps through the camera and then in front of the pinhole, acting as a no.25 red filter. Designed by Wayne for a photographic/geographic study of HIV sufferers. Aluminium, copper, titanium, acrylic, HIV-positive blood. 24" x 60"; (60 cm x 152.4 cm).

Left: *Bloodworks 7.* Gelatin silver print.

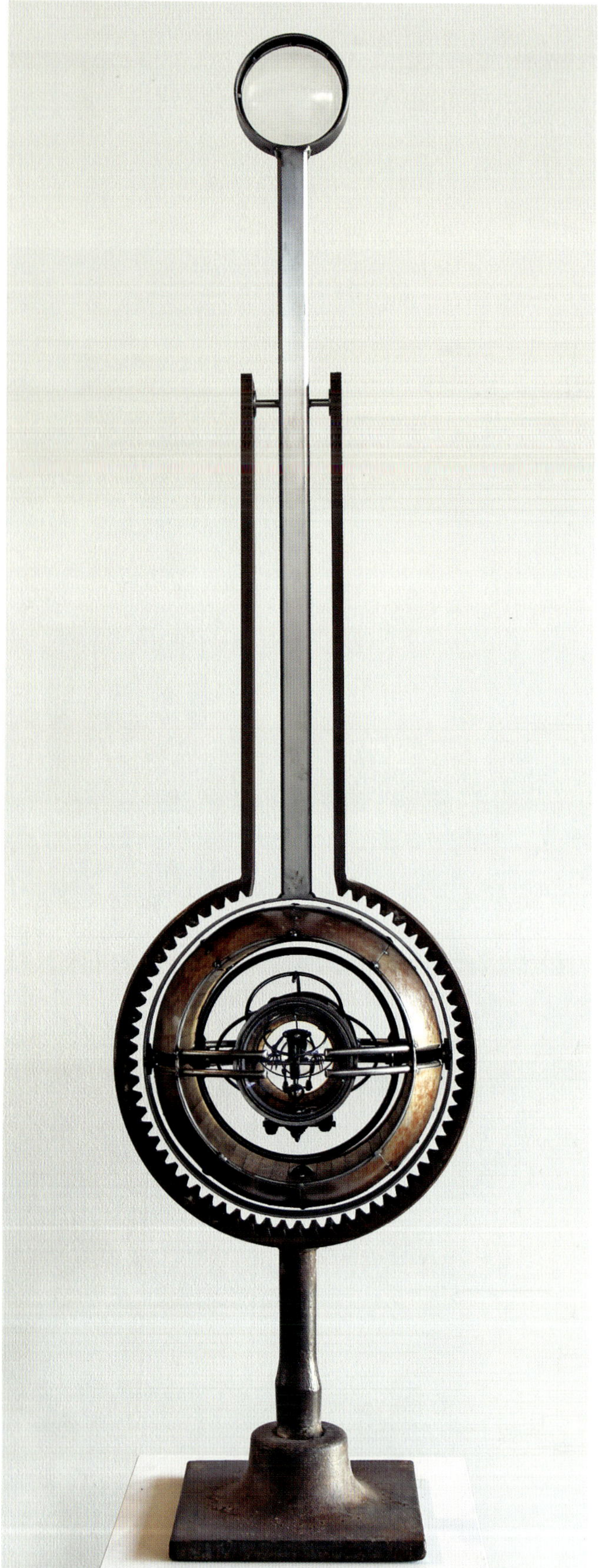

GREG BROTHERTON

"I have a vision: a post-industrial world, where a solitary being, tinkering away with silent genius, becomes the hope for the future." Growing up mostly in Utah and Colorado, Greg was experimenting with homemade explosives aged 12, was "ejected" from several schools, and then majored in Graphic Design at Colorado Academy of Art. There followed a highly successful career as a commercial artist in California. Simultaneously he was honing his skills as a brilliantly original sculptor: "The forms I present emerge from a disordered mechanical history, often revealed through a dystopian lens." Today his work is exhibited throughout the USA and is collected worldwide. In 2007 Greg was a featured artist at the prestigious TED conference in Monterey, CA.

Left: *Pendulum*, 2008. 47" x 13" x 9" (119 cm x 33 cm x 23 cm). Welded steel, teak, found lenses, planetary gear, jackhammer tamping bit and motor bearings.

Below and Right: Several views of *Chained to Earth*, 2010. 16" x 12" x 12" (41 cm x 31 cm x 31 cm). Welded steel, teak, typewriter parts and acrylic. Photo by Jen Jansen.

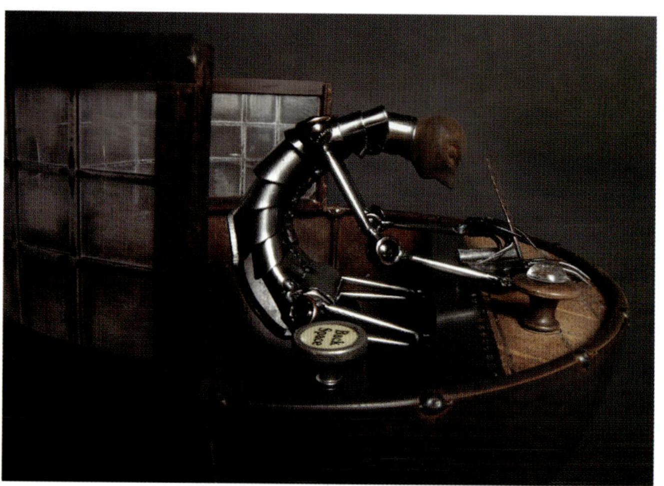

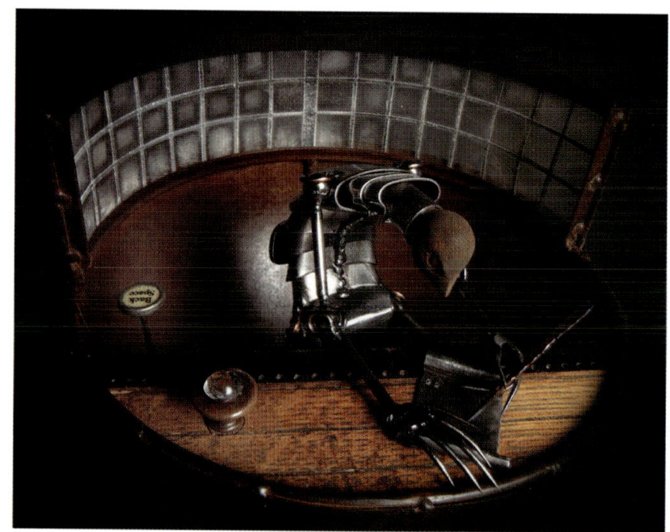

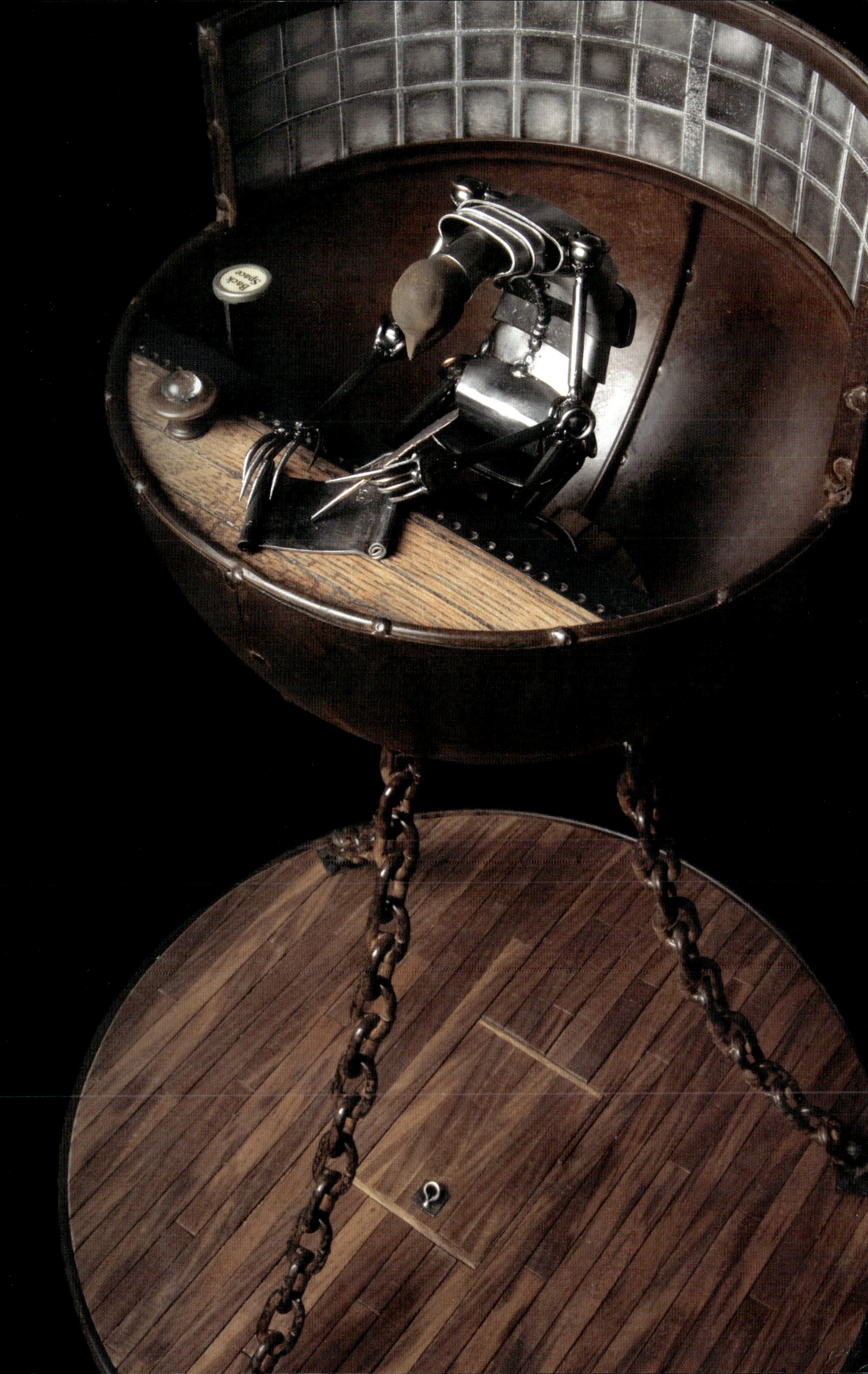
Back Space

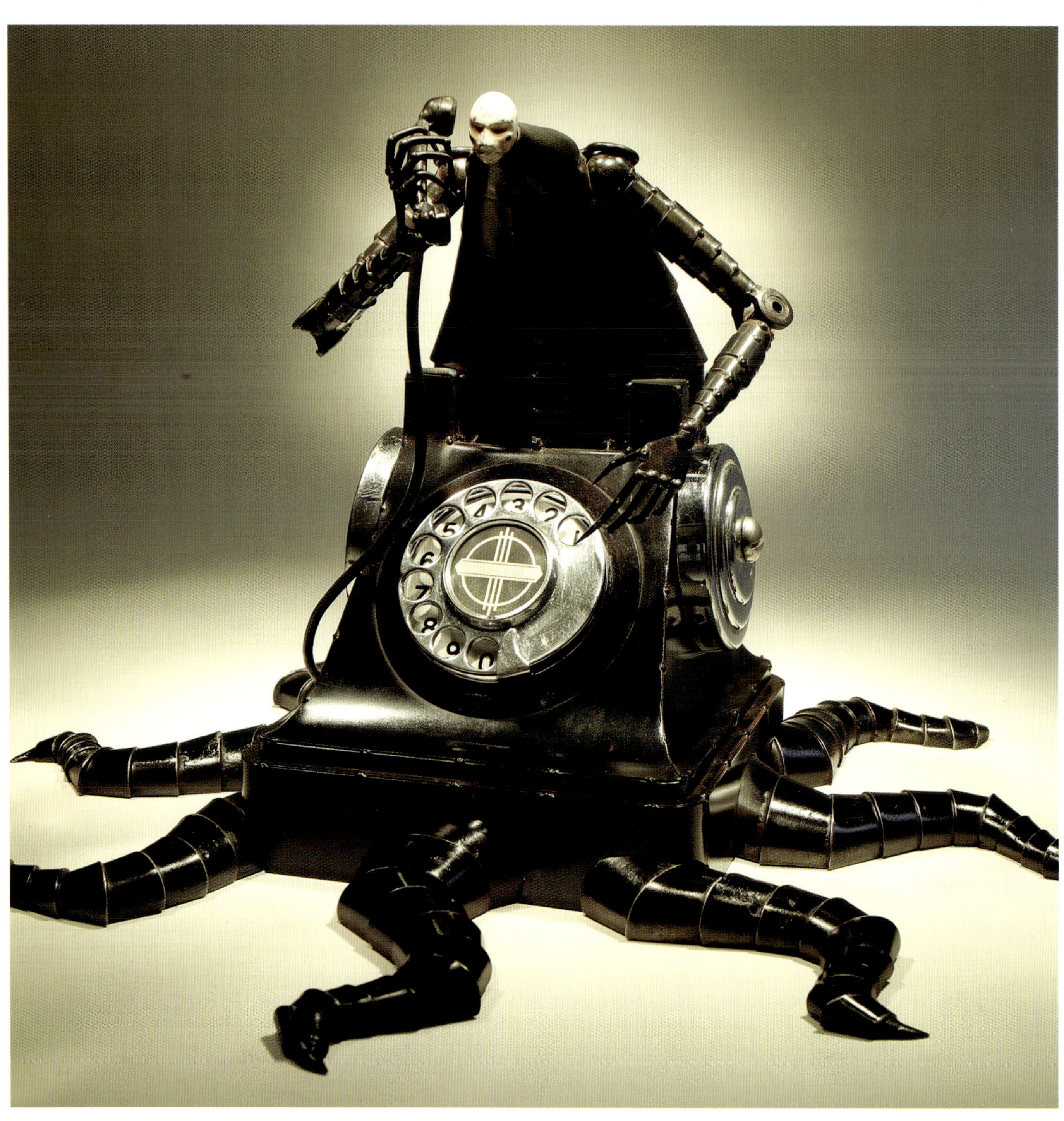

Above: *Listening In*, 2011. 12" x 18" x 18" (30.4 cm x 45.7 cm x 45.7 cm). Welded steel, cast pewter, payphone dial, parts from a beer tap and concrete.

Right: *Migraine Machine 1*, 2008. 12" x 18" x 18" (30.4 cm x 45.7 cm x 45.7 cm). Welded steel, teak, motor bearings, fisheye lenses and helicopter rotor gear.

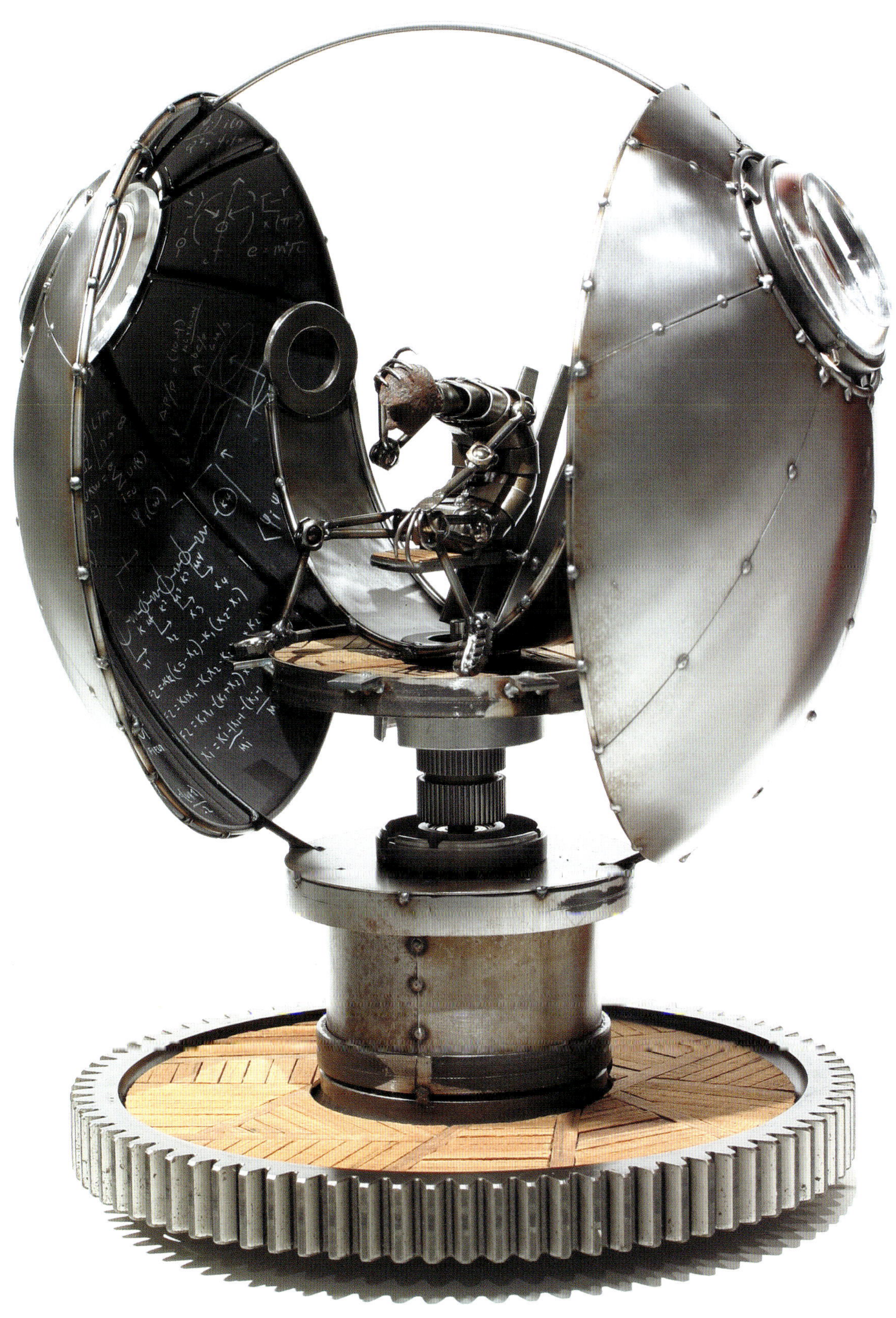

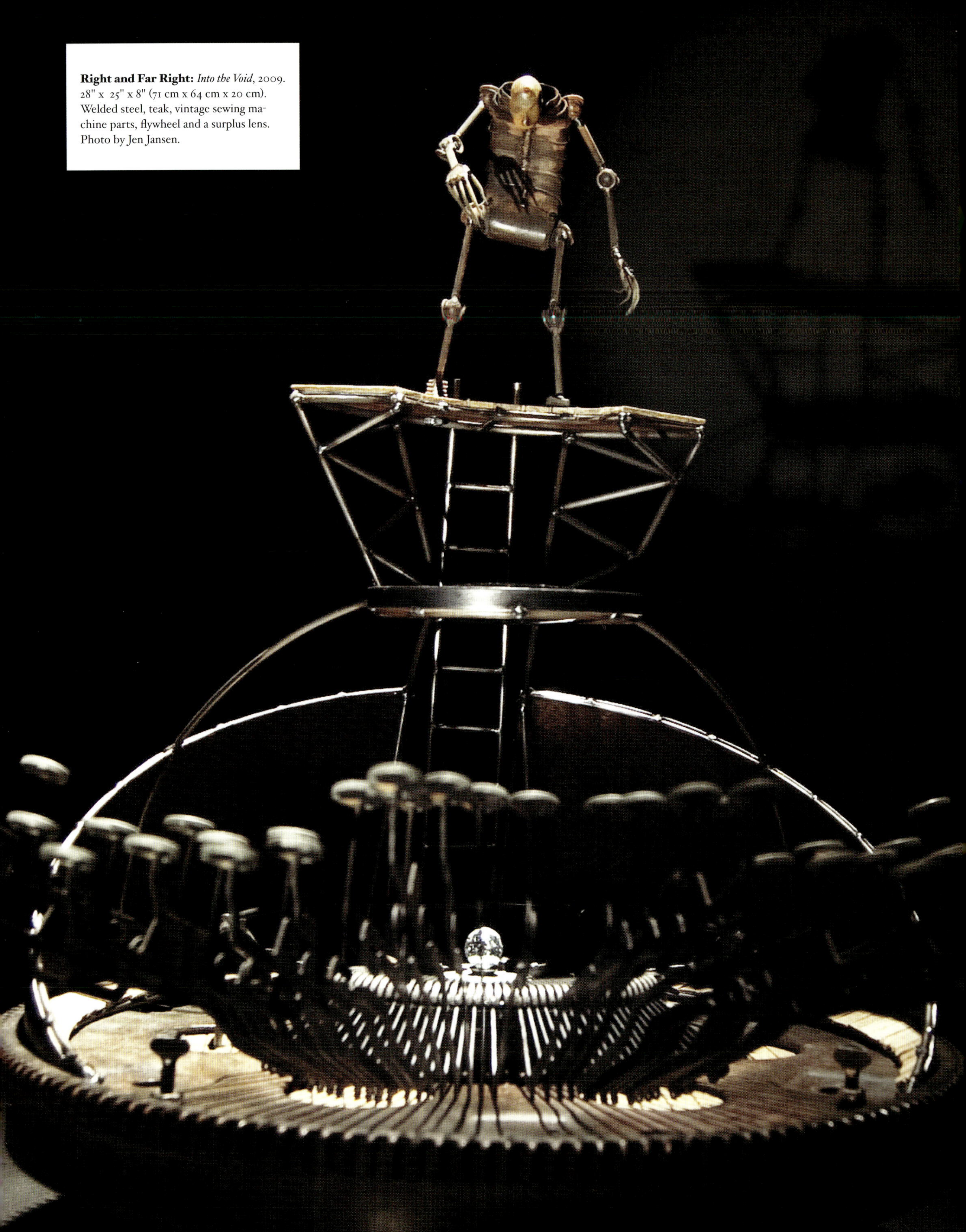

Right and Far Right: *Into the Void*, 2009. 28" x 25" x 8" (71 cm x 64 cm x 20 cm). Welded steel, teak, vintage sewing machine parts, flywheel and a surplus lens. Photo by Jen Jansen.

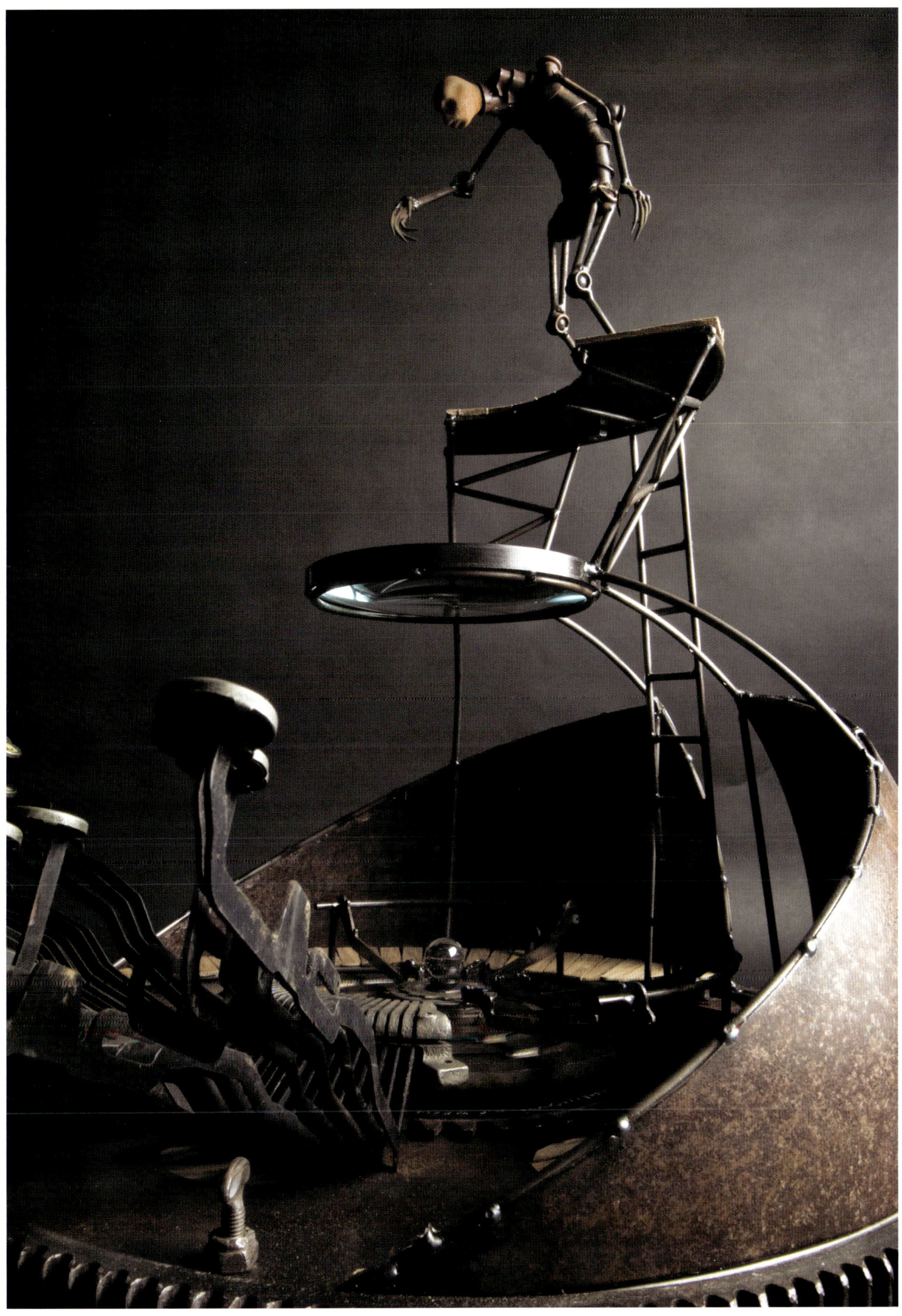

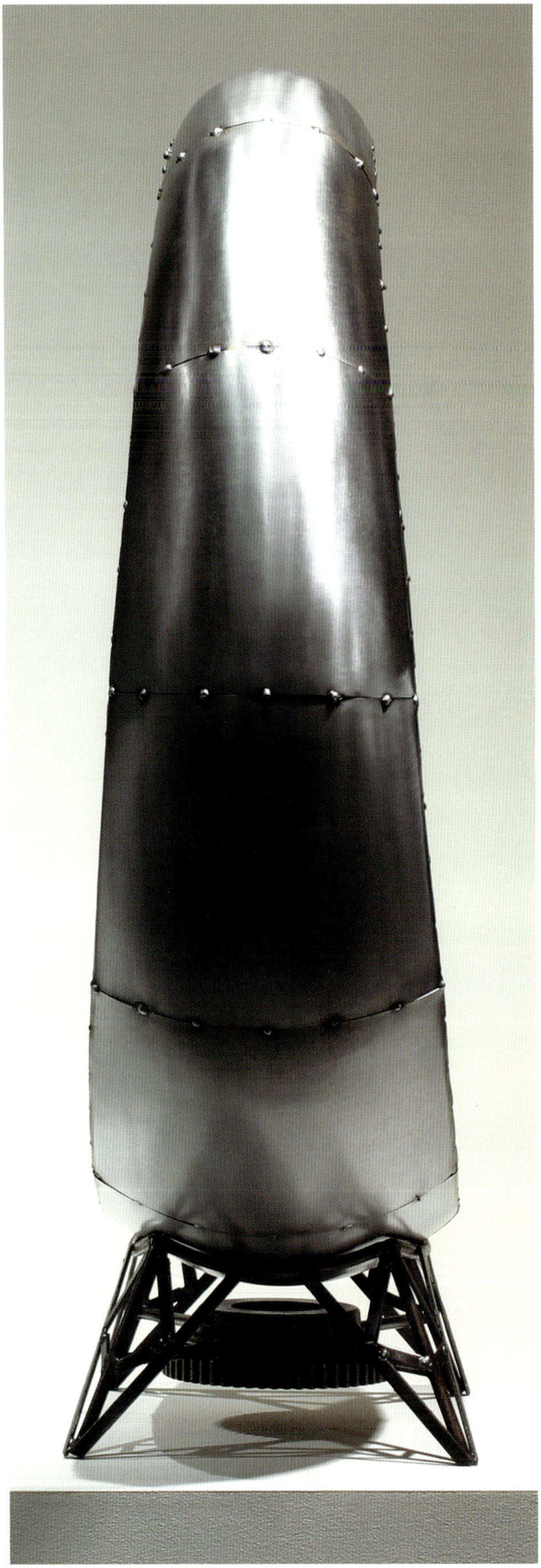

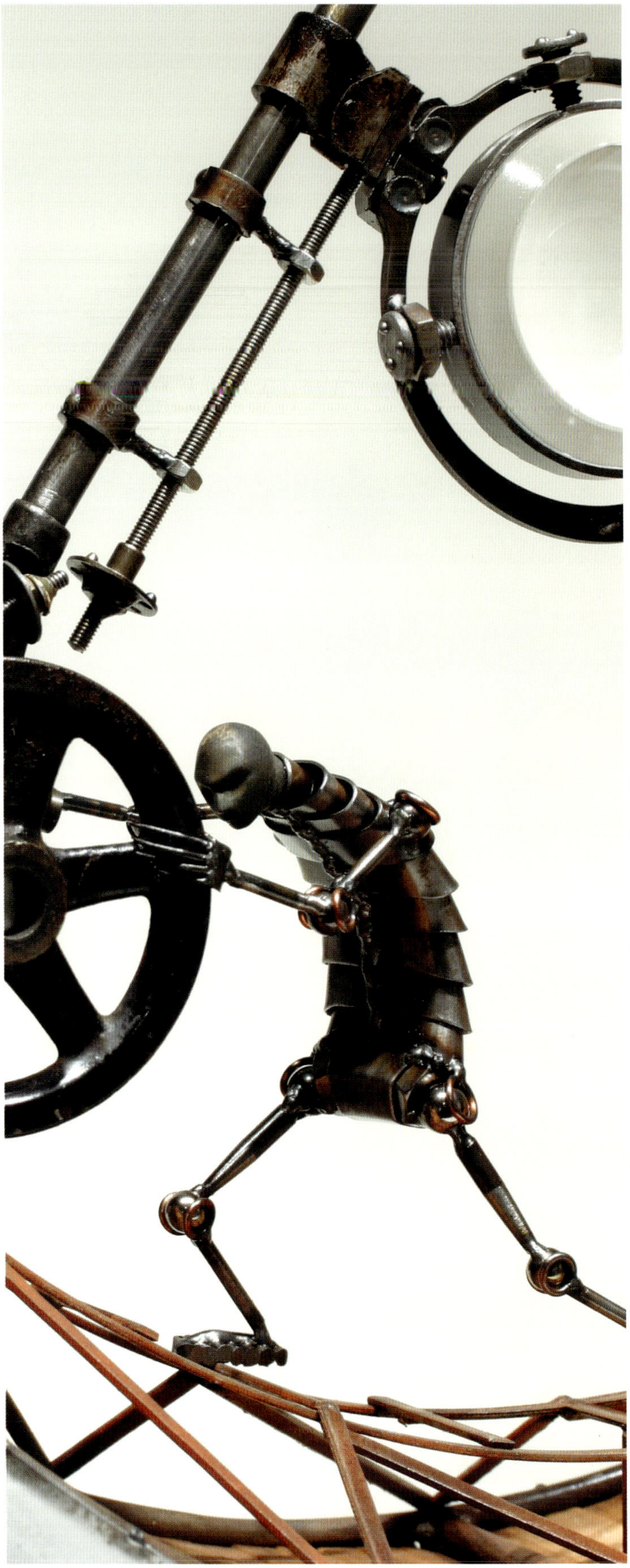

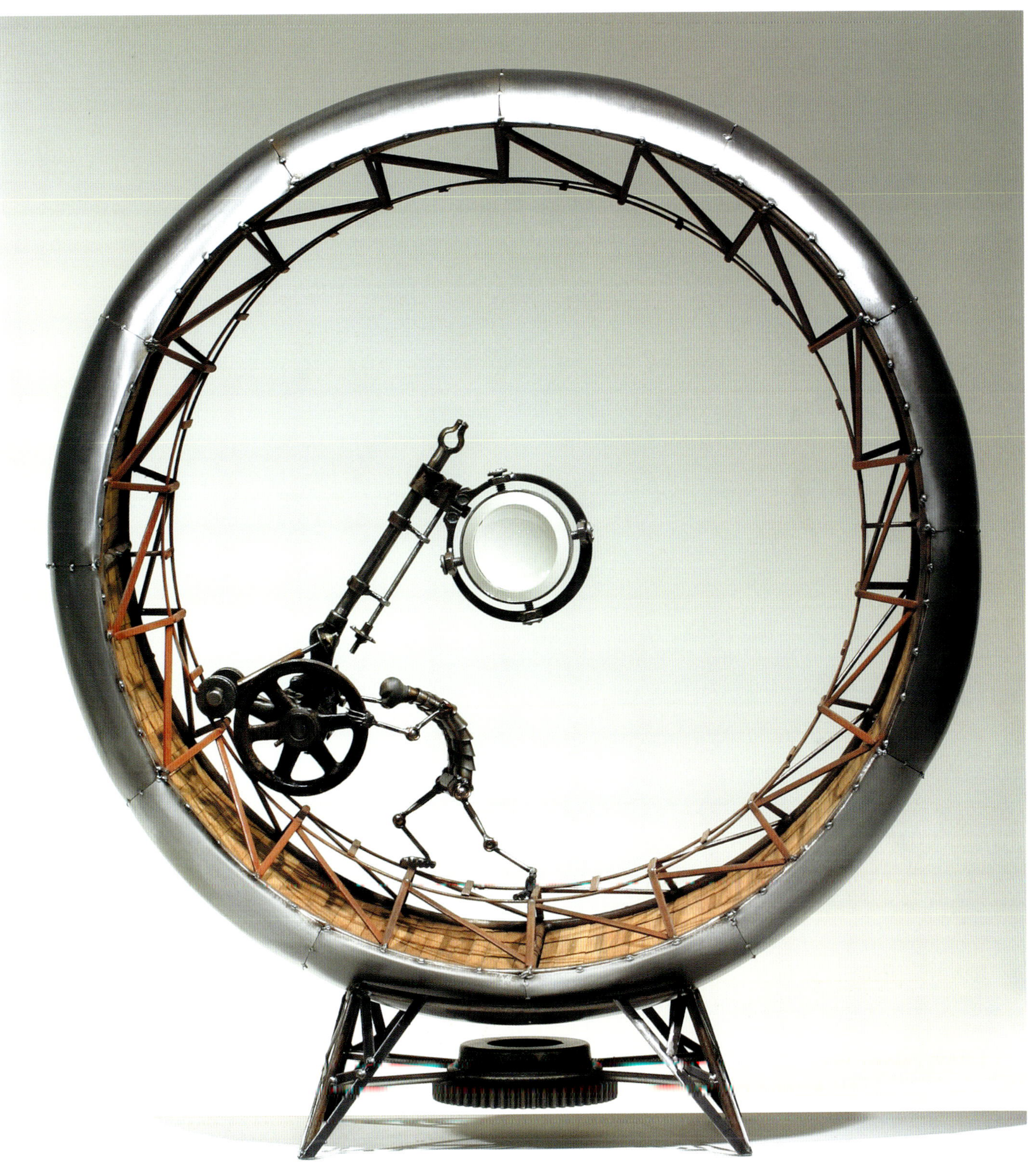

Above, Left and Far Left:
Pushed Around, 2009.
28" x 25" x 8" (71 cm x 64 cm x 20 cm).
Welded steel, teak, vintage sewing machine parts, found gear and a surplus lens.

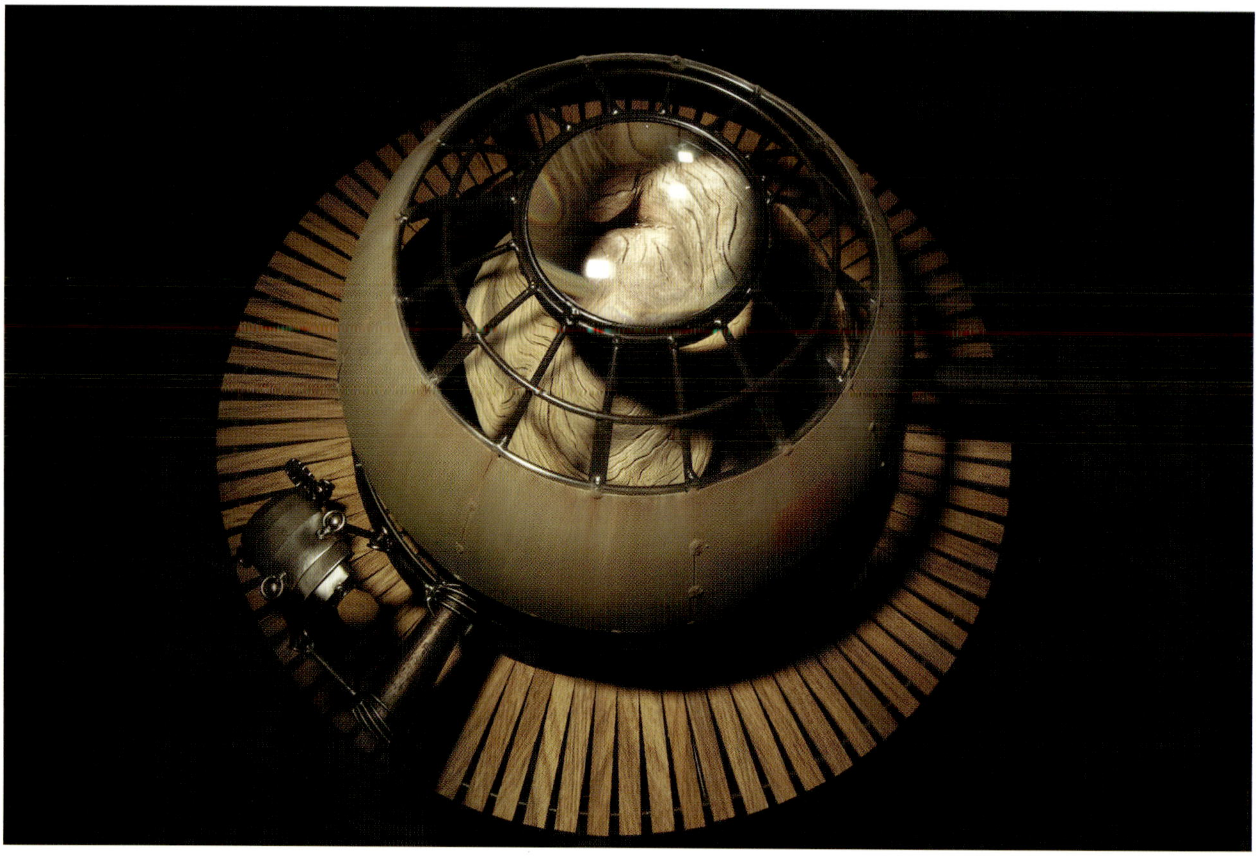

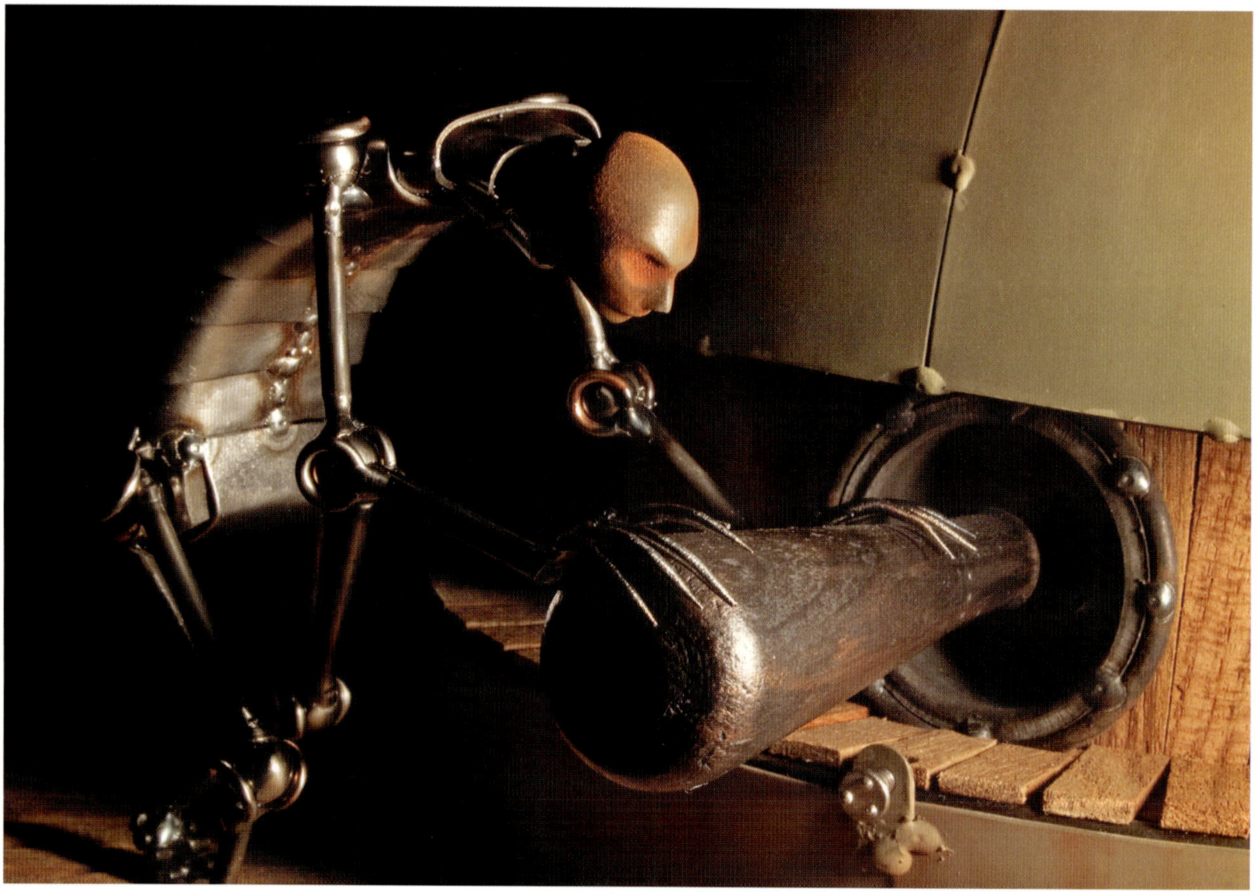

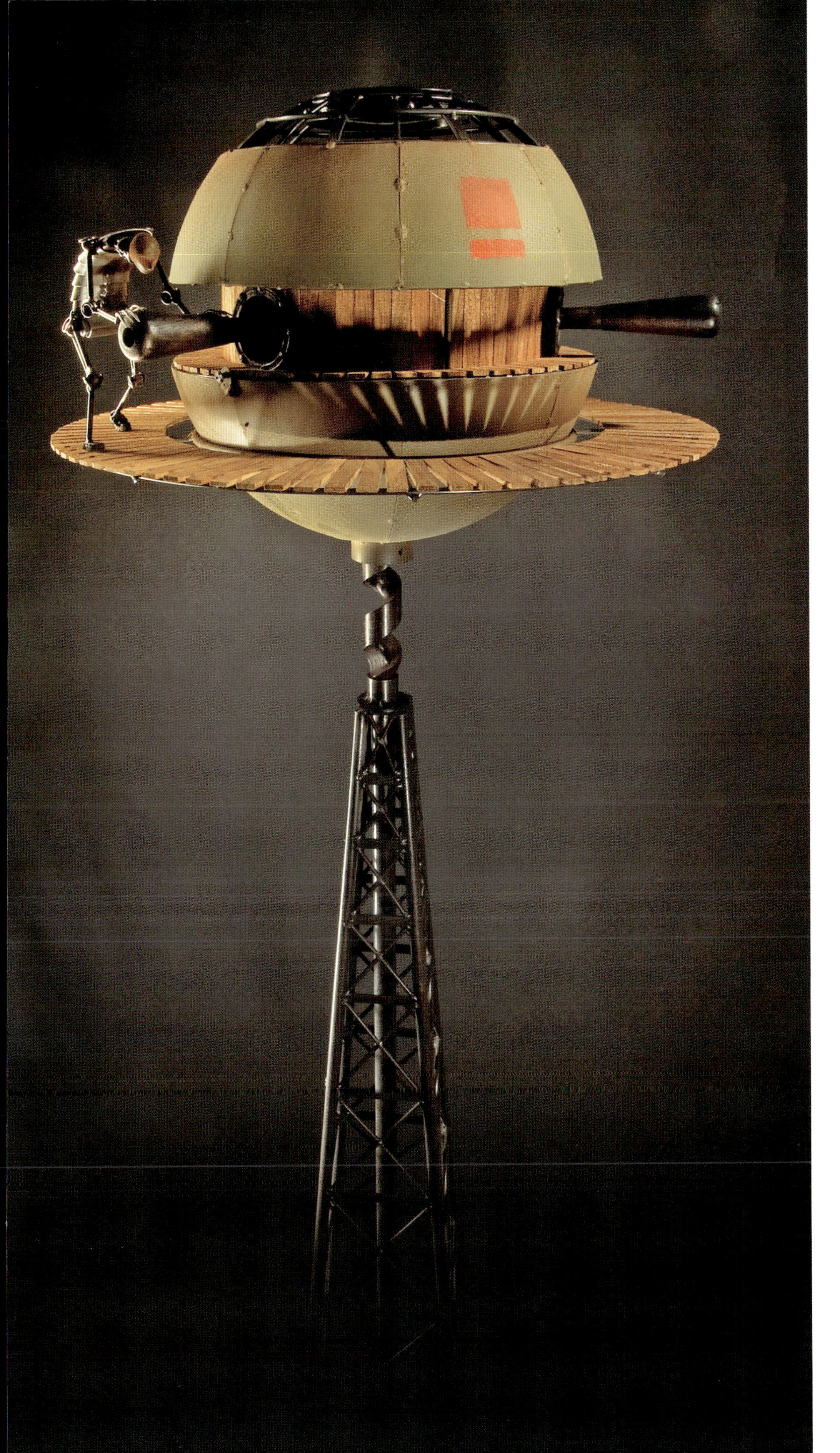

Left and Far Left:
Raising the Mind, 2010.
56" x 17" x 17"
(142 cm x 43 cm x 43 cm).
Welded steel, teak, root wood, antique file handles and a surplus lens.
Photo by Jen Jansen.

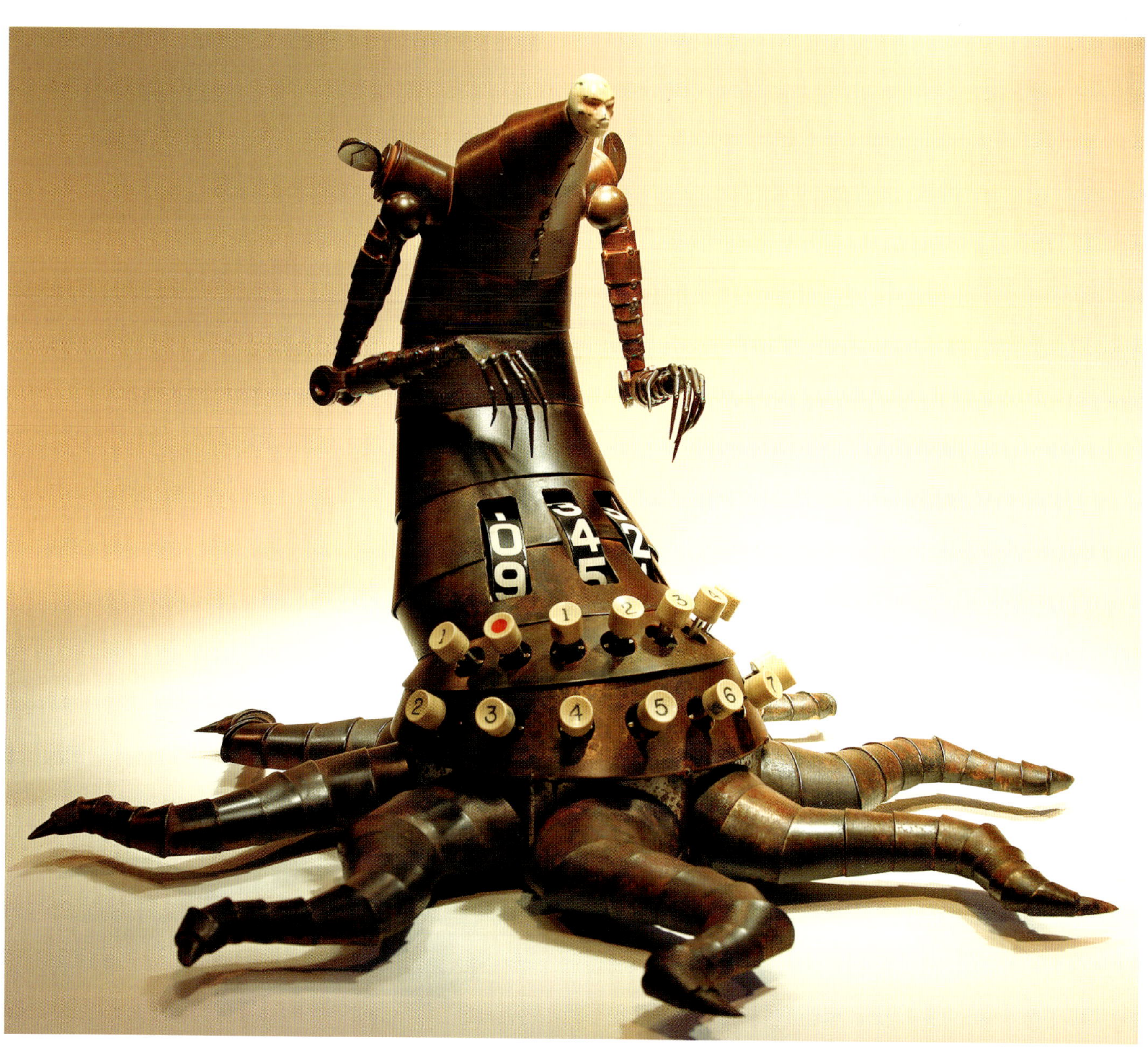

Above: *The Calculator,* 2011. 12" x 17" x 17" (31 cm x 43 cm x 43 cm). Welded steel, cast pewter, cash register parts and adding machine parts.

Right: *3-Wheeled Horn,* 2011. 20" x 24" x 10" (51 cm x 61 cm x 25 cm). Welded steel, concrete, French horn parts, sewing machine parts and a found gauge.

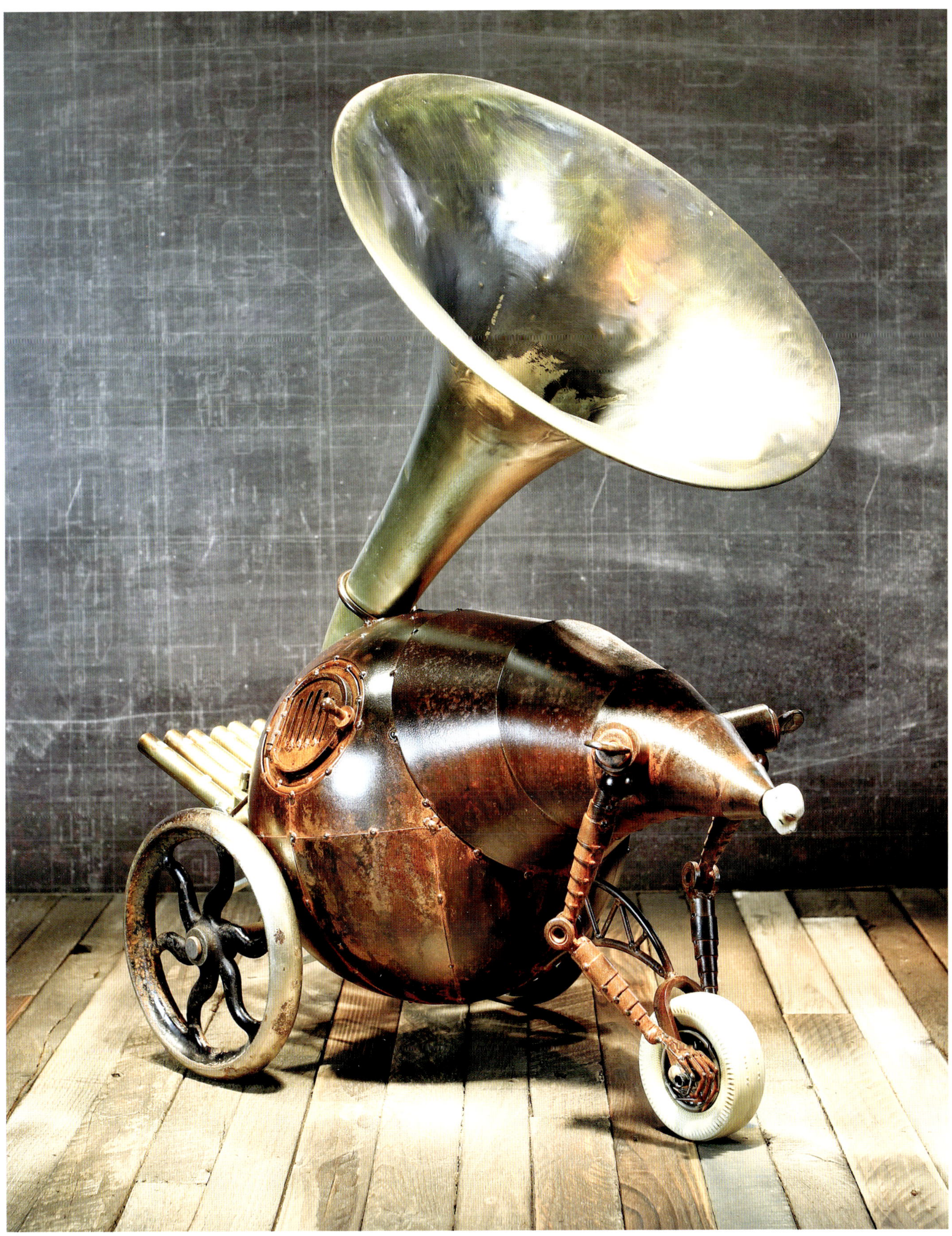

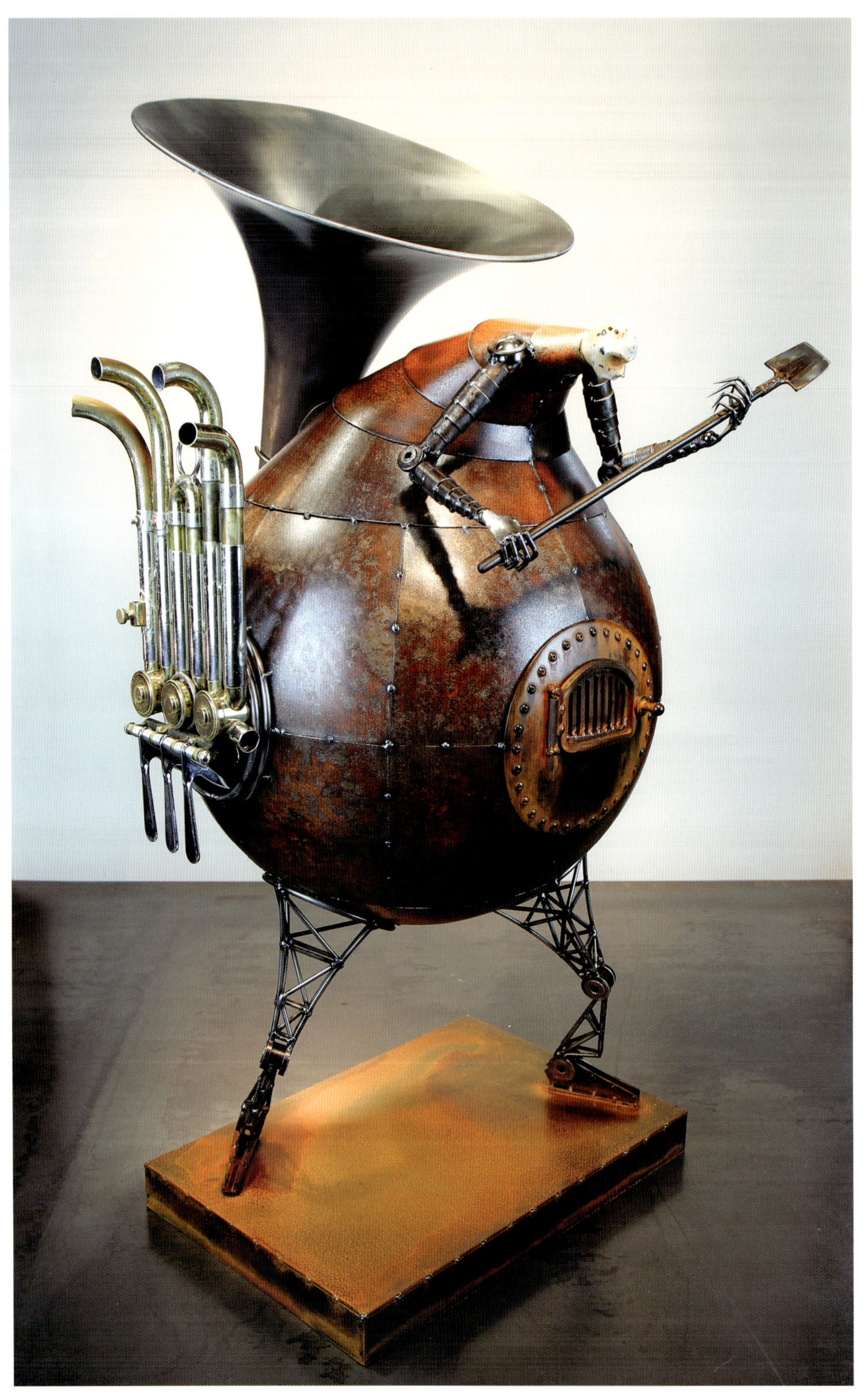

Left: *Sounding the Furnace*, 2010. 3" x 14" x 16" (7.6 cm x 35.6 cm x 40.6 cm). Welded steel, concrete and French horn.

Right, Top and Bottom: *Racer 8*, 2010. 25" x 13" x 6" (64 cm x 33 cm x 15 cm). Welded steel, concrete, teak, magnifying lens, wristwatches, ceramic, needle-nose pliers and a typewriter key.

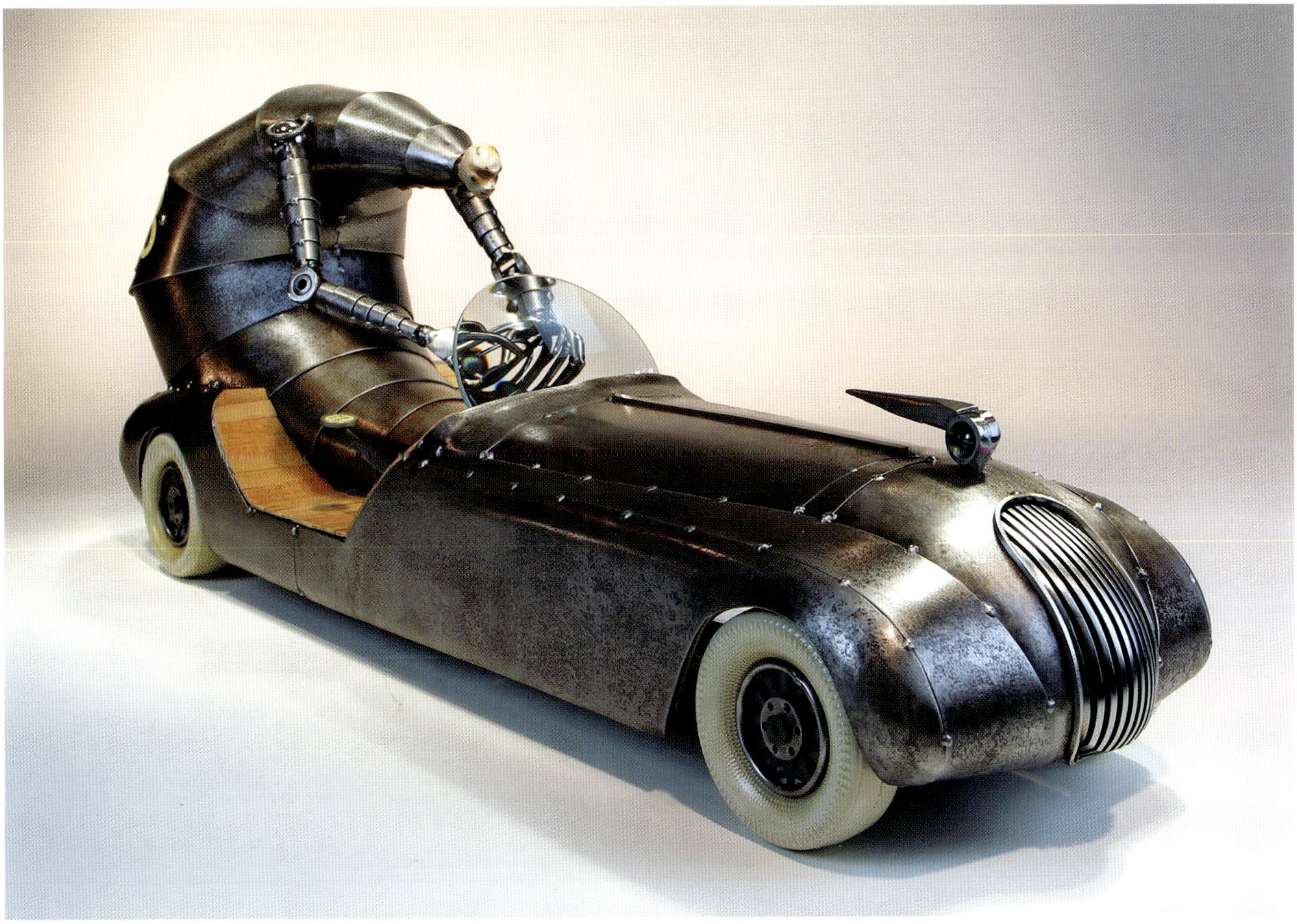

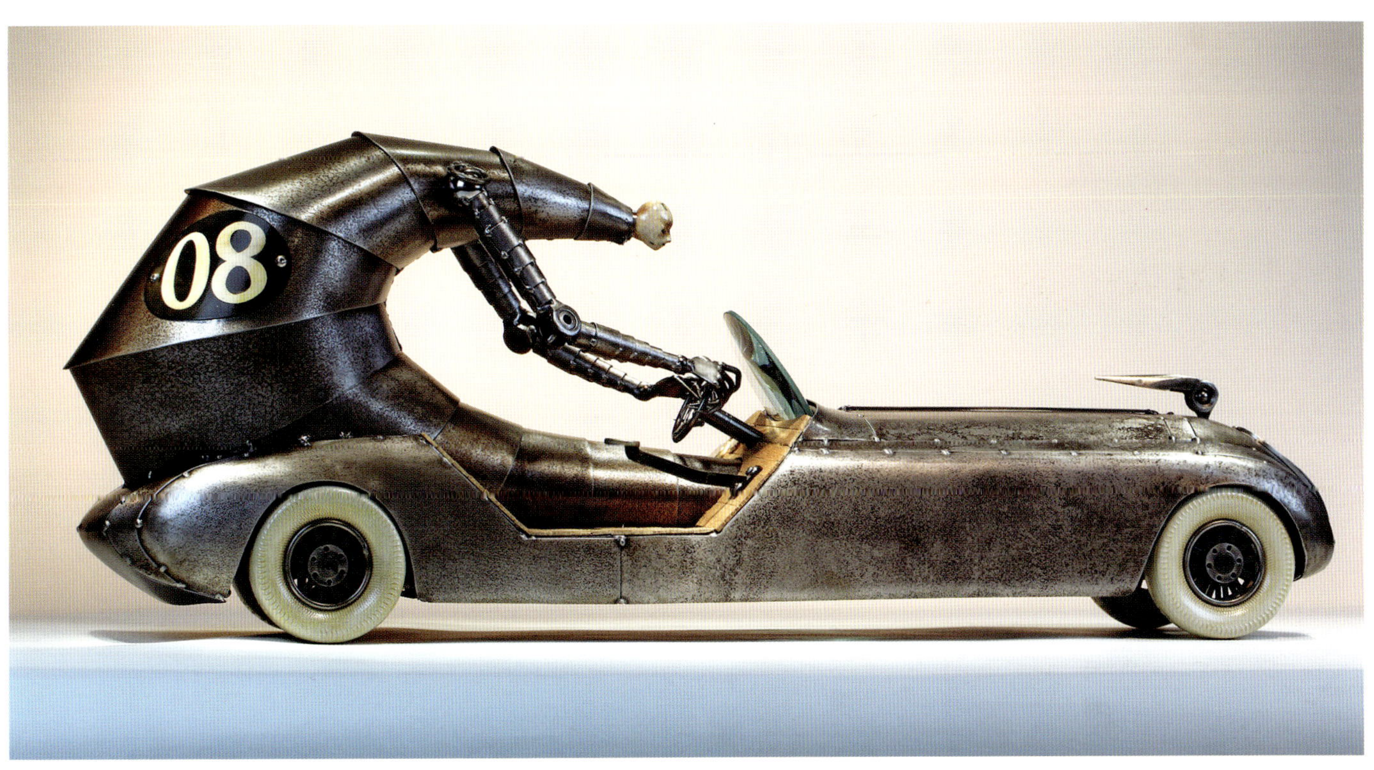
08

FRANK BUCHWALD

Based in Berlin, and a graduate of the University of the Arts in Berlin in Design, Frank Buchwald worked as a freelance painter and illustrator, before turning to creating his light objects and furniture exclusively in 2002. His creations are based on the notion that machines, on a level, acquire a life of their own: "there is a common mistake in our time that machines are solely products and artifacts of human planning. There is in fact an independent reality which withdraws itself from human access, exists behind the manifest appearances of mechanical objects and secretly determines the world of machines." Frank's creations are not the result of spontaneous inspiration, but rather of years of searching for the perfect form in each instance. He says, "I do not regard them as my own work, but as independent beings with their own natures."

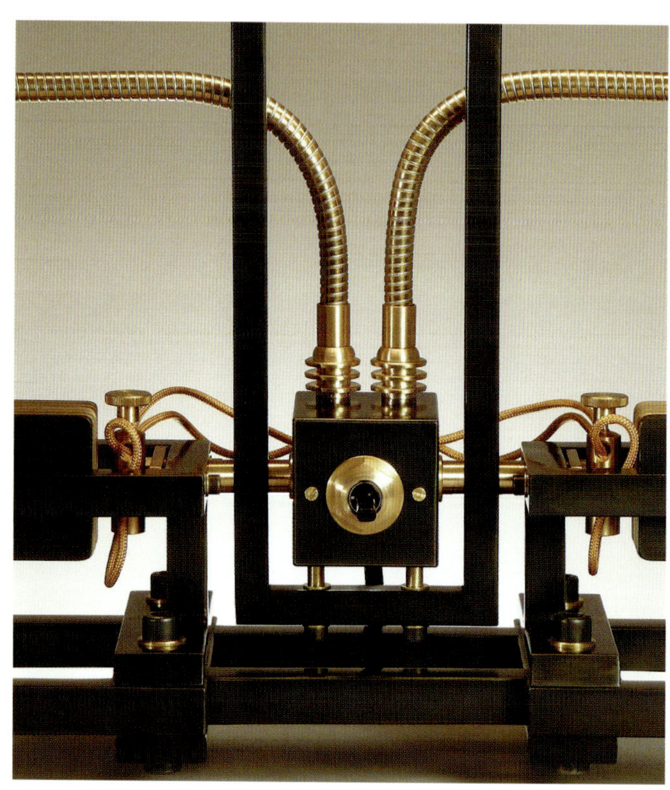

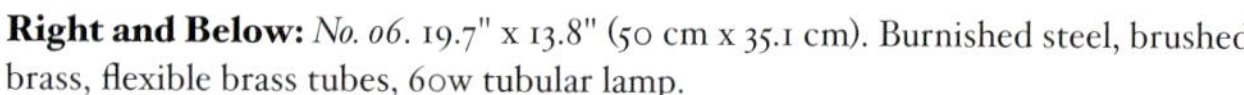

Right and Below: *No. 06.* 19.7" x 13.8" (50 cm x 35.1 cm). Burnished steel, brushed brass, flexible brass tubes, 60w tubular lamp.

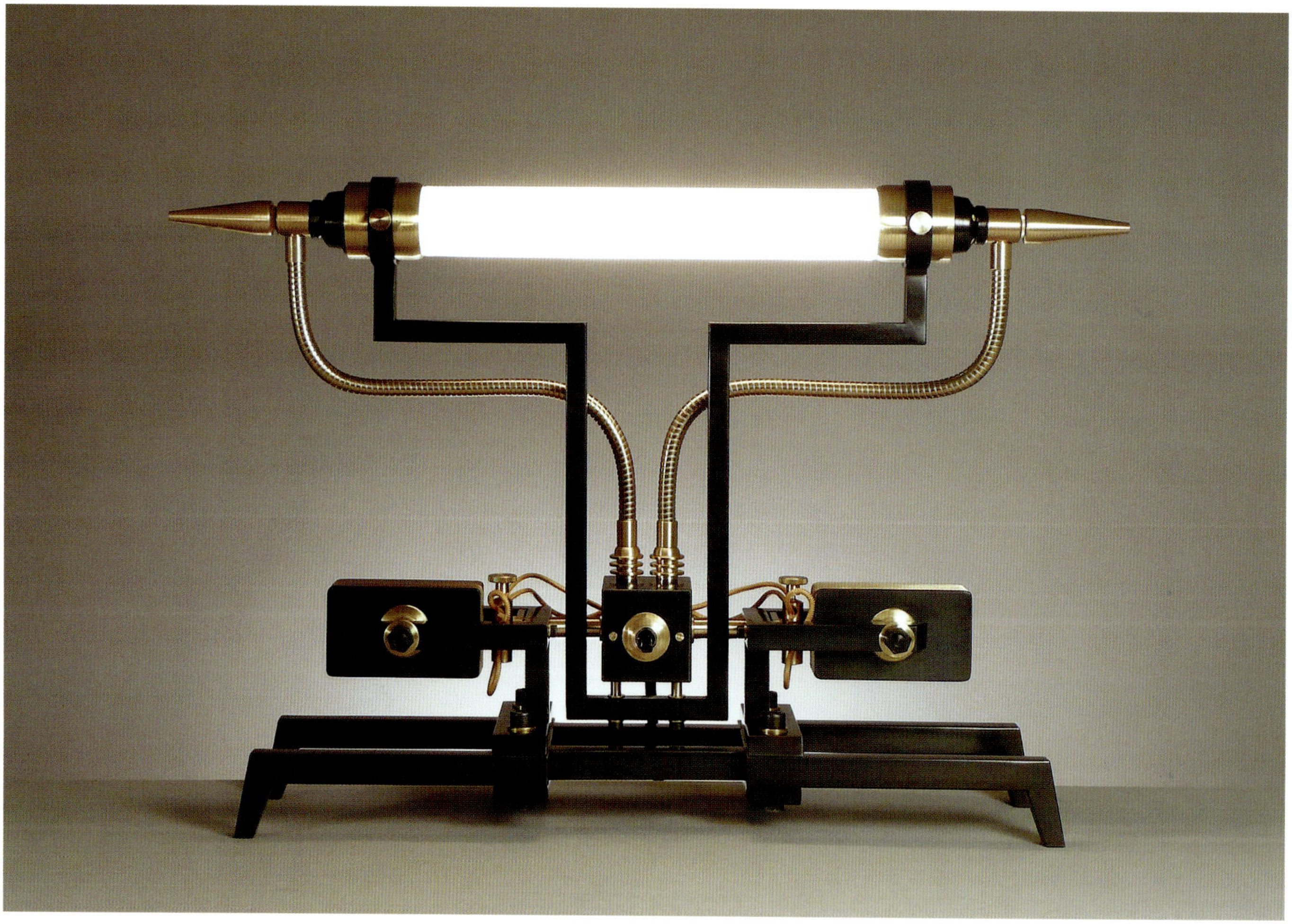

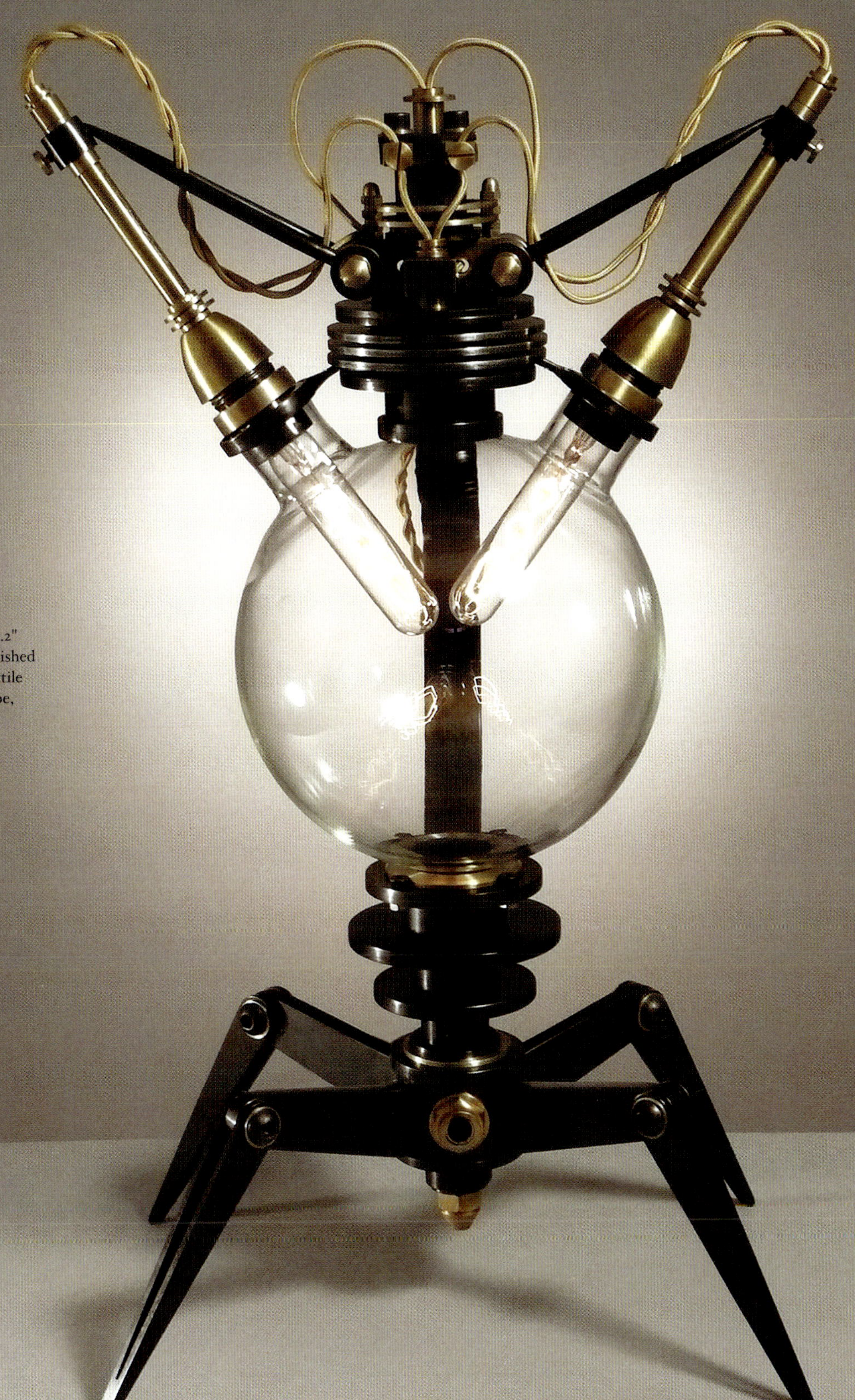

Right: *No. 01*. 19.2" x 12.2" (48.8 cm x 30 cm). Burnished steel, brushed brass, textile cables, hand-blown globe, 40w tubular lamps.

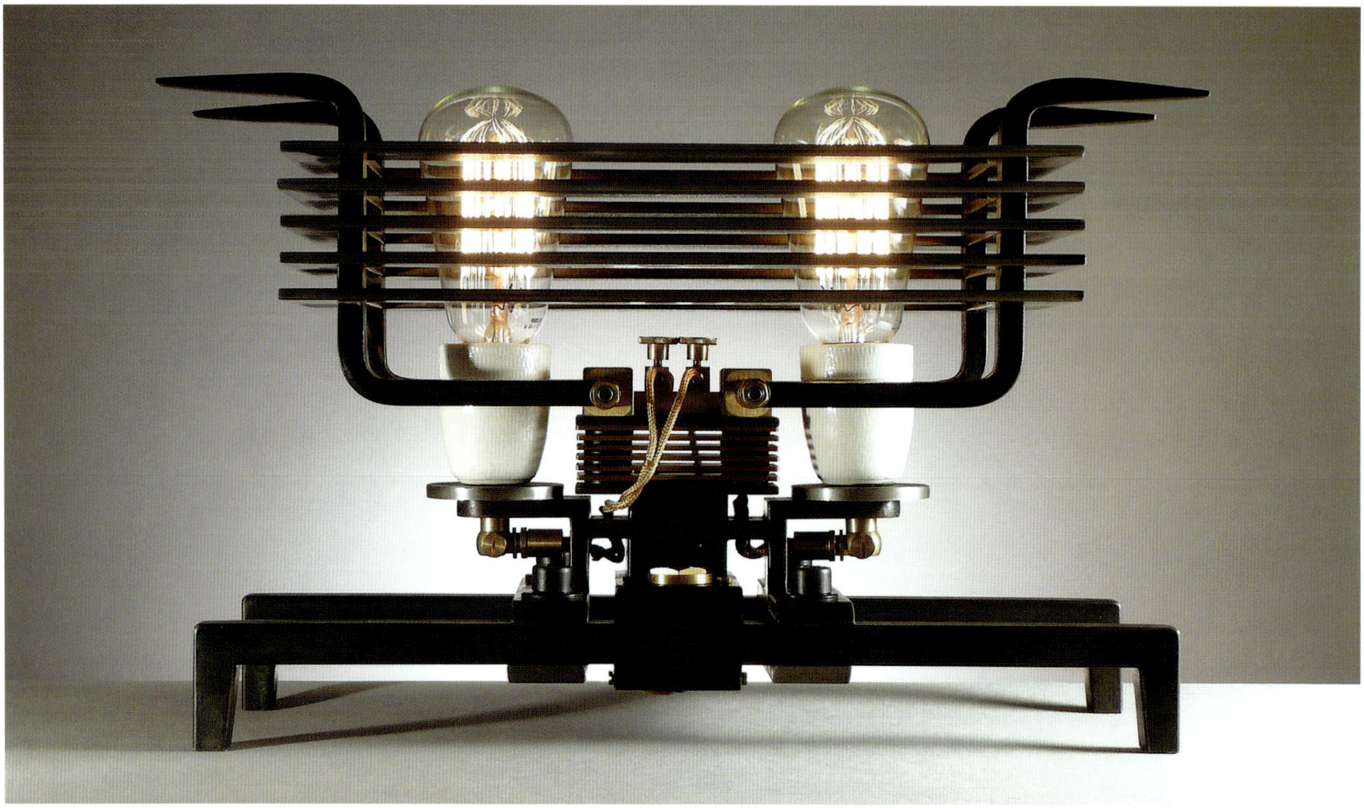

Above: *No. 04*. 10.6" x 15.8" (26.9 cm x 40.1 cm). Burnished steel, brushed brass, textile cables, 60w multiple filament bulbs.

Below and Right: *No. 05*. 15" x 25.2" (38.1 cm x 64 cm). Burnished steel, brushed brass, 40w spiral filament bulbs.

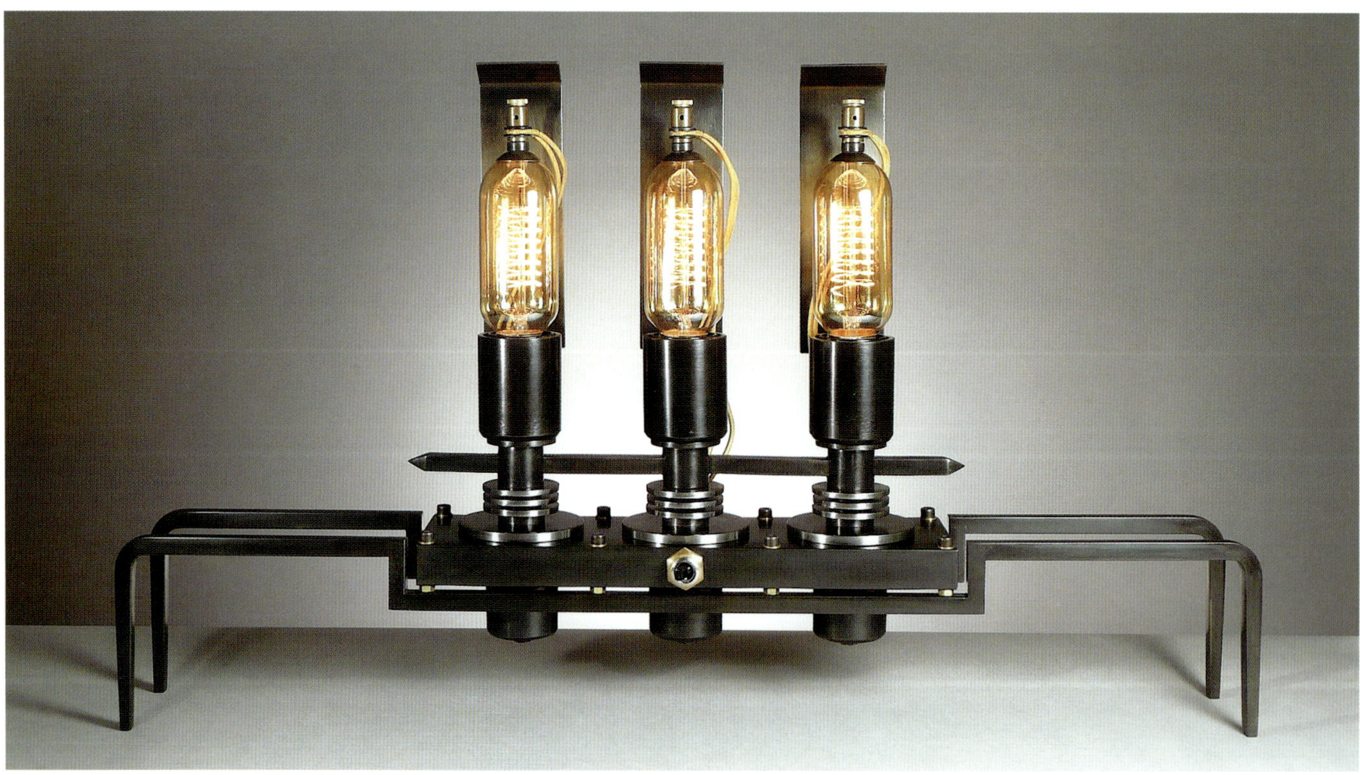

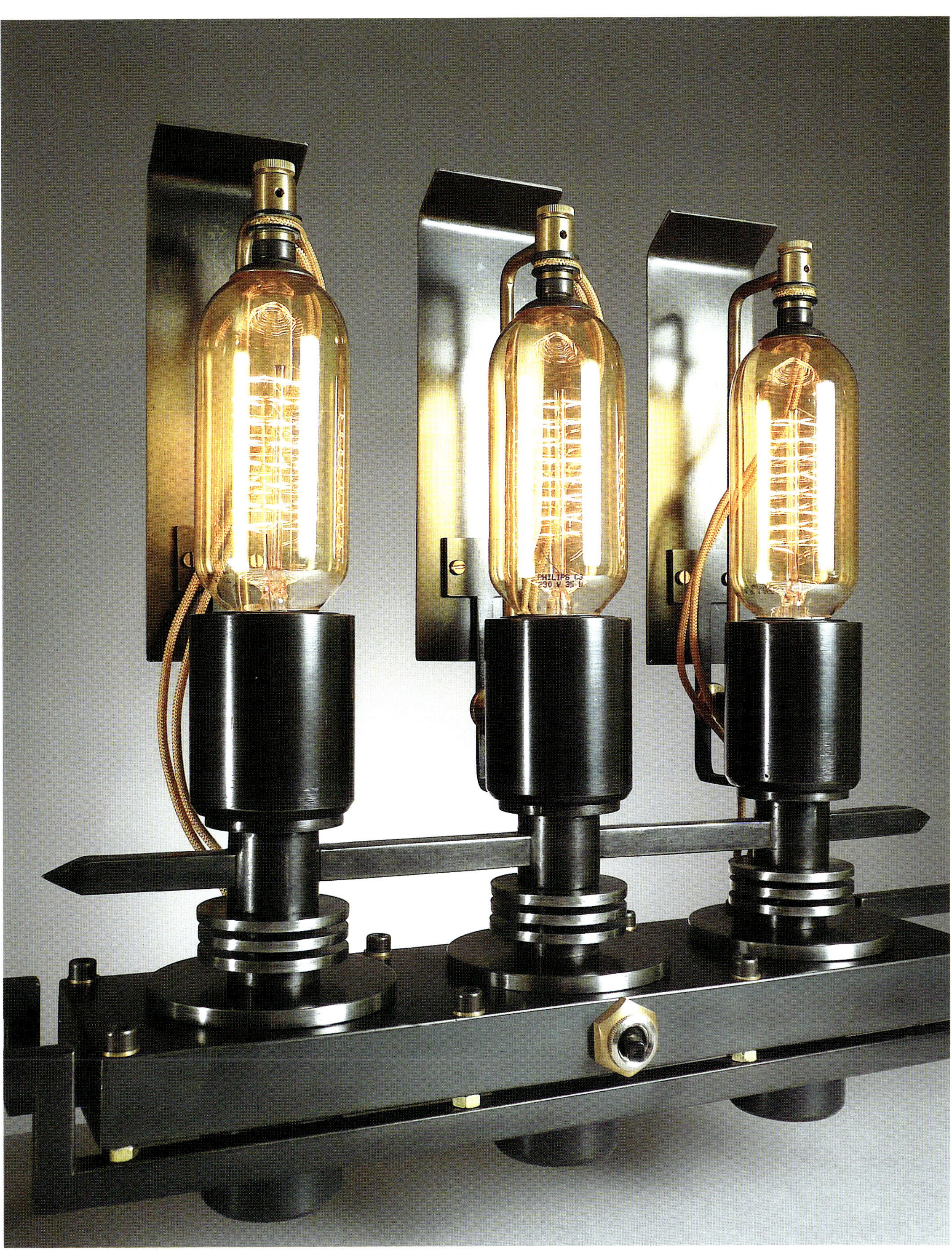
PHILIPS

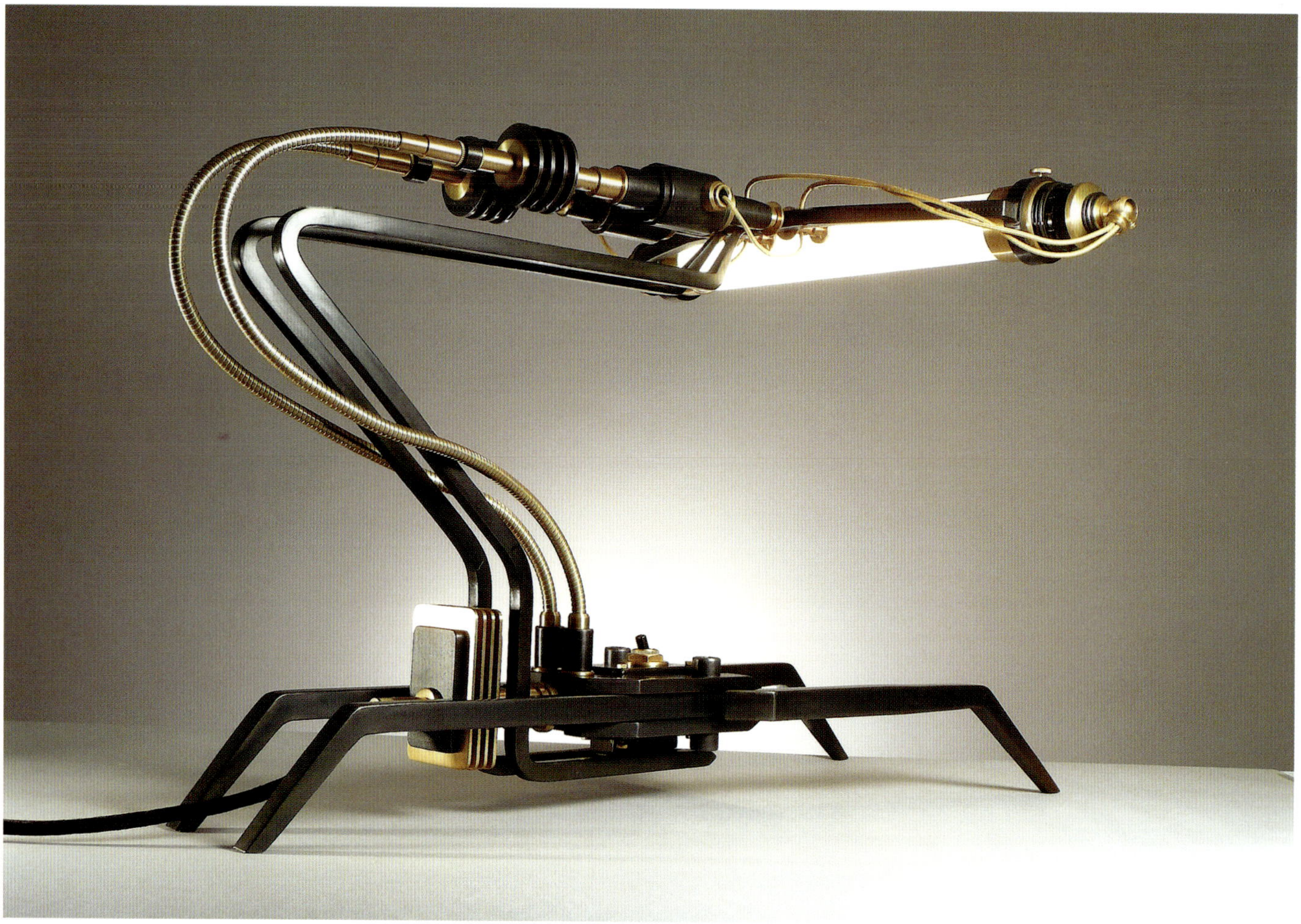

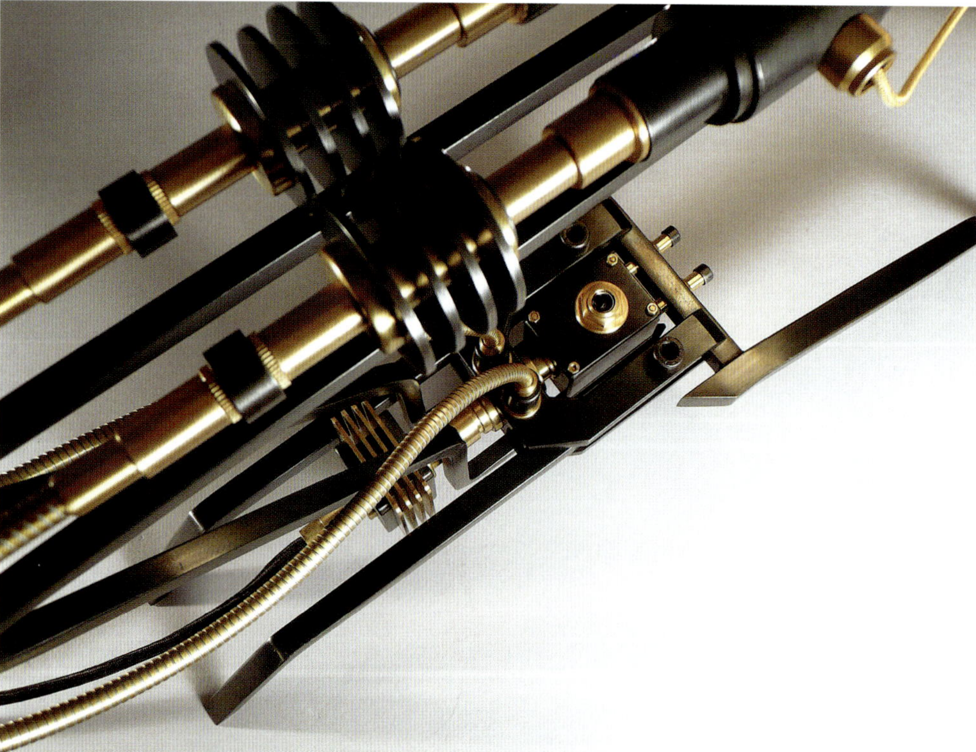

Above and Left: *No. 11*. 15.7" x 16.1" (38.1 cm x 64 cm). Burnished steel, brushed brass, textile cables, flexible brass tubes, 60w tubular bulb.

Right: *No. 12*. 17.5" x 17" (44.5 cm x 43.2 cm). Burnished steel, brushed brass, adjustable reflector shades, 40w globe bulbs.

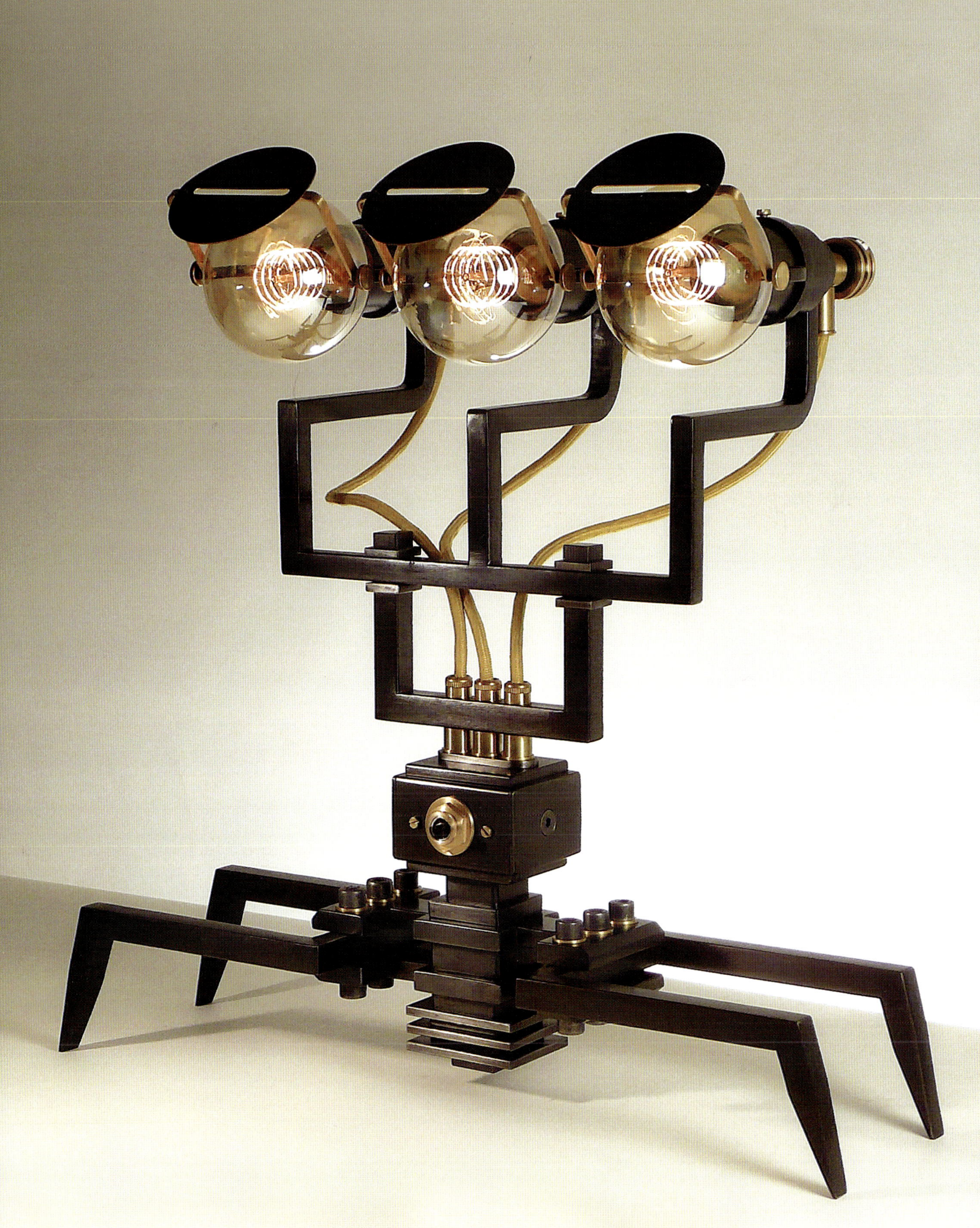

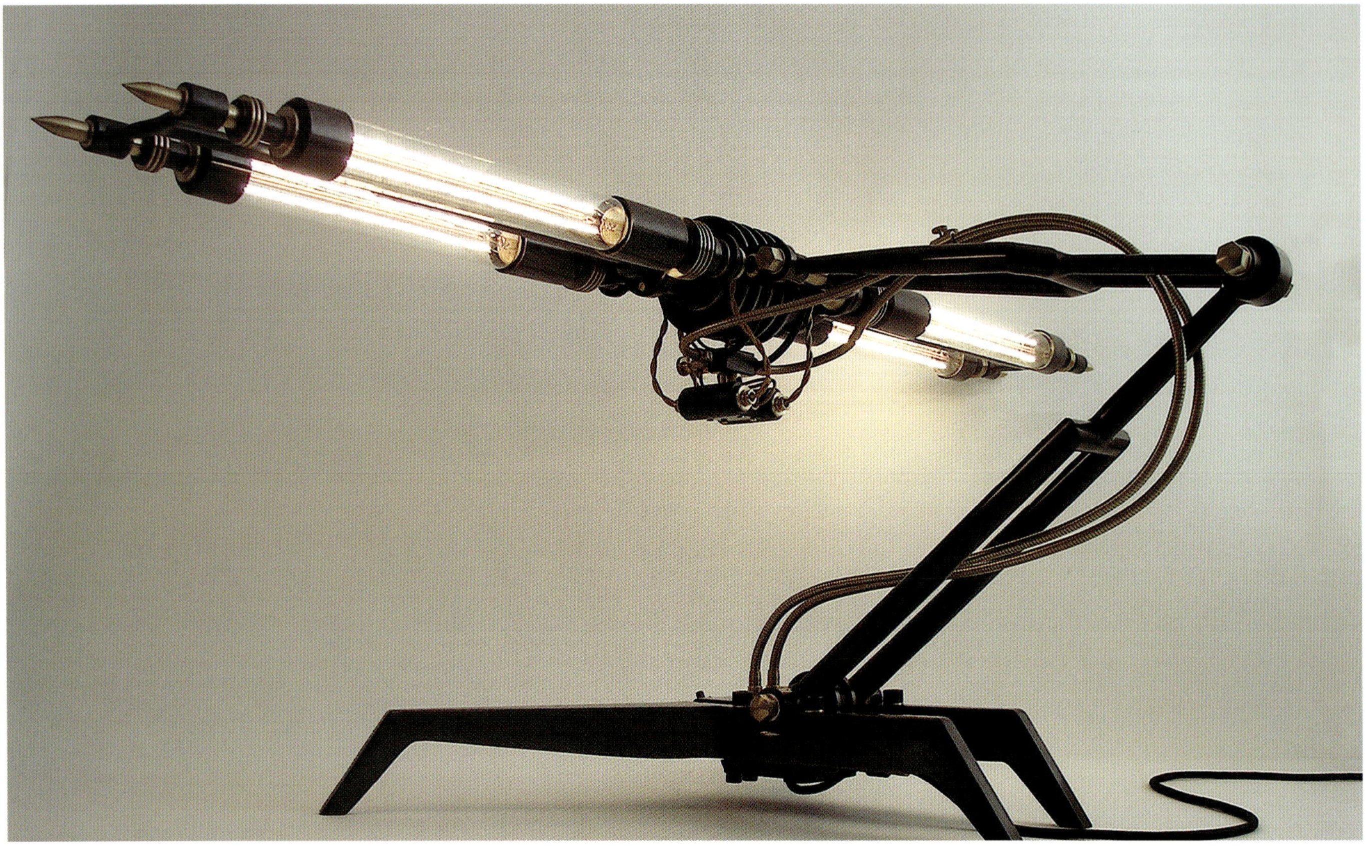

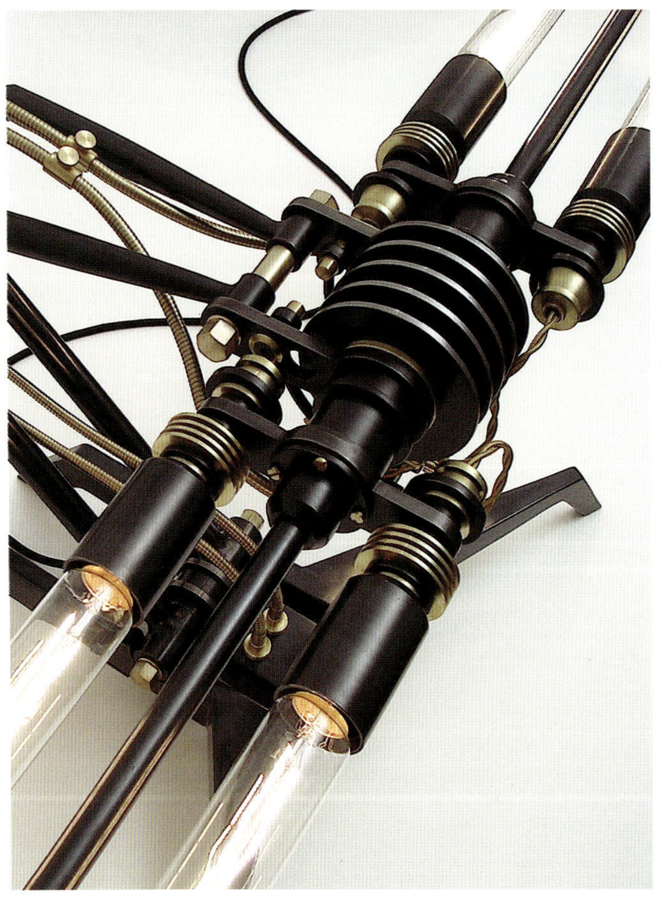

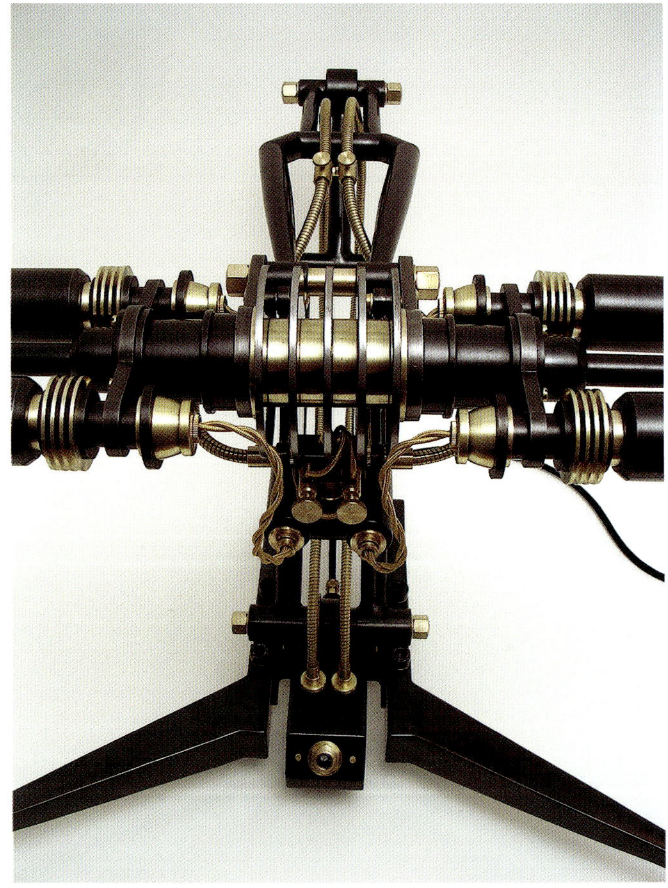

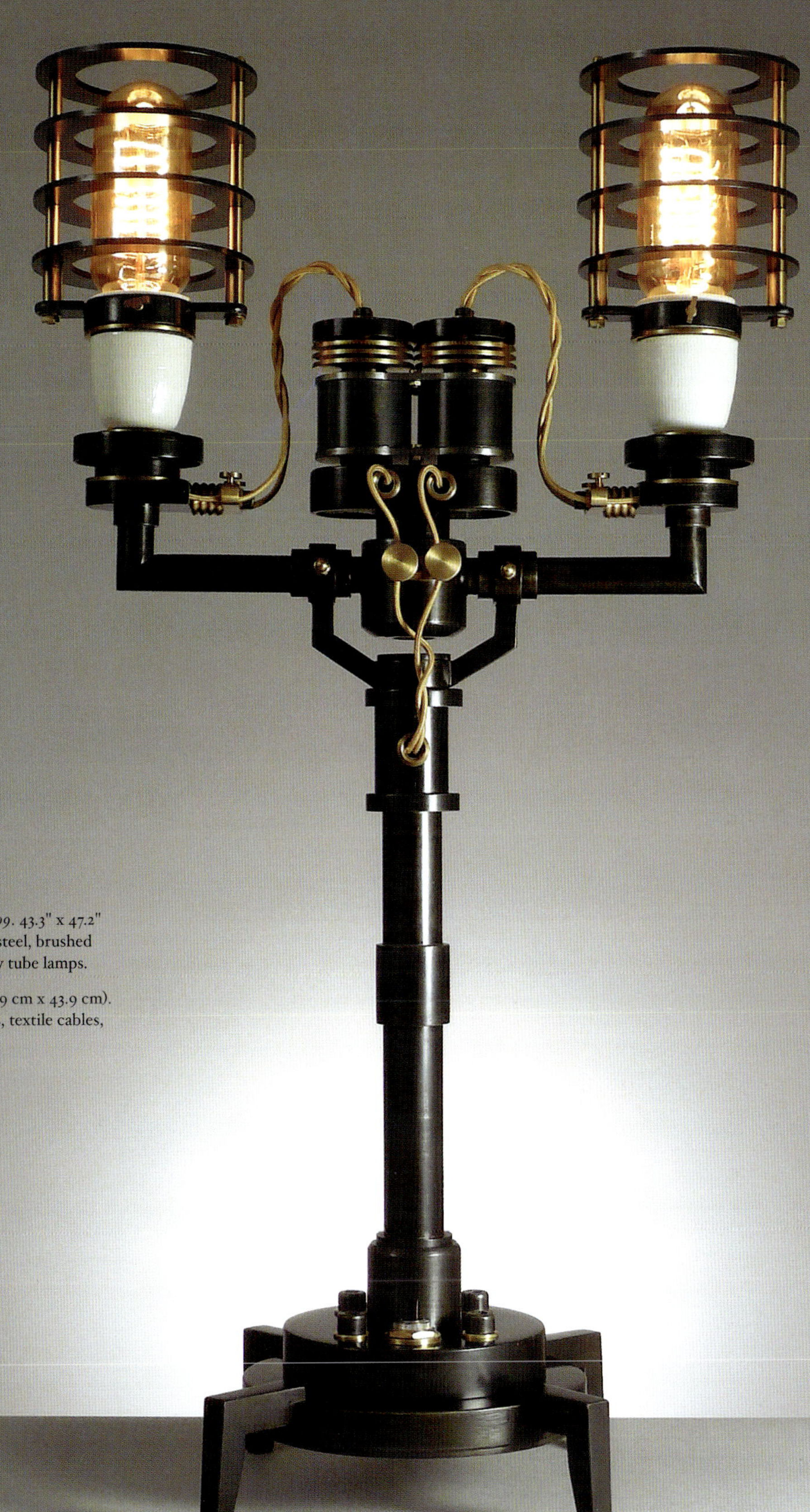

Left, Top and Bottom: *No. 09*. 43.3" x 47.2" (109 cm x 119 cm). Burnished steel, brushed brass, flexible brass tubes, 60w tube lamps.

Right: *No. 07*. 27.5" x 17.3" (69.9 cm x 43.9 cm). Burnished steel, brushed brass, textile cables, 40w spiral filament bulbs.

CHRIS CONTE

Born in Bergen, Norway, then moving to New York aged 6, Chris Conte majored in illustration at Pratt Institute in Brooklyn, where he also studied human anatomy. For 16 years he worked making prosthetic limbs, combining his interests in sculpture, medical science and biomechanics. In 2008 he turned artist full time. His work is influenced by robotics and technology (he often uses exotic aerospace industry materials and has worked with ex-Northrop Grumman engineers), but also employs ancient techniques, such as lost-wax bronze casting. Chris's pieces are unique, each sculpture taking many months to complete. His work has been exhibited at The National Museum, Washington DC and has featured on the Discovery Channel.

Below: *Chronos Version 2,* 2007.
Cast hand-finished acrylic resin skull and vintage components.
5" x 2" x 3.5"; (12.5 cm x 5 cm x 9 cm).
Photo by Amanda Dutton.

Right, Top and Bottom: *Steam II Insect,* 2009.
Cast bronze, machined brass and stainless steel.
6" x 2.5" x 6"; (15 cm x 6.5 cm x 15 cm).
Photos by Eric Vogel.

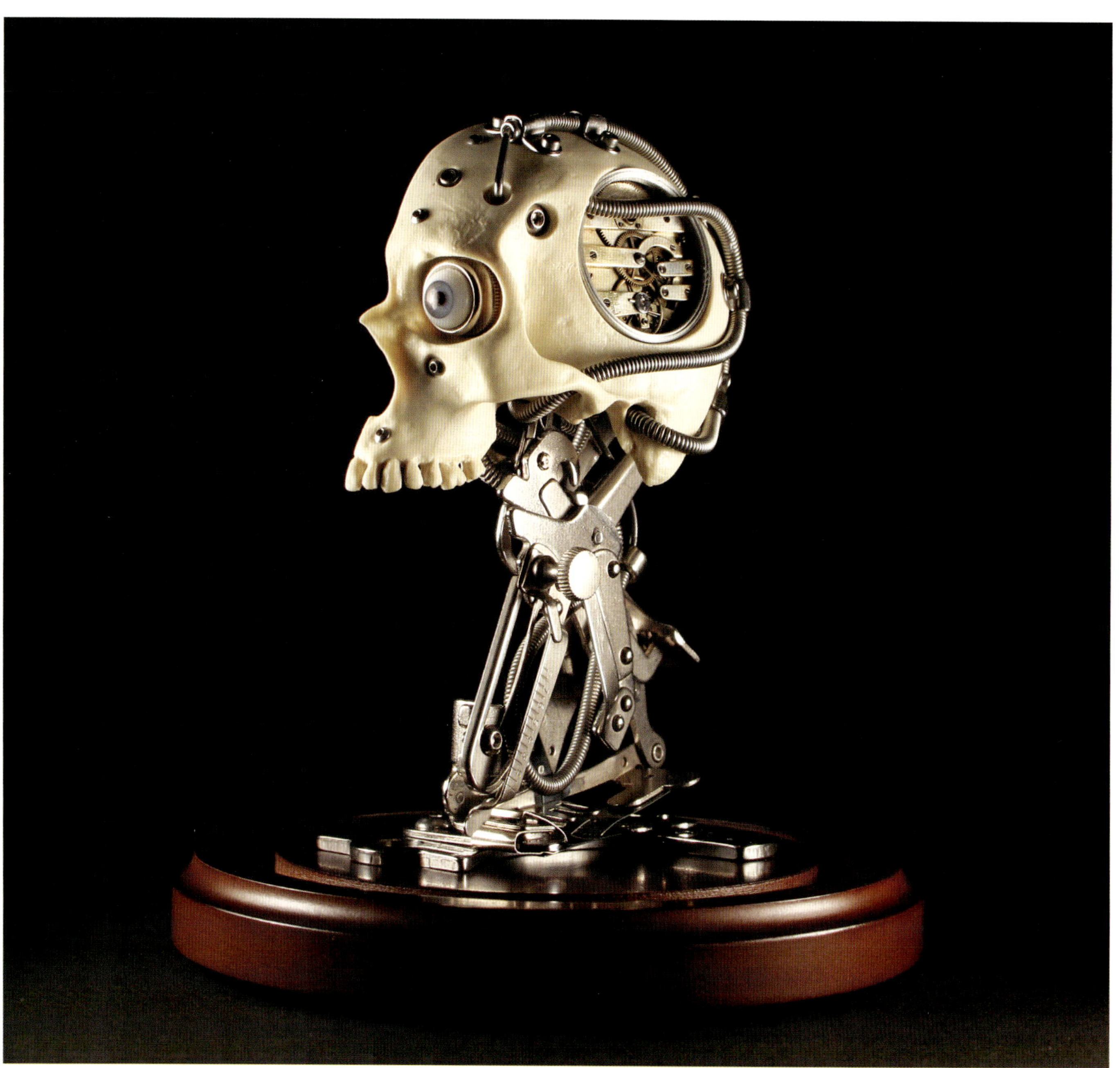

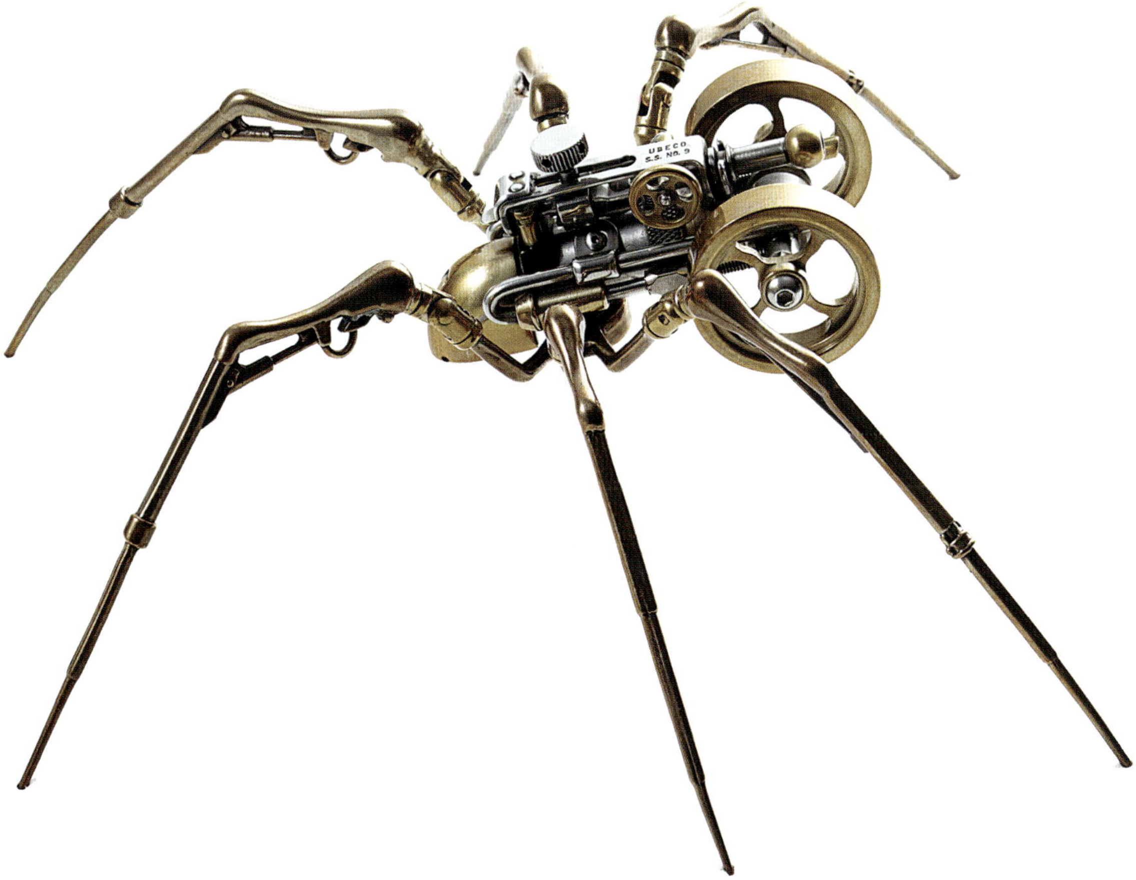

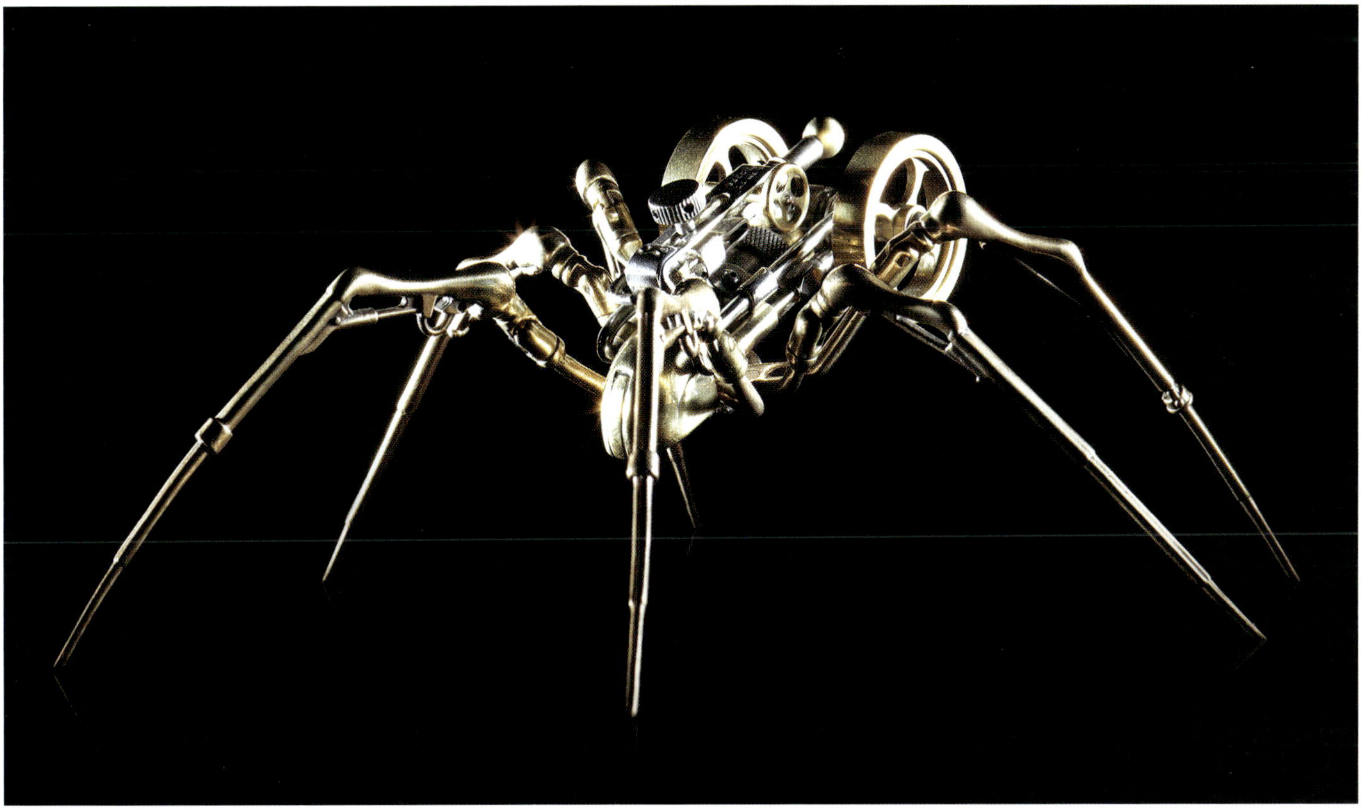

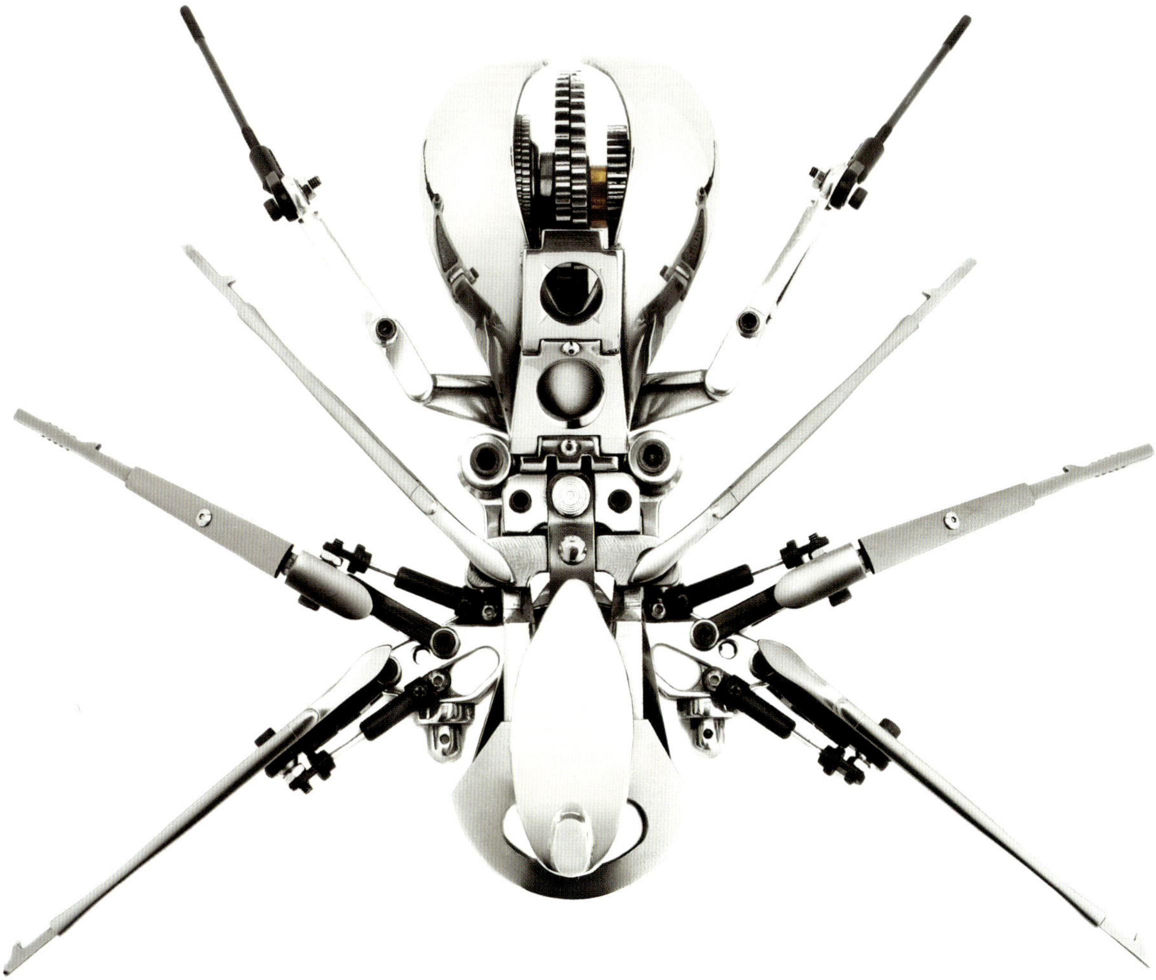

Steel Widow I, 2008.
Stainless steel, carbon steel, glass-filled nylon, aluminium and brass.
8" x 8" x 2"; (20 cm x 20 cm x 5 cm).
Photo by Robert Hakalski.

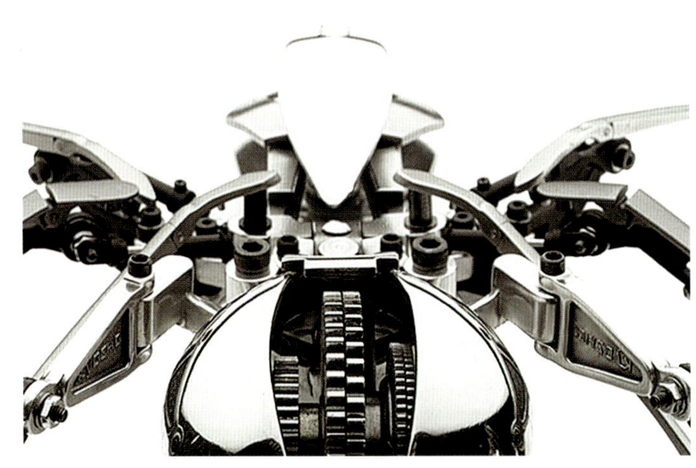

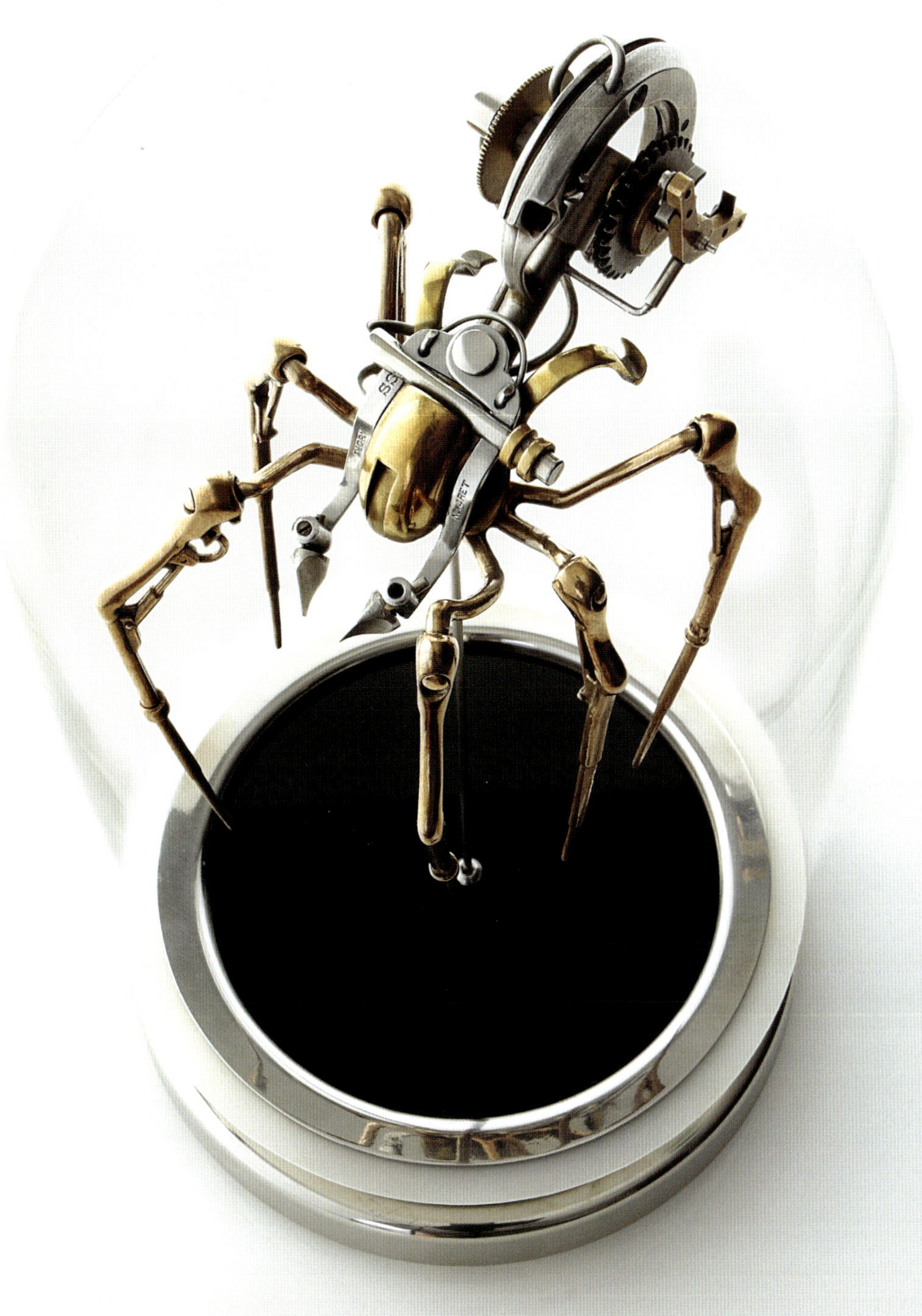

Decodroid, 2008.
Cast bronze with stainless steel and brass components.
3" x 5" x 3.5"; (7.5 cm x 12.5 cm x 9 cm).
Photo by Dennis Blachut.

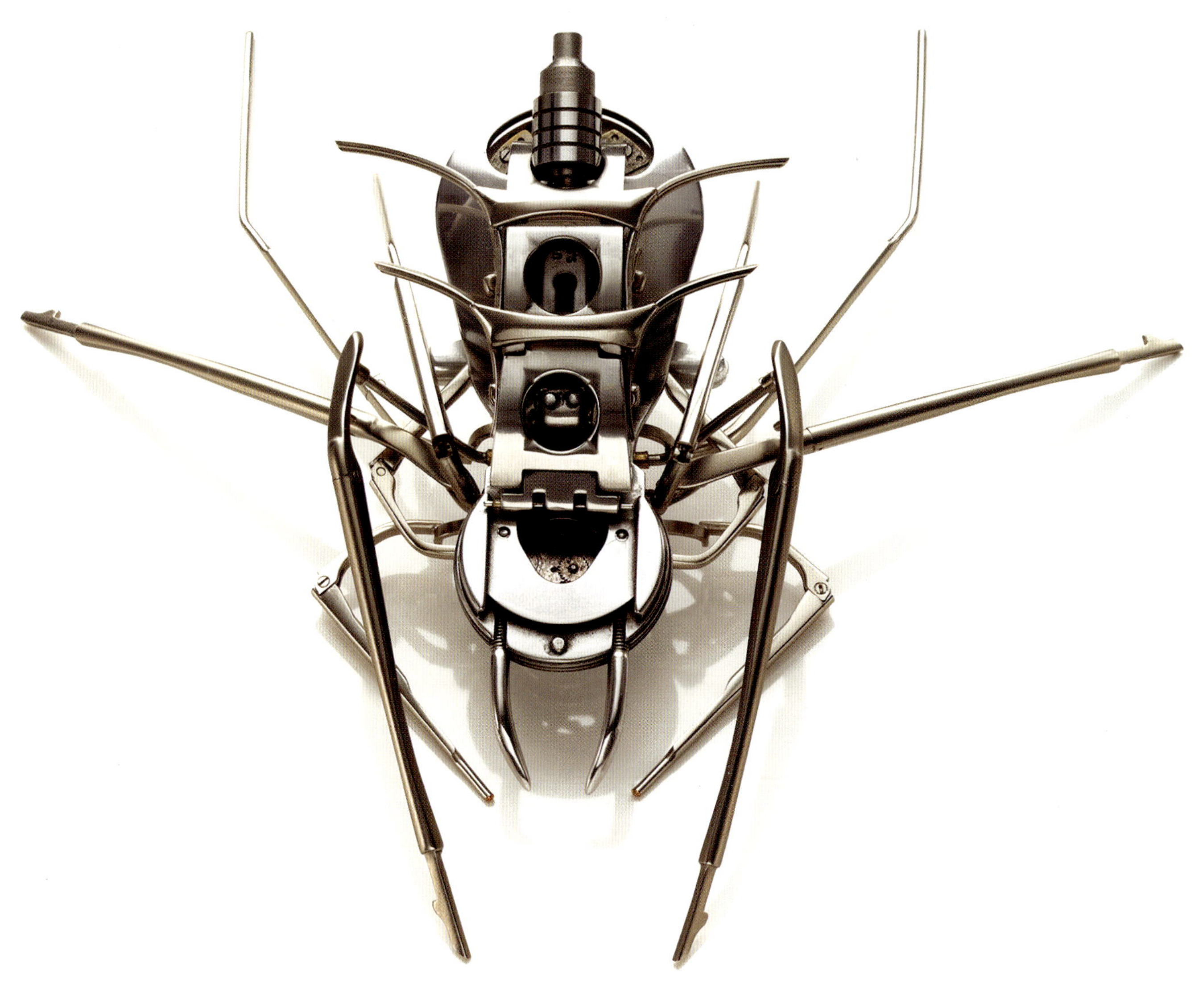

Above: *Steel Widow II*, 2009.
Stainless steel, plated brass and aluminium components.
6" x 6" x 2"; (15 cm x 15 cm x 5 cm).
Photo by Dennis Blachut.

Right: *Articulated Singer Insect*, 2005.
Antique mechanical parts and vintage Singer sewing-machine attachment.
8" x 6" x 4"; (20 cm x 15 cm x 10 cm).
Photo: Christopher Conte.

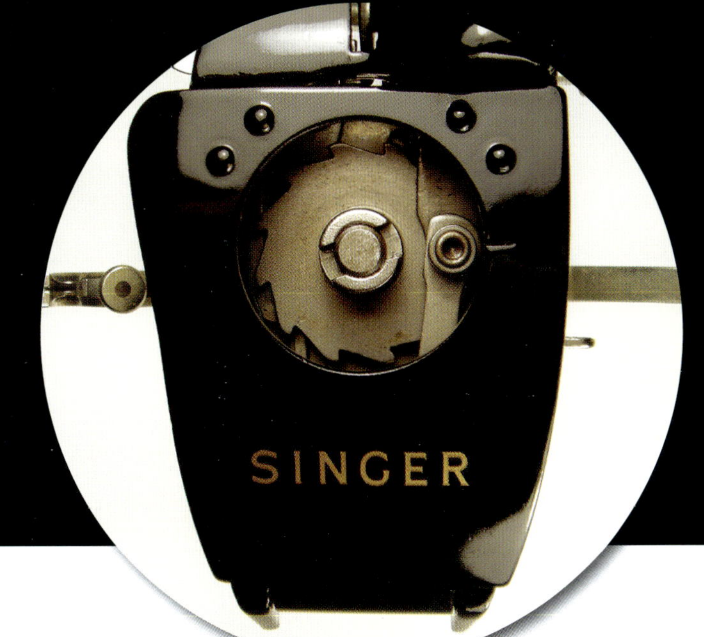
SINGER

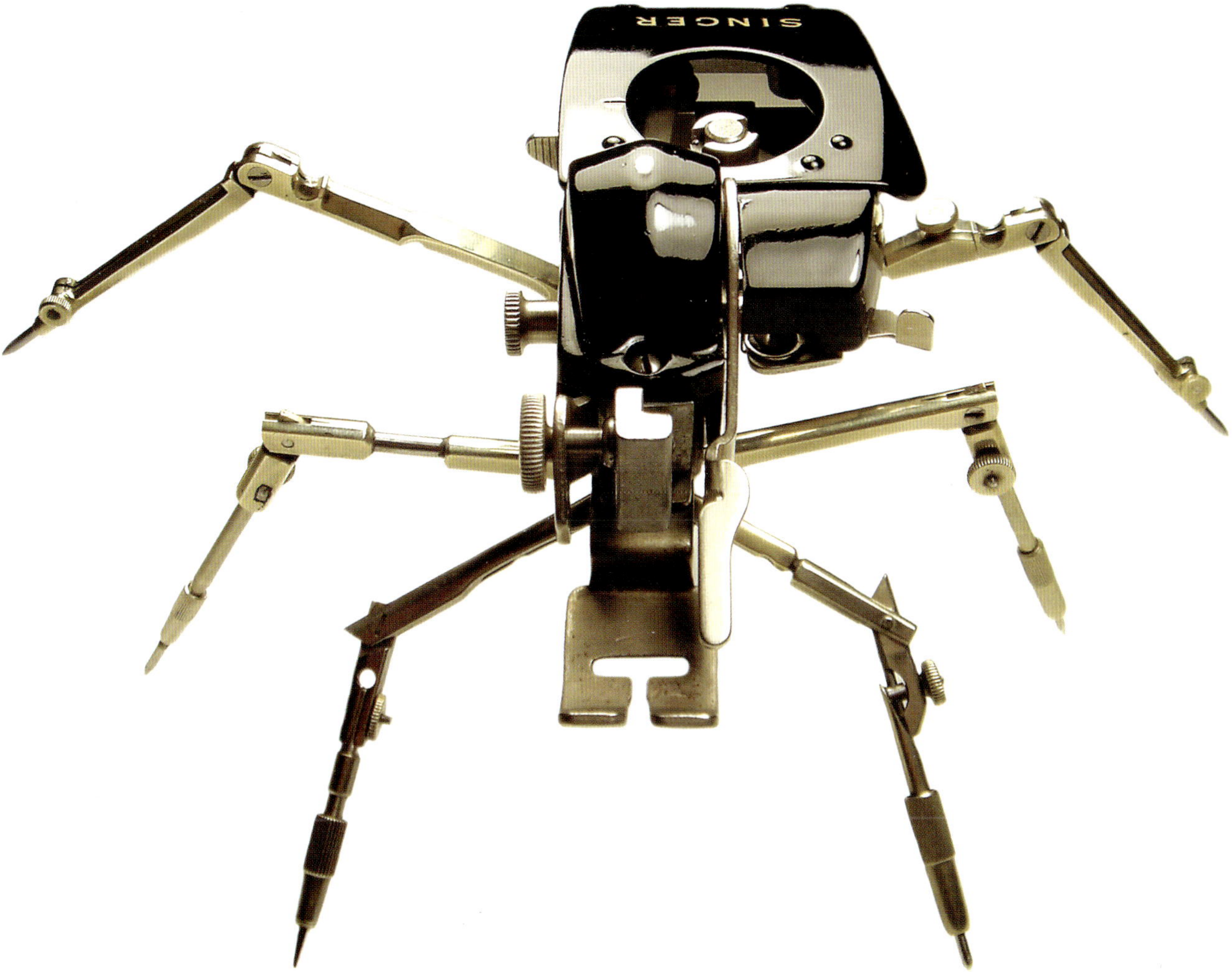

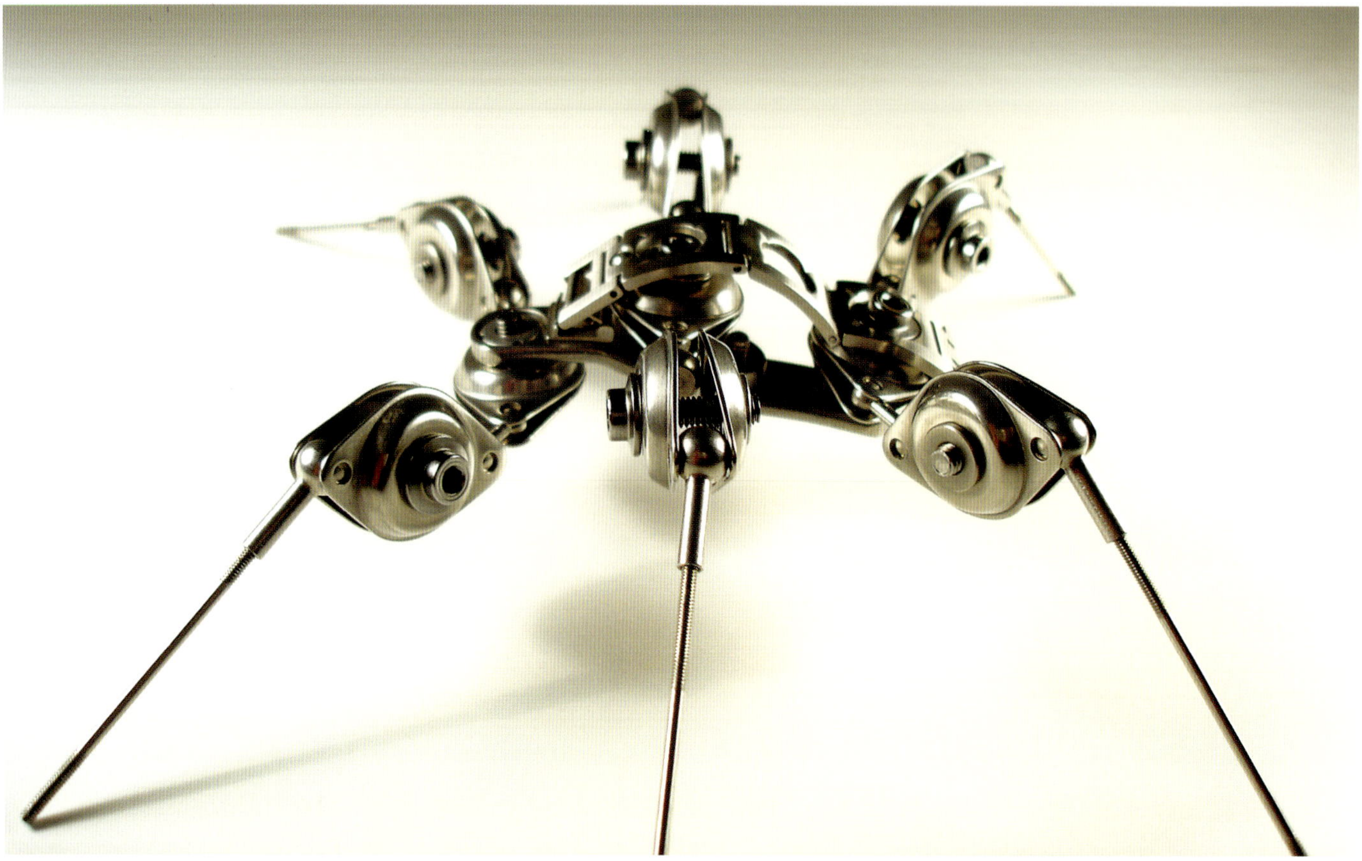

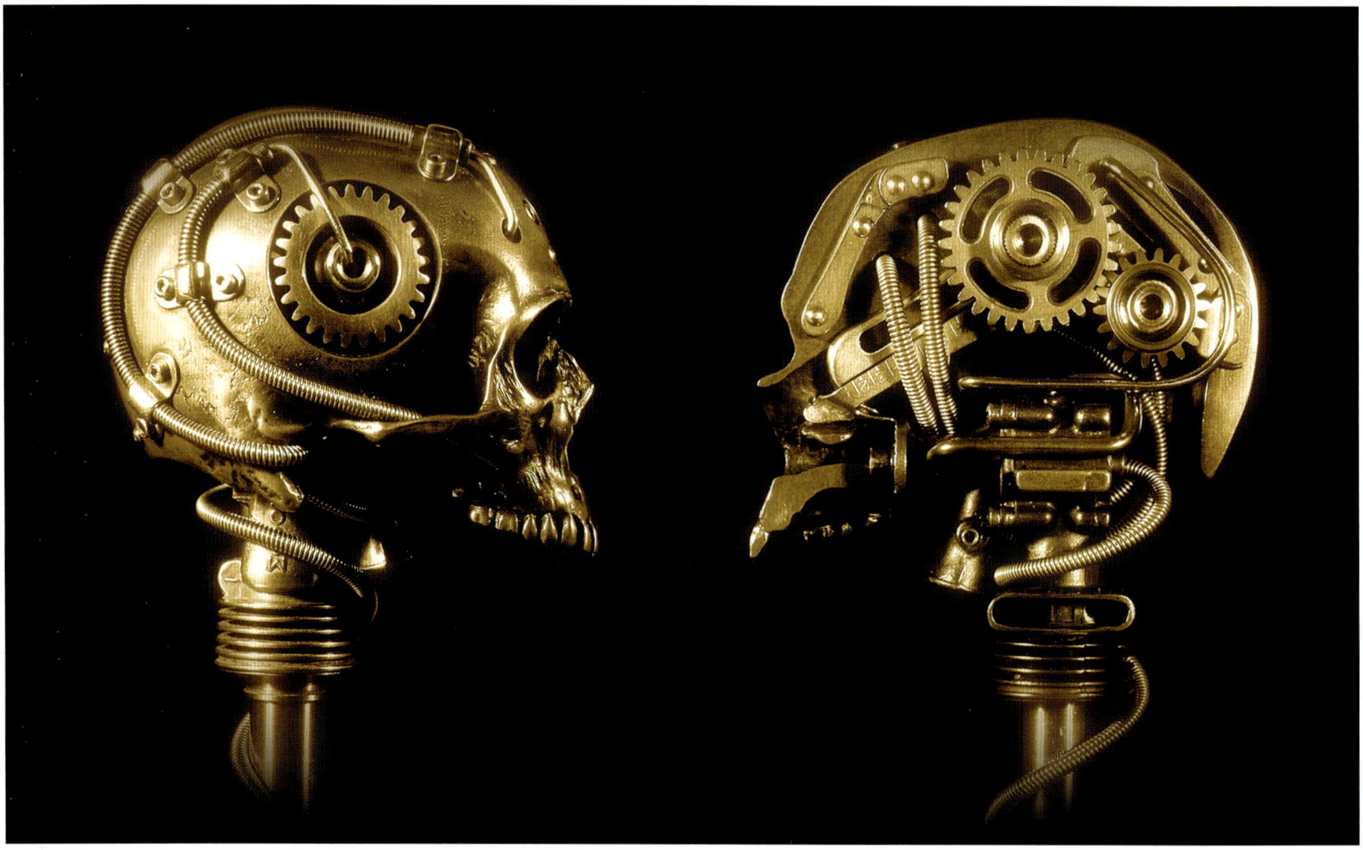

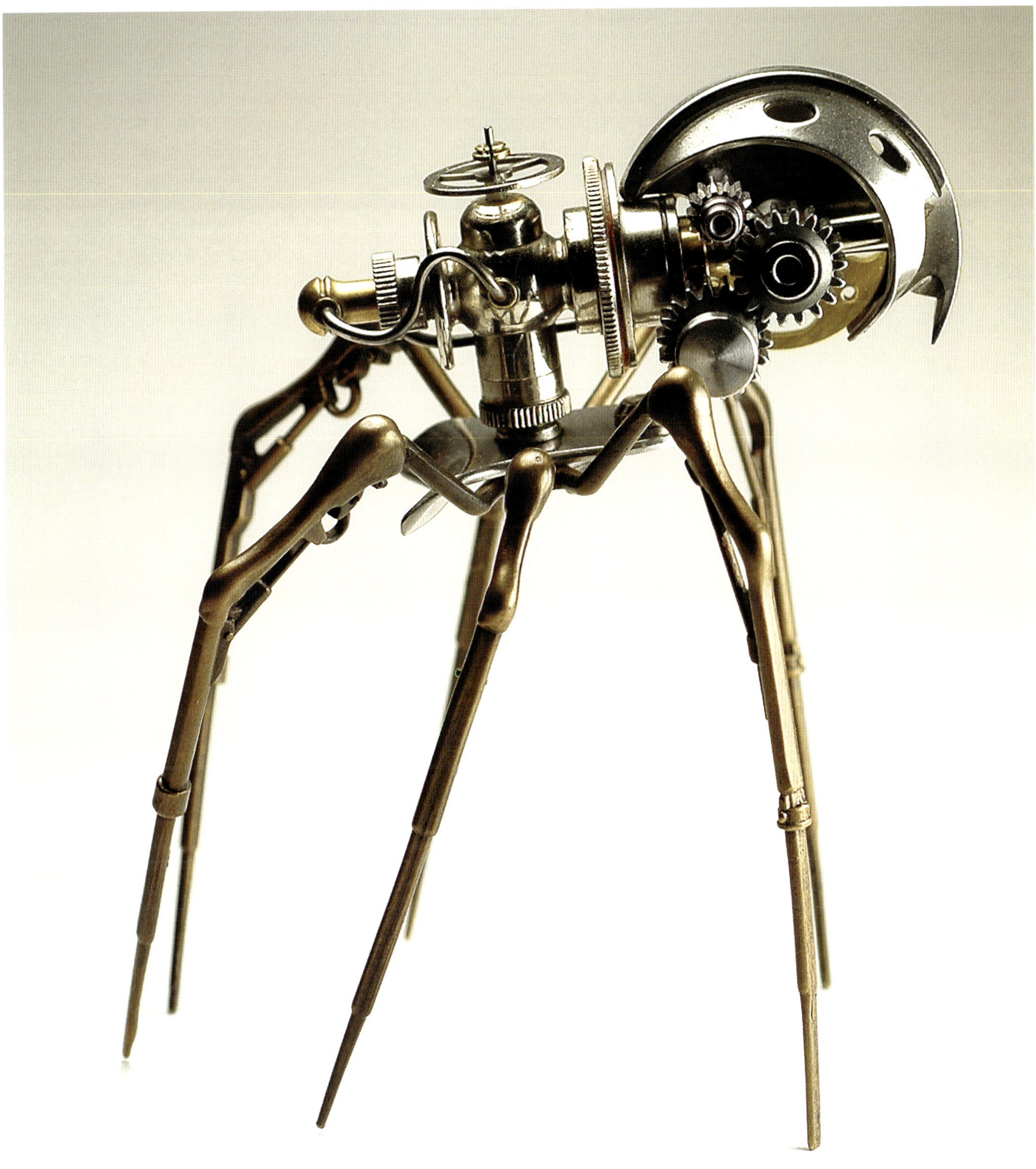

Above: *Steam Insect*, 2007.
Cast bronze with stainless steel components. 3" x 5" x 3.5"; (7.5 cm x 12.5 cm x 9 cm). Photo by Amanda Dutton.

Above Left: *Spider Armature*, 2003.
Recycled stainless steel parts, including part of Swatch wristband. 6" x 6" x 1.5"; (15 cm x 15 cm x 4 cm). Photo by Chris Conte.

Left: *Cog-nition*, *Version I*, 2007.
Cast hand-finished bronze with stainless steel components. 2" x 5" x 3.5"; (5 cm x 12.5 cm x 9 cm). Photo by Amanda Dutton.

DOKTOR A

Doktor A, a.k.a. Bruce Whistlecraft lives "under a hill on the Yorkshire Moors, from where I monitor the world's off-kilter culture and produce my dark, twisted dreams." Ray Harryhausen and Brian Froud were his early influences; today it's many artists, including Edward Gorey, H.P. Lovecraft, Terry Gilliam and Vivian Stanshall. Once told by his teachers "you'll never make a living drawing little men", he is now a full-time creator of robots and "other fantastical characters." Some are robot toys for toy companies, but mostly it's one-off fine art pieces, including his 'Mechtorians' (mechanical Victorians). His creative process involves defining the biography of a character with sketches, or is inspired by found objects, the character of the piece evolving as he builds; "I want my characters to have a certain level of 'wonk', which adds to their whimsy."

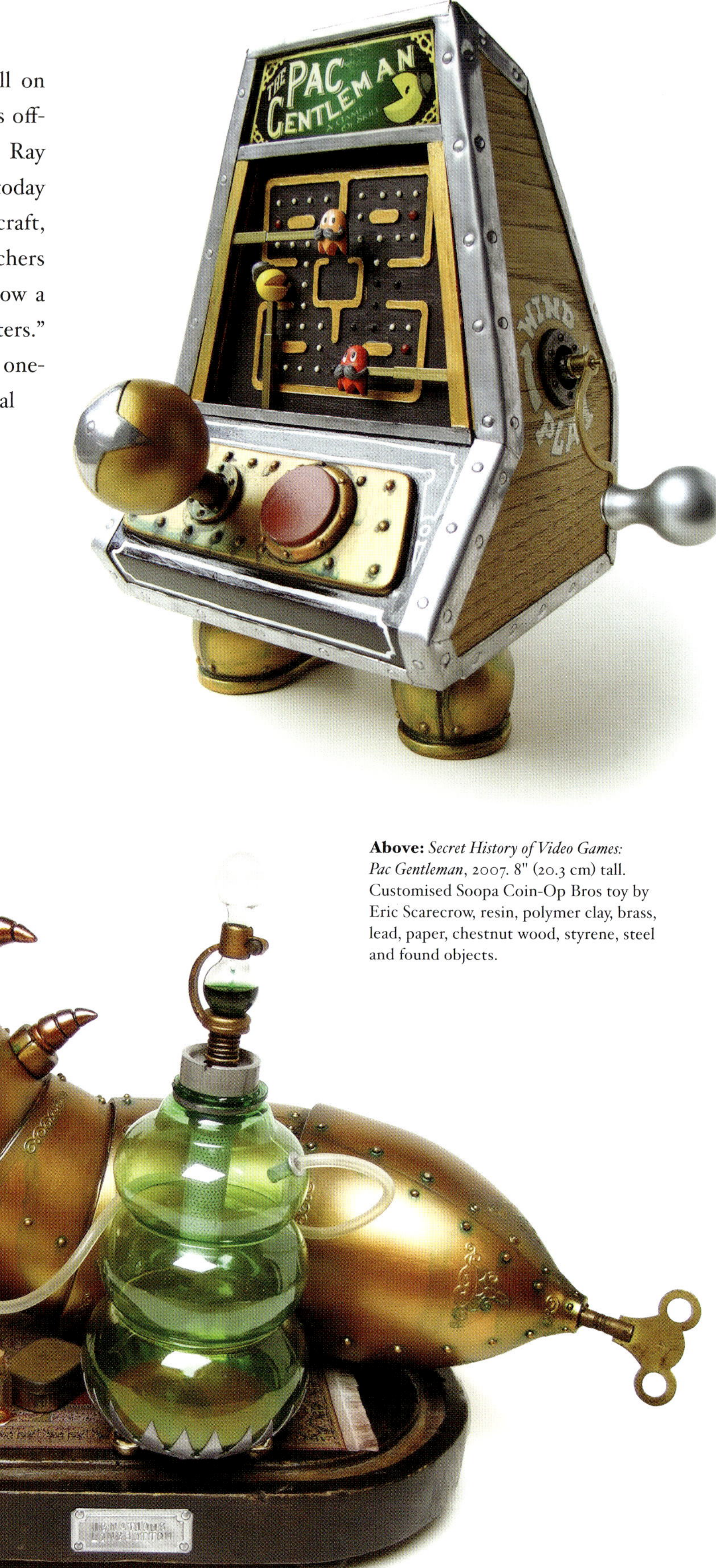

Above: *Secret History of Video Games: Pac Gentleman*, 2007. 8" (20.3 cm) tall. Customised Soopa Coin-Op Bros toy by Eric Scarecrow, resin, polymer clay, brass, lead, paper, chestnut wood, styrene, steel and found objects.

Right: *Ignatious Longbottom*, 2008. Mechtorian. 14" (35.4 cm) long. Acrylic, vinyl, lead, ABS, brass, styrene, polymer clay, steel, silicone rubber, wood, glass, paper and found objects.

"Ignatius is a professional daydreamer. He ponders the way of things, surmises patterns, and learns through the medium of smoke. To smoke a thing is to take it into yourself and to know its essence. Ignatious has a plan to smoke a little of everything so he may then better understand the relationships between all things. To this end he constructed a special piece of headgear, to maximize his immersion in his chosen miasma."

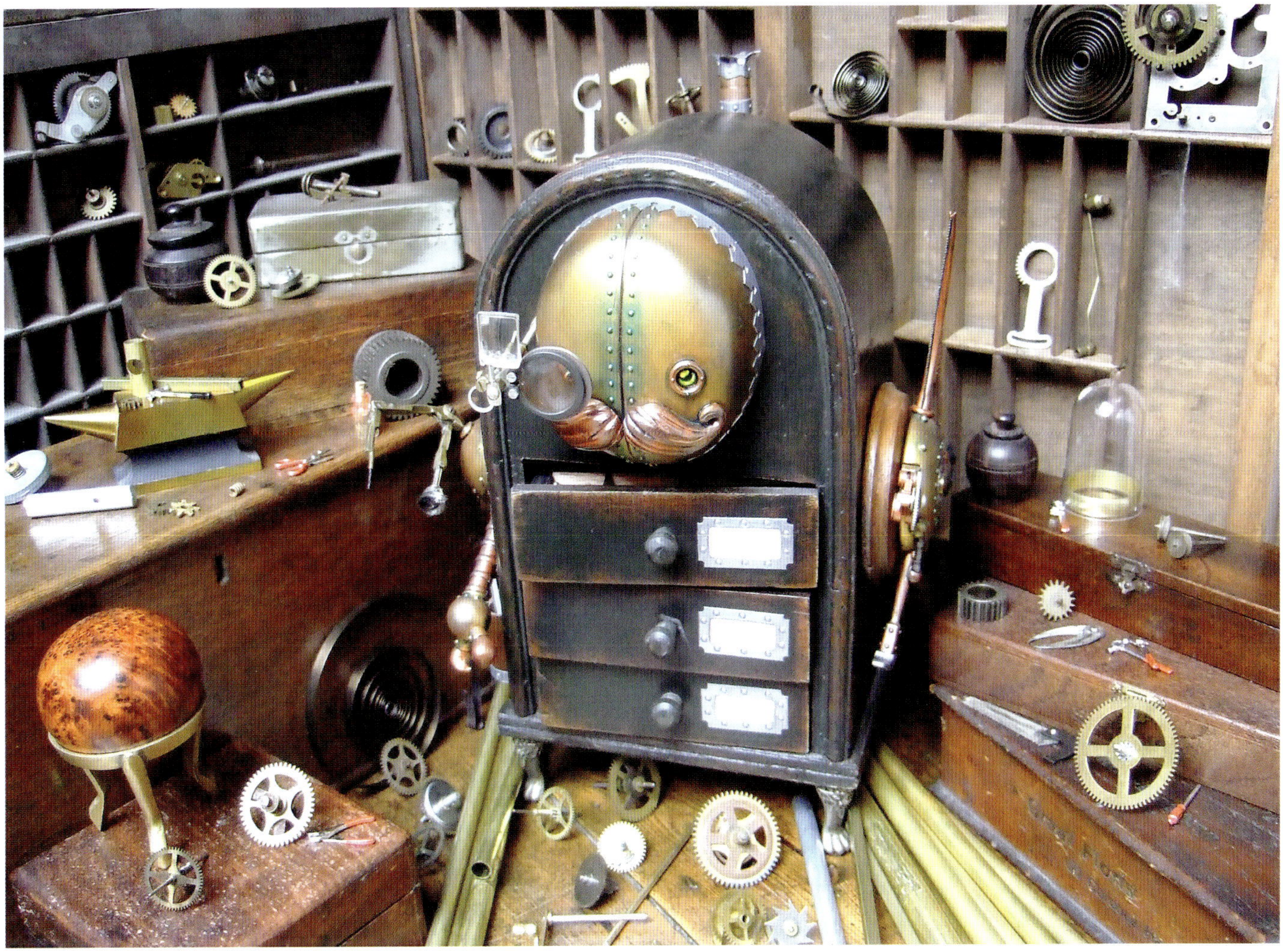

Above and Below: *Lester Molesworthy The Fixer*. Mechtorian. 9" (21.1 cm) tall. Wood, lead, ABS, brass, copper, aluminium, steel, felt, glass, polymer clay, paper and found objects. "One of the last remaining original builder Mechs. Long since outmoded by bigger, faster, smarter machines, he now resides with the circus, repairing the collective and tending to their eccentric needs. He regales them with tales of early Retropolis, a time when there was room to roam, and the hope that the makers would soon come was still present in all Mechs' minds. Now very few believe in the existence of the makers. But he remembers a time when there were still stocks of parts made by fleshy hands."

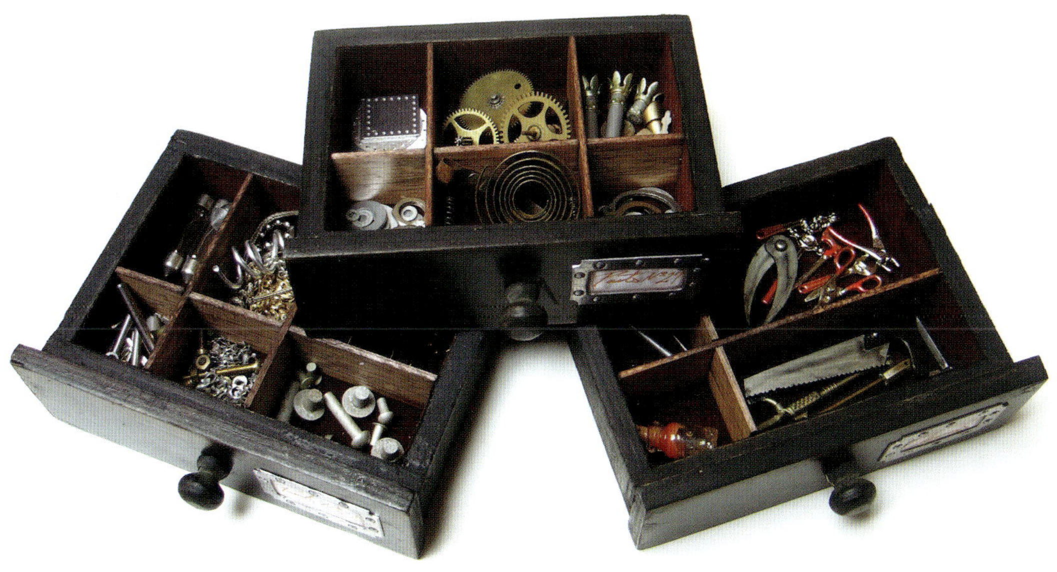

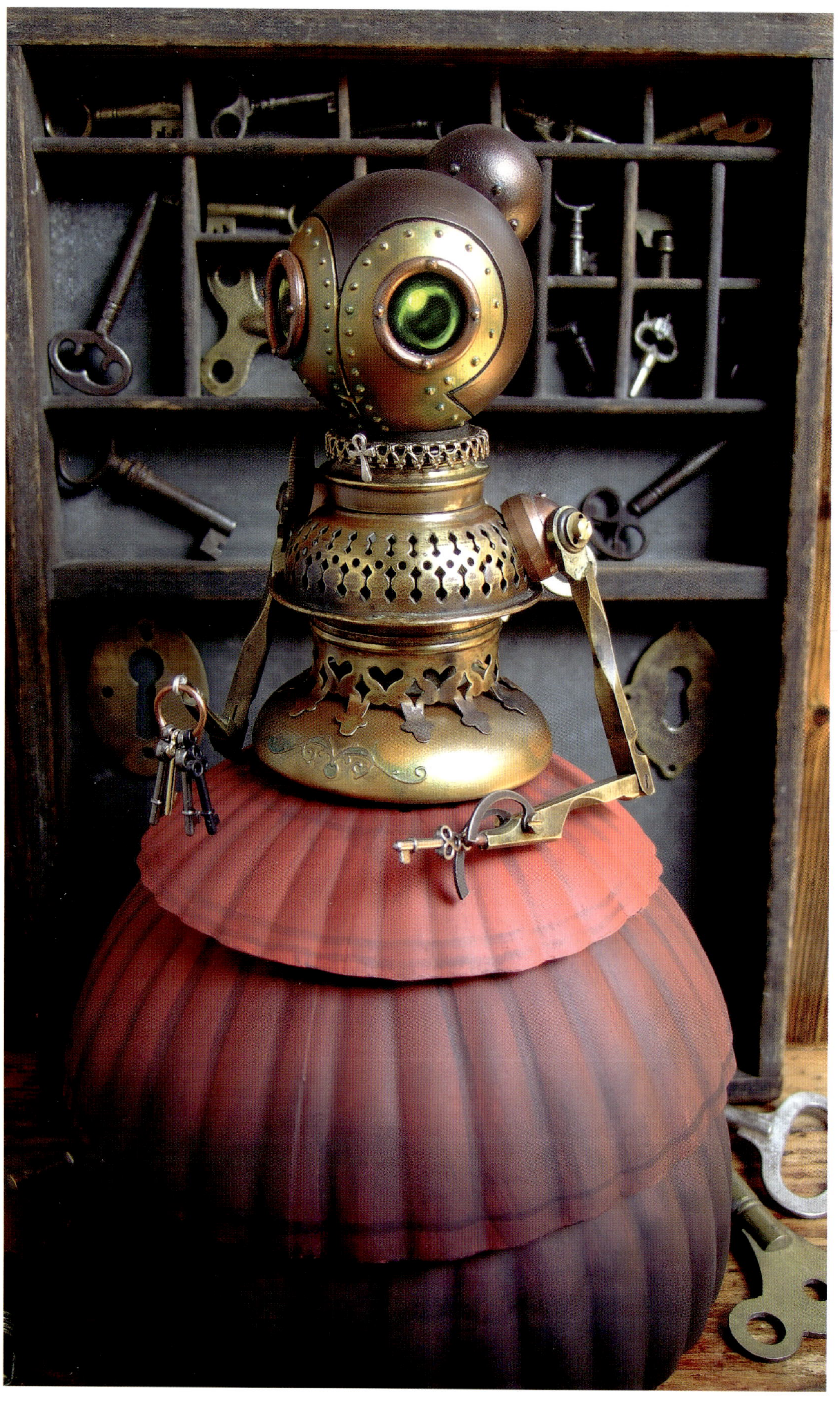

Left: *Amnesia Primm*. Mechtorian. 8" (18.7 cm) tall. Vinyl, rubber, lead, paper, ABS, brass and found objects.

Right, Left: *Nathaniel Herringbone, Biologist.* Mechtorian.

"Given the task of measuring, sketching and generally recording all information about any new species encountered by the Expedition, Nathaniel is, however, easily bored and distracted. This low attention span makes him prone to flights of fancy, which results in most of his animal renderings sporting gratuitously fashionable waistcoats."

Right, Middle: *Erasmus Swift, Entomologist.* Mechtorian.

"If it's small and creeps or flutters, then Erasmus is intrigued: how do these little things move about without the need for winding key or furnace stoking? Surely a proper study of the non-mechanical native species of the planet Victoria could provide a wealth of new technologies. Plus the prettier specimens look so arresting mounted up in little frames in one's study."

Right, Right: *Hugo Wattleberry, Botanist.* Mechtorian.

"Founder of the Royal Herbology Society, Hugo is attempting to catalogue every type of flora he can. In the process he hopes to discover which makes the best pot of tea."

Below Right and Far Right: *Sinister & Dexter Robe Maudsley*. Mechtorians. Each 7" (16.4 cm) tall. Vinyl, ABS, rubber, lead, polymer clay, paper, copper, brass, steel and found objects.

"Not Half the Man He Used to Be. His parents wanted identical twins! In fact that's what they commissioned. But when, due to a clerical error, only one little bundle of joy was delivered to them things got heated. All the funds for children were spent. Another baby was out of the financial question, not to mention the fact that another one made seperately from the first would never be quite the same. Arguments and threats of legal action, against the workshop that made him, did nothing to alter the situation. So Sinister's father took drastic action. Driven to the edge of desperation and logic, he did his best to turn their one offspring into two. He was not a craftsman and the job was not neat or skillful, but it worked. Sinister is the more driven-by-logic of the twins. He is a good businessman and a fine mathematician."

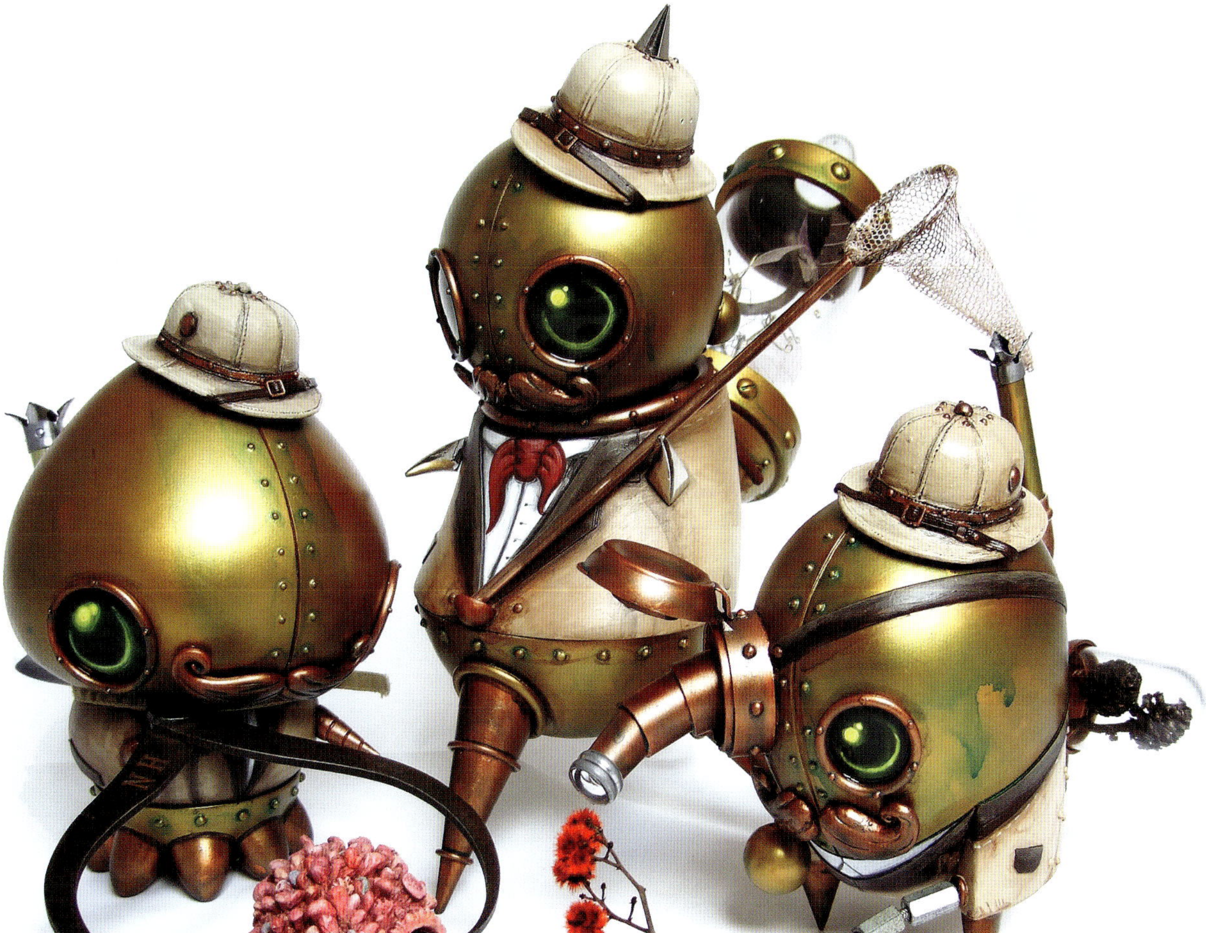

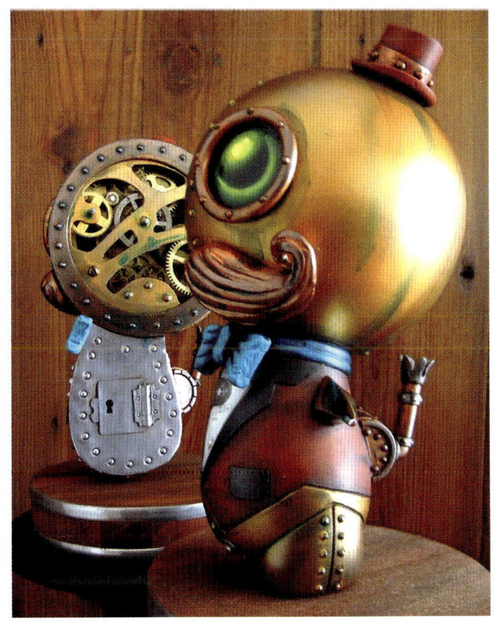

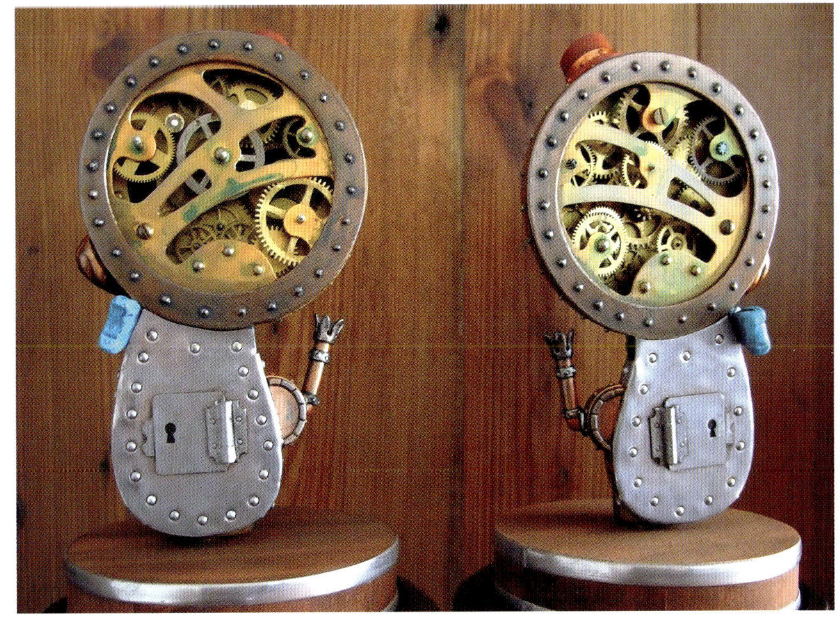

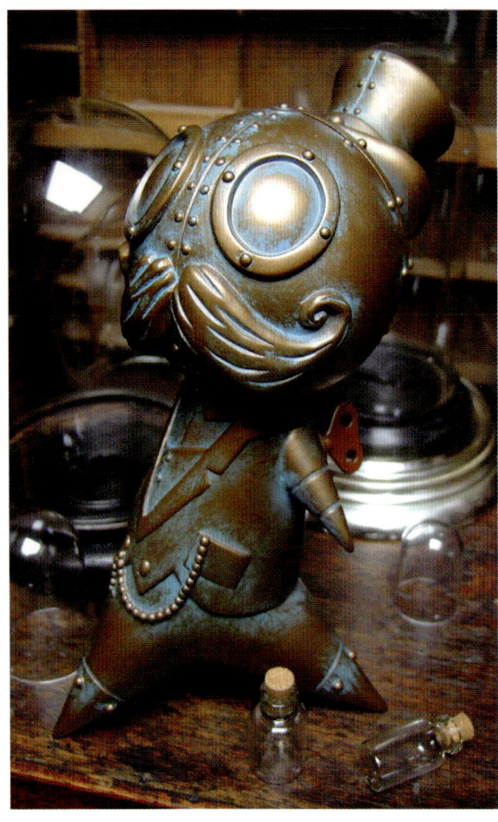

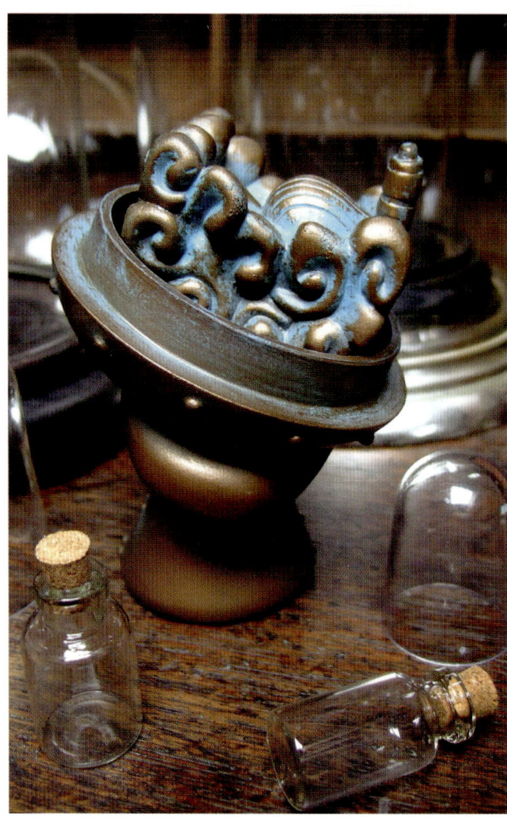

Left, Above and Below: *Humphrey Mooncalf.* Mechtorian. 8" (18.7 cm) tall. Vinyl. Limited edition by Pobber toys.

"Humphrey had a reoccurring problem with his Travithick No. 4 Nano-clockwork brain. Repeated trips to the watch-smith proved a great success: the pain was held at bay by loosening his cranial rivets. This however means that he can no longer look up. Such a shame, as he does so love the moon."

Page Opposite, Clockwise from Top Left (all Mechtorians)**:**

Sir Shilling Copperpenny. 4" (9.4 cm) tall. Vinyl and ABS in a window box.

"Sir Shilling is the Manager at the Bank of Retropolis. He has deep pockets and short arms. Although his heart is large, he loves his coin collection above all else... he has even toyed with the idea of having his beloved coins fashioned into a spouse."

The Whipple Brothers. 8" (18.7 cm) tall.

"When Ronson Travithick first introduced his revolutionary NanoClockwork brains they were all the rage. It was the height of fashion to be seen sporting one of these. Twin brothers Arthur and Simeon Whipple hit upon the idea of pooling their money and purchasing one between them. Unable to come up with an agreeable rota of usage for their new acquisition they instead took the unusual decision to fuse their two bodies and share the brain simultaneously."

Roderick "Tin Nosed" Magee. 8" (18.7 cm) tall. Vinyl, lead, steel, wood, brass, copper, polymer clay, styrene and found objects.

"A commanding officer who lost his nose in a munitions-loading accident. His bagman rustled him up a makeshift replacement from a sugar spoon, which he wears to this day. He greatly dislikes the nickname given to him by his men. The spoon, you see, was silver..."

The Ringmaster. 8" (18.7 cm) tall. Vinyl, rubber, lead, polymer clay, paper, ABS, brass, steel and found objects.

"Barnabus T. Barnabus, the Hawker, Barker and Ringmaster of the show he's been with from the beginning. Originally "The 'Orrible Legless Boy", he purchased some wheels and worked his way up to run the whole shebang. His eye for the peculiar made him and the circus a monumental success. Many dispossessed Mechtorians now arrive at the Freak Show's doors seeking fame and fortune. They have to be chosen by Barnabus to make the cut; he can probably be bribed with a packet of Custard Creams."

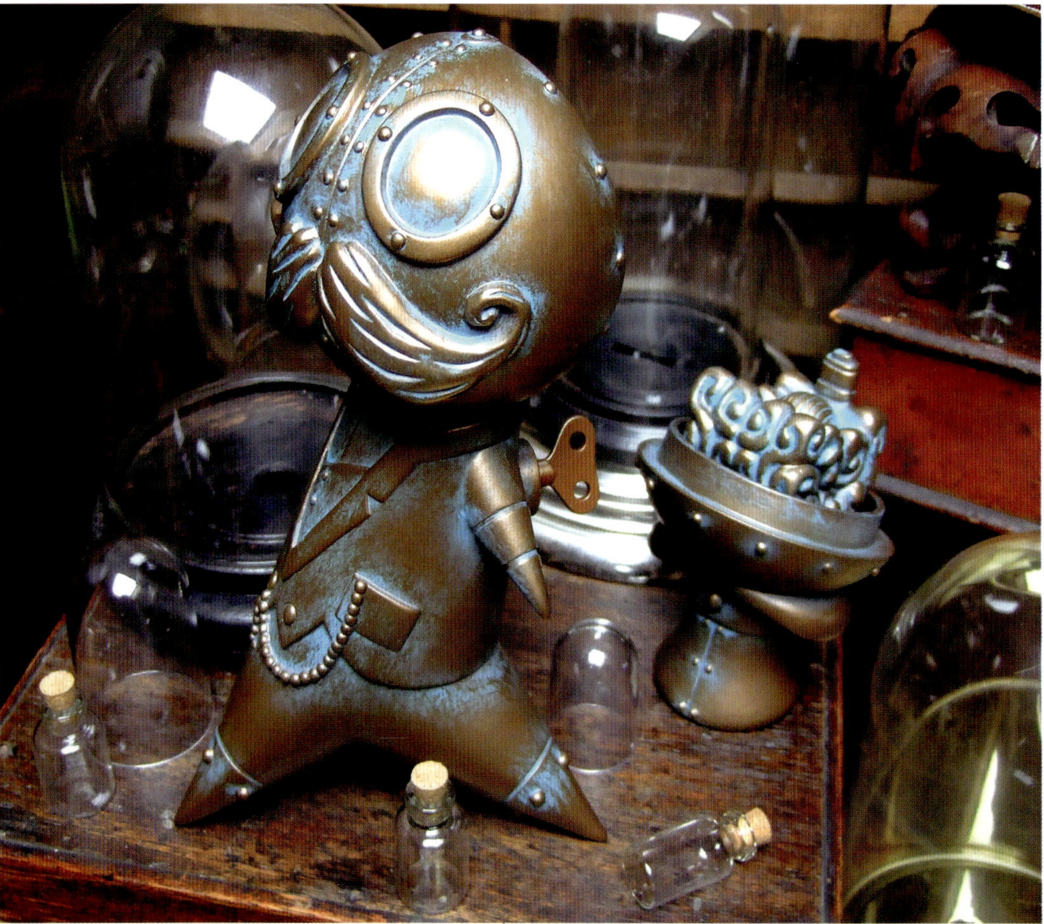

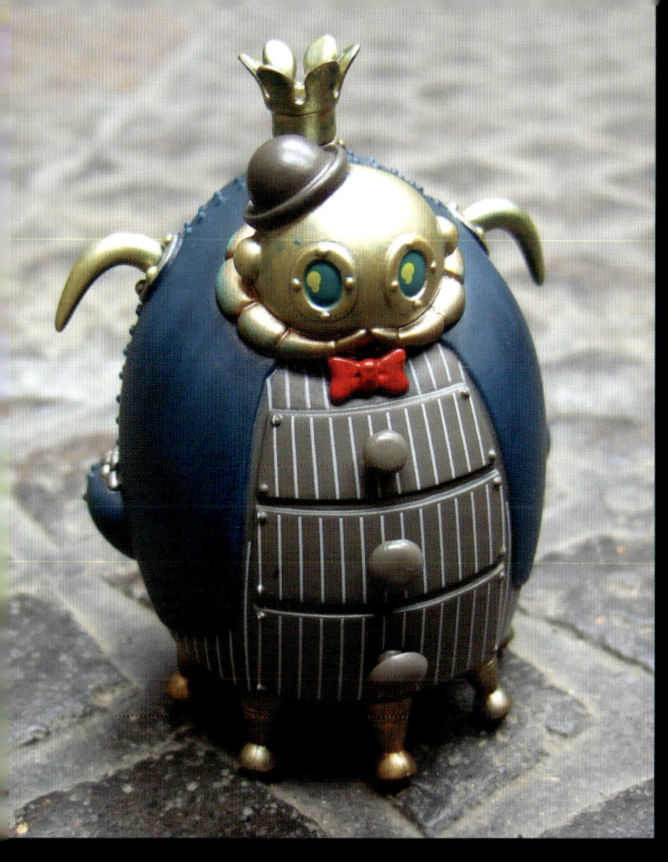
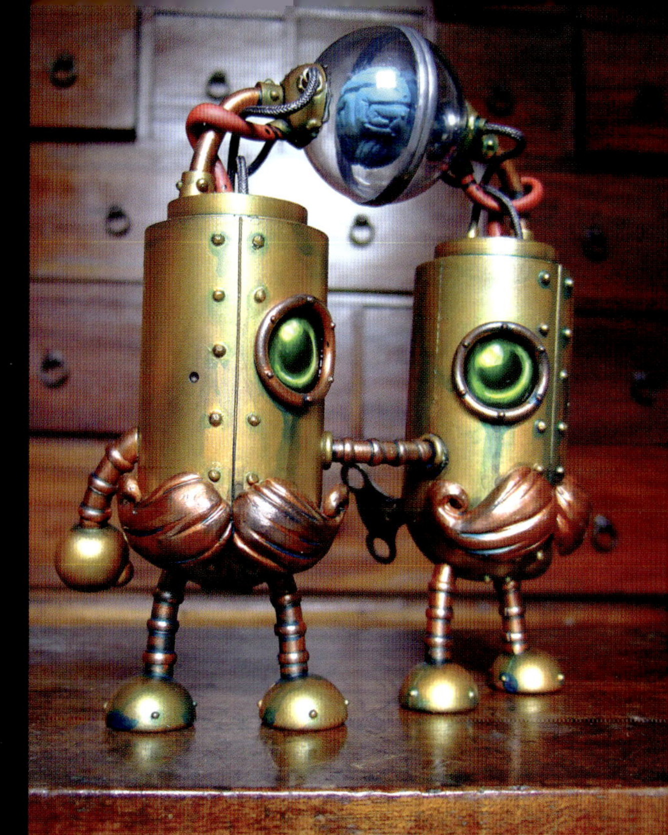
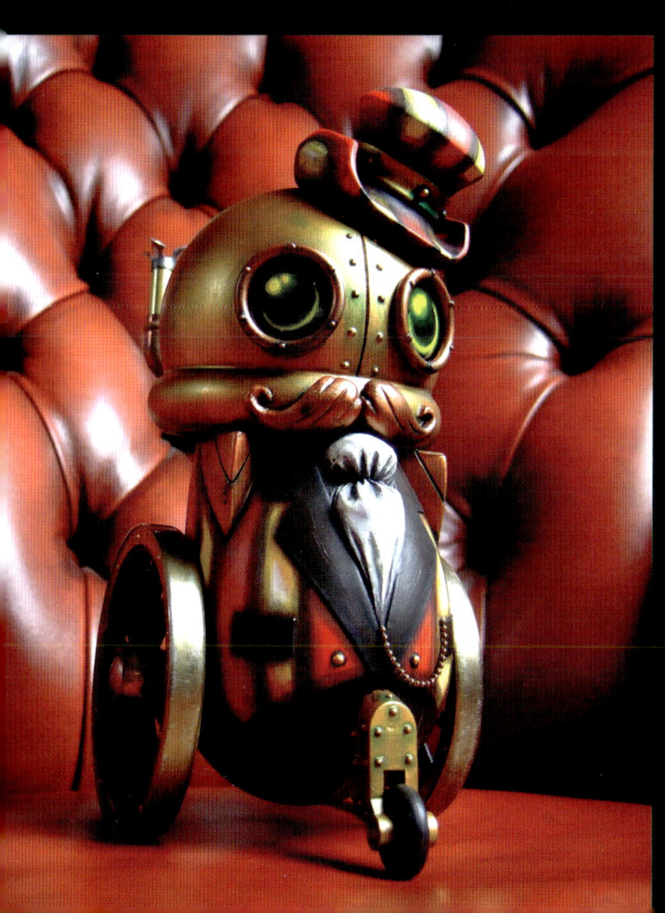
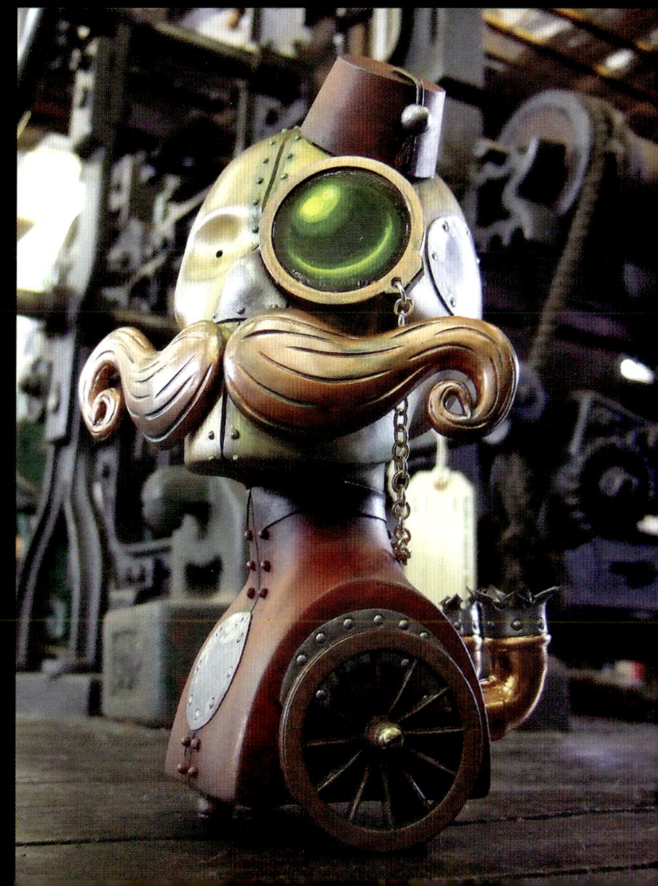

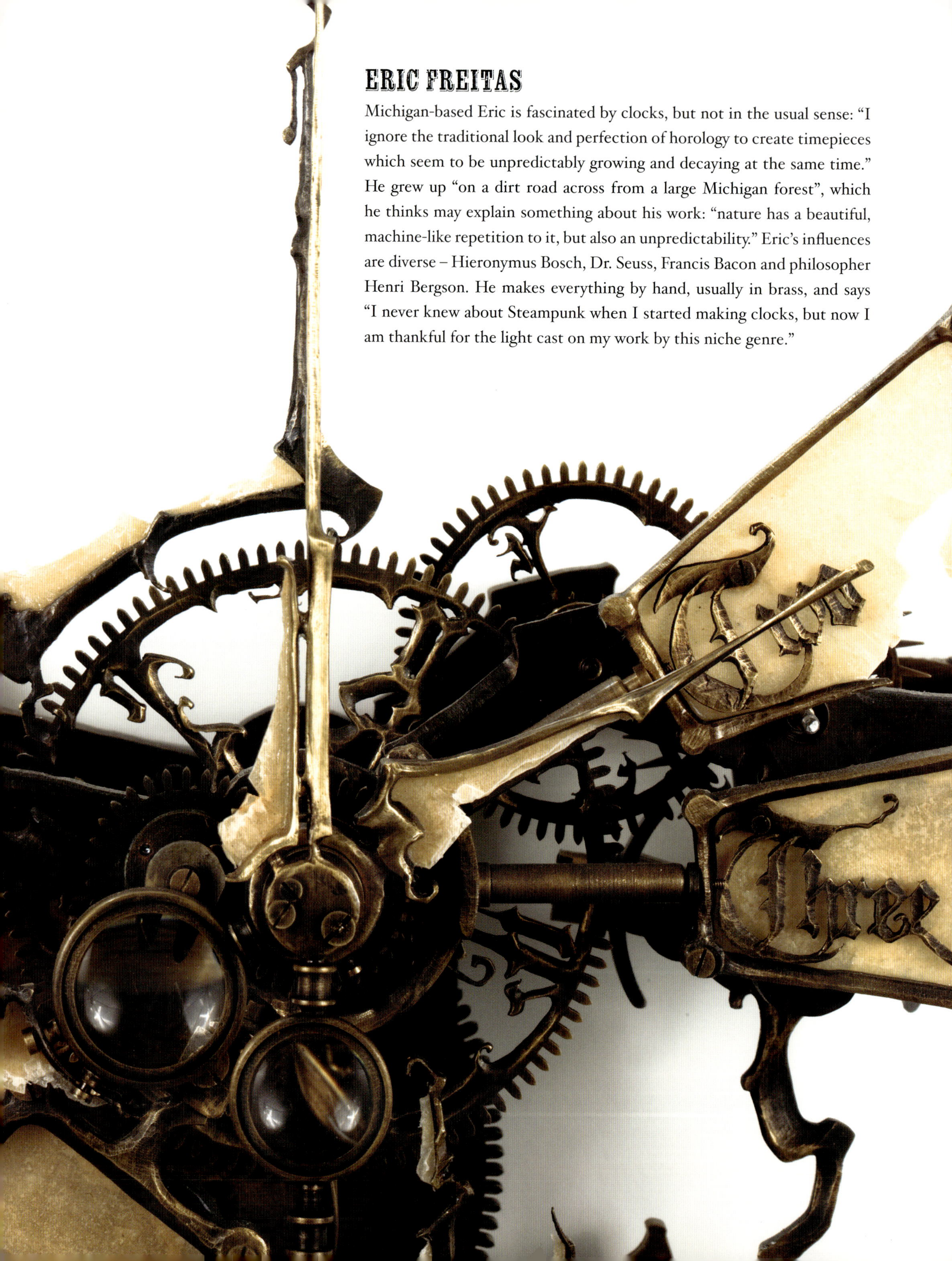

ERIC FREITAS

Michigan-based Eric is fascinated by clocks, but not in the usual sense: "I ignore the traditional look and perfection of horology to create timepieces which seem to be unpredictably growing and decaying at the same time." He grew up "on a dirt road across from a large Michigan forest", which he thinks may explain something about his work: "nature has a beautiful, machine-like repetition to it, but also an unpredictability." Eric's influences are diverse – Hieronymus Bosch, Dr. Seuss, Francis Bacon and philosopher Henri Bergson. He makes everything by hand, usually in brass, and says "I never knew about Steampunk when I started making clocks, but now I am thankful for the light cast on my work by this niche genre."

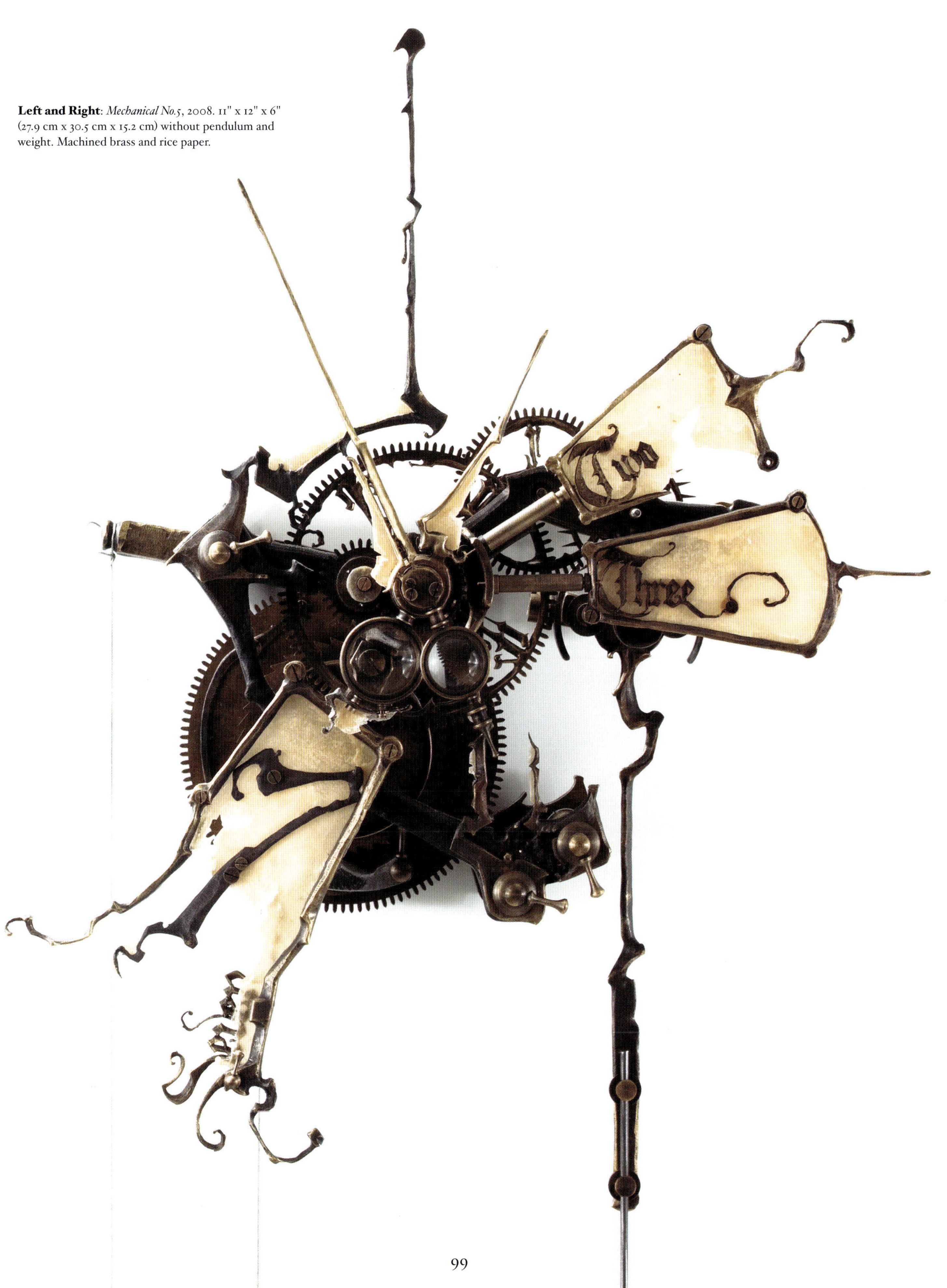

Left and Right: *Mechanical No.5*, 2008. 11" x 12" x 6" (27.9 cm x 30.5 cm x 15.2 cm) without pendulum and weight. Machined brass and rice paper.

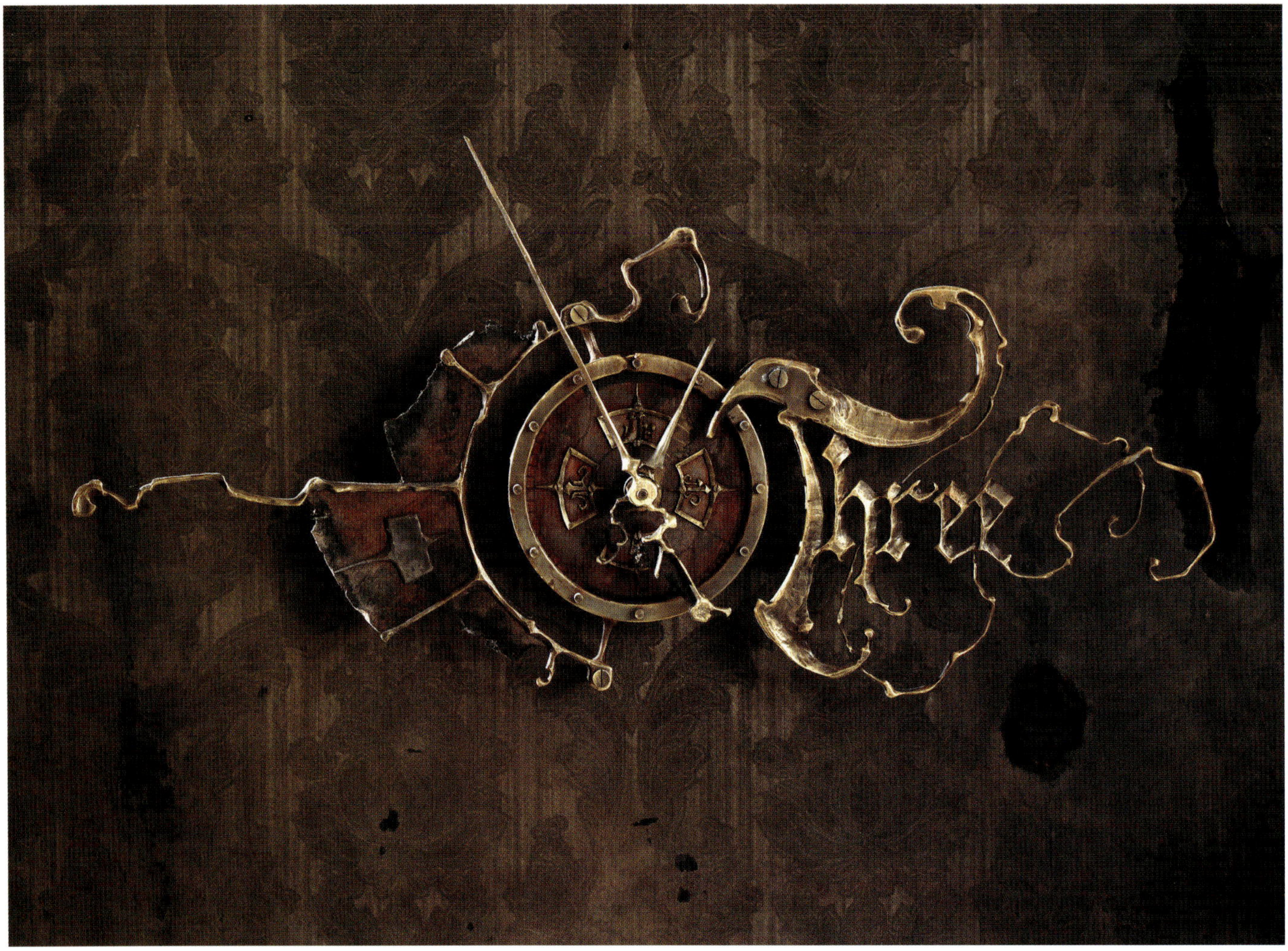

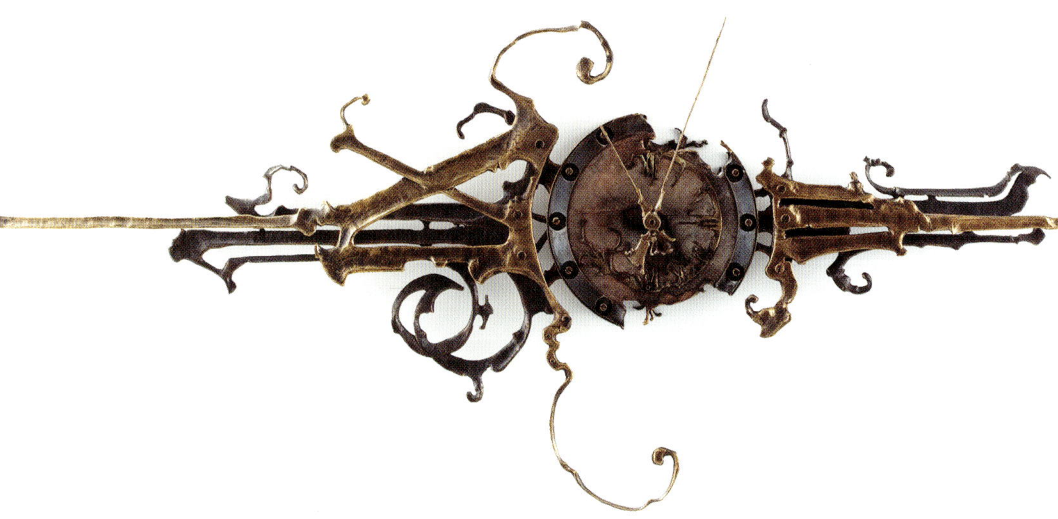

Top: *Quartz 6*, 2008. 16.5" x 7" x 2" (41.9 cm x 17.8 cm x 5.1 cm). Machined brass and rice paper.

Above: *Quartz 10*, 2009. 37" x 13" x 2.5" (93 cm x 33 cm x 6.4 cm). Machined brass and rice paper.

Right: *Mechanical No.6*, 2009. 7.5" x 22" x 5.5" (19.1 cm x 55.9 cm x 14 cm), excluding chain. Machined brass and rice paper.

Far Right: *Quartz 9*, 2009. 7" x 20" x 2" (17.8 cm x 50.8 cm x 5.1 cm). Machined brass and rice paper.

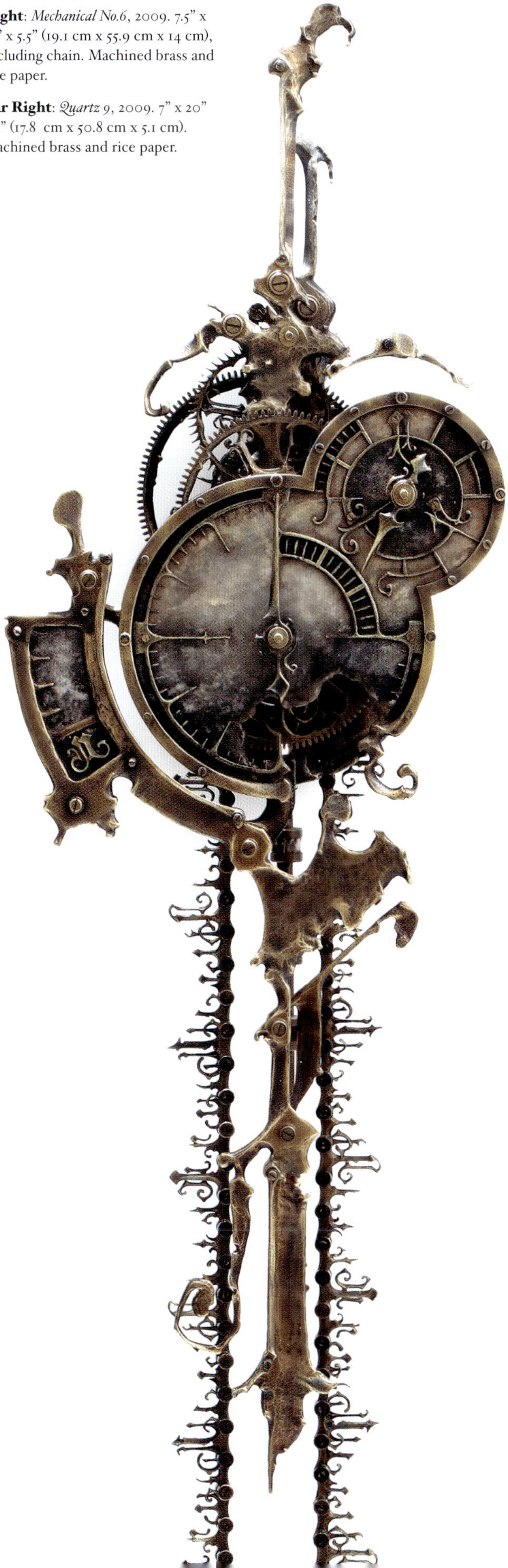

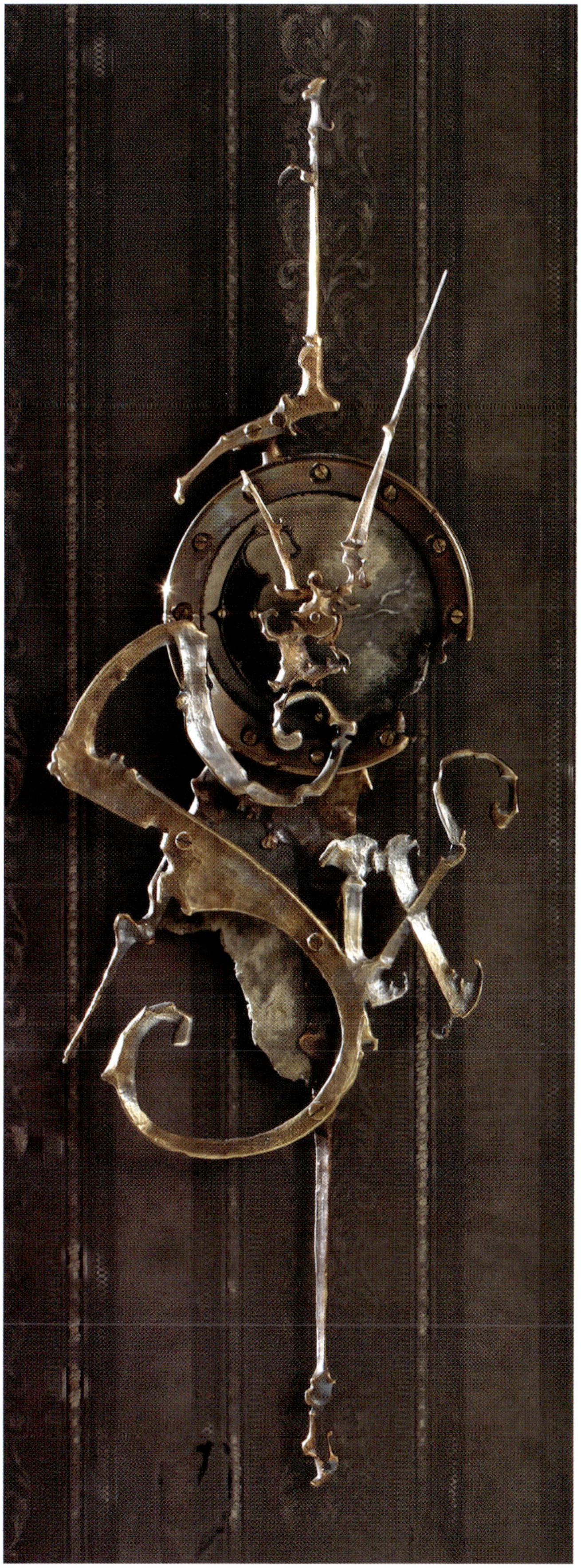

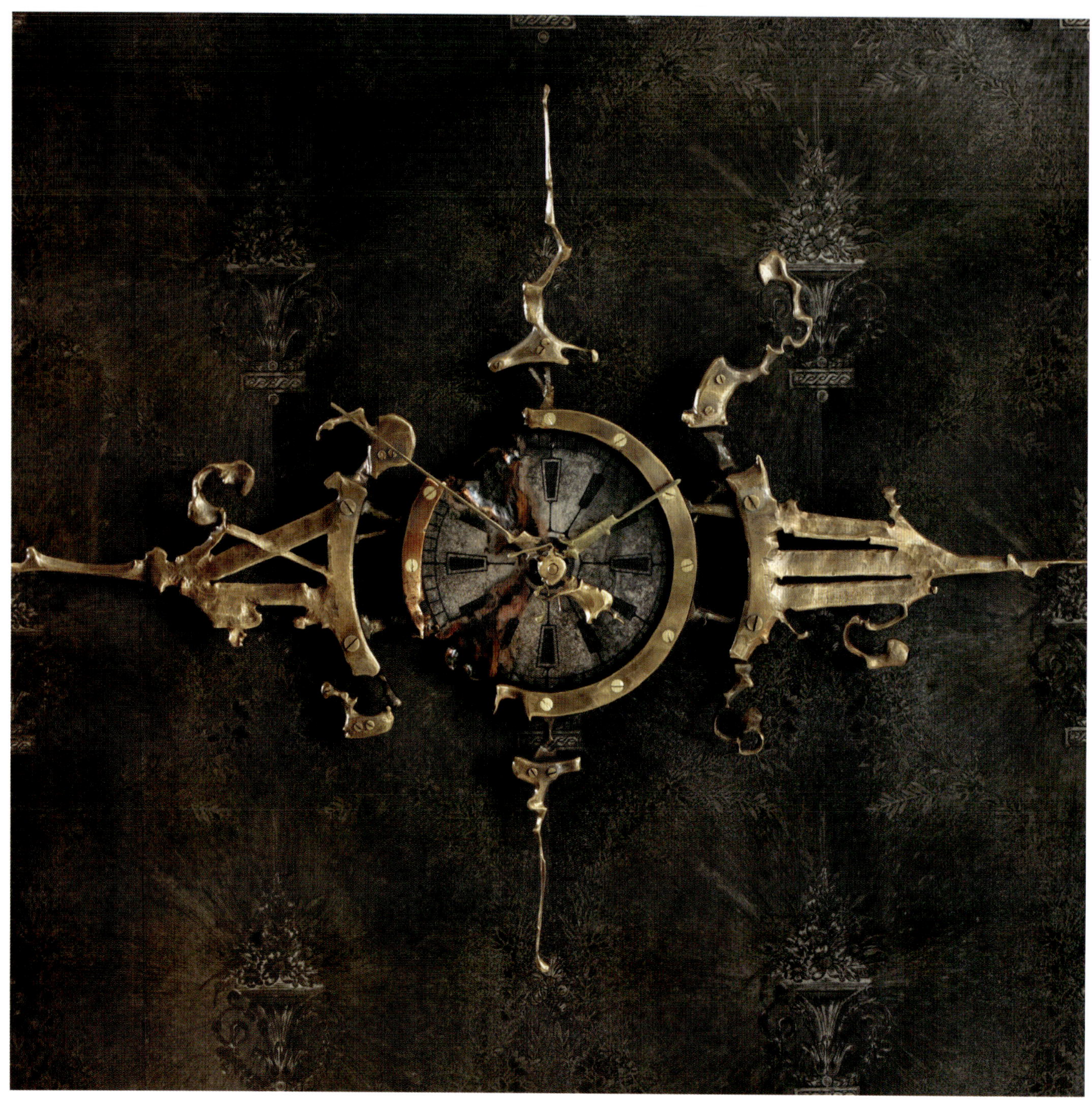

Above: *Quartz 8*. 17" x 12" (43.2 cm x 30.5 cm). Machined brass.

Right: *Mechanical No.7* (detail). 5' x 3' x 1' (152 cm x 91 cm x 30 cm).

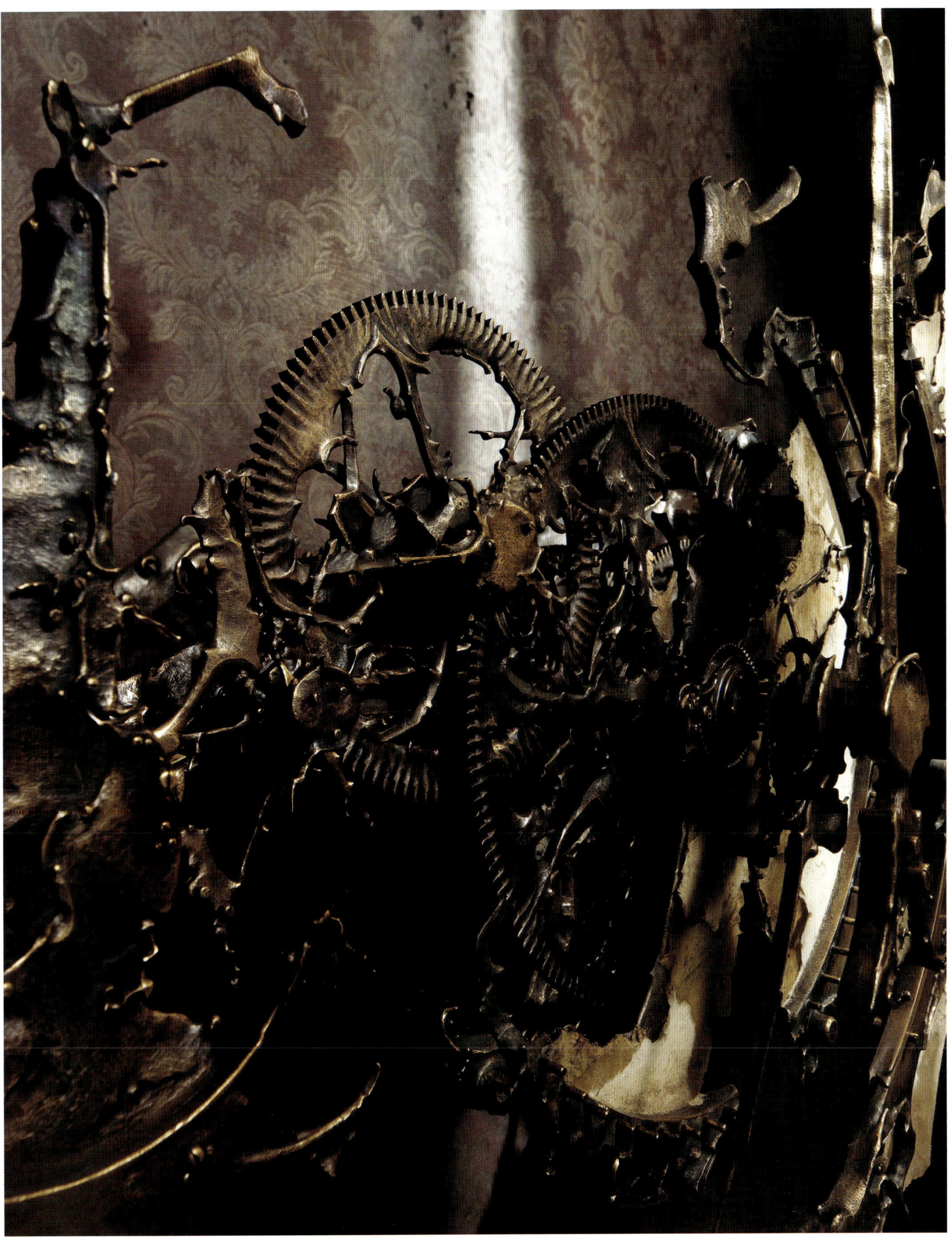

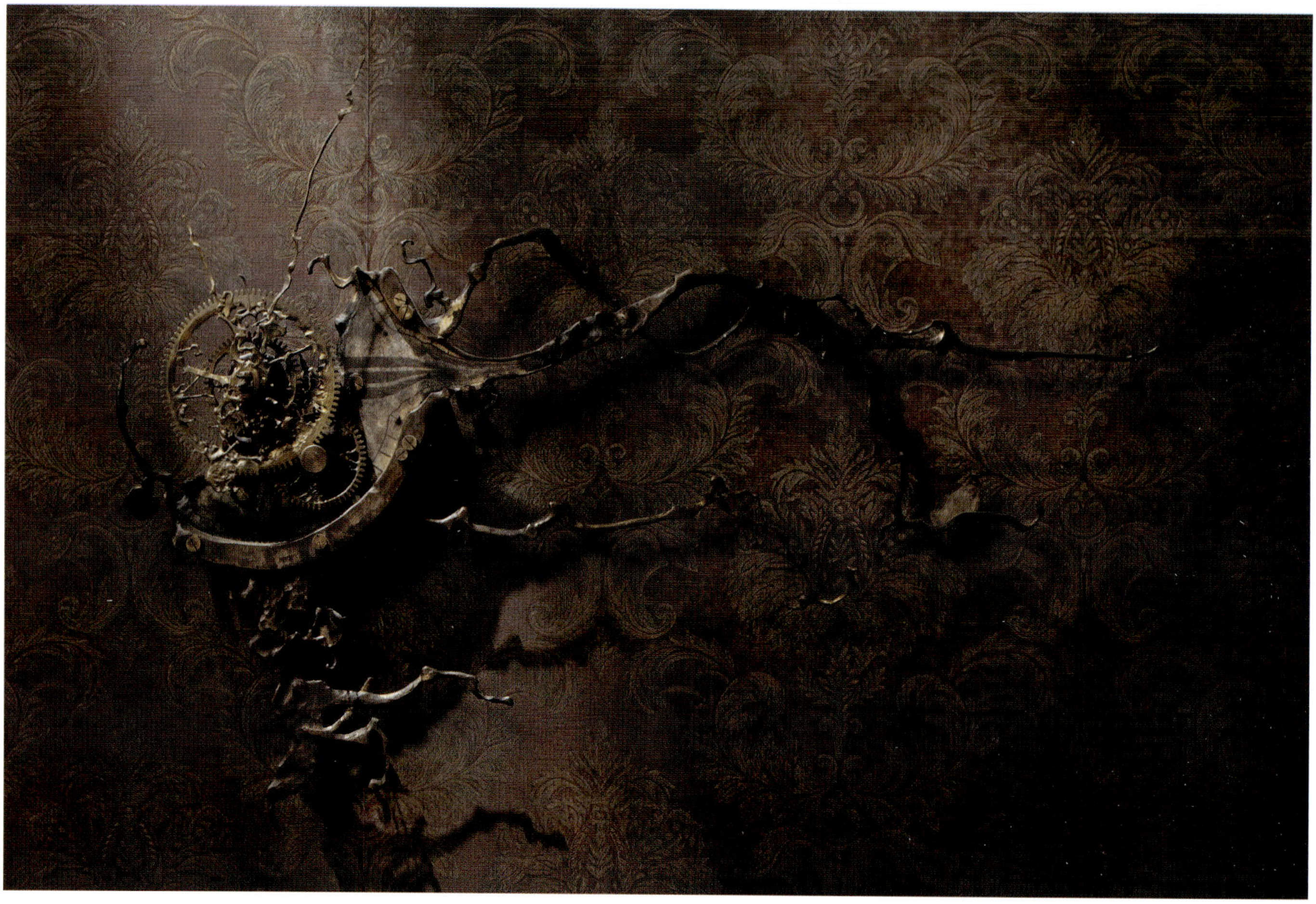

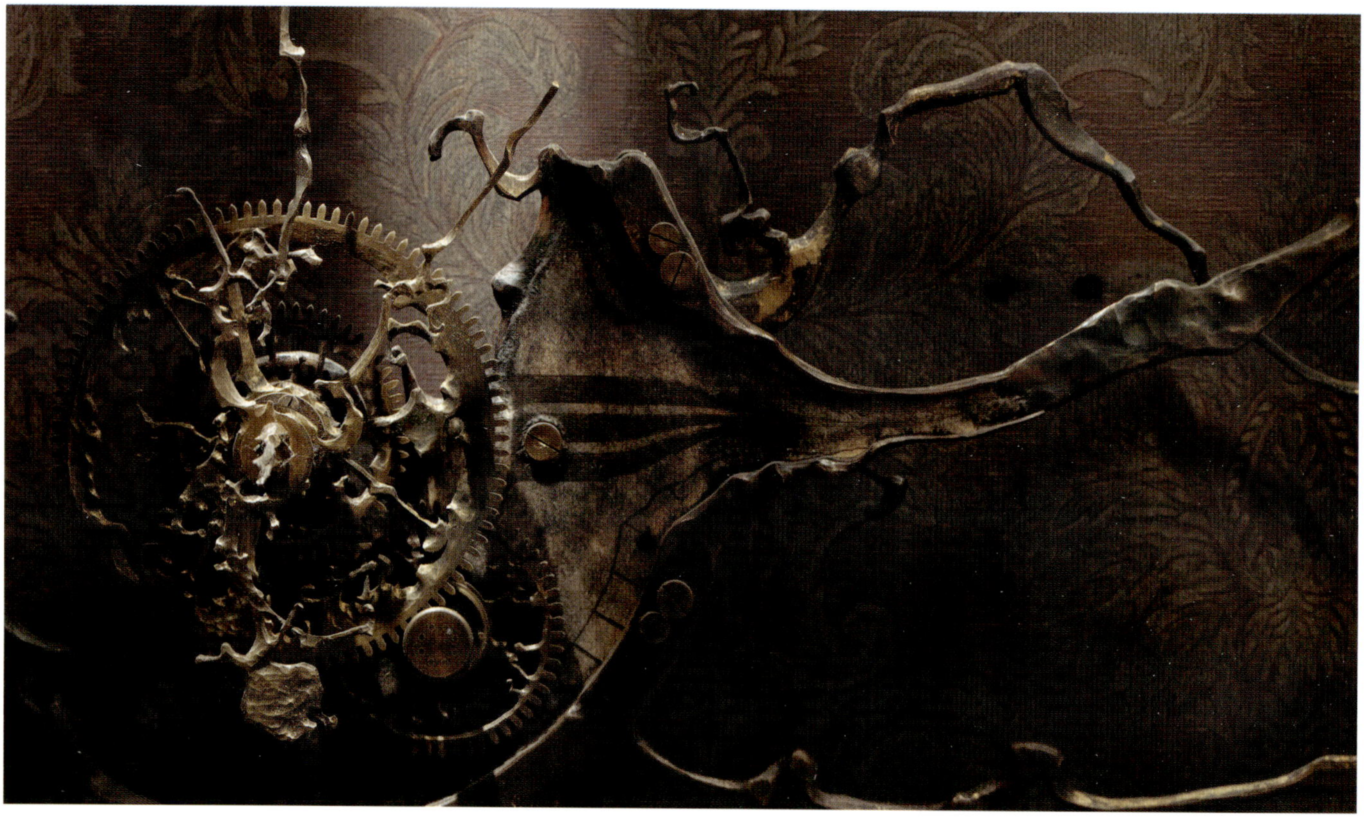

Left: *Quartz 7*. 18.5" x 12" (47 cm x 30.5 cm). Machined brass.

Left, Bottom: *Quartz 7* (detail).

Right: *Quartz 11*. 16" x 12" (40.6 cm x 30.5 cm). Machined brass.

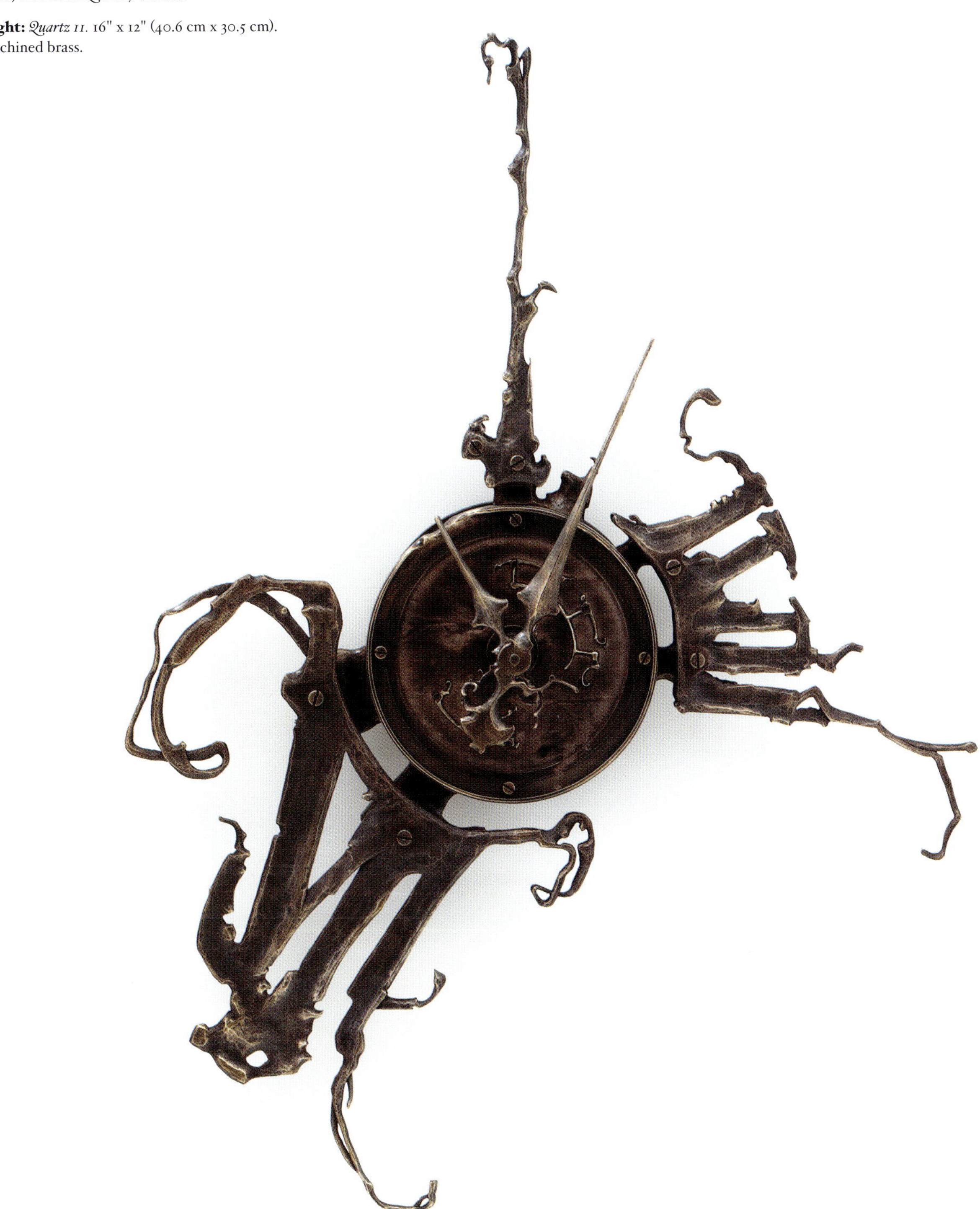

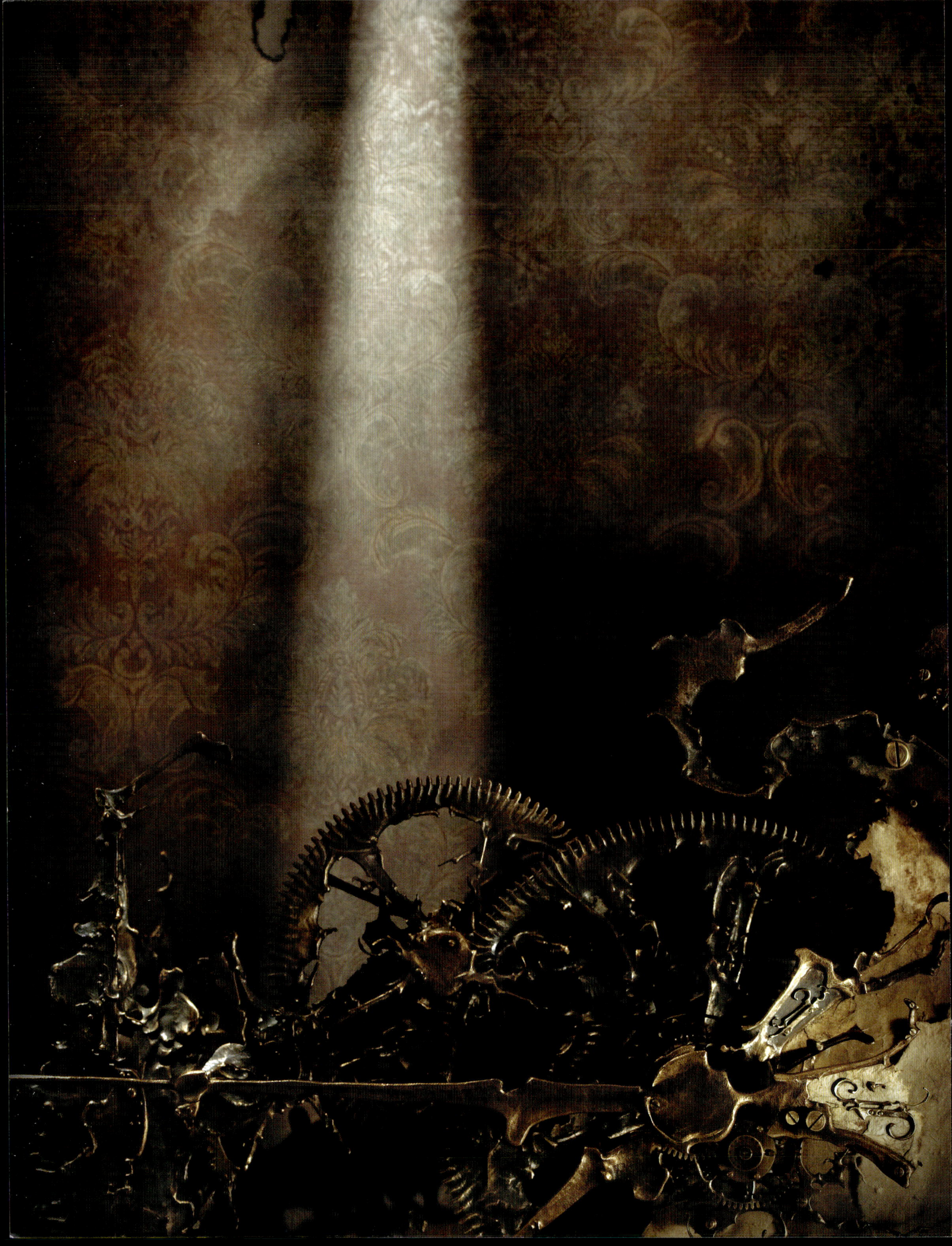

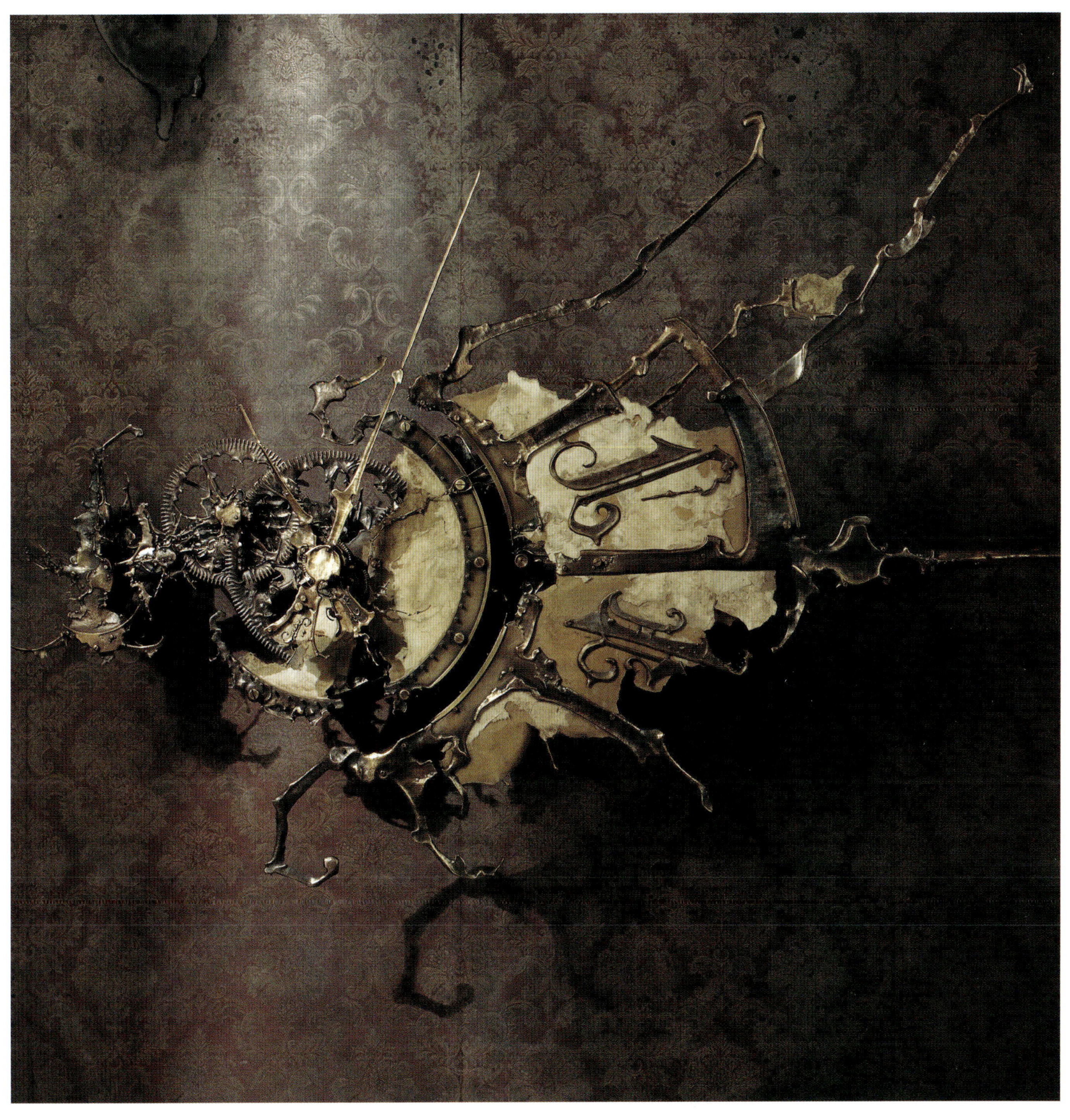

Left and Above: *Mechanical No.7*, 2011. 5'x 3' x 1' (152 cm x 91 cm x 31 cm). Machined brass and rice paper.

DOCTOR GRORDBORT

The character of Dr Grordbort is one of the inventions of New Zealand's remarkable Oscar-winning ideas and 'creator of worlds' factory, Weta. Founded by Peter Jackson, Richard Taylor and Jamie Selkirk, Weta is based in the very Hollywood-sounding Miramar in Wellington. Their film credits are astounding and include *The Chronicles of Narnia*, *King Kong* and, of course, *Lord of the Rings*, the last two directed by Peter Jackson. Grordborts' creator is Greg Broadmore. Greg was a designer and sculptor on *Black Sheep*, *Kong* and *Narnia*, before becoming the concept designer on the *District 9* project, where he art-directed the prop, vehicle and costume builds and designed the movie's techonology, ships, armour, weaponry and robotics. In 2006 he was co-designer and art director of Wellington's massive Tripod Sculpture, a celebration of the city's local film industry.

That same year, Weta revealed the first of their Dr Grordbort's rayguns, entirely dreamt up and designed by Greg. These 'Infallible Aether Oscillators' were an instant hit, and sold out as their existence propagated across the Internet. *Wired Magazine*, *Boing Boing* and *IO9* got in on the act. Describing himself as a "Male shaped human with a tendency to draw pictures and make up stories", Greg has helpfully published two Grordbort books, *Dr Grordbort's Contrapulatronic Dingus Dictionary* and *Victory*. The world of Grordbort he says "is a retro-Science Fiction (whatever that means) universe of sex, satire and violence. OK, so maybe there's no sex in it. Maybe in the next book." More of Grordbort's world can be seen in the touring show, *Dr Grordbort's Exceptional Exhibition*.

Right Top: *Pearce 75* (atom ray gun). 8.7" x 14.6" x 3.1" (22 cm x 37 cm x 8 cm). Imitation metal ("a lightweight compound that looks and feels remarkably like plastic under Earth conditions").

Right Bottom: *Righteous Bison* (indivisible particle smasher). 10.4" x 15.7" x 3.1" (26.5 cm x 40 cm x 8 cm). Metal and metal components.

Below: *Saturn 17 Raygun Cut-away*. Dr Grordbort's raygun poster.

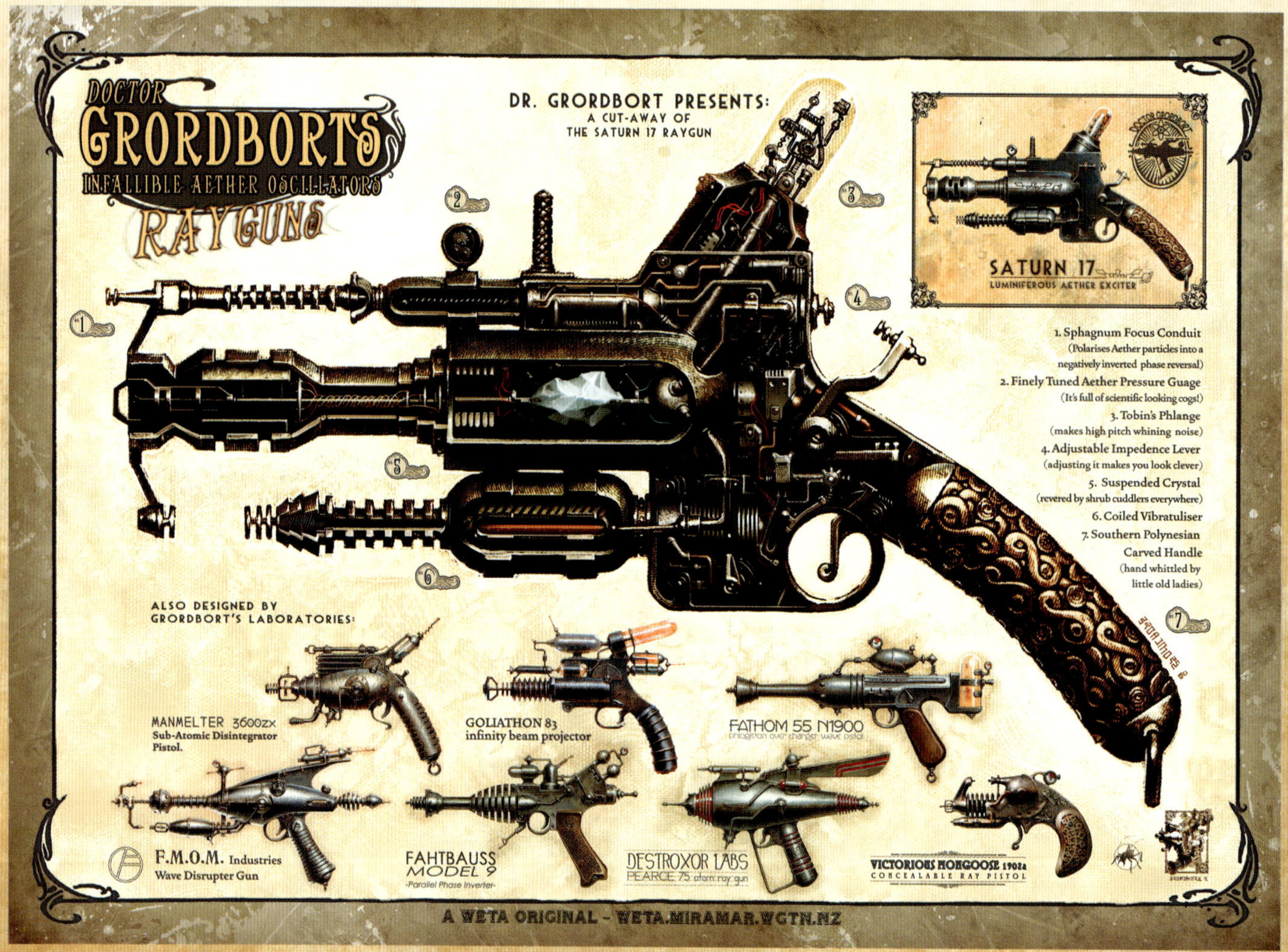

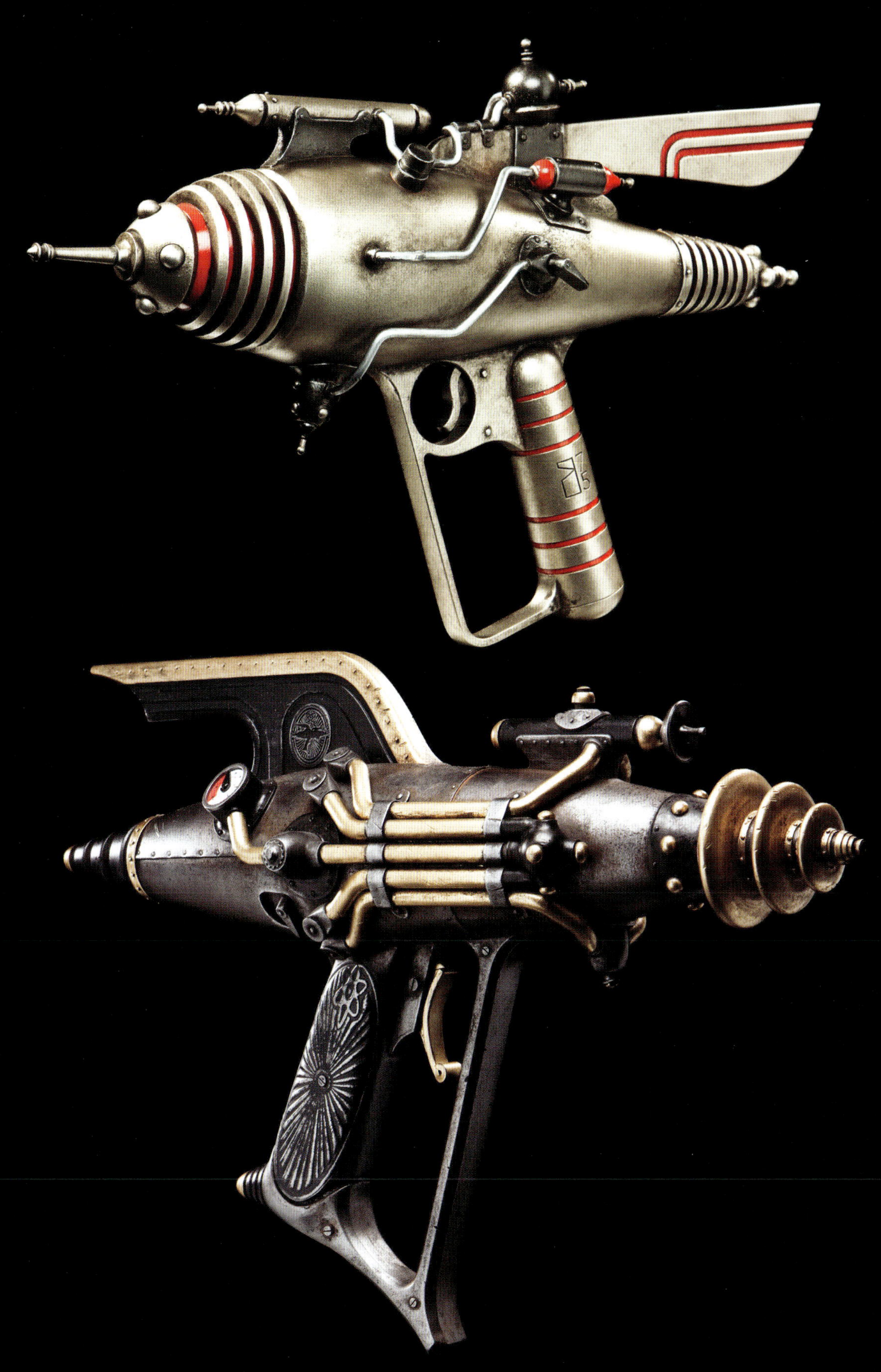

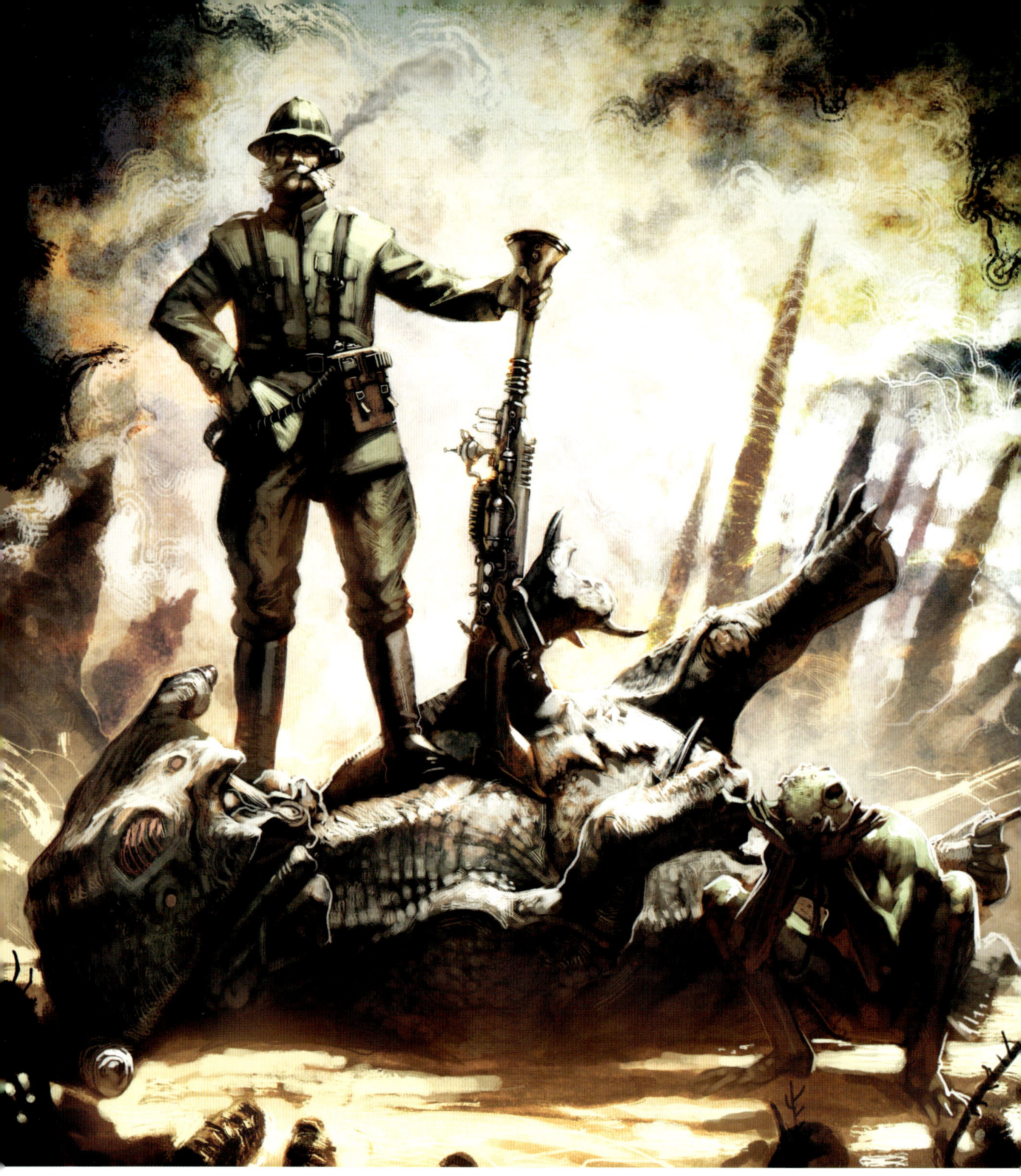

Above: Greg Broadmore, *Lord Cockswain* ("renowned naturalist, pillock of the community and revered hero.")

Top Right: The Unnatural Selector (miniature version), 2007. 3.9" x 11.4" x 2" (10 cm x 29 cm x 5 cm). Various metals and Venusian Worm Oak ("a compound that contains traces of not actual wood.")

Right: F.M.O.M (wave disrupter gun), 2007. 9.8" x 16.9" x 4.1" (25 cm x 43 cm x 10.5 cm). Metal and glass parts.

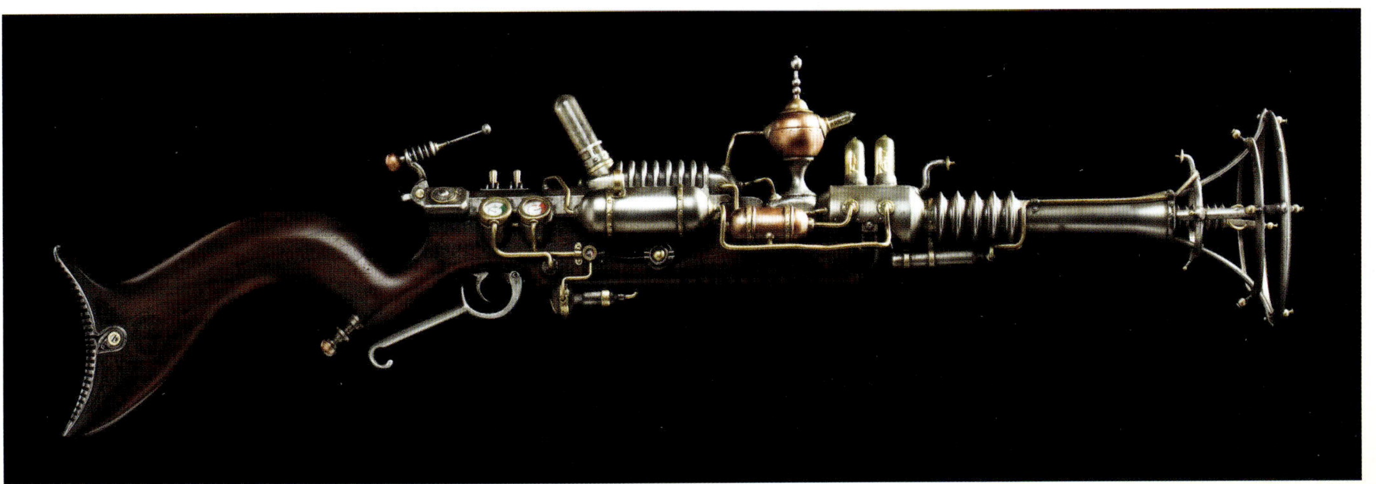

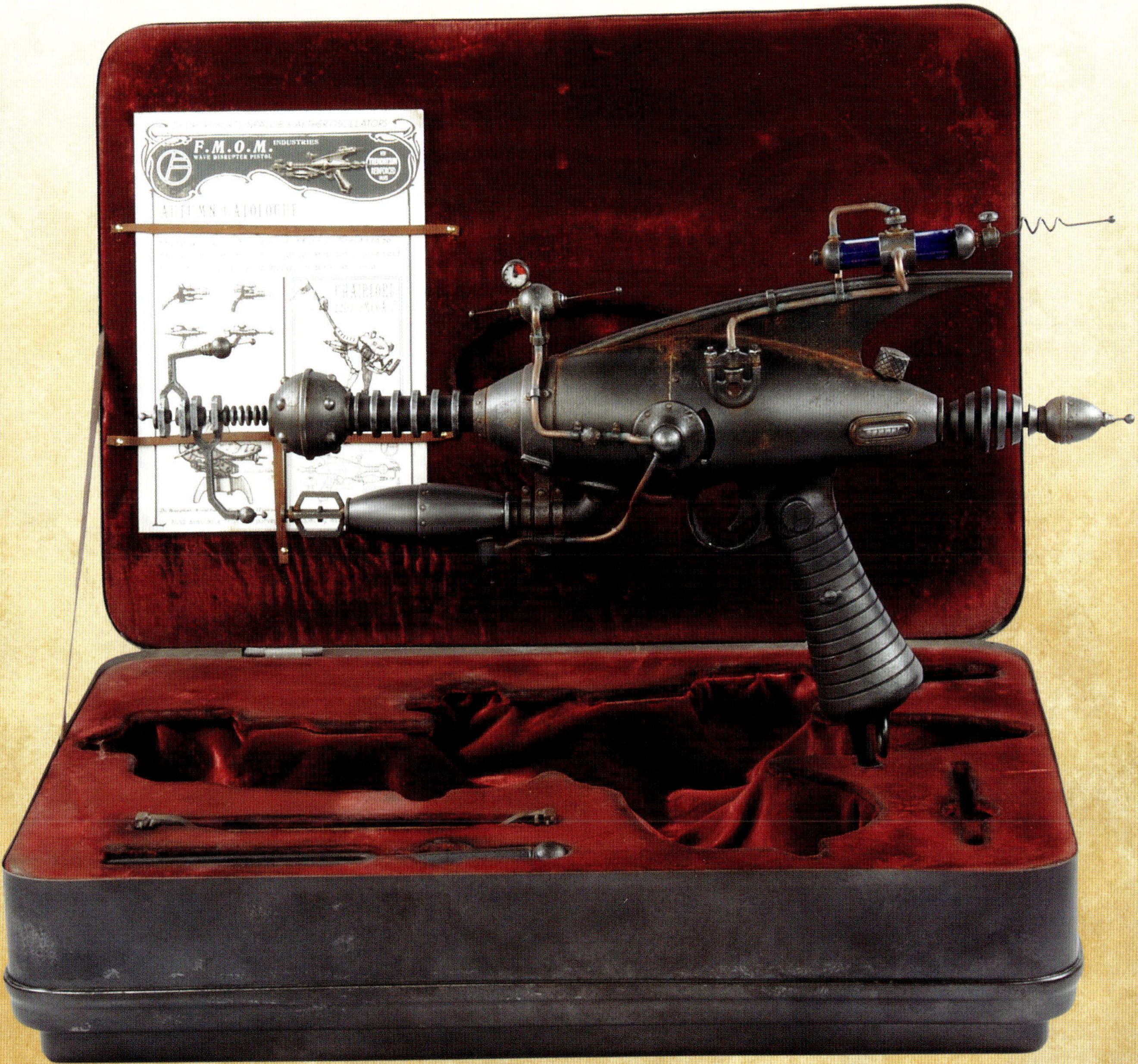

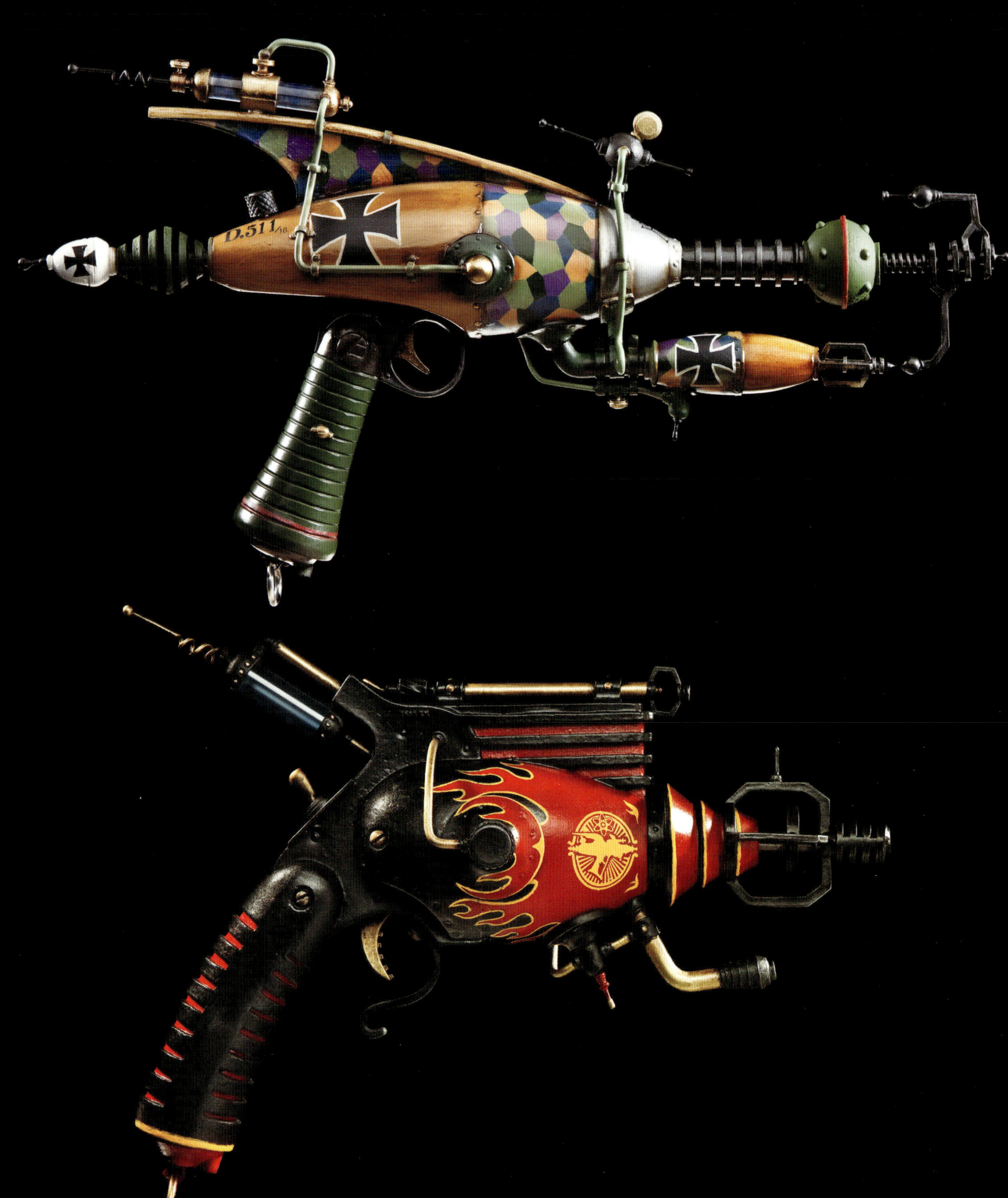
D.511/18

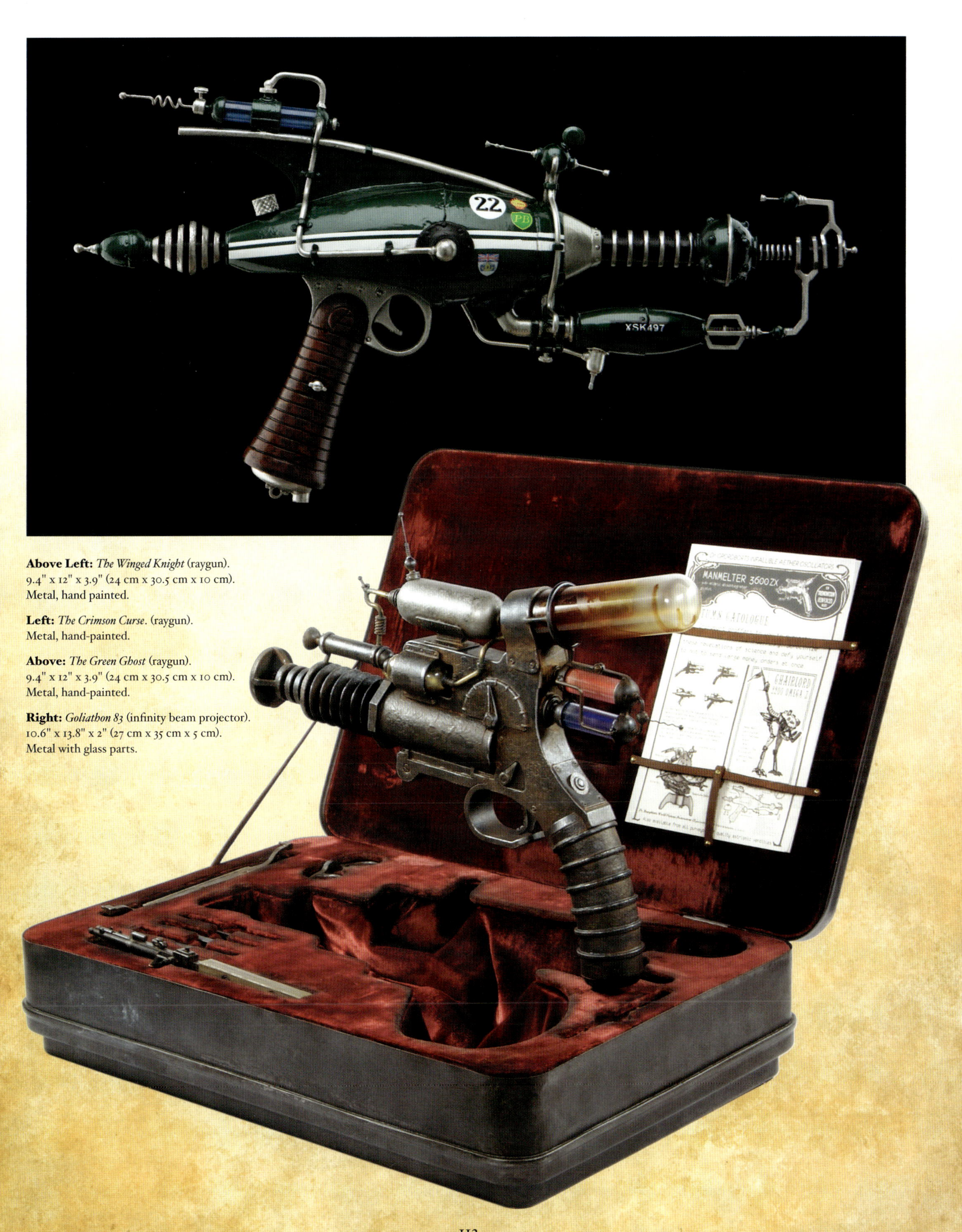

Above Left: *The Winged Knight* (raygun).
9.4" x 12" x 3.9" (24 cm x 30.5 cm x 10 cm).
Metal, hand painted.

Left: *The Crimson Curse*. (raygun).
Metal, hand-painted.

Above: *The Green Ghost* (raygun).
9.4" x 12" x 3.9" (24 cm x 30.5 cm x 10 cm).
Metal, hand-painted.

Right: *Goliathon 83* (infinity beam projector).
10.6" x 13.8" x 2" (27 cm x 35 cm x 5 cm).
Metal with glass parts.

STÉPHANE HALLEUX

"My style was formed by the films, books, comic strips and novels that fascinated me... and then by chance inspiration from strange pieces I come across in the assembly process." Based in Naumur, in the Belgian countryside, Stéphane Halleux studied art and drawing in Liège. He became fascinated with plans, blueprints for strange mechanisms and robots, and began constructing what he was drawing. A job as a layout artist at a comics studio in Luxembourg followed. Disgusted by the lack of creativity there, he left after seven grinding years and went to work at a repo antique store, where he refound his passion for sculpture. Since 2008 he has turned to sculpting full-time. "My work has often been defined as Jules Verne meets Tim Burton, which is a huge compliment; others see Panamarenko or Tingeli... I love all that, even if I don't always see the similarities!" Stéphane is fascinated by robotics, and the increasing influence of robots on mankind. He works meticulously, each piece taking three or more weeks of intense effort. "I like crazy mixtures" he says "unlikely associations of advanced technology mixed with the mechanisms of long ago. It is the old elements, full of history, that give a past and a soul to the finished work."

Right and Below: *Frankenstein.*

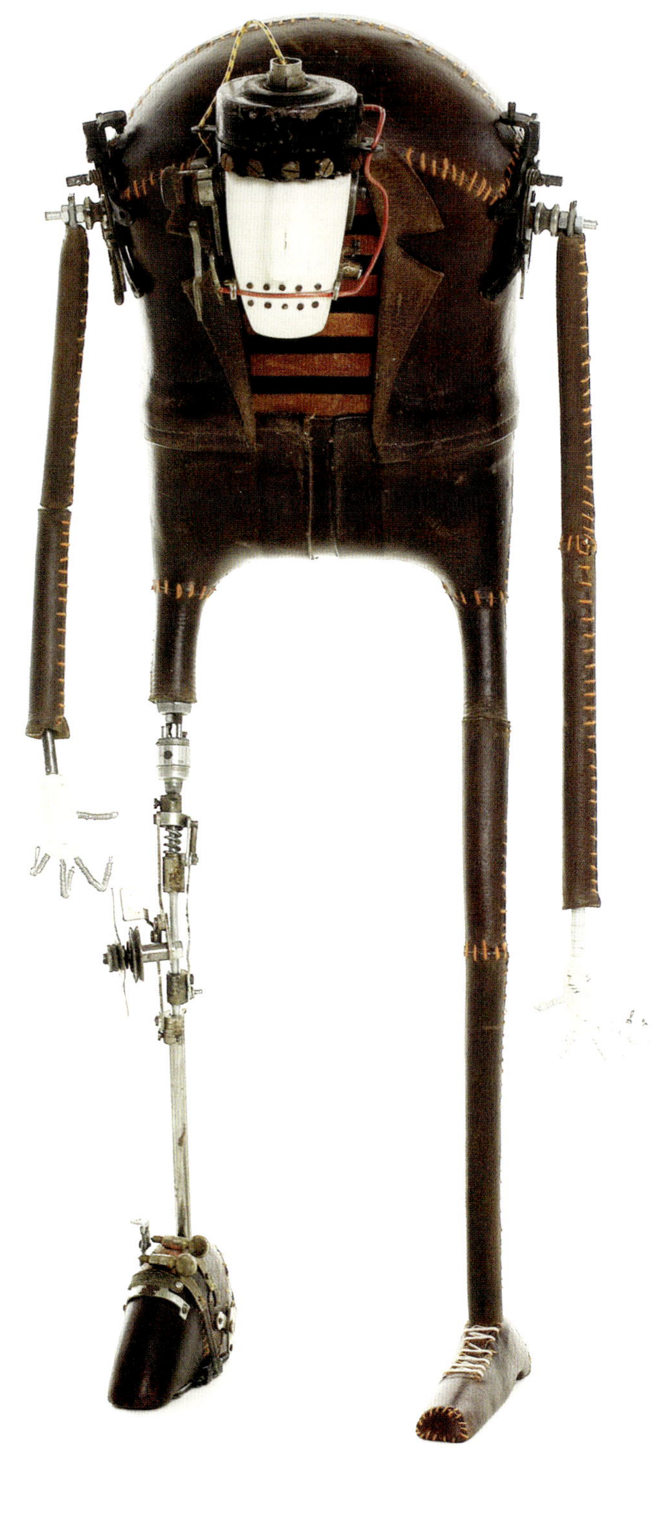

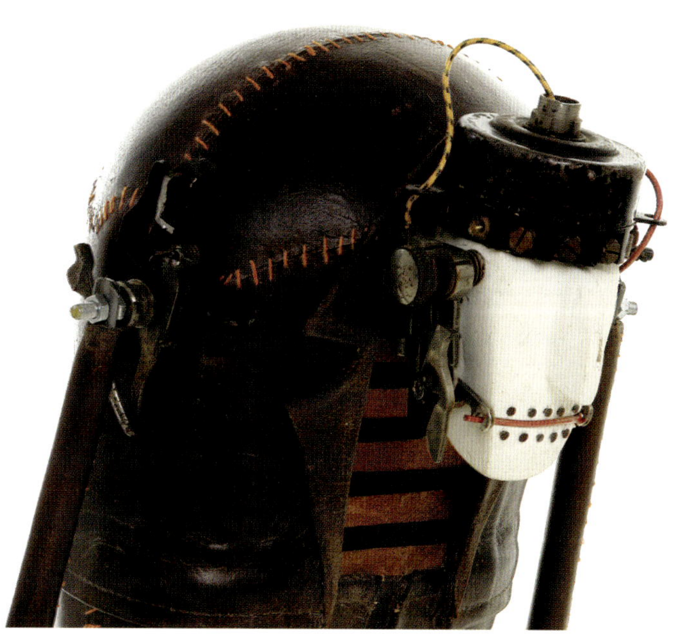

Left: *Electric Chair.*

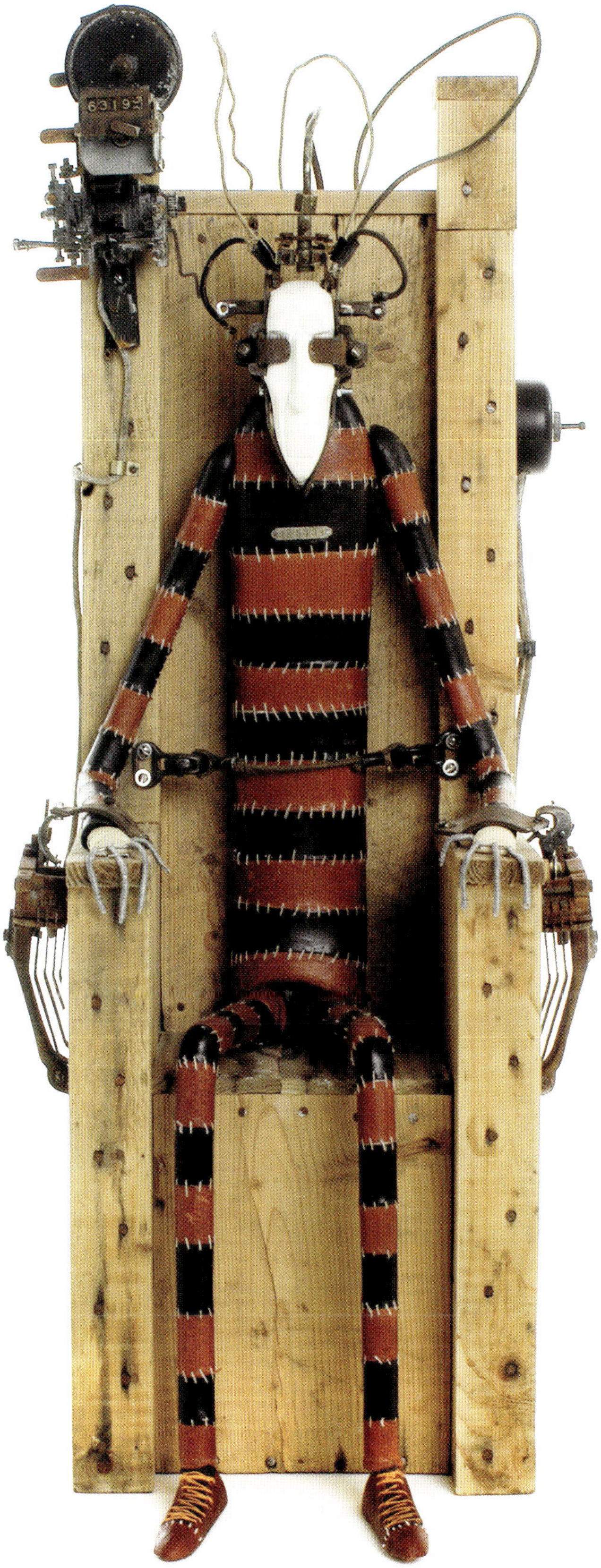

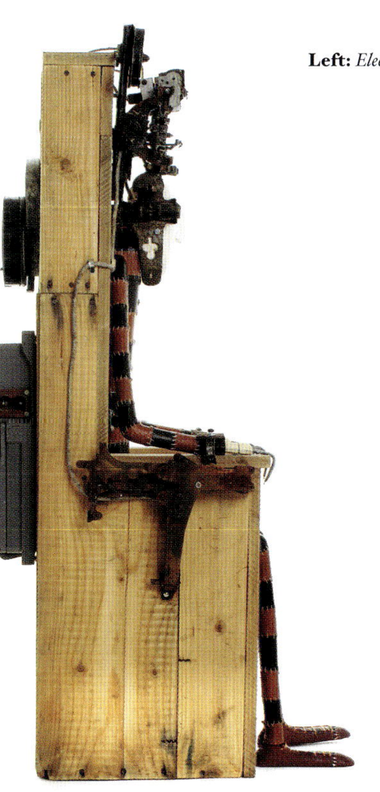

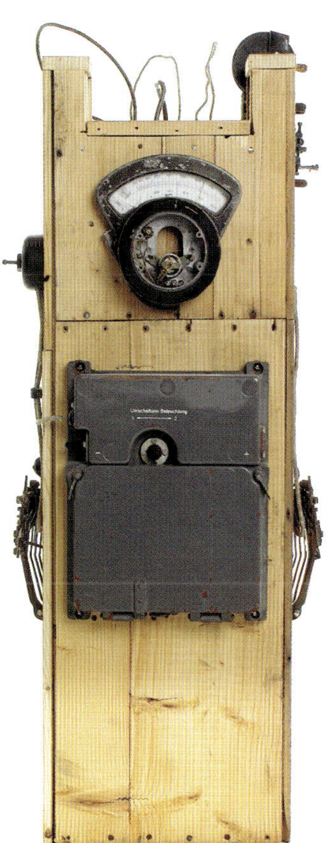

Right: *Convoyeur* (Escort).

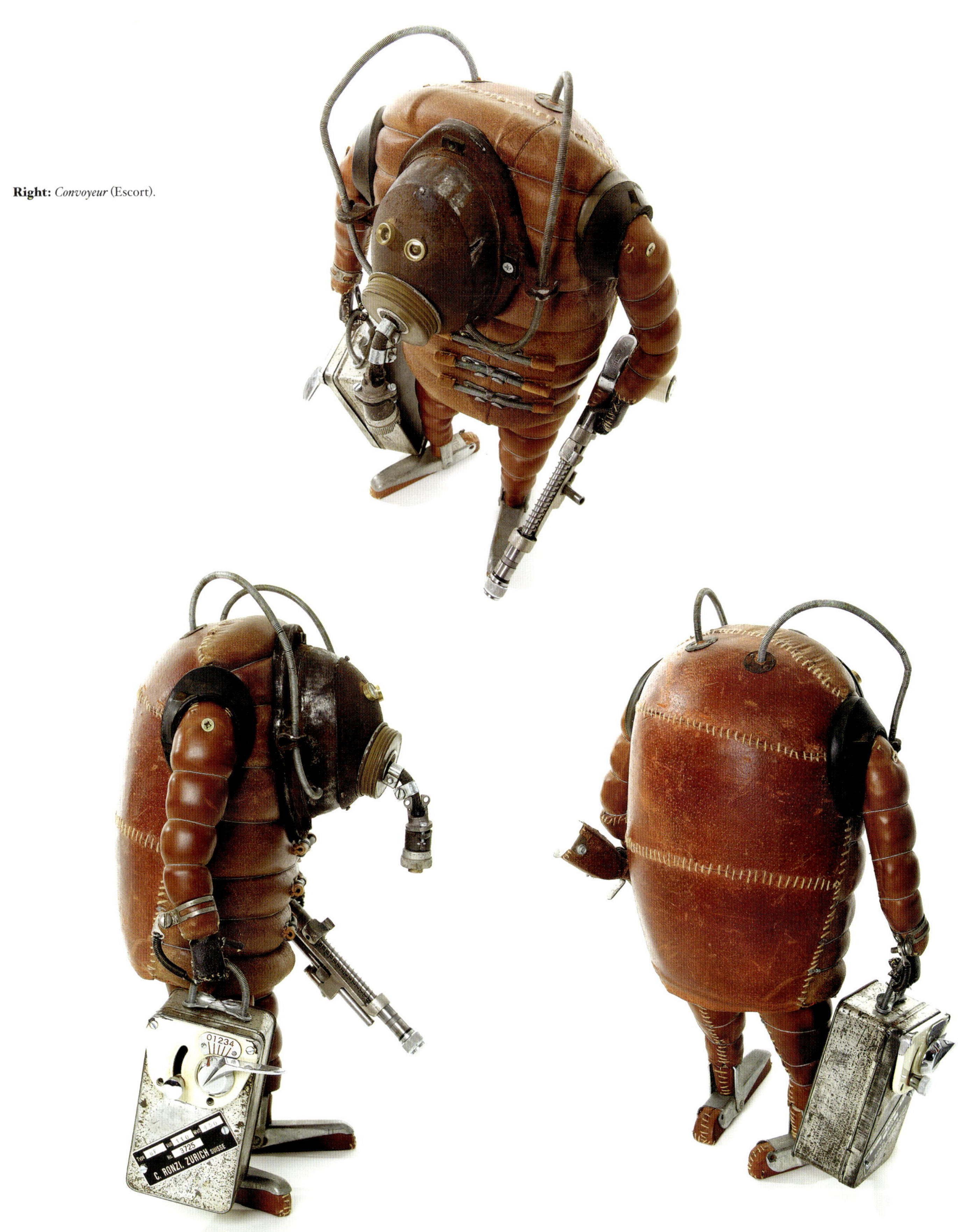

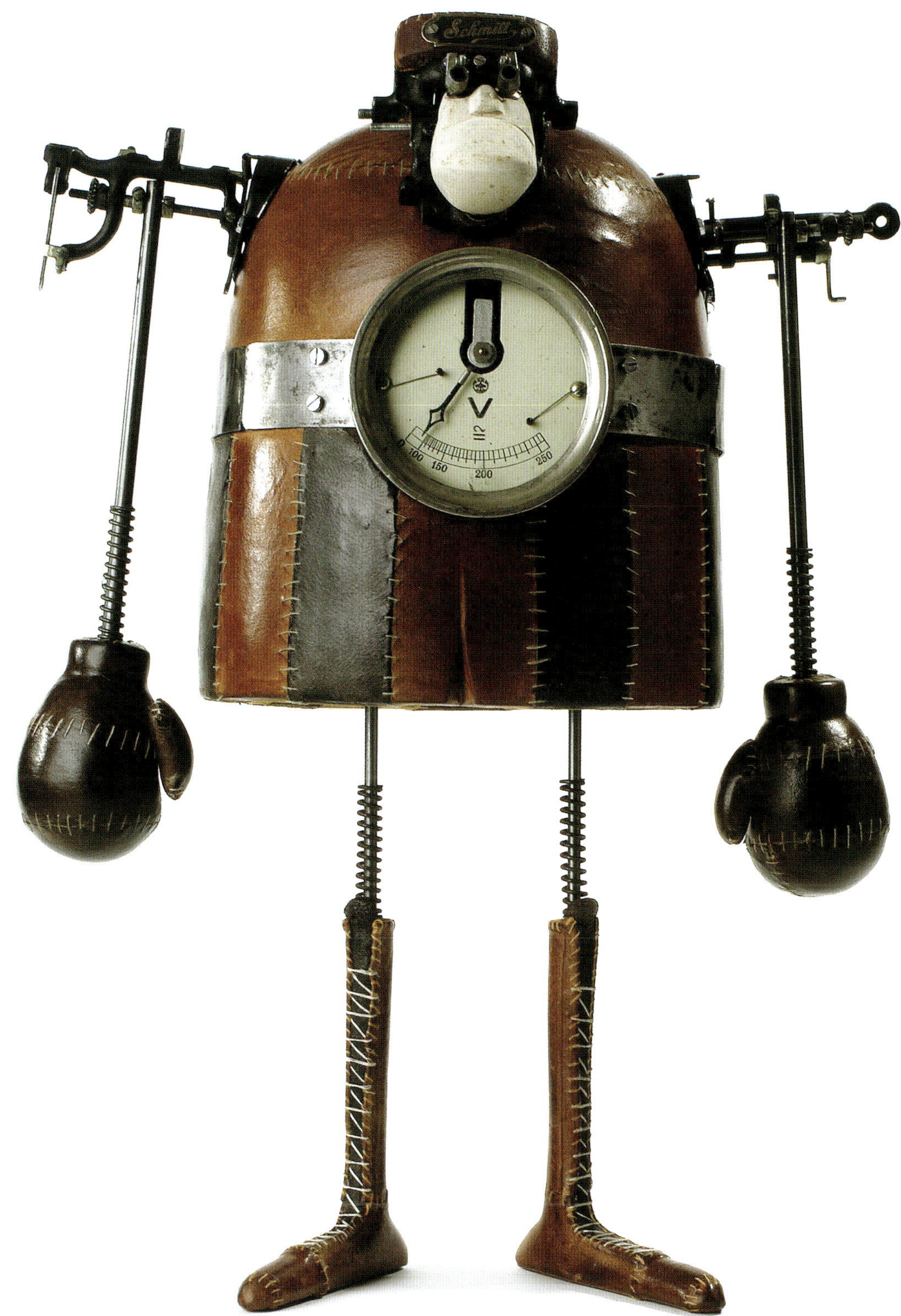

Right: *Boxer*.

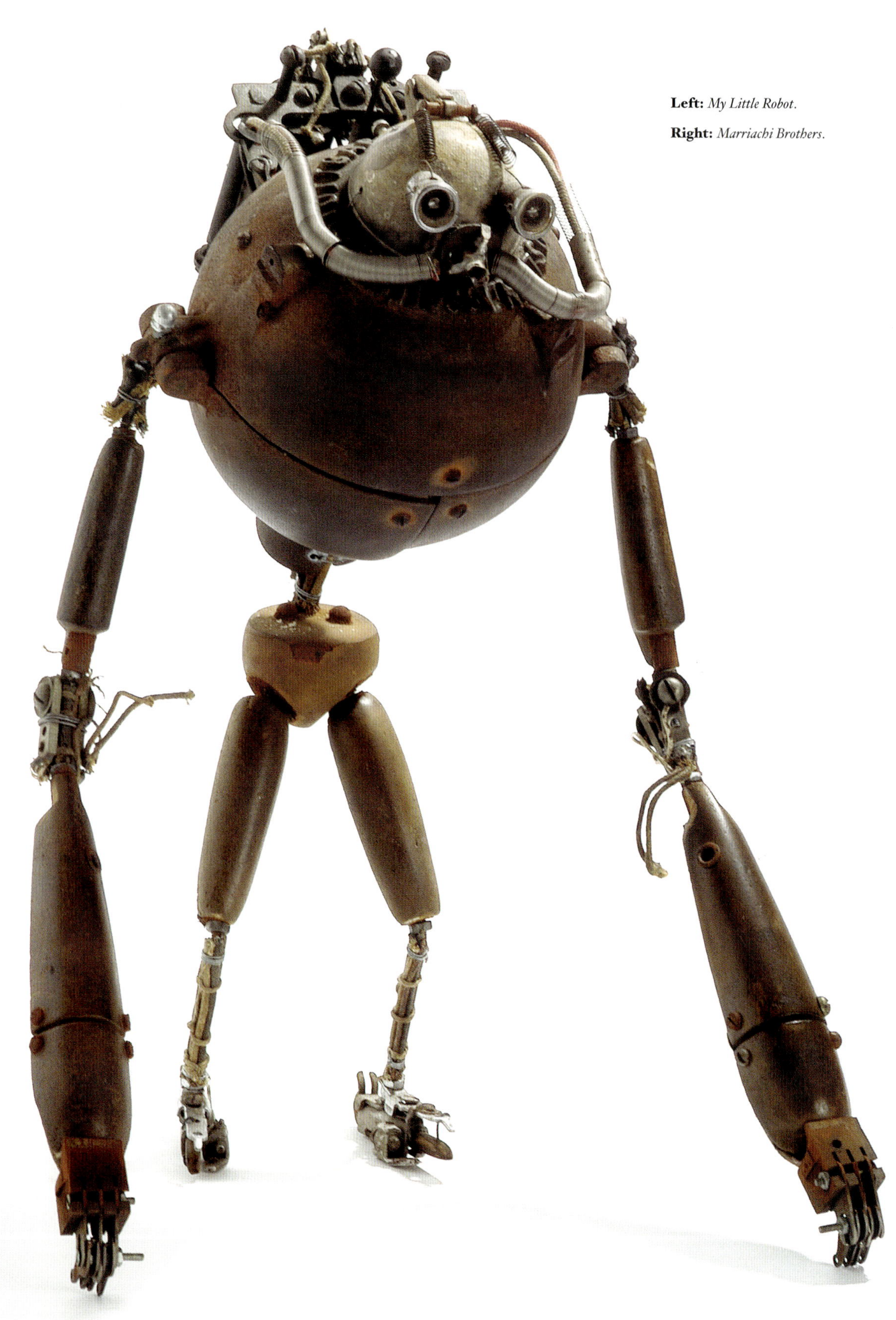

Left: *My Little Robot.*

Right: *Marriachi Brothers.*

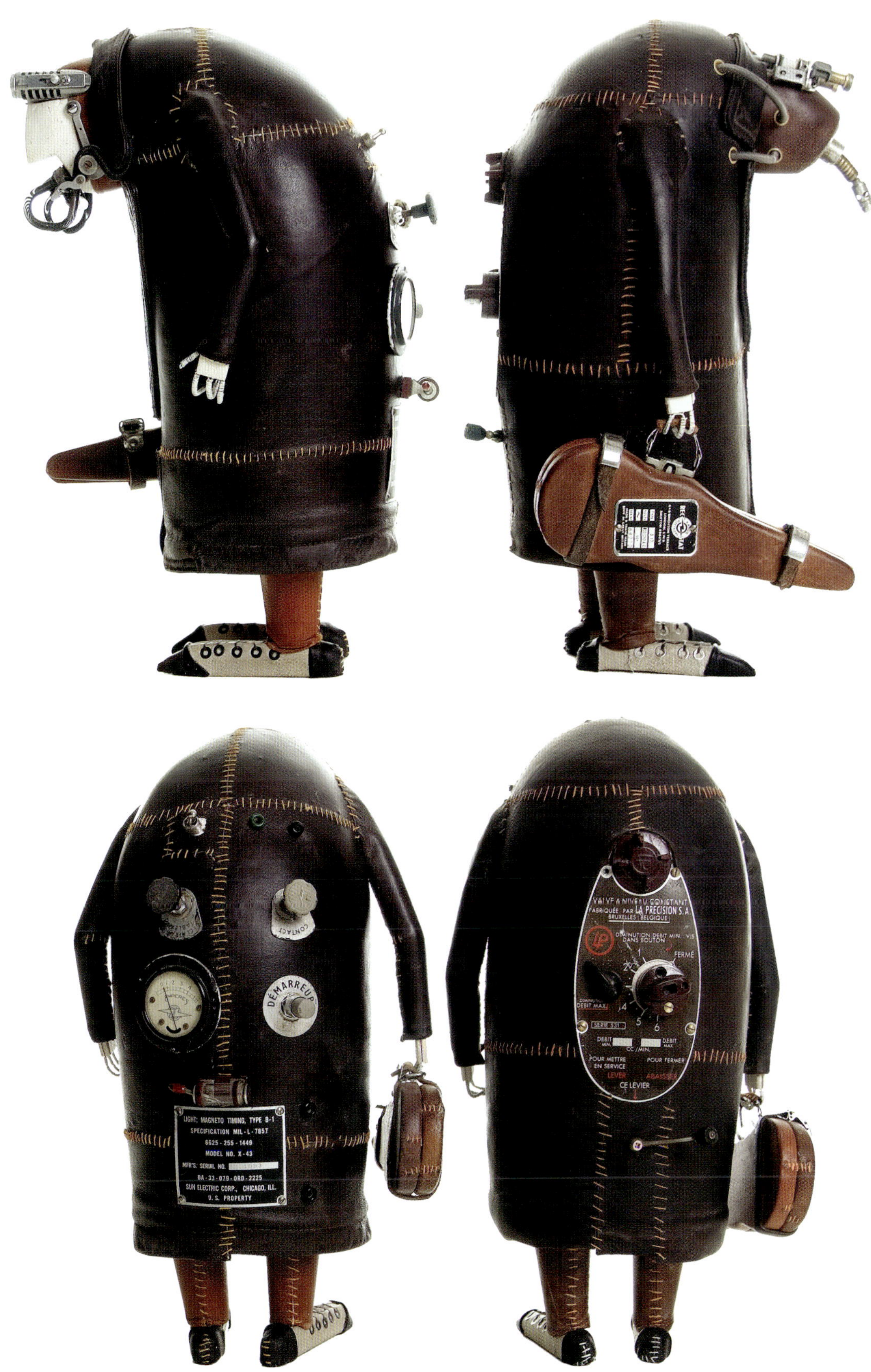
CONTACT
DÉMARREUR
LIGHT; MAGNETO TIMING, TYPE B-1
SPECIFICATION MIL-L-7857
6625-255-1449
MODEL NO. X-43
MFR'S. SERIAL NO.
DA-33-079-ORD-2225
SUN ELECTRIC CORP., CHICAGO, ILL.
U. S. PROPERTY
FABRIQUÉE PAR LA PRECISION S. A.
BRUXELLES BELGIQUE
LP
DIMINUTION DEBIT MIN. VIS
DANS BOUTON
FERMÉ
1
2
DEBIT MAX.
4
5
6
SERIE 531
DEBIT MIN.
CC/MIN.
DEBIT MAX
POUR METTRE
EN SERVICE
POUR FERMER
LEVER
ABAISSER
CE LEVIER

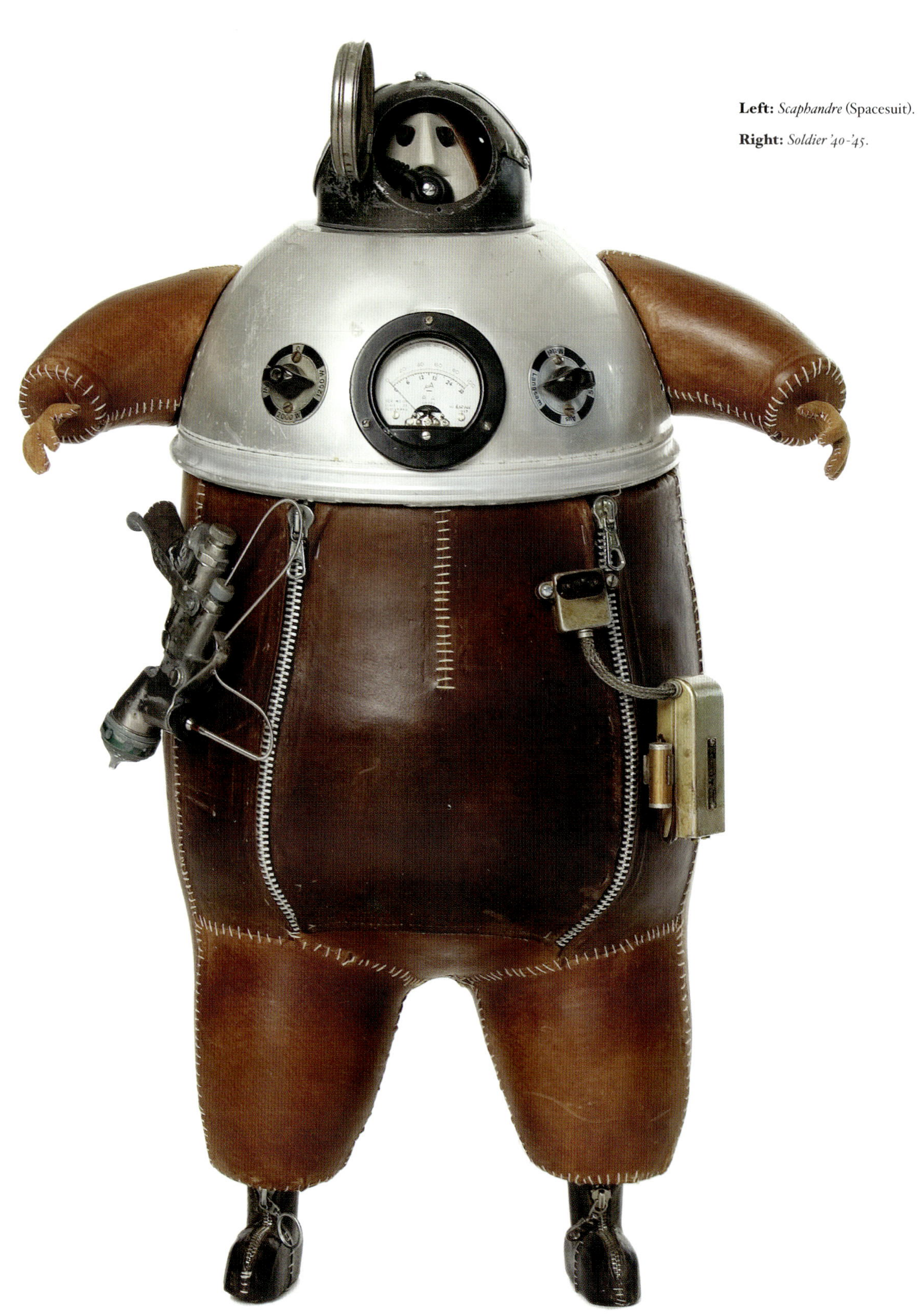

Left: *Scaphandre* (Spacesuit).

Right: *Soldier '40-'45.*

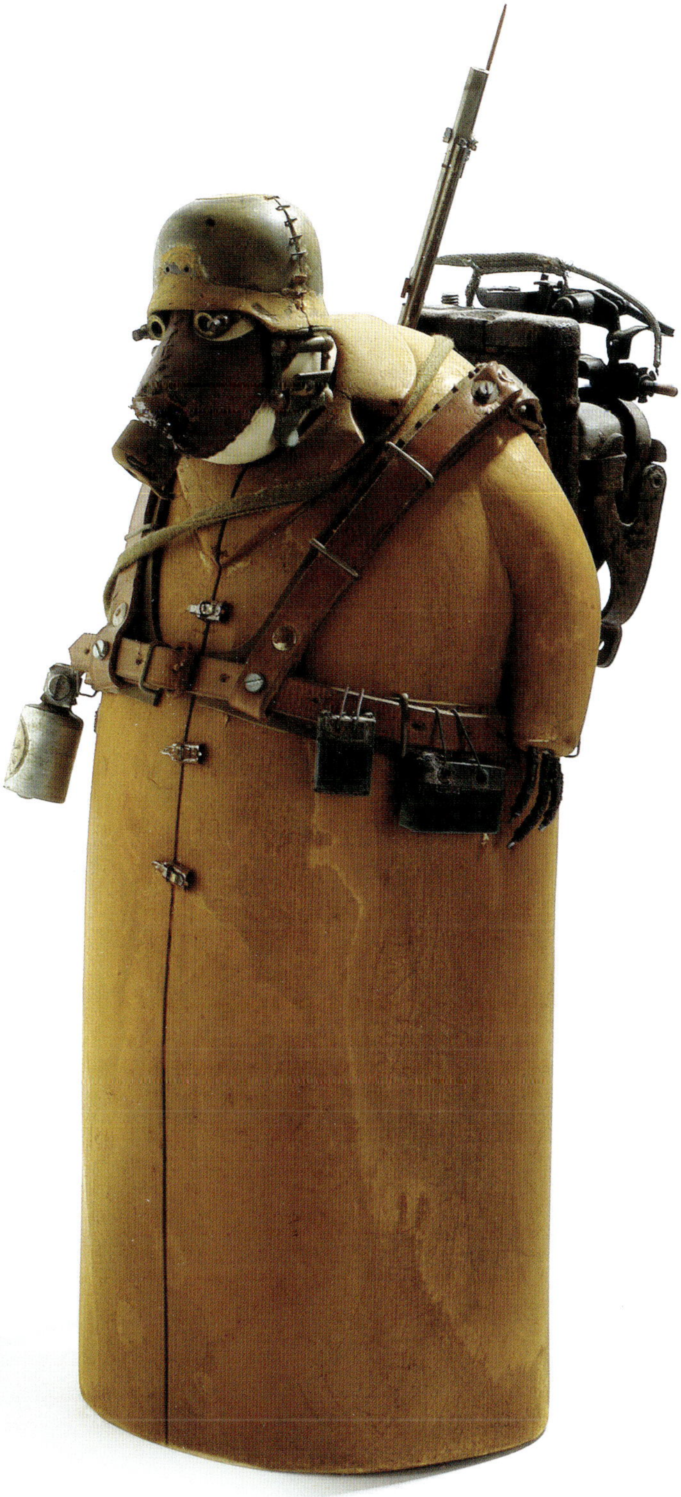

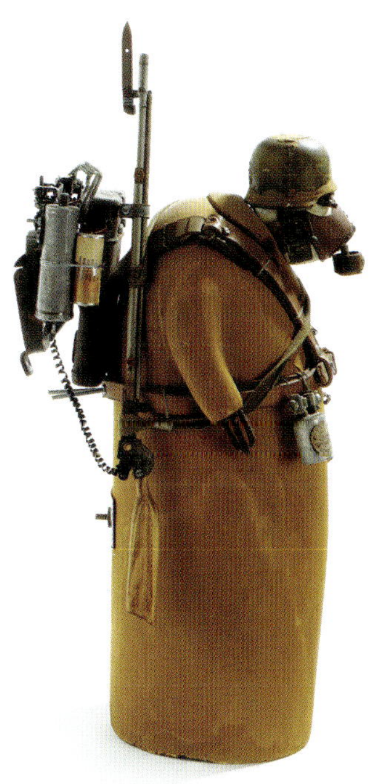

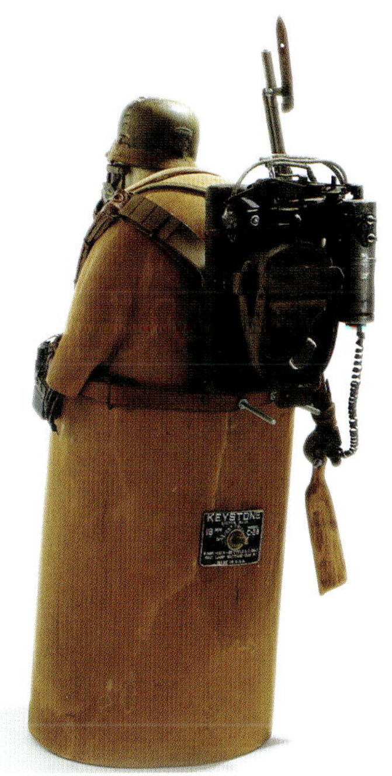

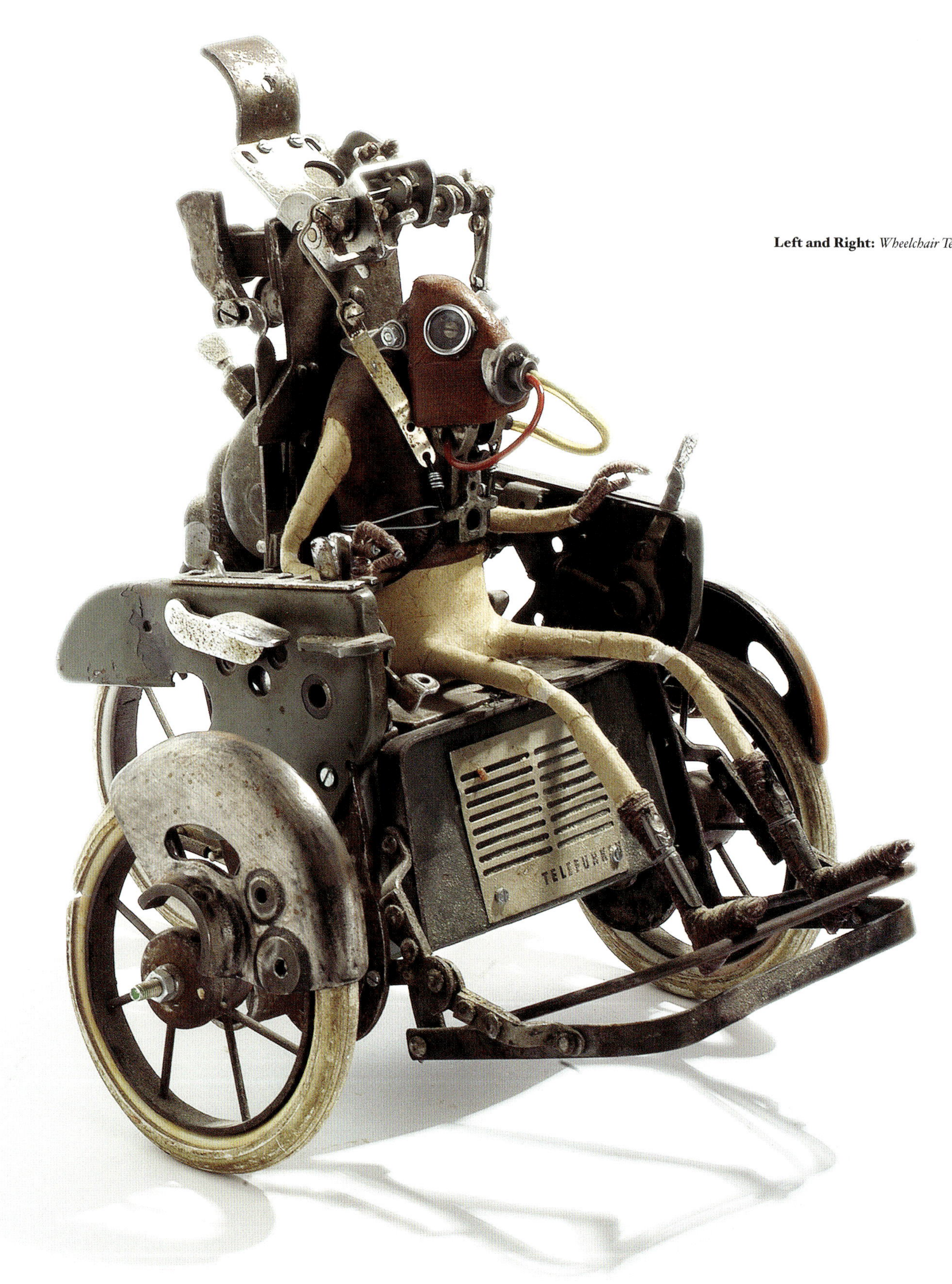

Left and Right: *Wheelchair Telefunken.*

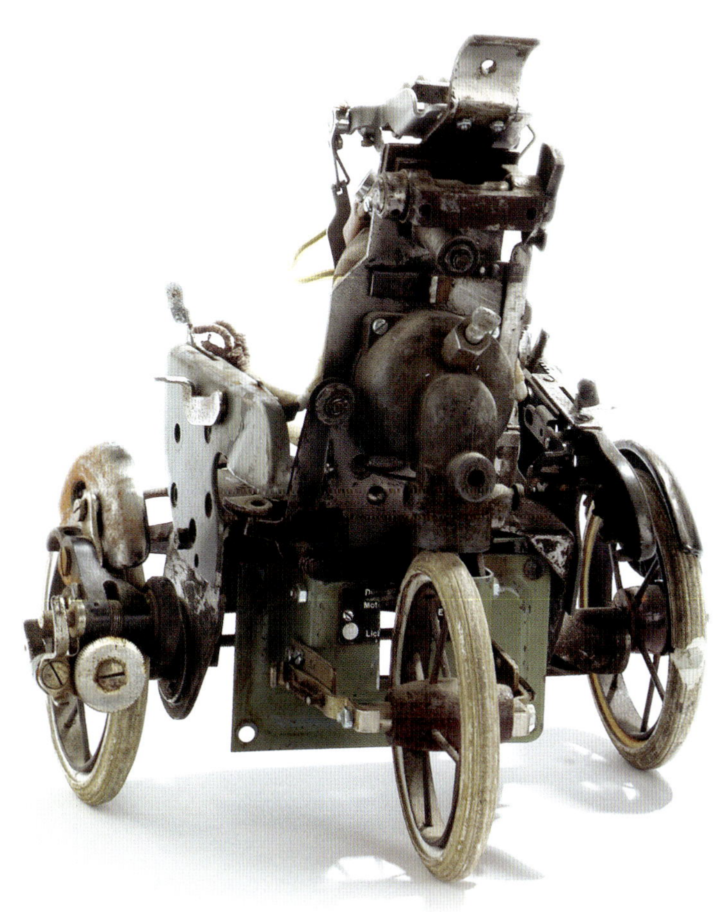

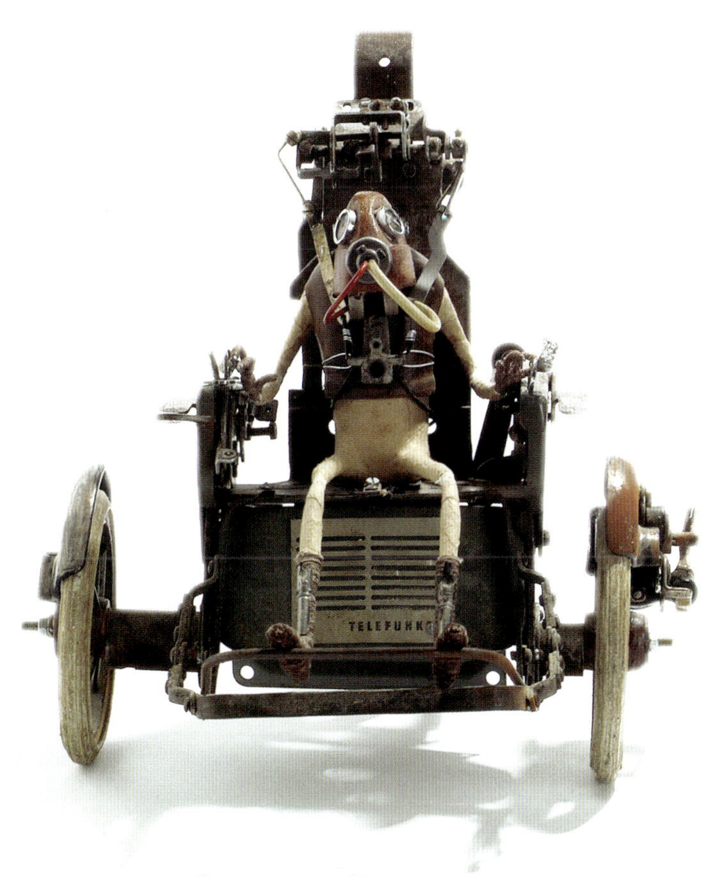
TELEFUNK

MIKE LIBBY

A graduate in sculpture from Rhode Island School of Design (RISD), Mike describes himself as a multi-disciplinary artist exploring themes of science, nature, fantasy, history and autobiography "highlighting illogical and acute correspondences between the real and the unreal." His fascination with insects and their technological applications – "NASA scientists are finding that nature can be the source of the most manoeuvrable and efficient design features... and they're looking at 'swarm theory' probes for planetary exploration" – has informed his Insect Lab works. Here Mike marries real insect specimens with antique watch parts: "my insect sculptures are not intended to function, but to slyly suggest that they could." Based in South Portland, Maine, Mike has exhibited extensively (including at The Smithsonian) and his work is carried by a number of exclusive boutiques in Europe as well as the US.

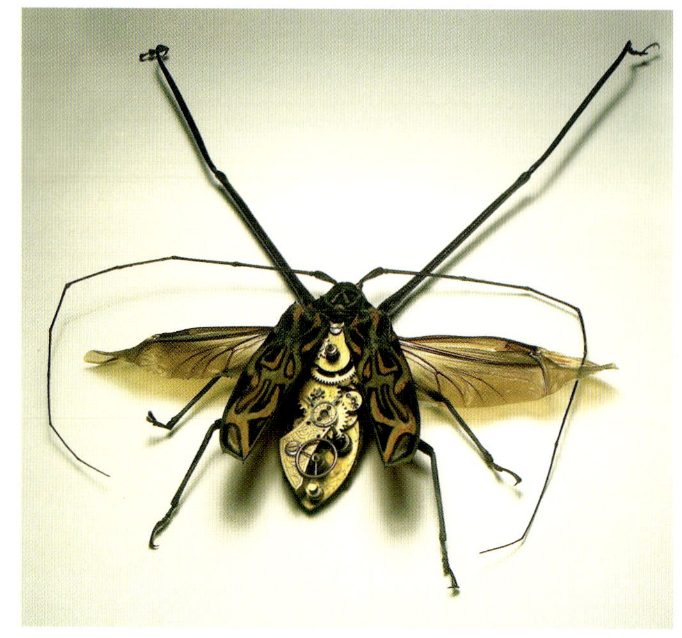

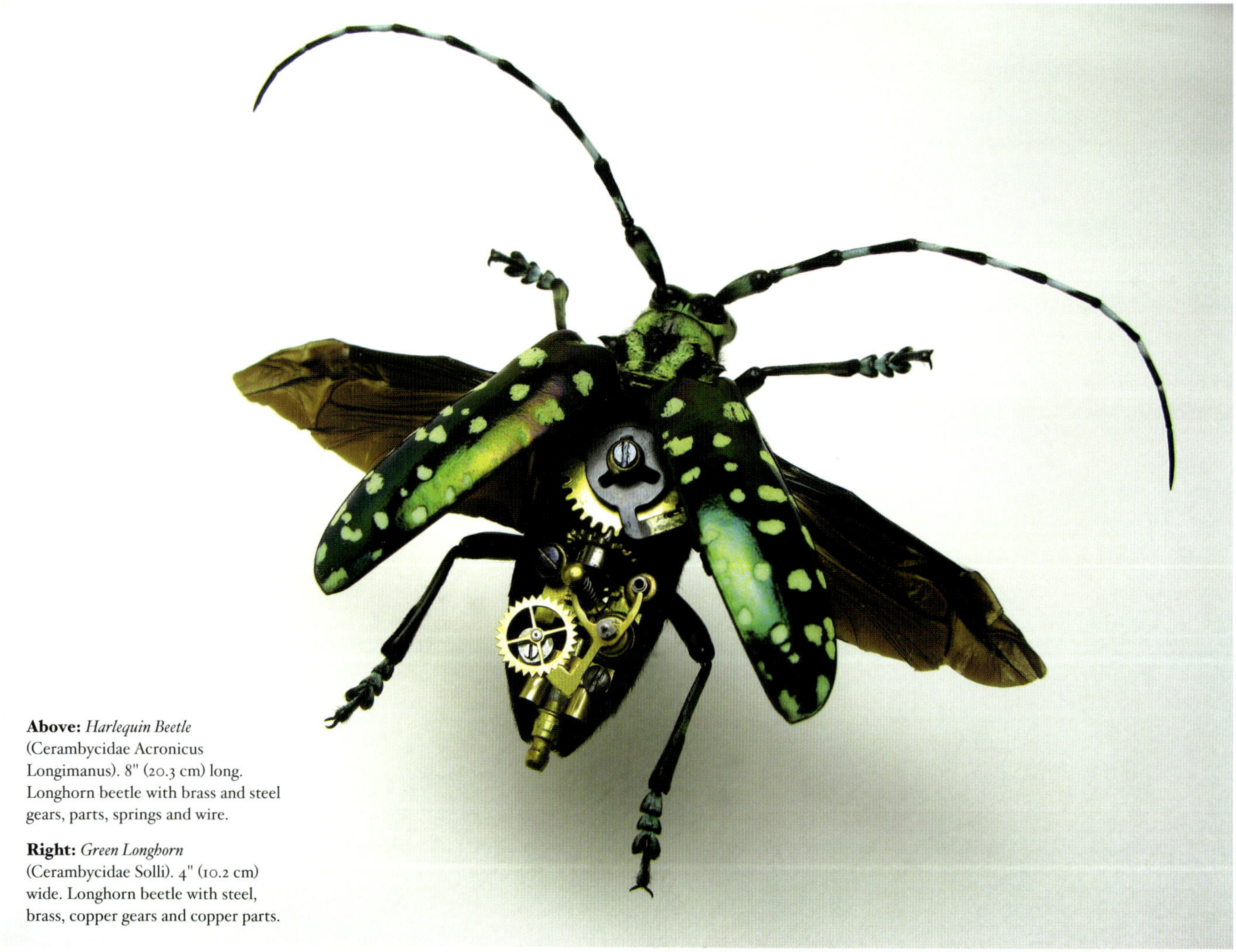

Above: *Harlequin Beetle* (Cerambycidae Acronicus Longimanus). 8" (20.3 cm) long. Longhorn beetle with brass and steel gears, parts, springs and wire.

Right: *Green Longhorn* (Cerambycidae Solli). 4" (10.2 cm) wide. Longhorn beetle with steel, brass, copper gears and copper parts.

Right: *Rhino* (Xyloryctes Jamaicensis). 4.5" (11.4 cm) wide. Rhino beetle with brass watch parts and gears.

Below: *Longhorn* (Cerambycidae Solli). 4.5" (11.4 cm) wide. Longhorn beetle with brass watchparts and gears.

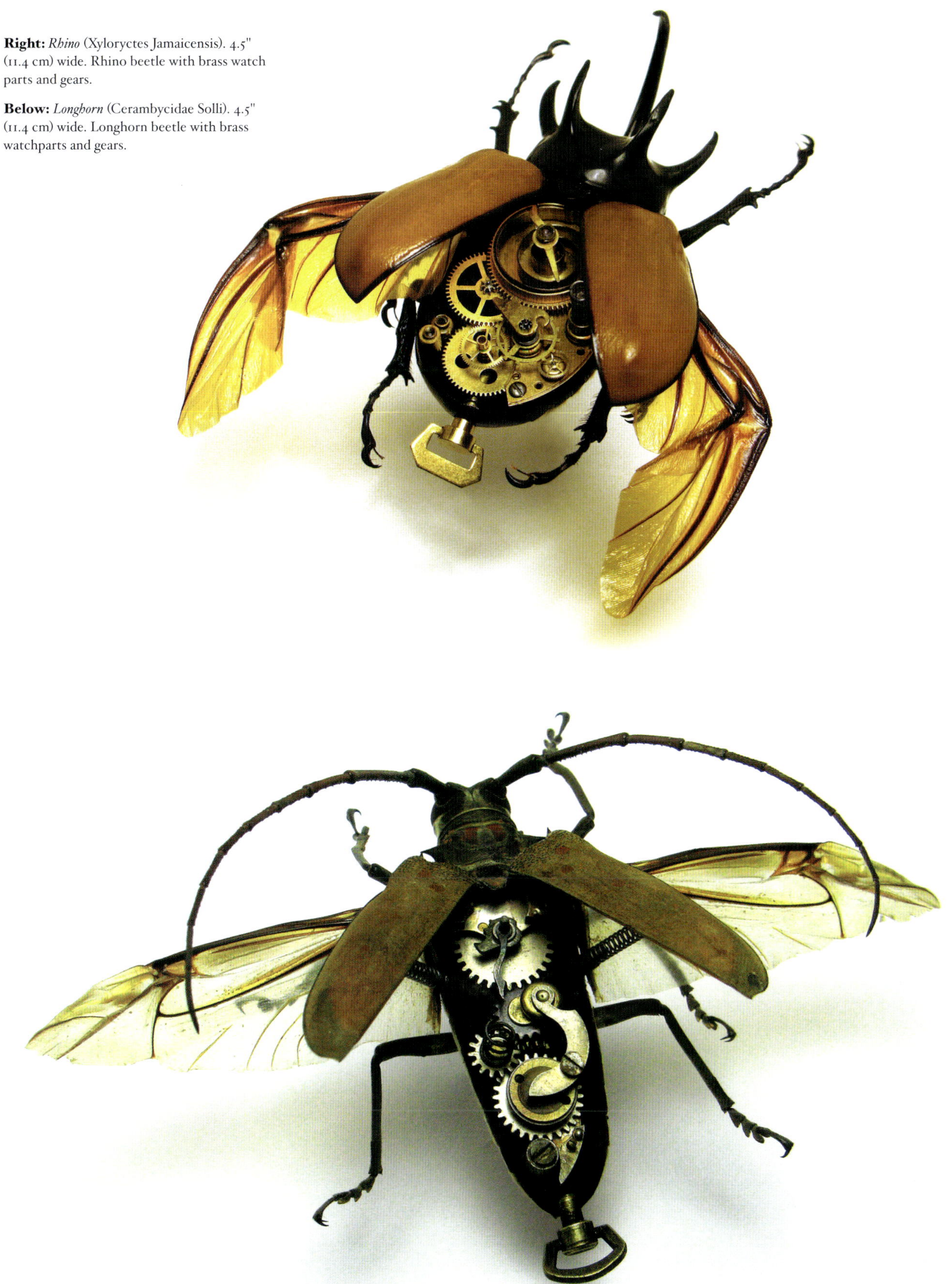

Right: *Tarantula* (Arachnidae Roseus). 3.5" (8.9 cm) wide. Tarantula with brass and steel gears.

Below: *Blue Butterfly* (Morphidae Achilles Patrocles). 4.5" (11.4 cm) wide. Butterfly with brass and steel gears, parts, springs and blue L.E.D..

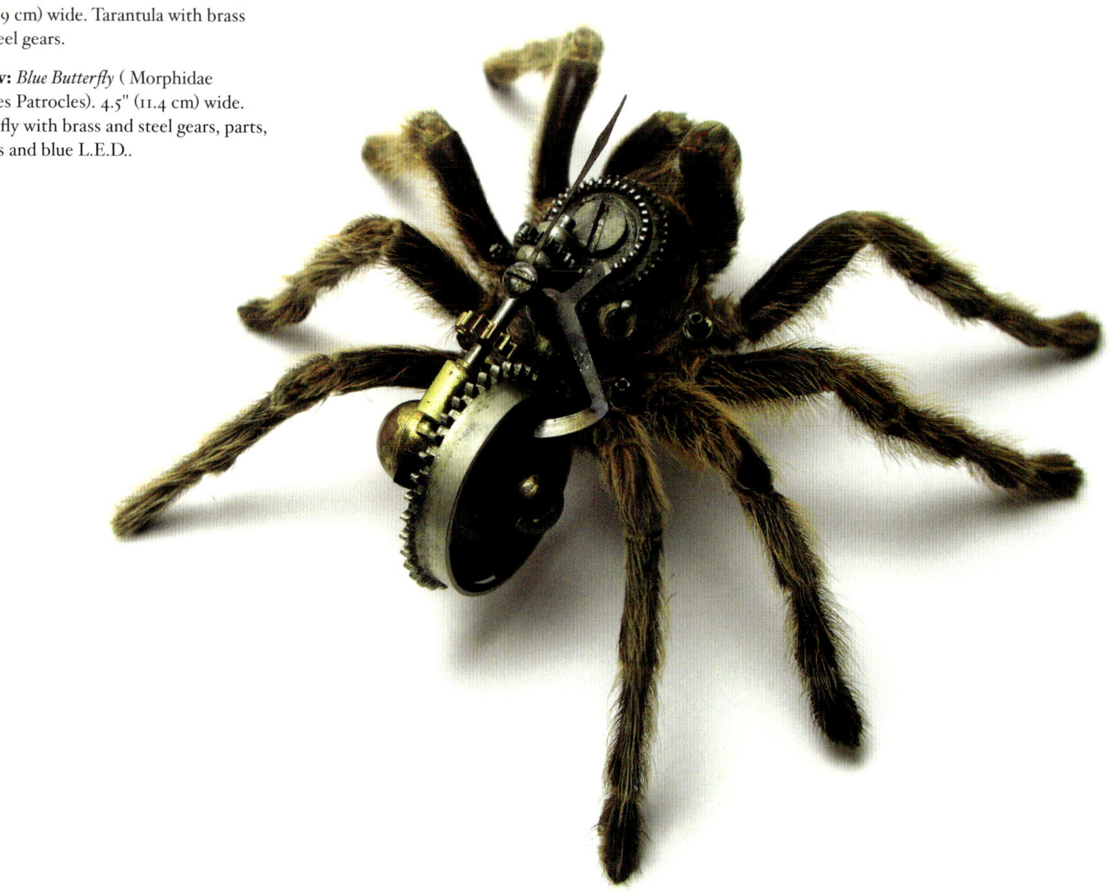

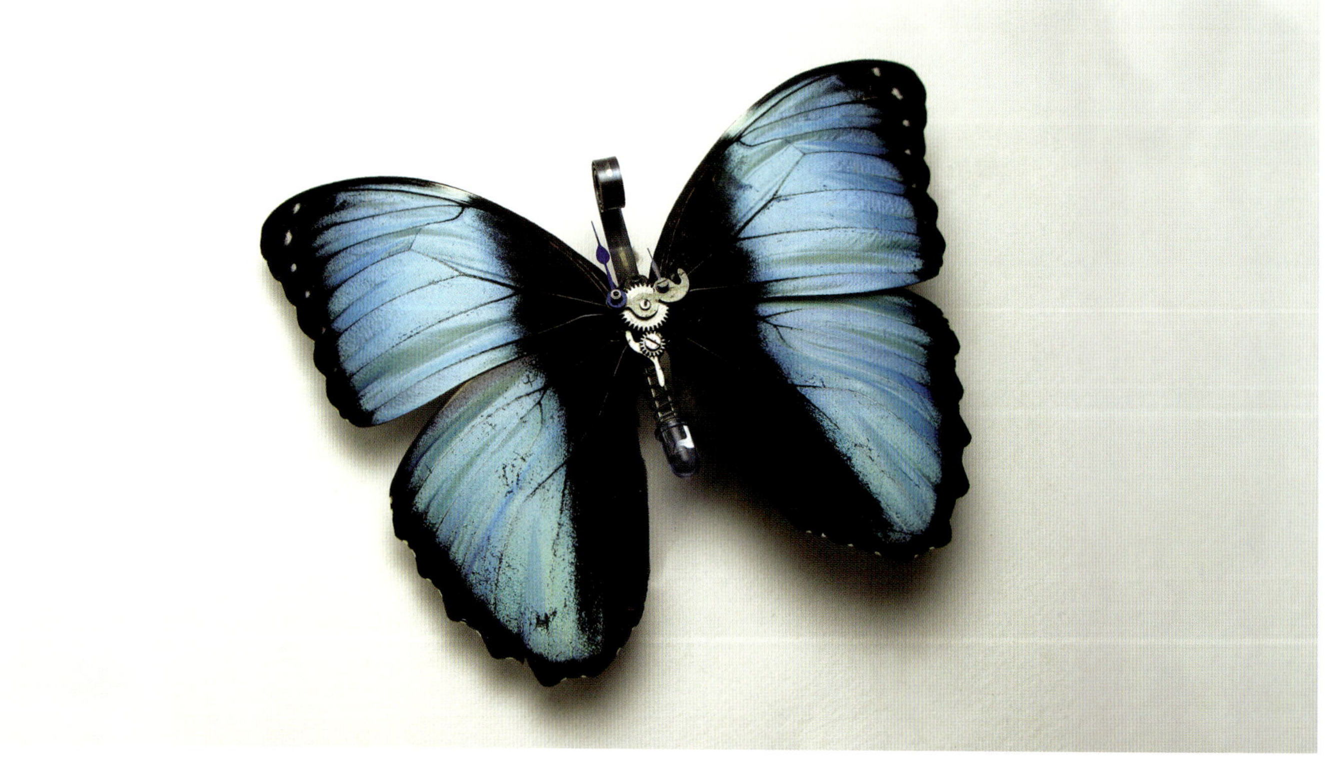

Right: *Buprestidae* (Buprestidae Euchroma Gigantea). 3.5" (8.9 cm) wide. Jewel beetle with brass watch parts and gears.

Below: *Green Beetle* (Cetonidae Dicrapheneous Obertherni). 4.5" (11.4 cm) wide. Flower beetle with brass and steel watch parts, gears and dial.

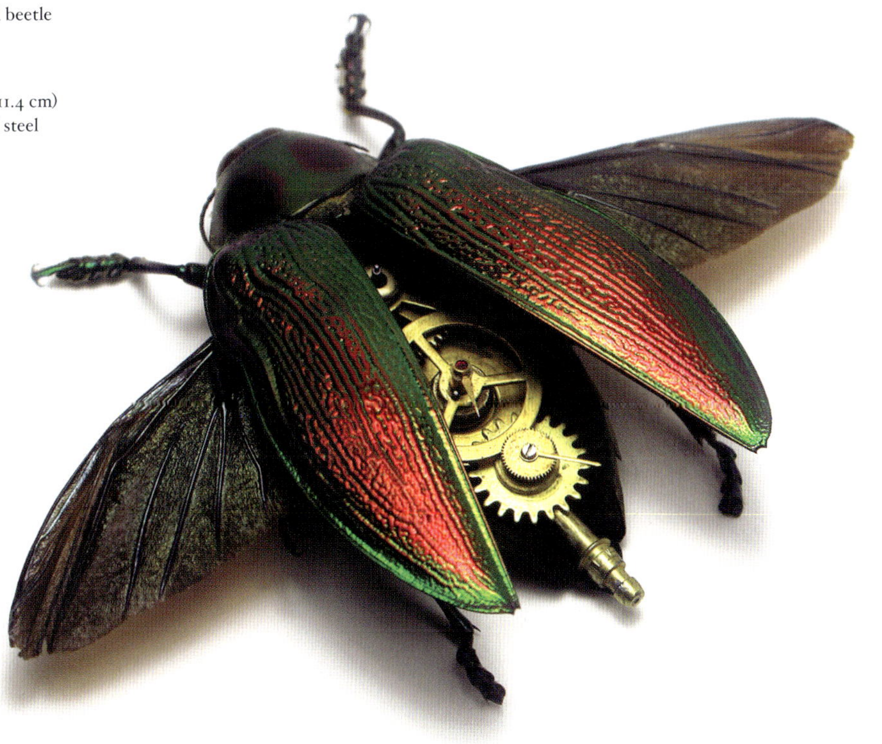

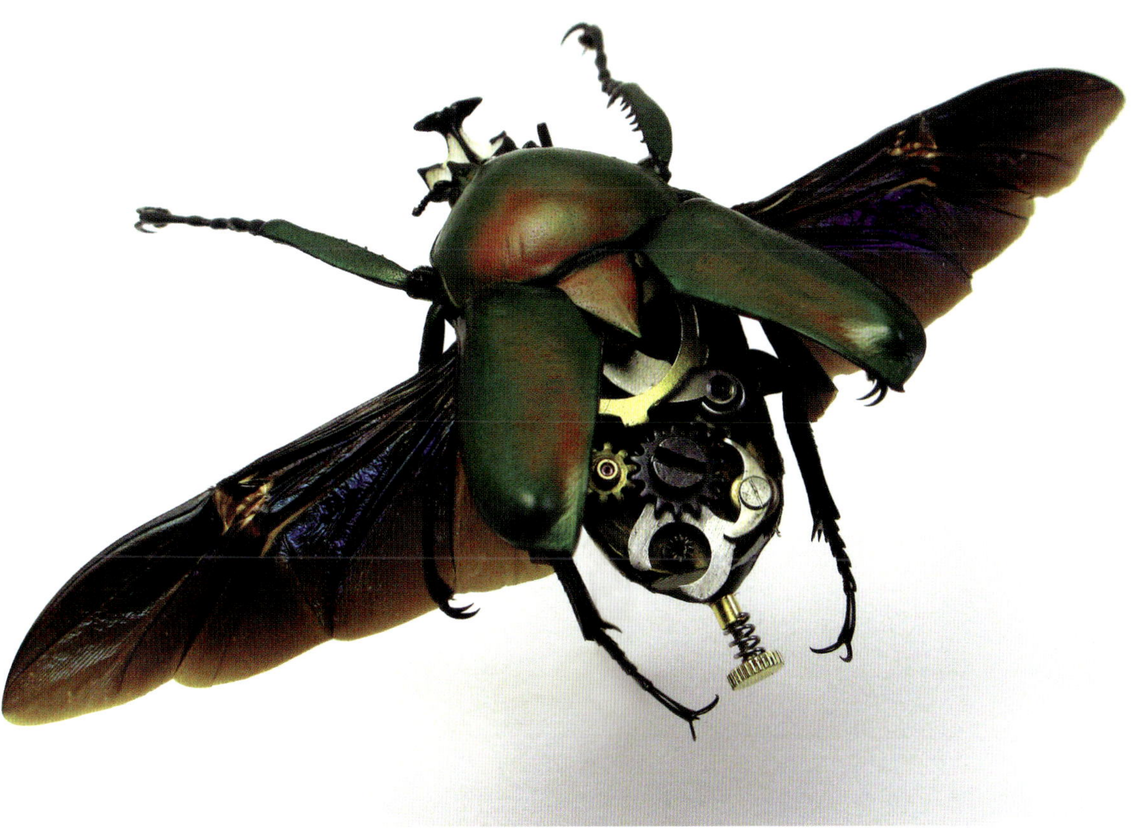

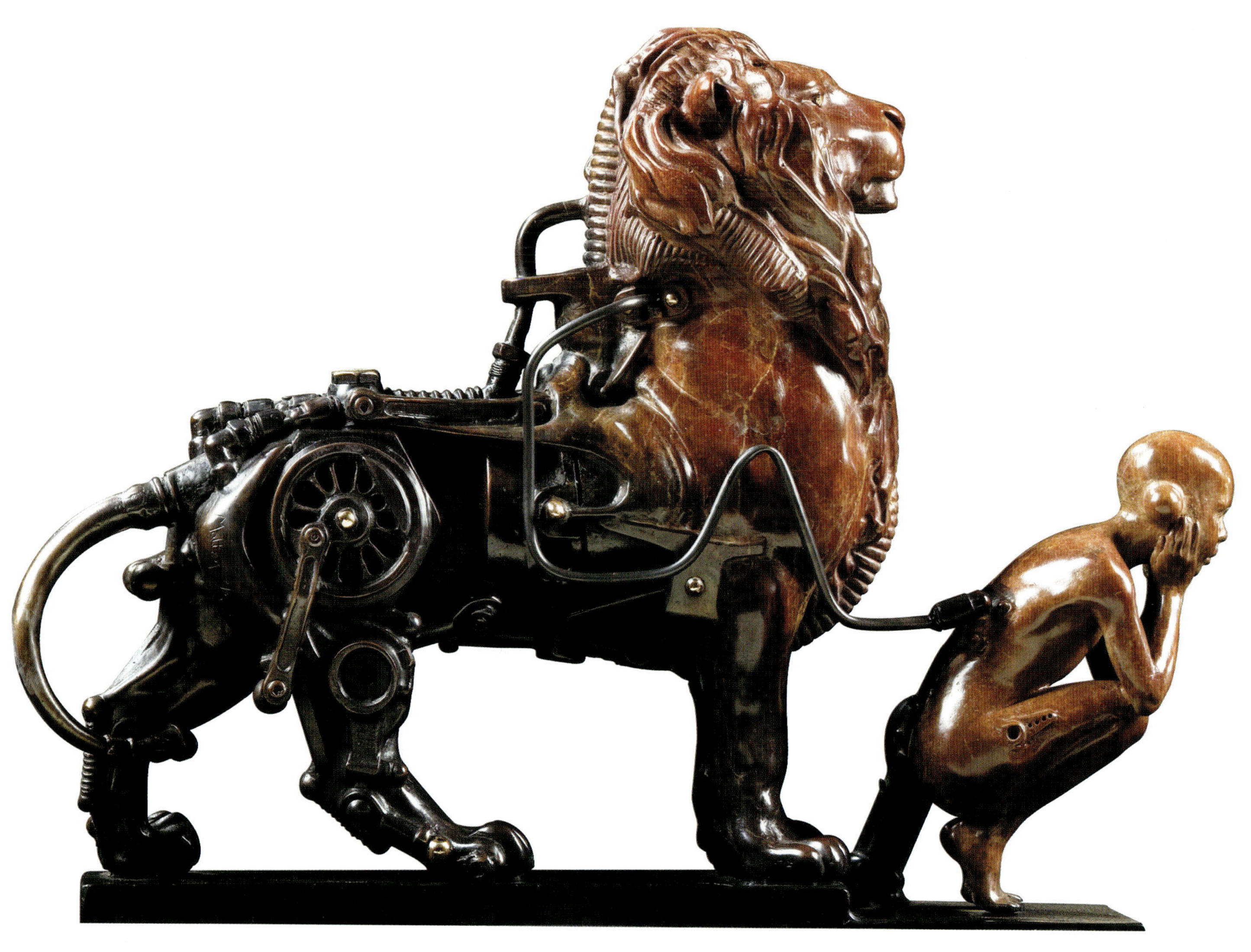

PIERRE MATTER

"I draw my inspiration from the way nature is being changed by science, from the hybridization of humans and animals and machines", says Pierre Matter. Based in Buhl, France, near the Swiss border, Pierre was a "mystical child, then a tormented teenager" studying mathematics. Via a series of twists and turns, he ended up turning to the "mystical world of art", working with a host of media (oil on canvas, gouache, ink – including comic strips – and bas relief on stone), before settling on three-dimensional volumes. Today Pierre works mostly with scrap metals and recycled objects, using welders, plasma cutters, laser cutters and grinders to shape and sculpt. "I am a kind of salvager. I feel like a child in a heap of sand, but instead of sand, there's a lot of recycling and scrap, full of magnificent objects. Often, the sculptures which emerge from these scraps of metal speak to us of who we are and how our future might be." His main influences are Bilal, Giger, Jodorowsky and Dali. Pierre's work is highly collectable and has been shown in Paris, London, New York, Miami, Hong-Kong, Shanghai and Dubai, to name a few.

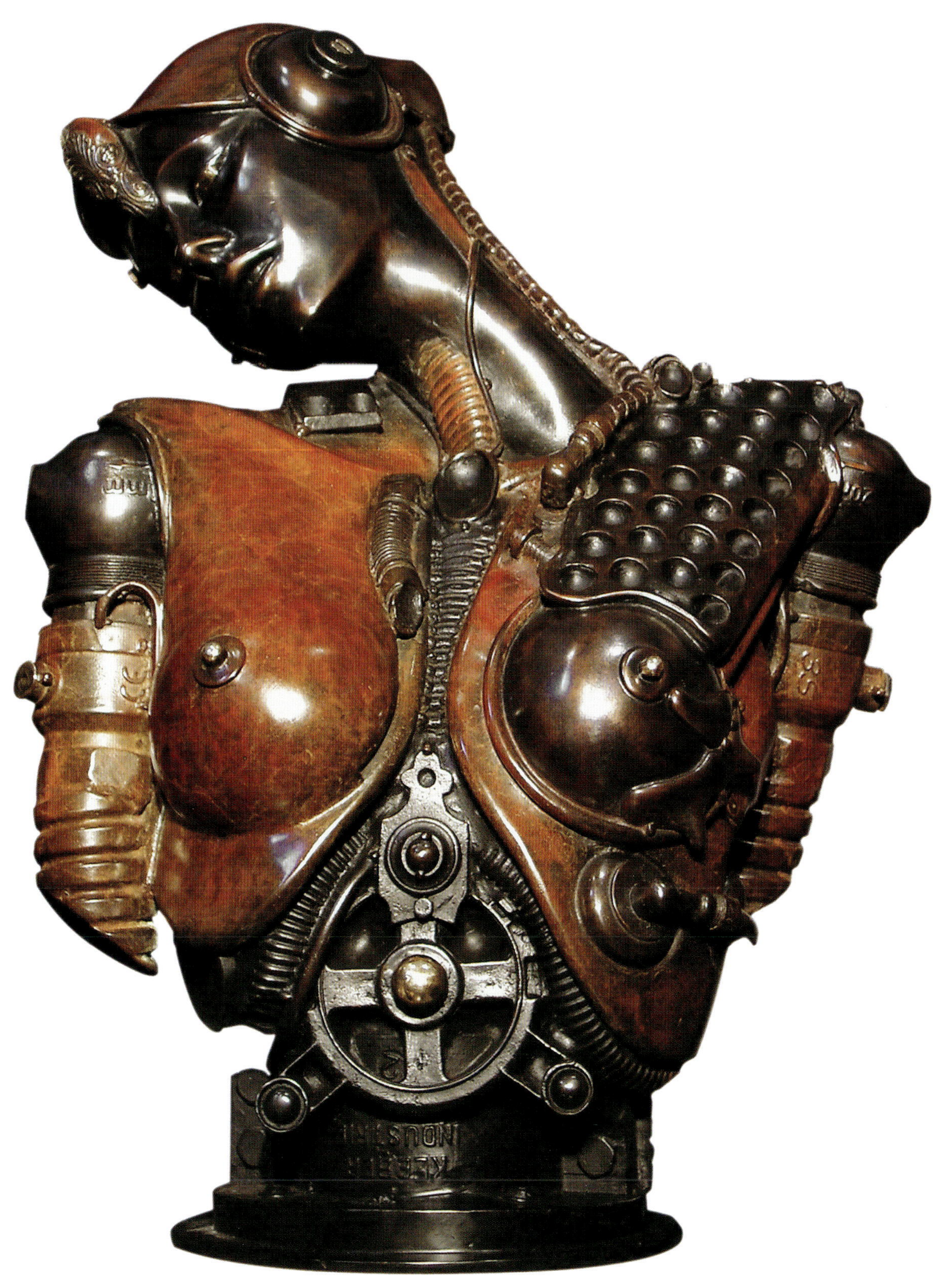

Above: *Diane le buste,* 2008. 27.5" x 19.6" x 15.7" (70 cm x 50 cm x 40 cm). Bronze.

Left: *Unbalanced Friendship*, 2010. 14.5" x 19.6" x 4.7" (36 cm x 50 cm x 12 cm). Bronze.

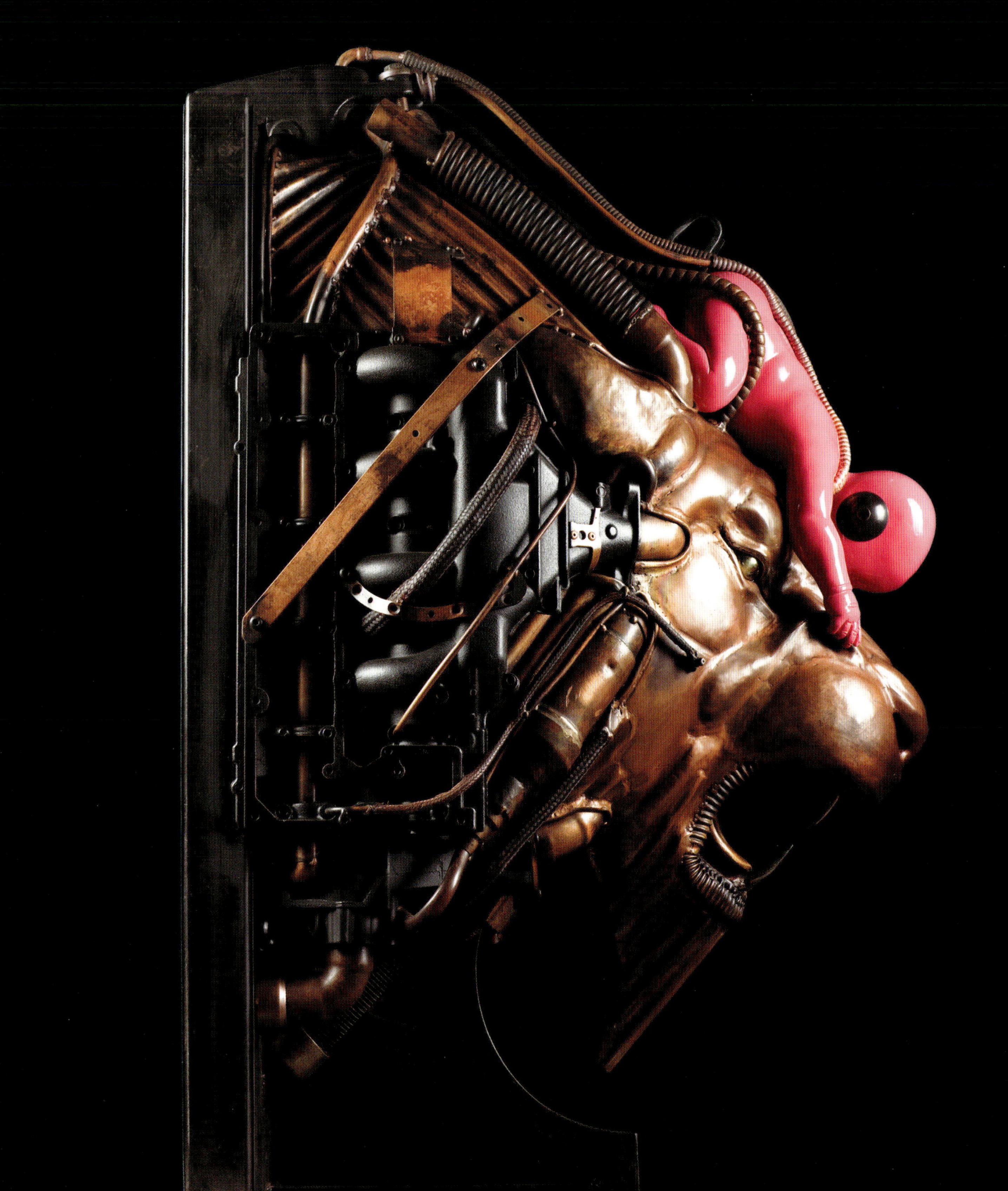

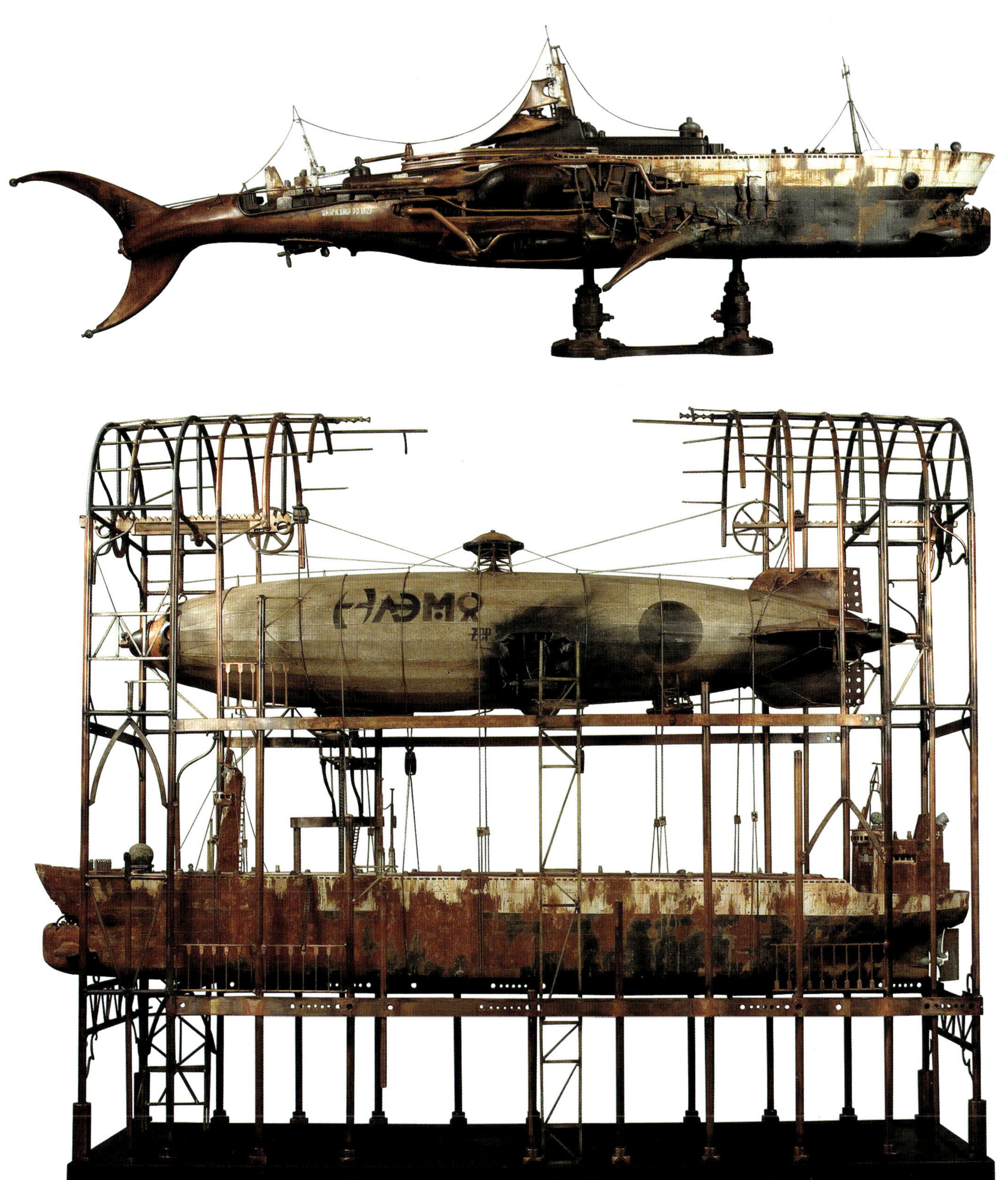

Top: *Sharkship*, 2006. 34.2" x 133" x 33.5" (87 cm x 297 cm x 85 cm). Copper, bronze and salvaged material.

Above: *Le vaisseau désert* (The Deserted Vessel), 2005. 93.7" x 89.4" x 23.6" (238 cm x 227 cm x 60 cm). Copper, salvaged metal, bronze and fabric.

Left: *Riding the Storm*, 2009. 44.9" x 29.1" x 24.8" (114 cm x 74 cm x 63 cm). Copper, resin and salvaged metal.

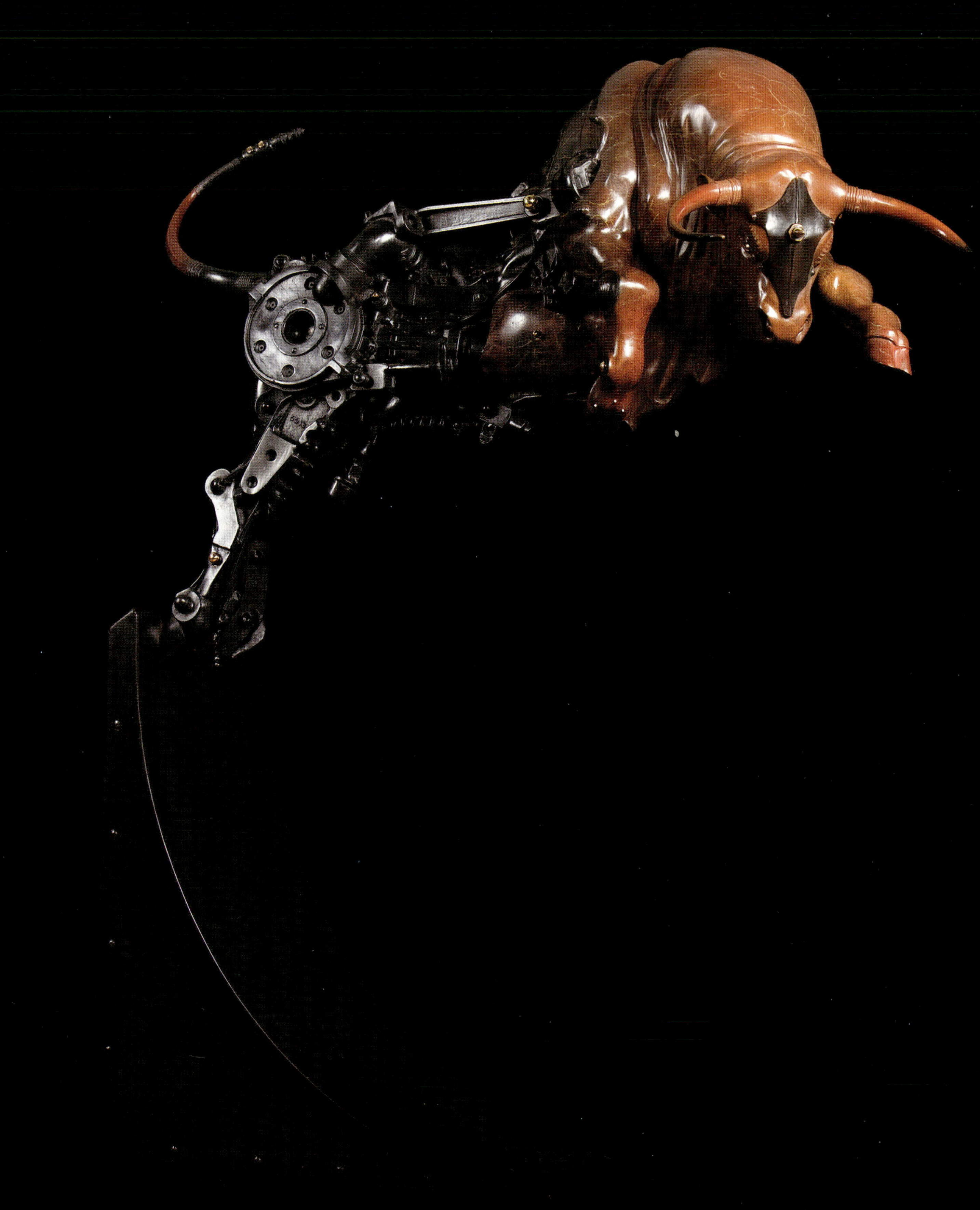

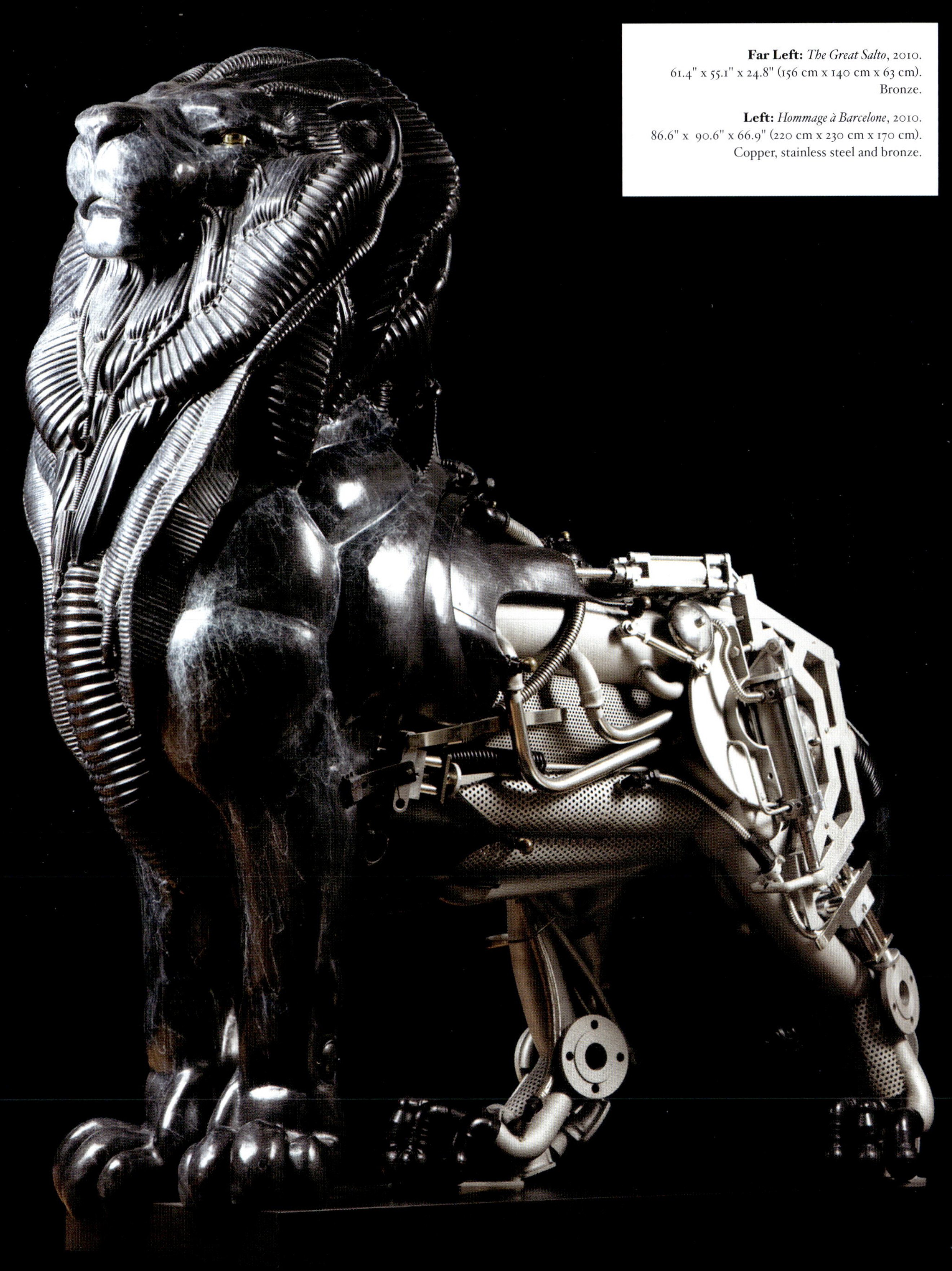

Far Left: *The Great Salto*, 2010.
61.4" x 55.1" x 24.8" (156 cm x 140 cm x 63 cm).
Bronze.

Left: *Hommage à Barcelone*, 2010.
86.6" x 90.6" x 66.9" (220 cm x 230 cm x 170 cm).
Copper, stainless steel and bronze.

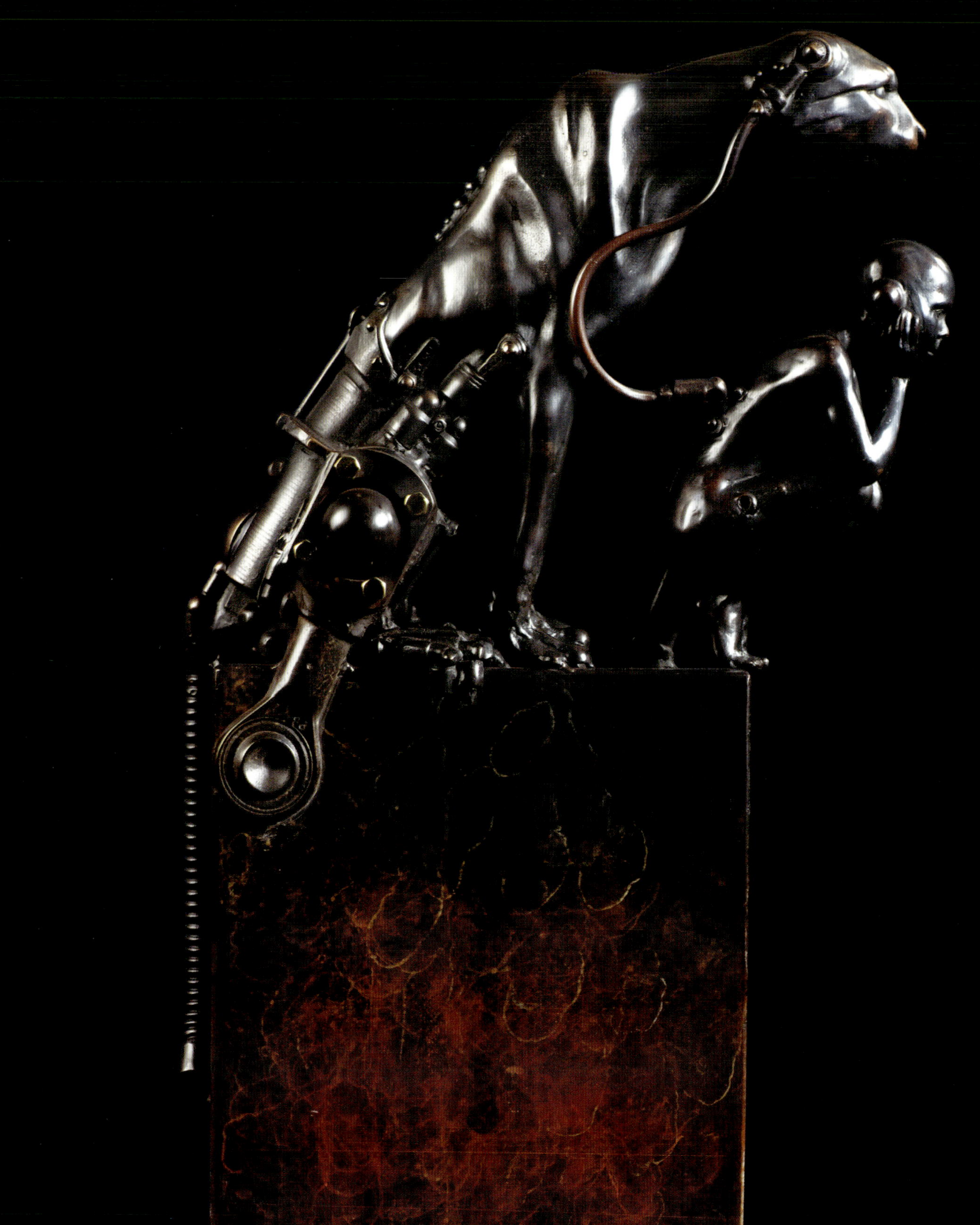

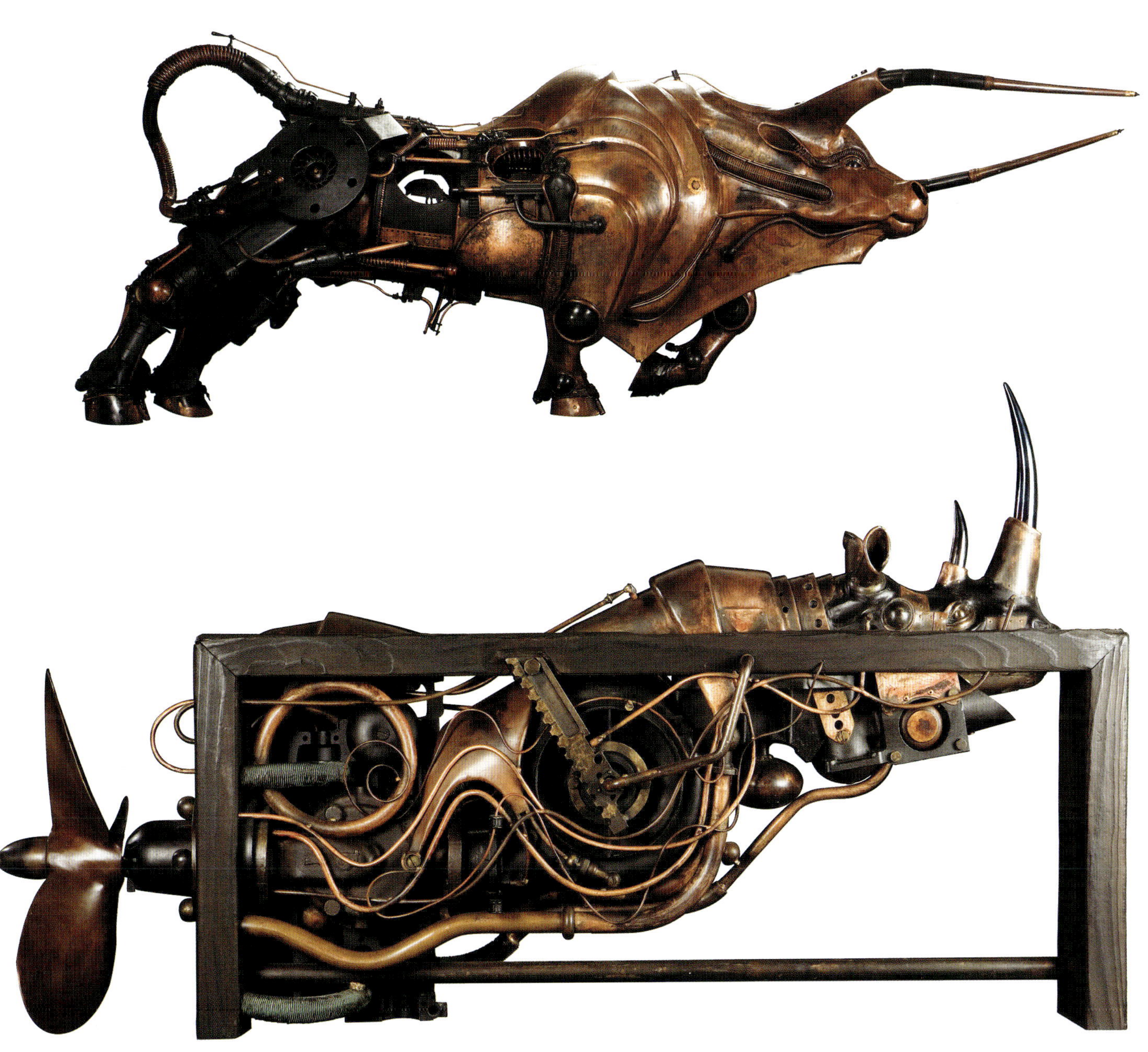

Top: *Bull Spirit*, 2005. 70.9" x 195.7" x 51.2" (180 cm x 497 cm x 130 cm). Copper, stainless steel, bronze and salvaged metal.

Above: *Bath*, 2006. 32.7" x 57.5" x 17.7" (83 cm x 146 cm x 45 cm). Copper, salvaged metal and wood.

Left: *The Horizon*, 2010. 21.2" x 13.7" x 5.1" (54 cm x 35 cm x 13 cm). Bronze.

KAZUHIKO NAKAMURA

Based in Kawasaki City, Japan, Kazuhiko, a.k.a. Almacan, was influenced early on by the 16th Century Italian painter, Archimboldo. "There was something fascinating in his 3-D renderings, in which he drew human faces from a combination of various objects. I wanted to create a new illusionism combining Archimboldo with scenes from Kafka's *Metamorphoses*, which I had read aged 16." The resultant series, *Metamorphoses*, was first shown in 2005, and the themes were continued by Kazuhiko in his *Automaton* series in 2006, which has clear Steampunk half human/half machine motifs, also recalling Fritz Lang's *Metropolis*; "I am also influenced by surrealism and Cyberpunk and I'm drawn to 19th Century machine designs." Kazuhiko evolves his works organically, achieving transformations – "like the ecdysis of an insect" – as he puts it; "Reborn these images are mechanical mirages in a desert of pixels."

Below: *Requiem for Industry*, 2007. Inspired by *Frankenstein* (The 1931 film version with Boris Karloff). Digital artwork: Shade and Photoshop.

Right: *Brain Tower*, 2009. Digital artwork: Photoshop and ZBrush.

Following Pages: *Automaton (Other)*, 2006. Mannequin-robot 'torture machines' inspired by the puppets in films by Jan Svankmajer and The Quay Brothers. Digital artwork: Shade, Total Textures and Photoshop.

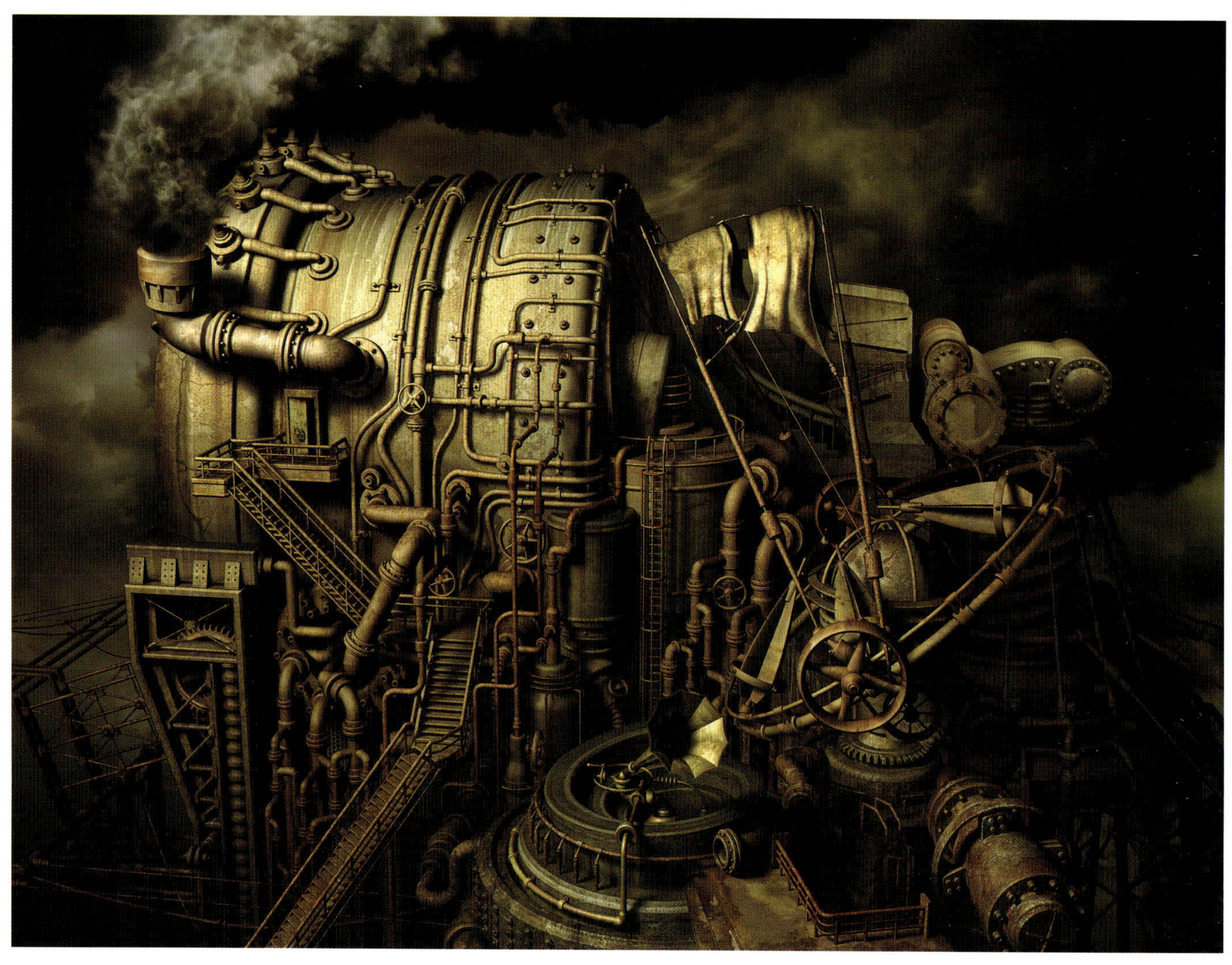

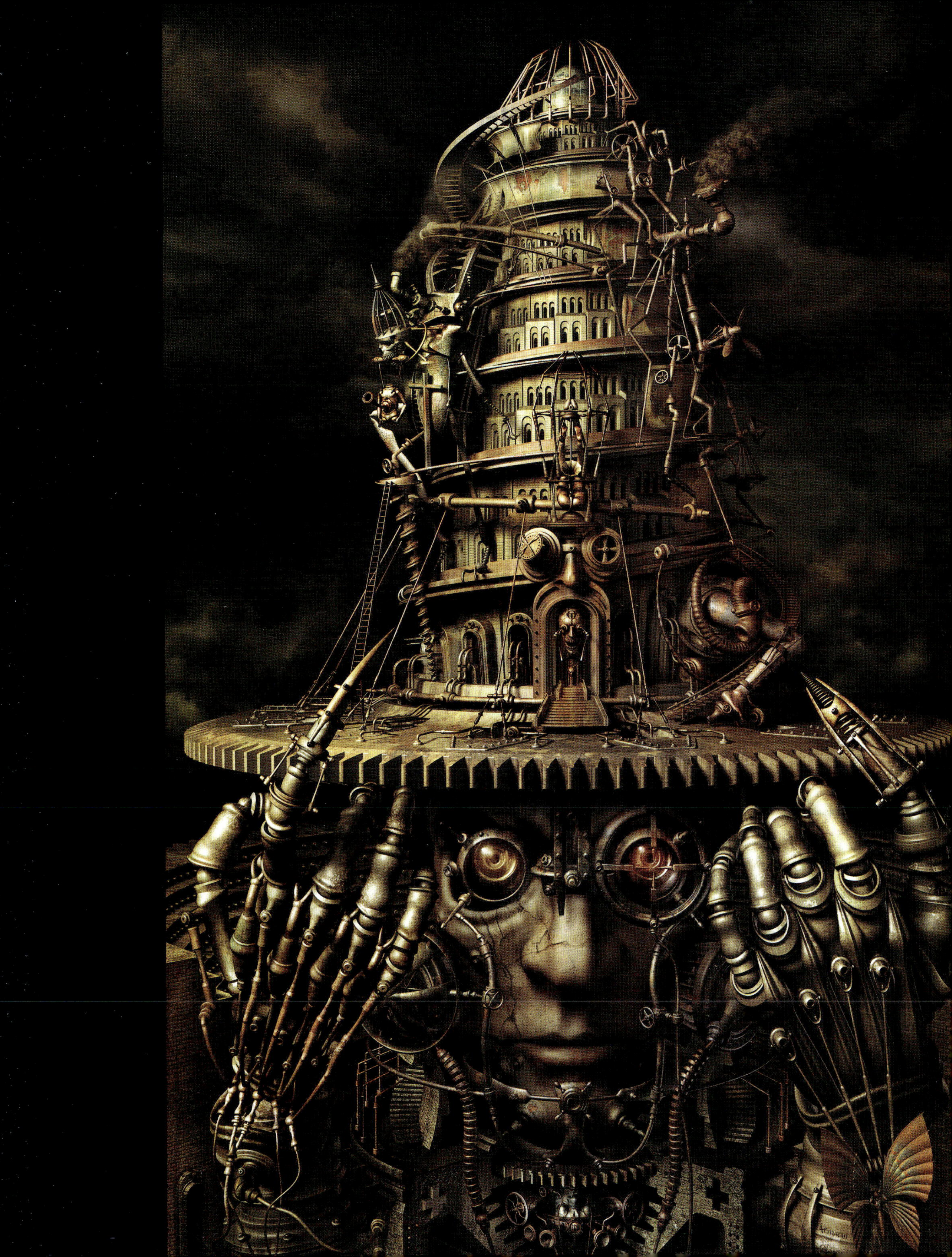

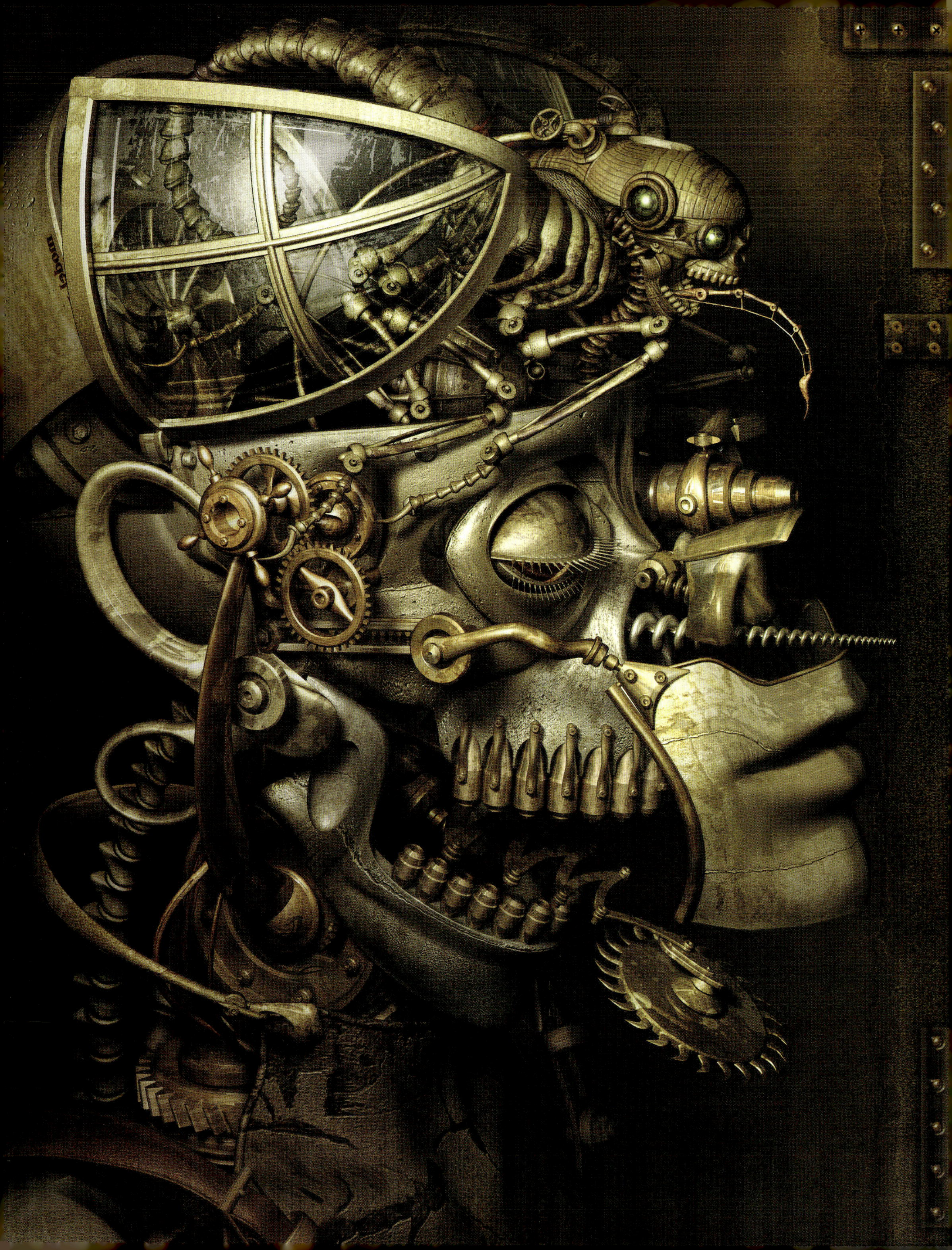

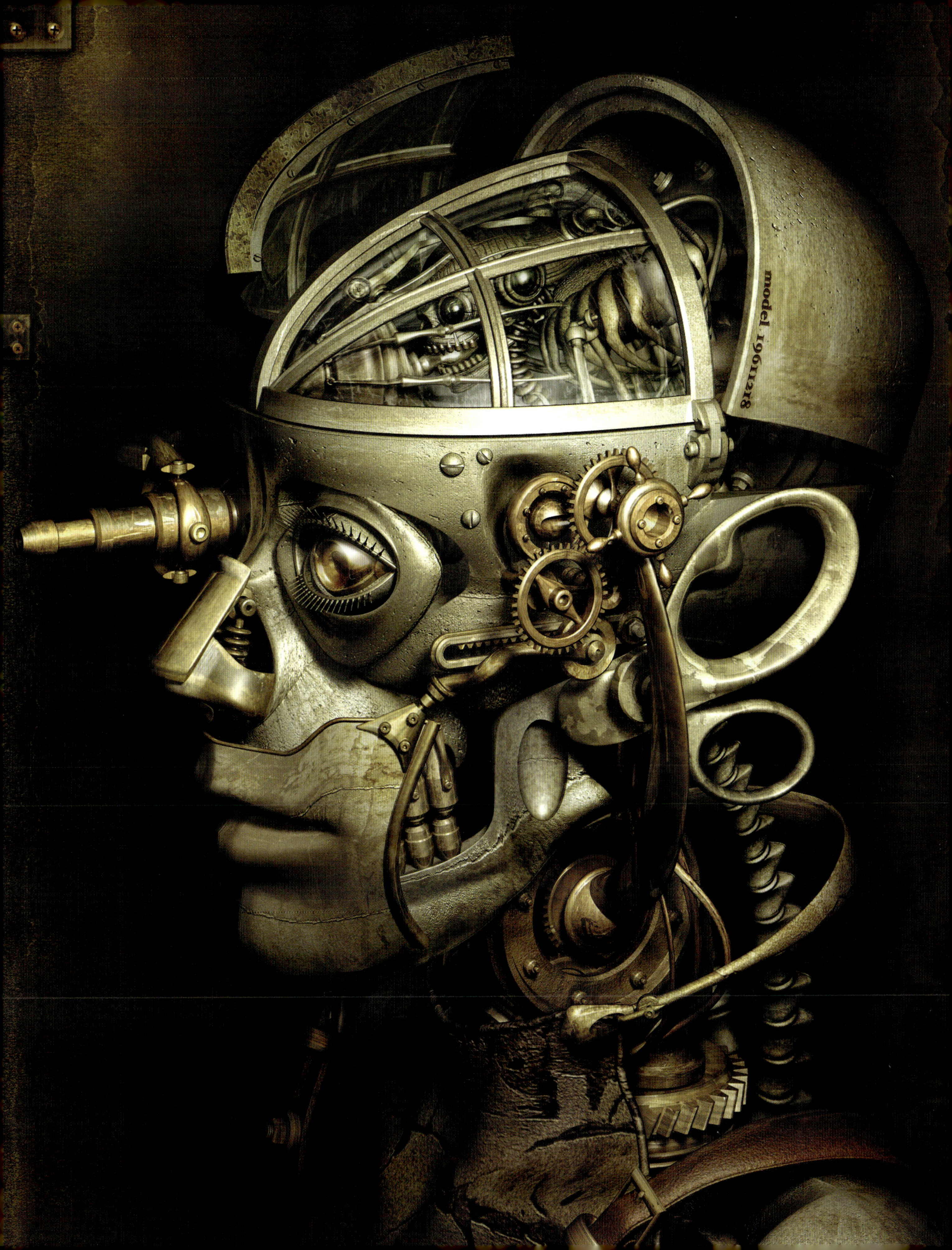
model 19611218

JAMES NG

A master of the representation of Steampunk anachronisms, James Ng (pronounced 'Ing') likes to imagine a world where the Chinese had the first industrial revolution, which they exported to the West: so rather than China becoming Westernized, the West became China-ized. He was born in Hong Kong and as a child was obsessed with drawing robots and monsters and creating toys. Today he is a full-time concept artist and illustrator who divides his time between Hong Kong, Vancouver, New York, Chicago and London. "I am fascinated by the Qing Dynasty (1644-1912), the last Chinese dynasty" he says, and the imagery from this period has informed his *Imperial Steamworks* series. James's ultimate goal is to make a movie from all his characters. In the meantime he exhibits widely, his work is being used to decorate 50 double-decker buses in Hong Kong and has even inspired a piece by classical composer Patrick Hutchings.

Below: *Court Band*. From the *Imperial Steamworks* series.
Right: *Key Keeper*. From the *Imperial Steamworks* series.

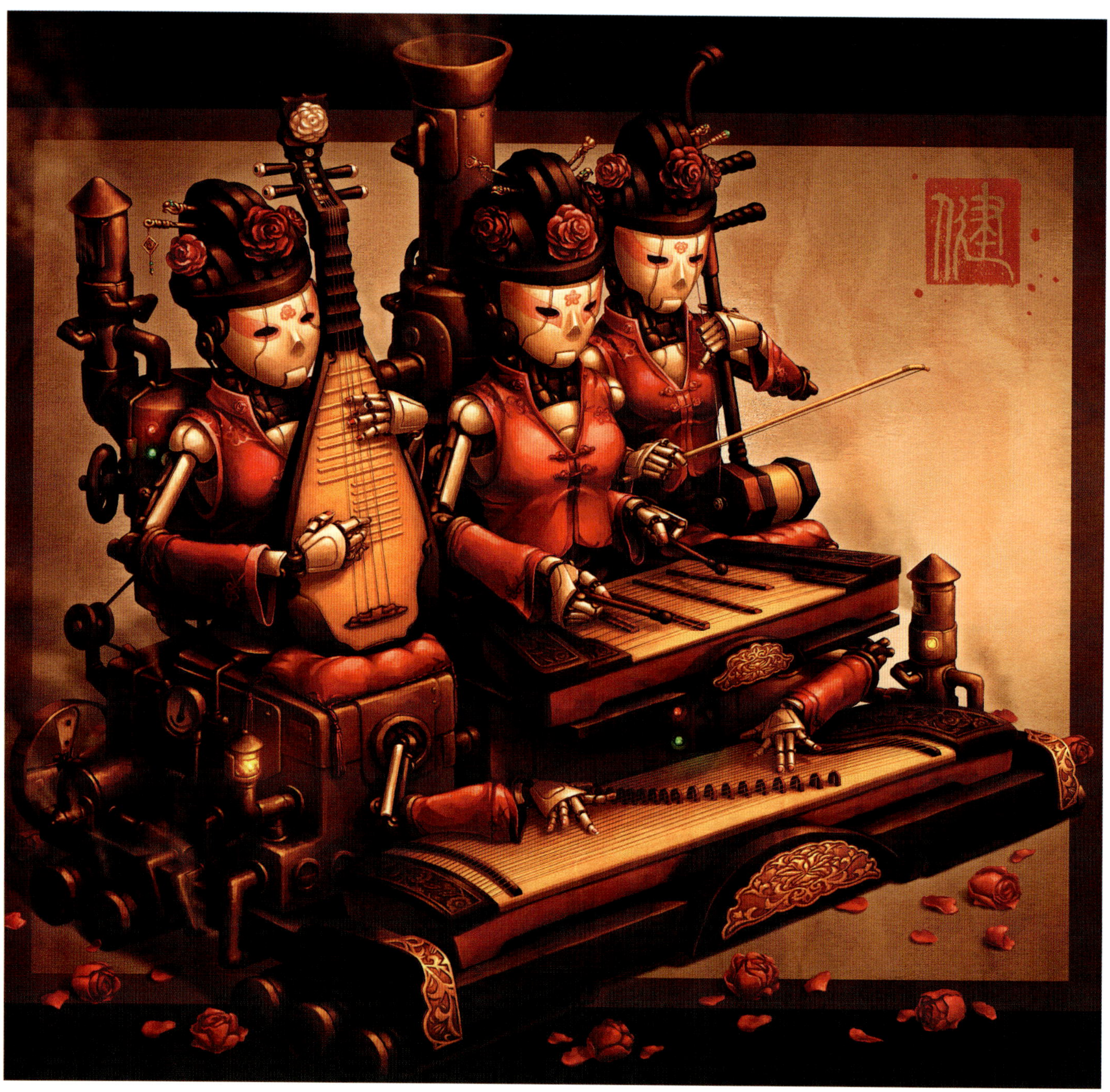

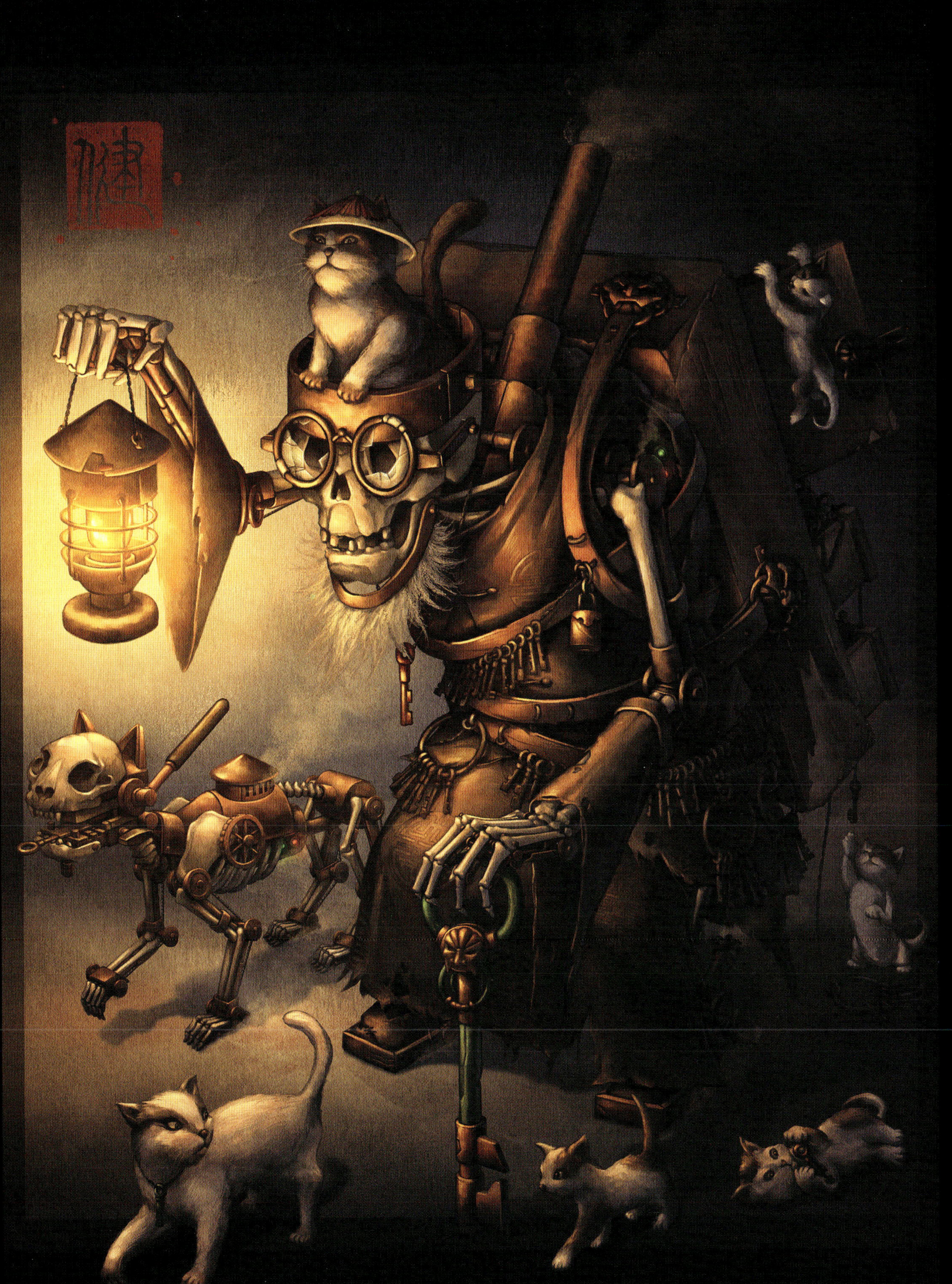

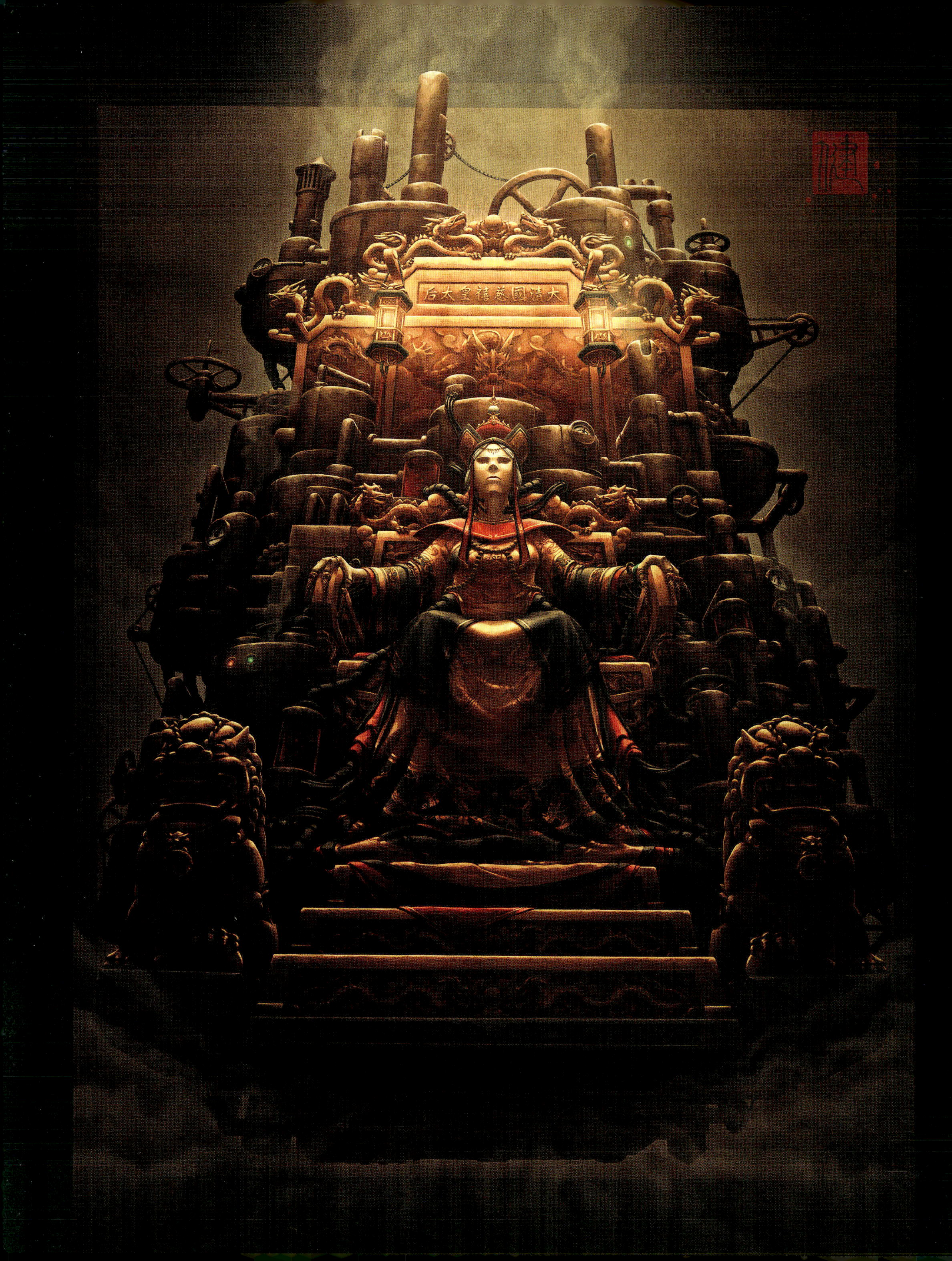
大清國慈禧皇太后

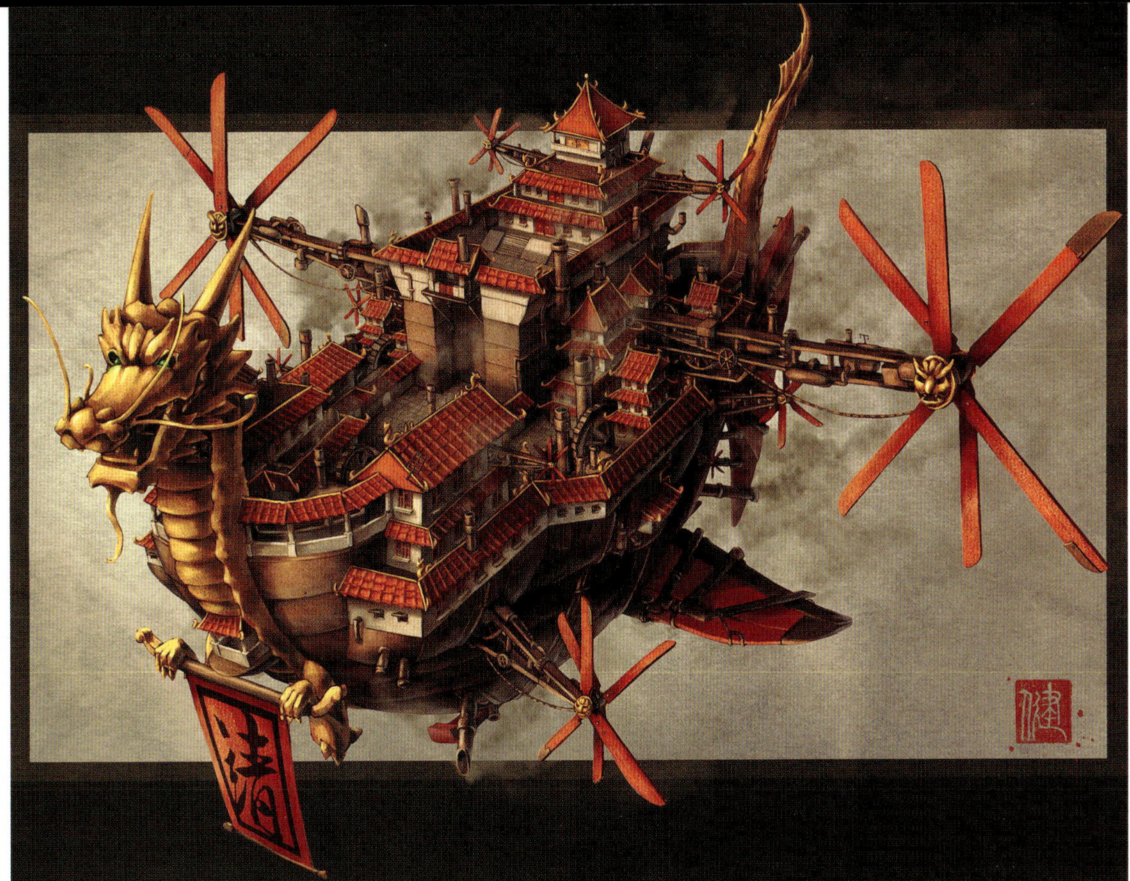

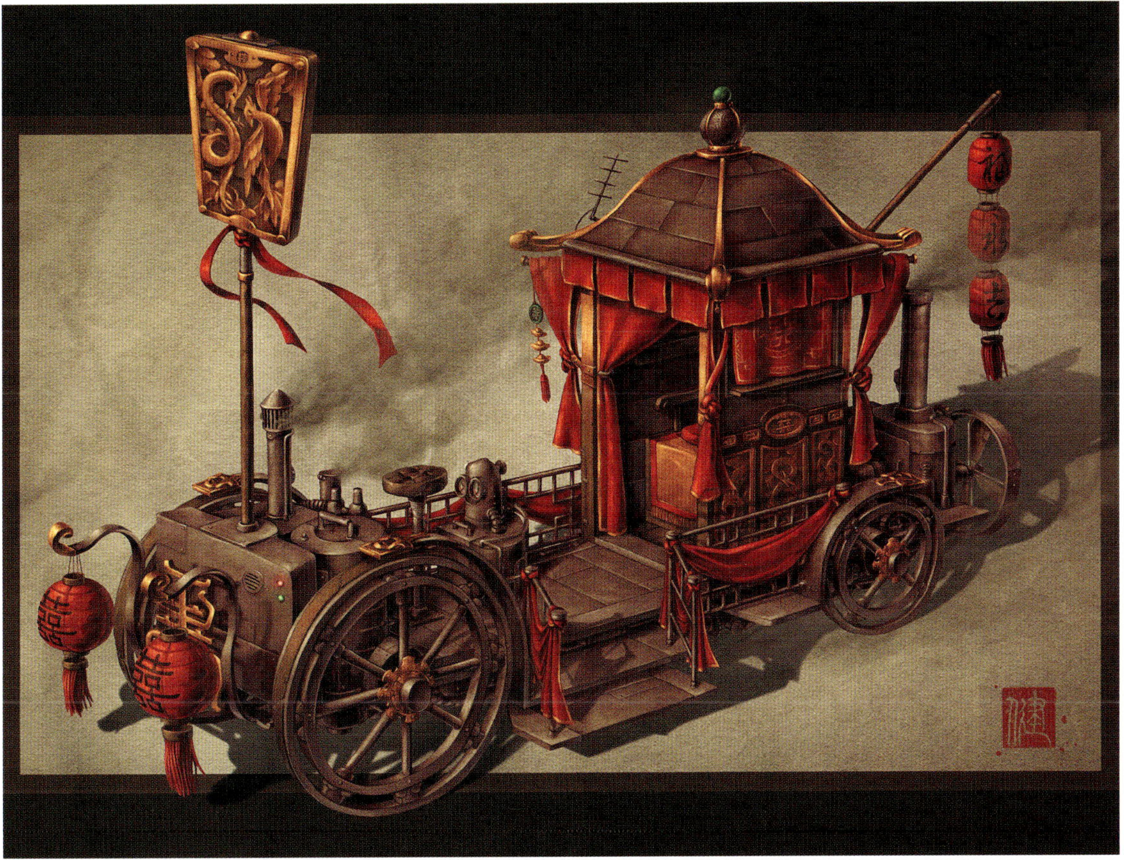

Above Top: *Imperial Airship*. From the *Imperial Steamworks* series.

Above: *Bridal Carriage*. From the *Imperial Steamworks* series.

Left: *Immortal Empress*. From the *Imperial Steamworks* series.

SAM VAN OLFFEN

Born and still based in Montpellier, in the south of France, Sam read a lot of Franco-Belgian and US comics as a kid. "I wanted to be George Pérez, Gil Kane or John Byrne, from whose work I learnt the power of the line." He always wanted to draw – "my marks in art were always great" – but somehow ended up repairing photocopiers. He continued drawing privately, and then the advent of image-editing software changed everything. "Rather than drawing, I began to assemble photographic elements into compositions. I think of it as 'visual sampling', playing with imagery as a DJ plays with sound, translating what starts as a metaphysical signal into something tangible." He is hugely inspired by Gustave Doré – also self-taught, he points out – classical painters such as Van Eyck and Rembrandt, Sci-fi films and the special effects of Ray Harryhausen and Richard Edlund. Sam has exhibited extensively, in the US as well as Europe.

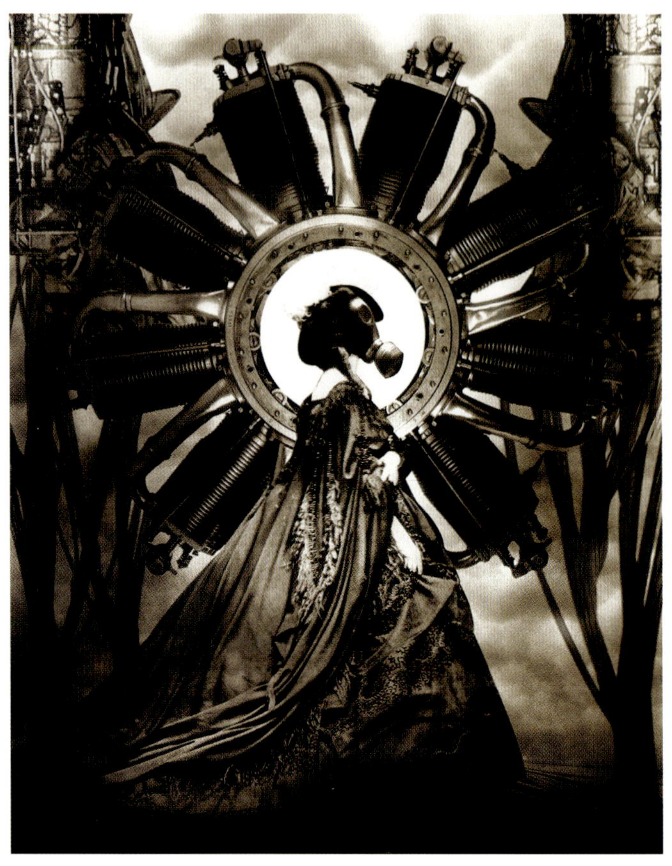

Right: *Courtisane* (Courtesan), 2007.

Below: *Cours lapin, cours!* (Run Rabbit, Run!), 2008.

Far Right: *Steampunk Family,* 2008.

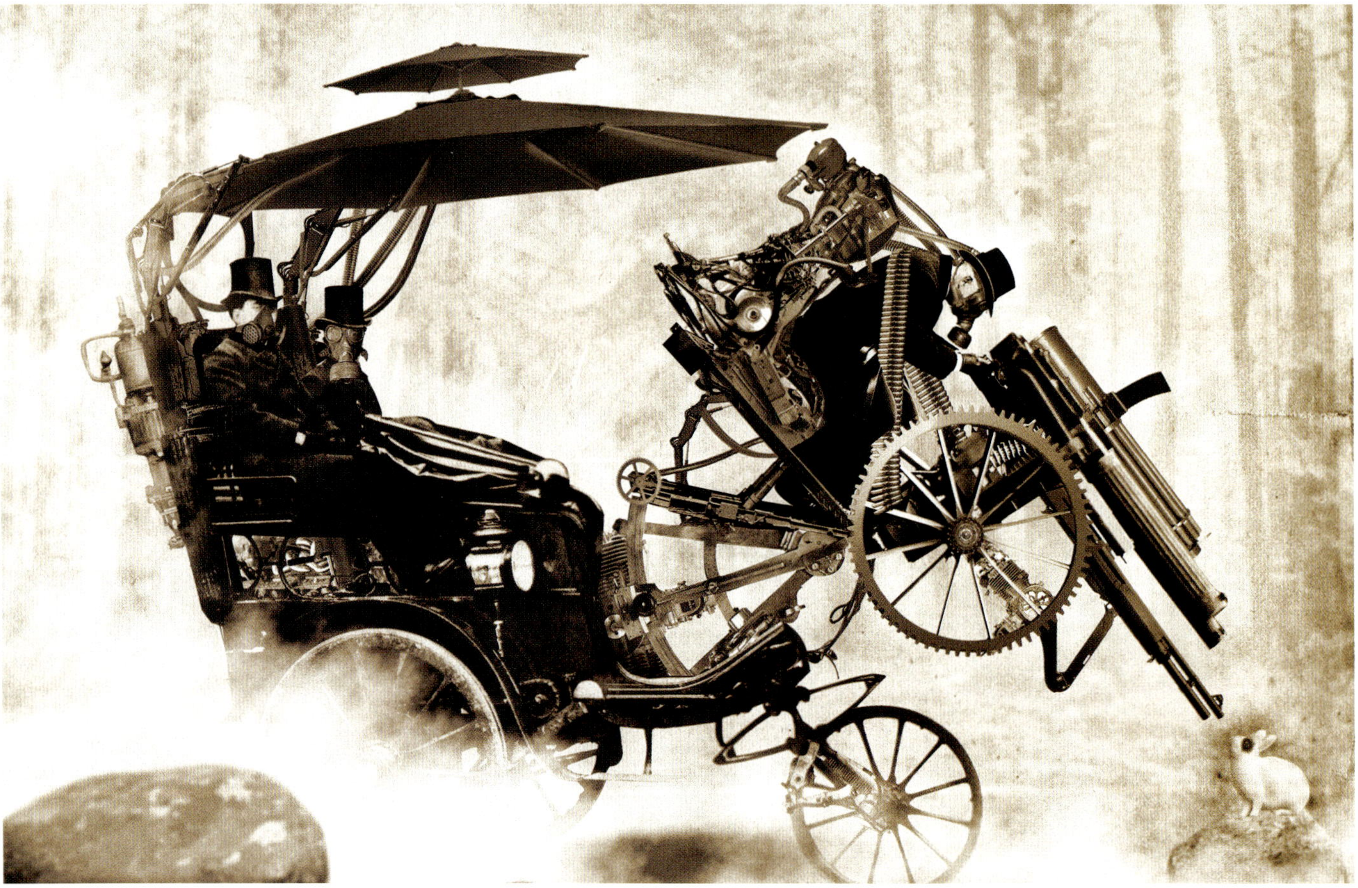

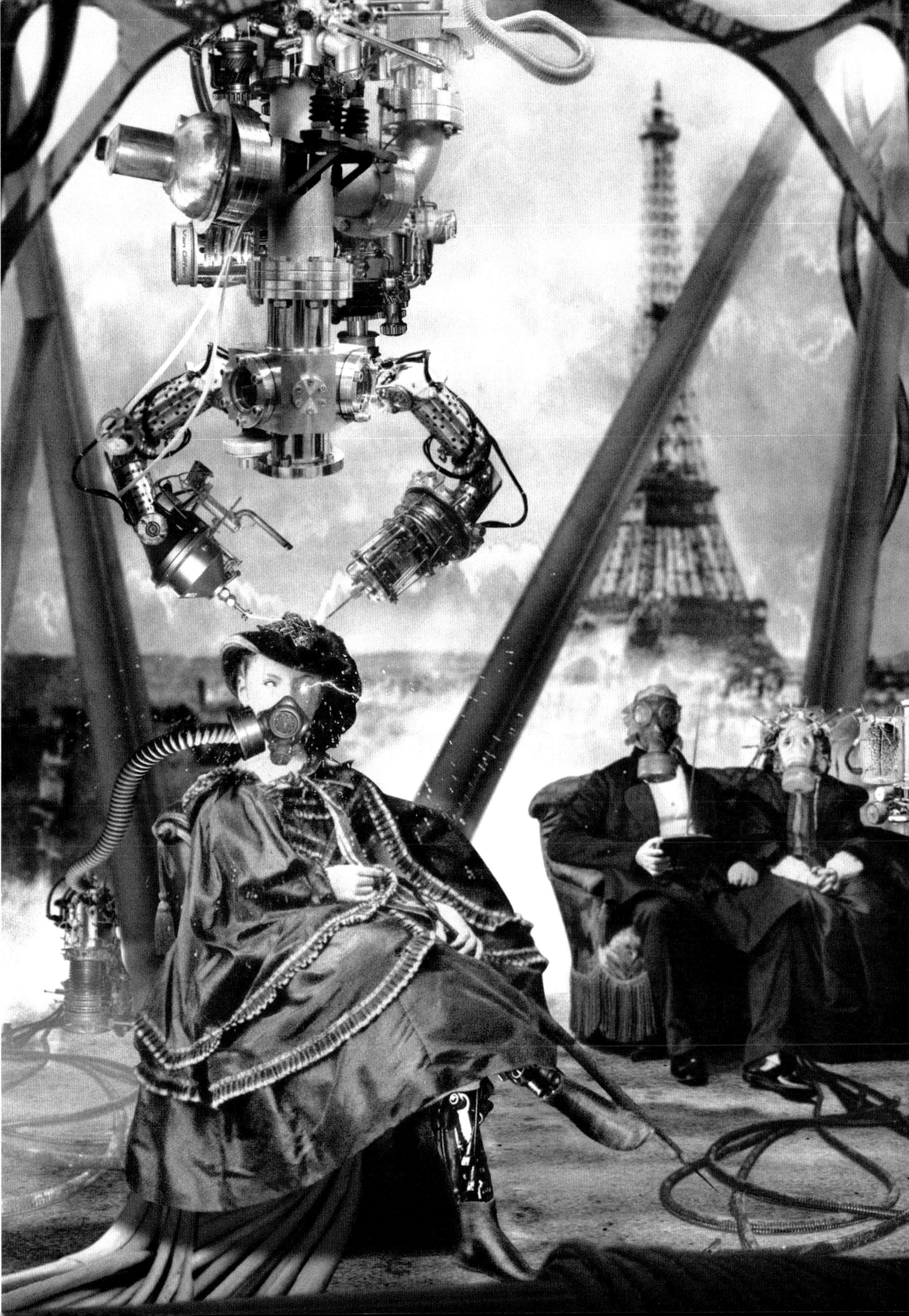

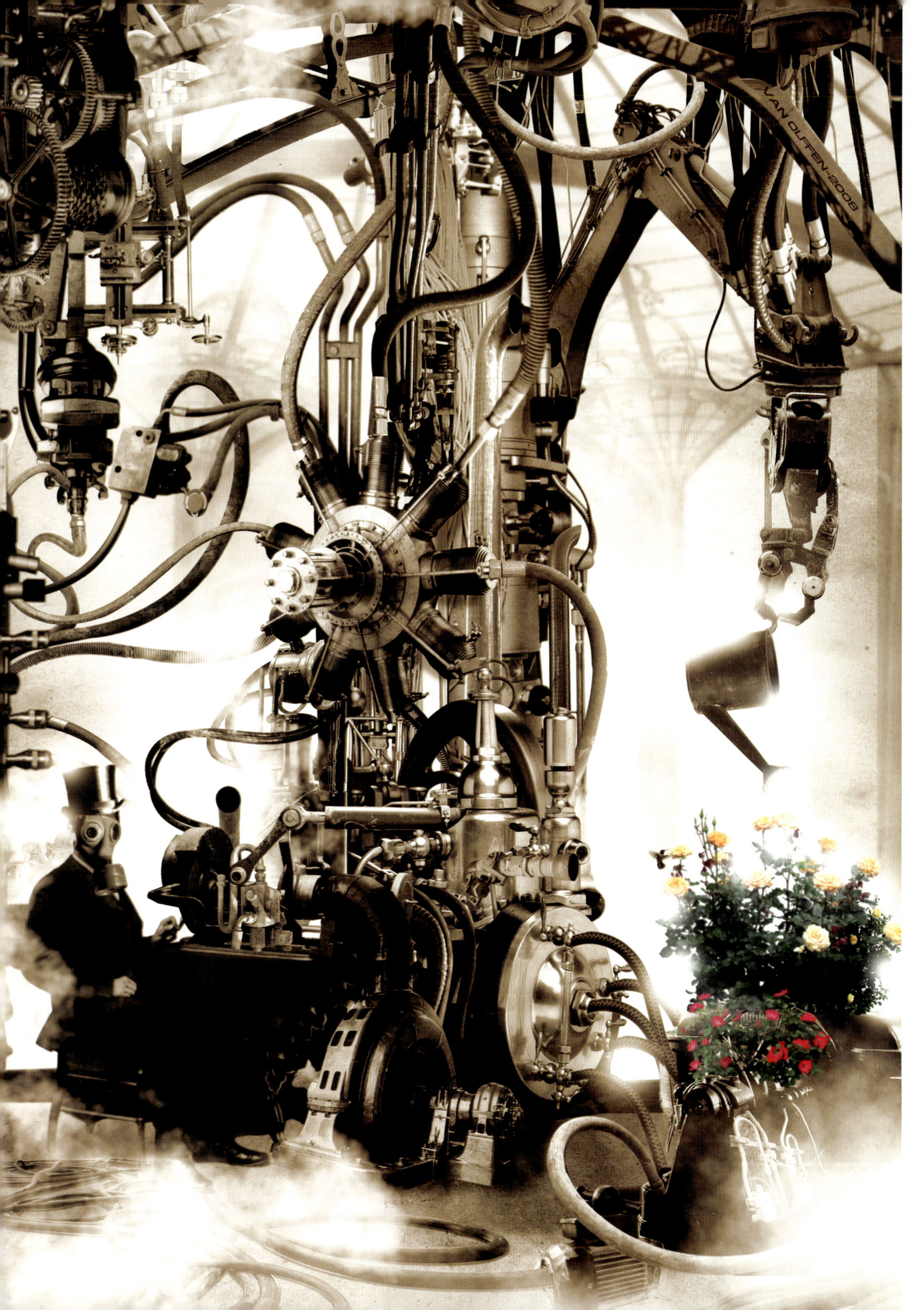
VAN OLFFEN-2008

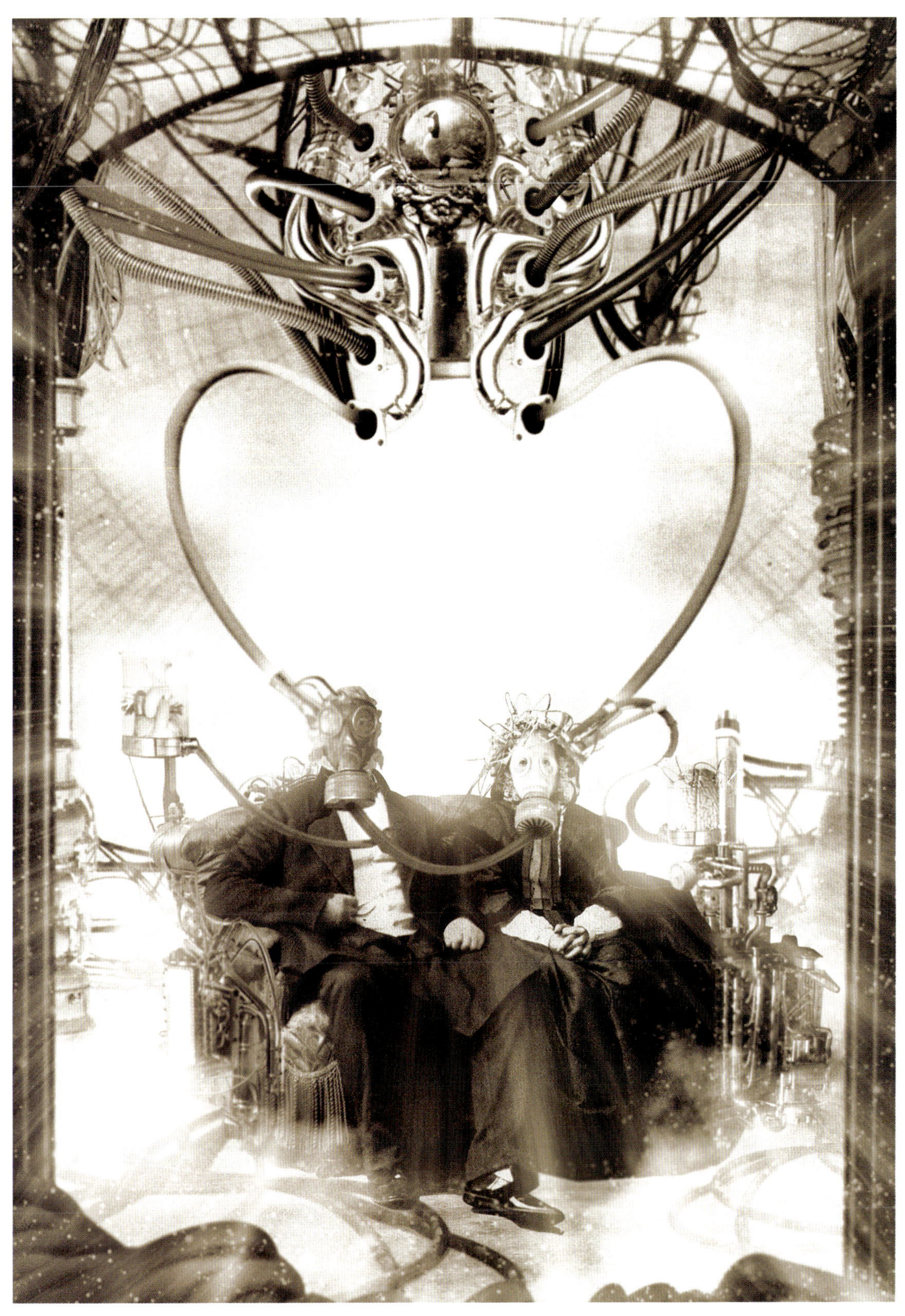

Above: *Les vieux amants* (The Old Lovers), 2008.

Left: *Le Mécatron* (The Mecatron), 2008.

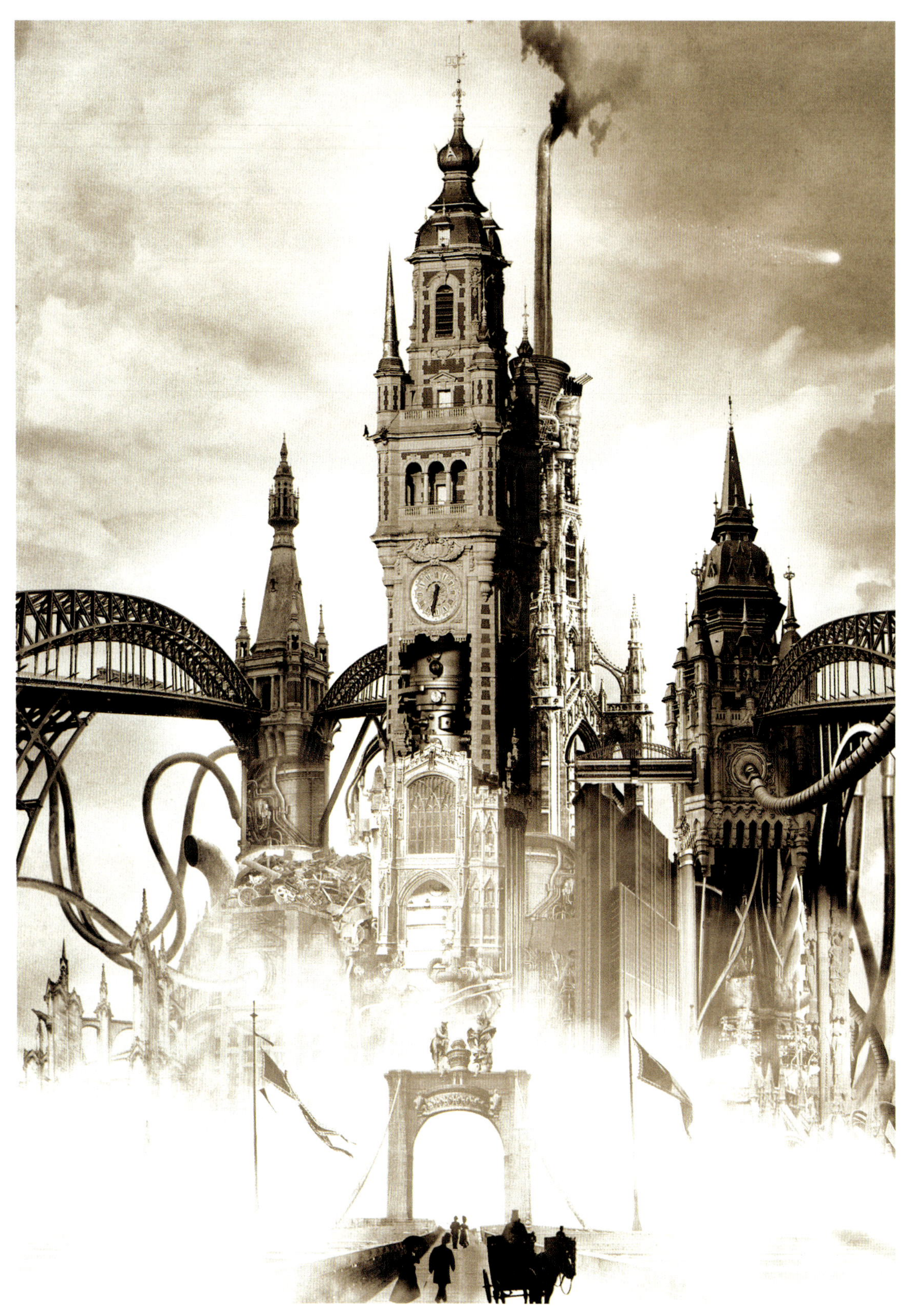

Above: *Lille Megaville – Les beffrois de l'effroi* (The Belfries of Dread), 2008.

Right: *Le tunnel du mystère* (The Tunnel of Mystery), 2008.

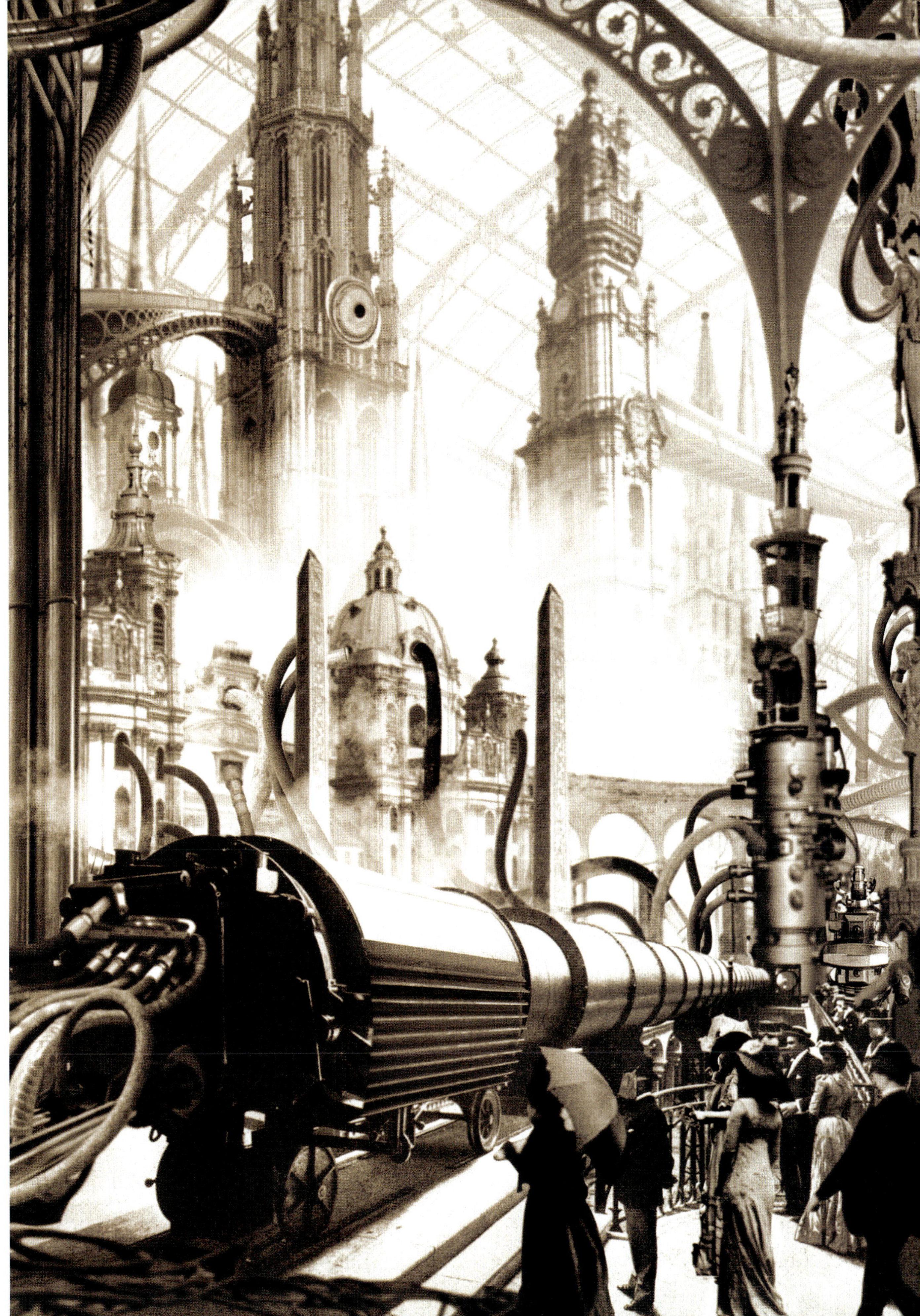

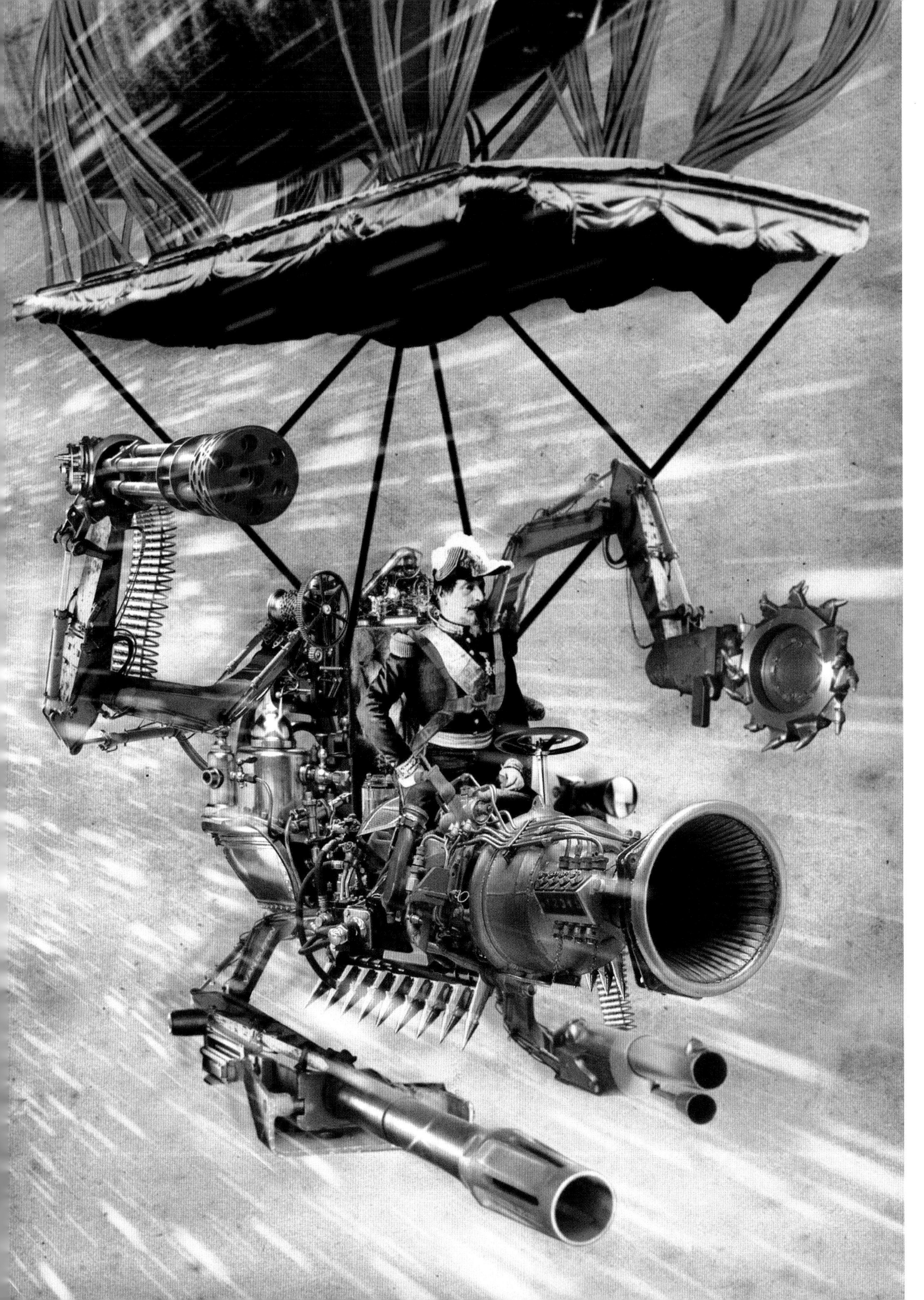

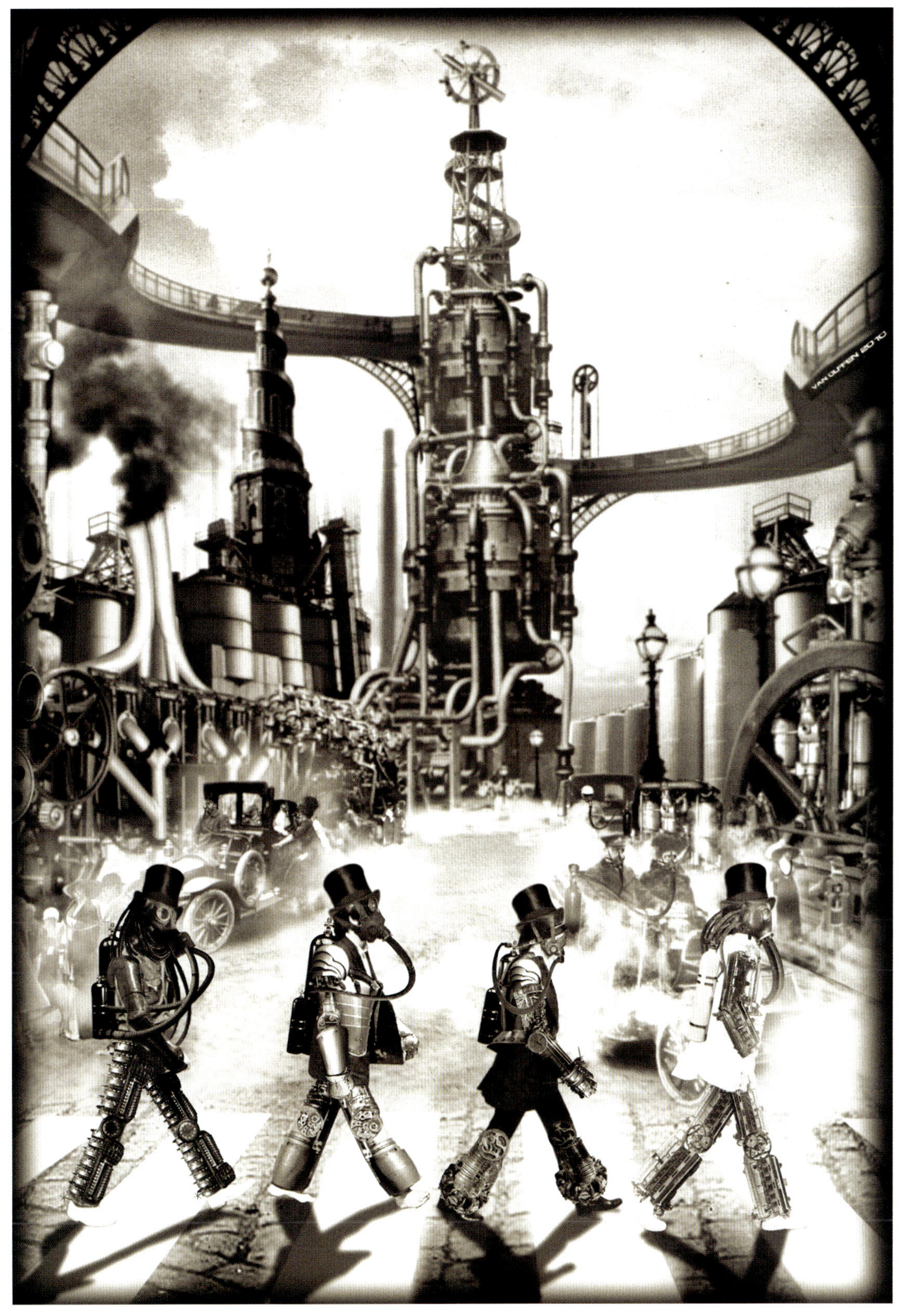

Above: *Abbey Road*, 2010.

Left: *Napoleon III contre-attaque!* (Napoleon III Counter-attacks!), 2008.

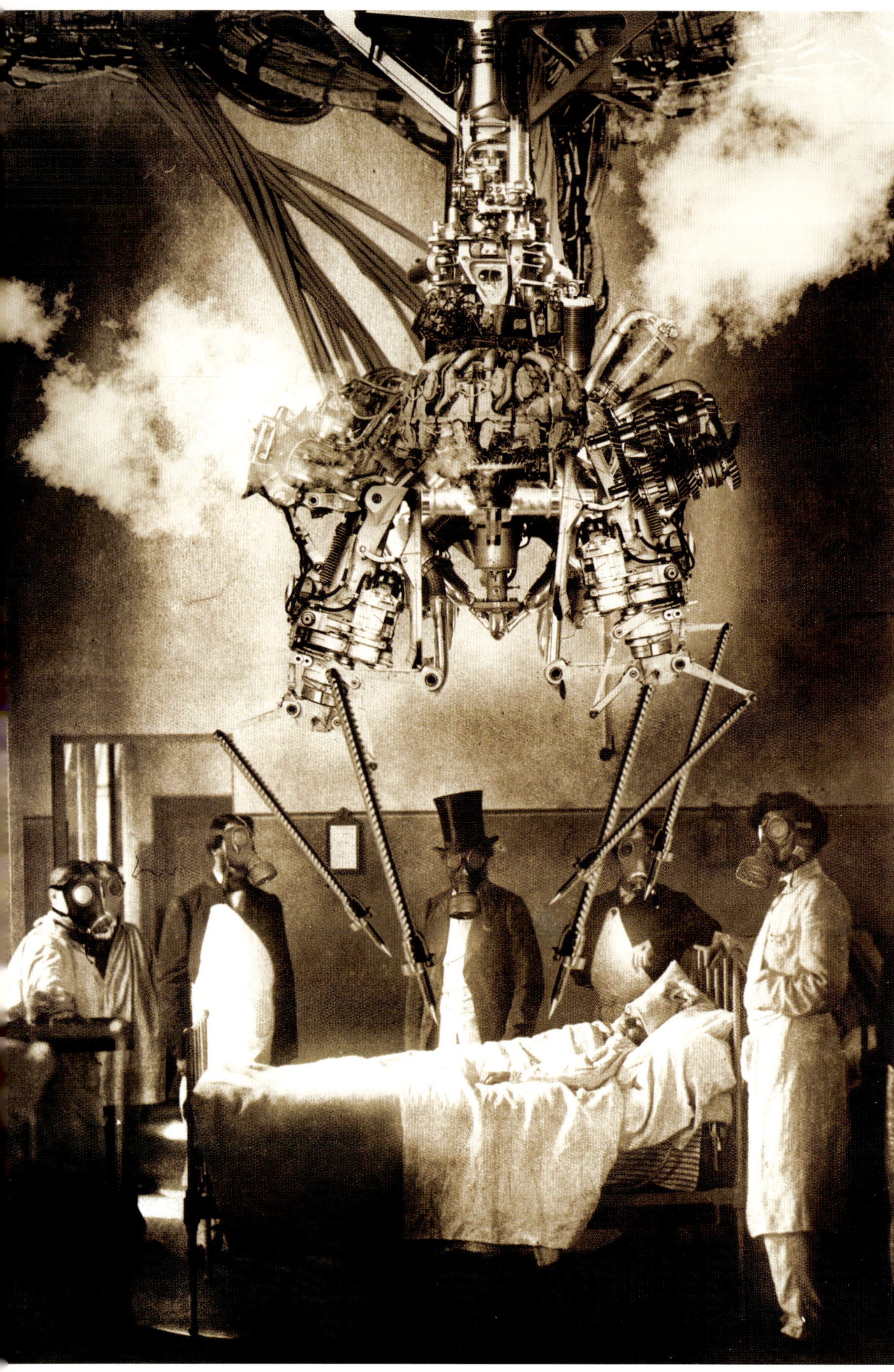

Left: *Dissecator,* 2007.

Right: *Chapelier* (Hatter), 2005.

Far Right: *Madame Bovary, Steampunk version*, 2007.

Below Right: *Chaoscopic Movie Stars: J.C.V.D.*, 2010.

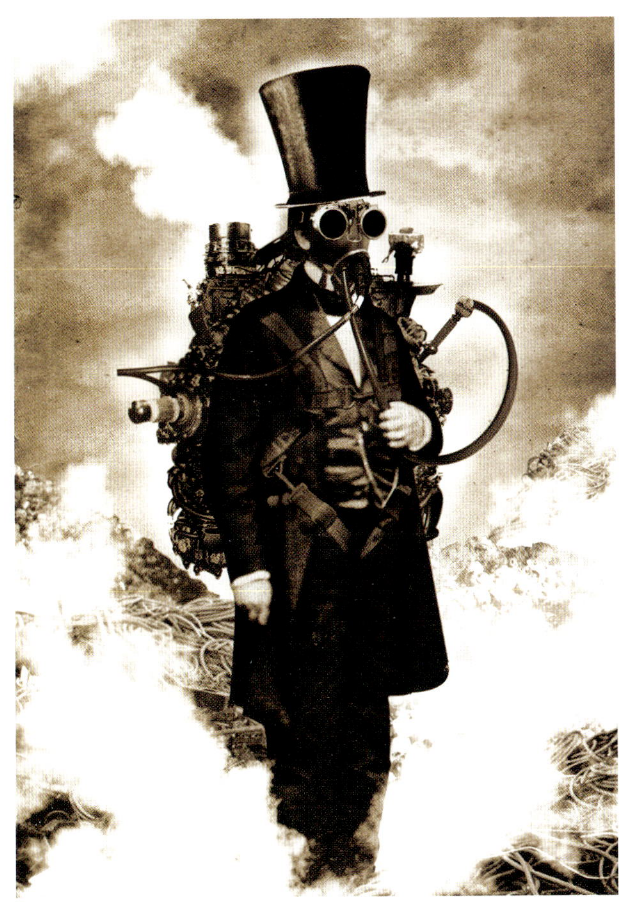

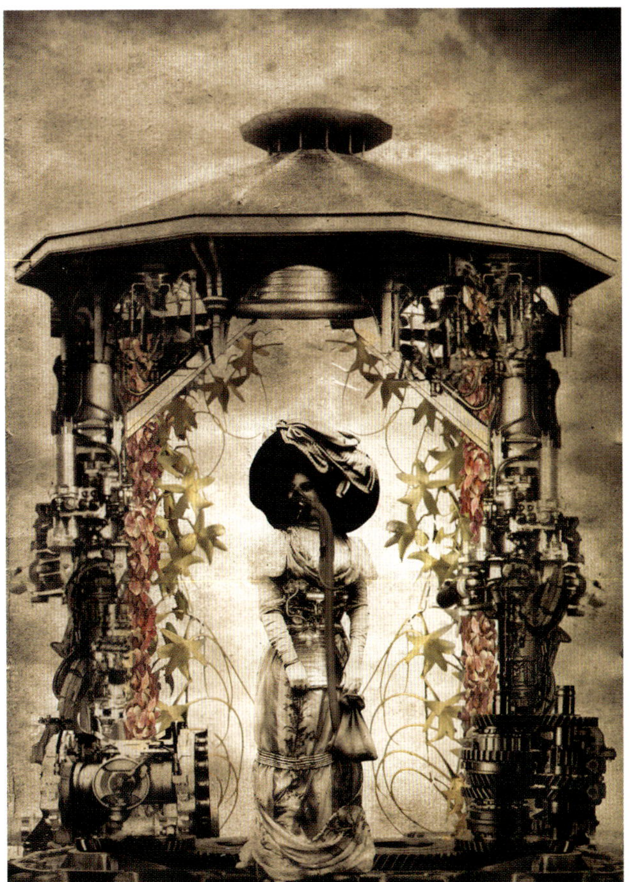

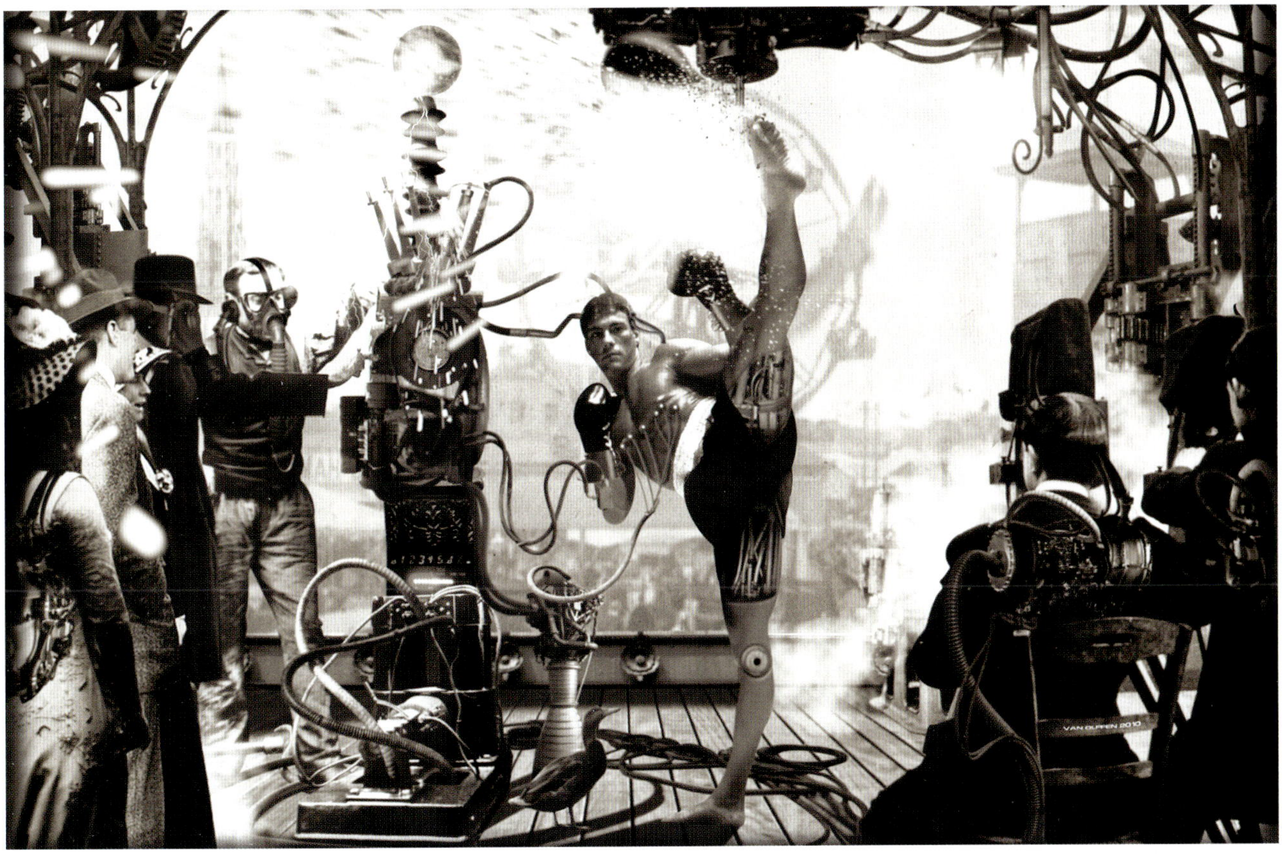

NOZOMU SHIBATA

Based in Aichi, Japan, Nozomu says of his work "My admiration is for mechanical objects that have a heartbeat, rather than for modern digital culture." At the age of 18, Nozomu was sent to an extraordinary school in Norway. Part of the training required that he build a sailing craft from trees he had felled himself: "that was a formative experience, living in nature and creating a work from nature's raw materials, having to sail a vessel I had made." Today he works mostly with sheet metal (usually copper, brass or tin) using hammers to raise the material, a process known in Japan as 'Tankin'. He then elaborates with found objects – clock parts, knives or old saucepans. The inspiration for his 'biomechanical' sculptures remains the natural world: "I decide on a series of motifs or themes and then try to add something original of my own. I want every piece to reflect my imagination and the sheer enjoyment of the creative process." Nozomu shows his work at the Yatsugatake Club and at the annual Matsumoto Craft Fair.

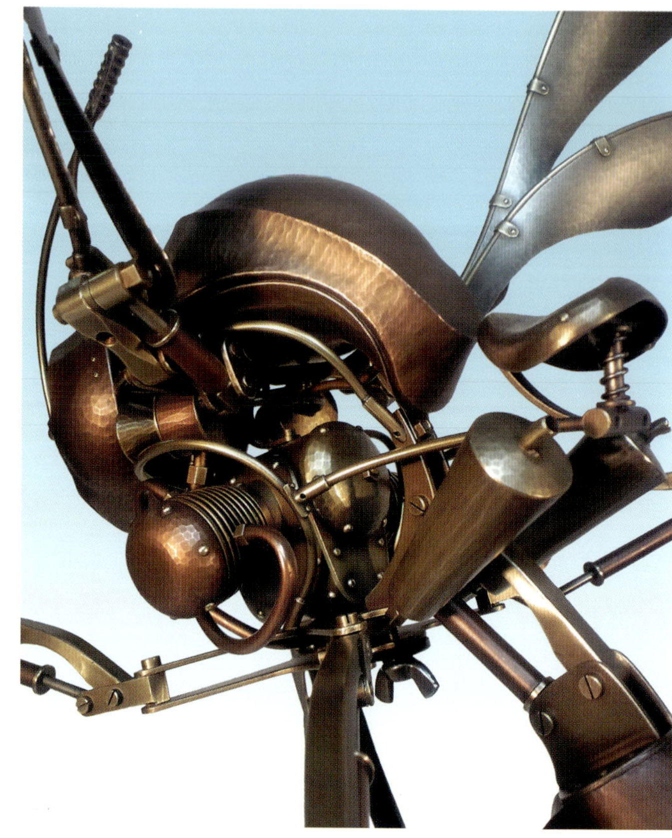

Right, Below and Far Right: *Beeke 6*, 2010. 17.6" x 27.3" x 21.5" (45 cm x 70 cm x 55 cm). Copper, brass and nickel.

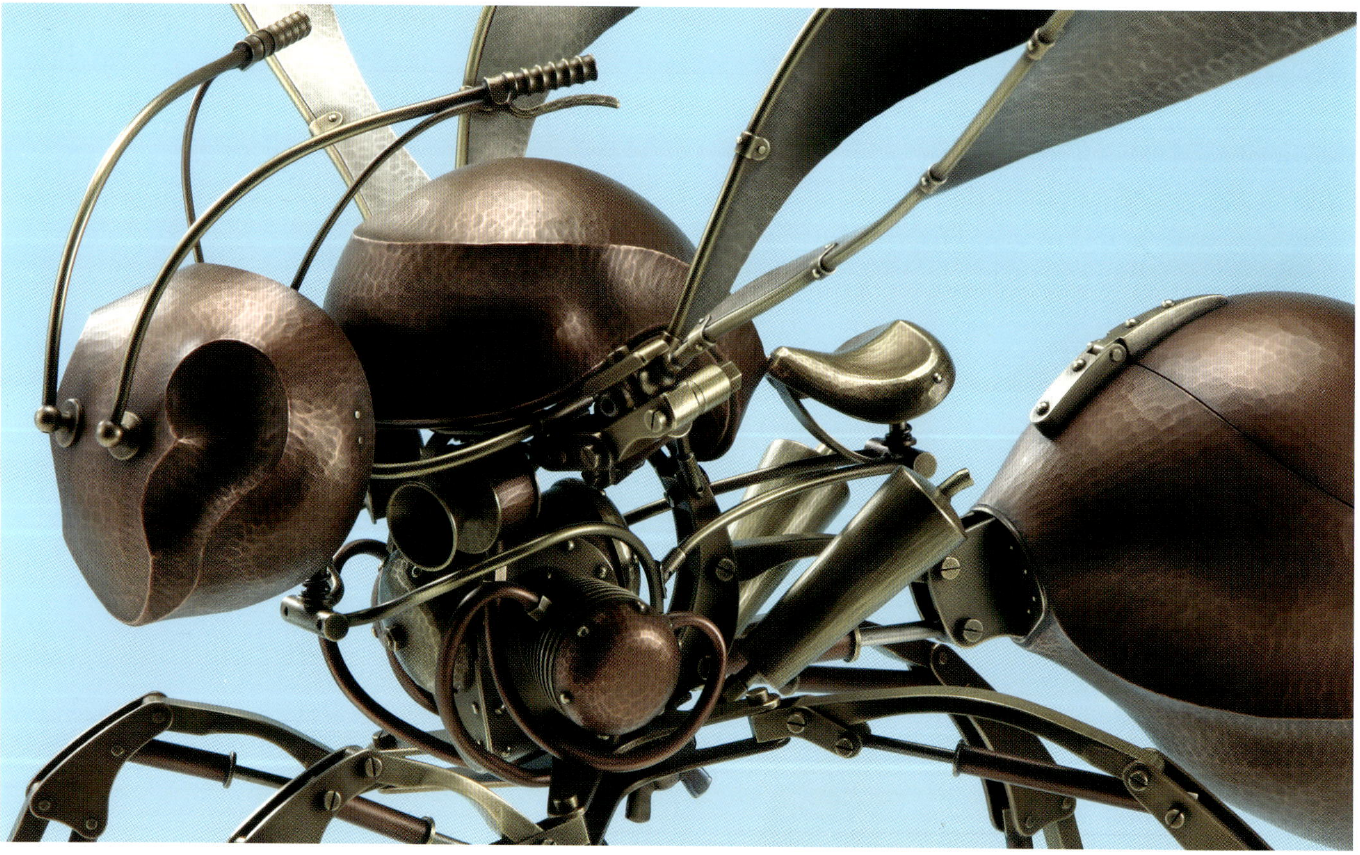

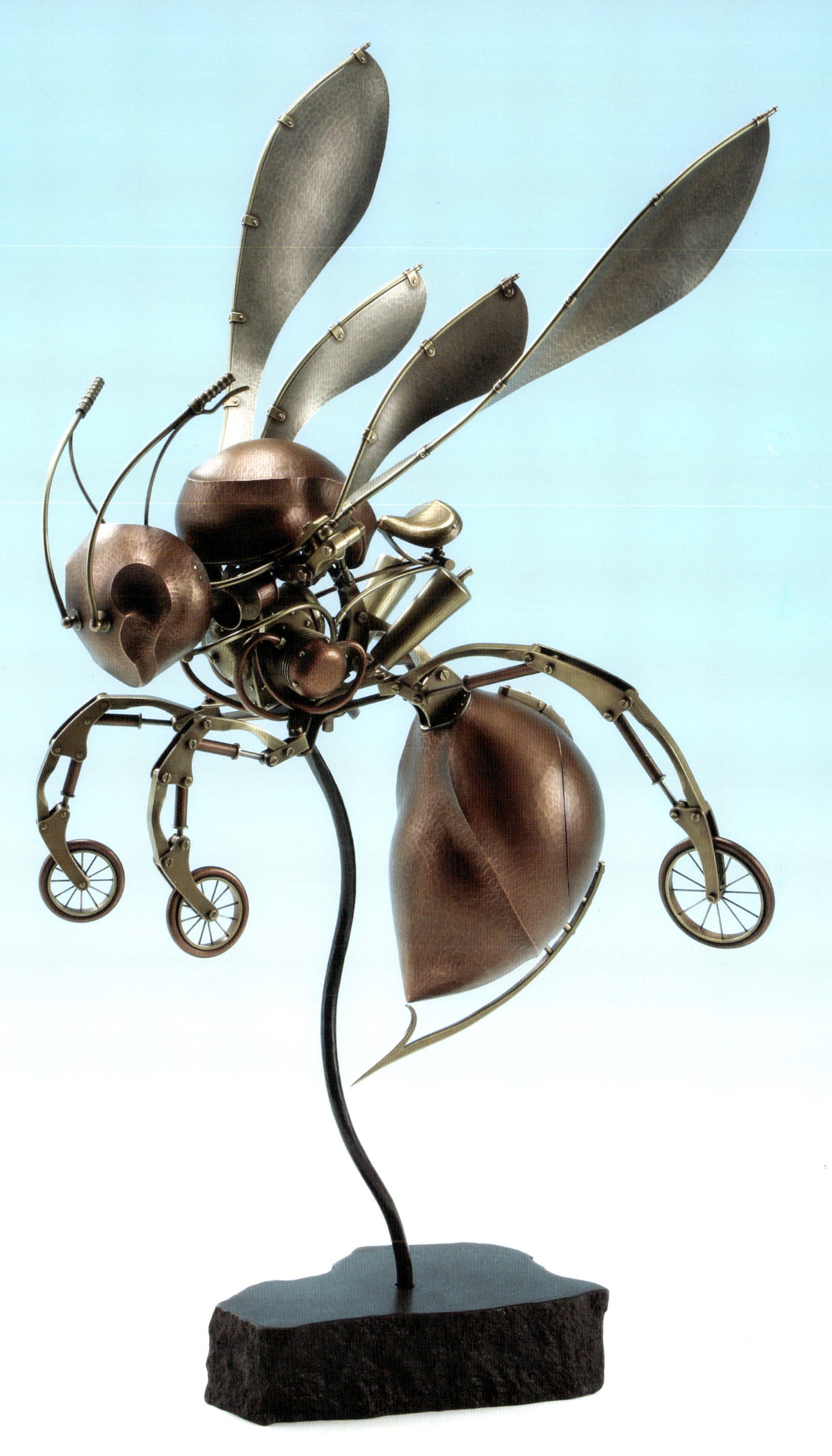

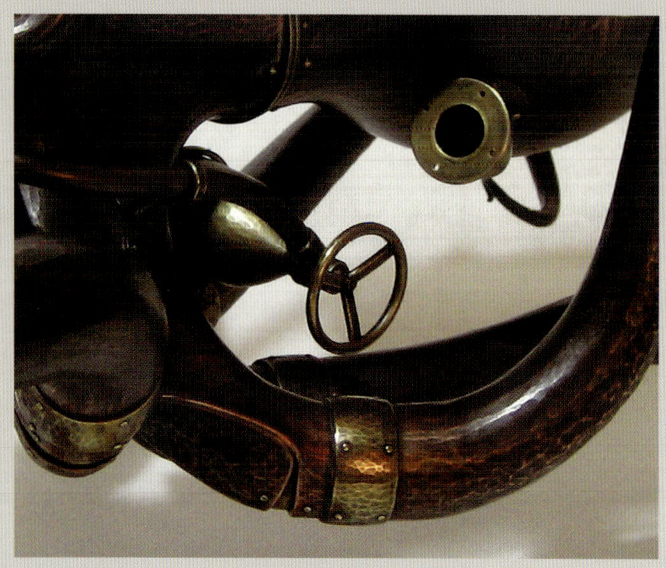

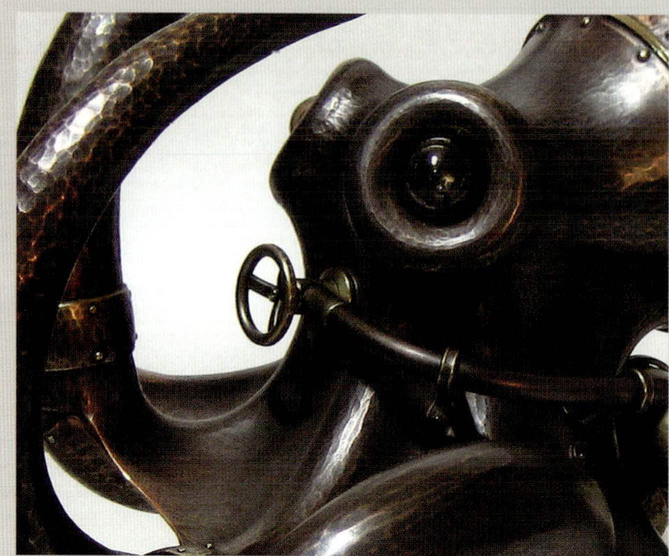

Above, Right and Below: *Top Heavy (Rise)*, 2008.
15.6" x 13.7" x 11.7" (40 cm x 35 cm x 30 cm). Copper, brass, glass and acrylic.

Far Right: *Top Heavy (Dive)*, 2008.
15.6" x 13.7" x 11.7" (40 cm x 35 cm x 30 cm). Copper, brass, glass and acrylic.

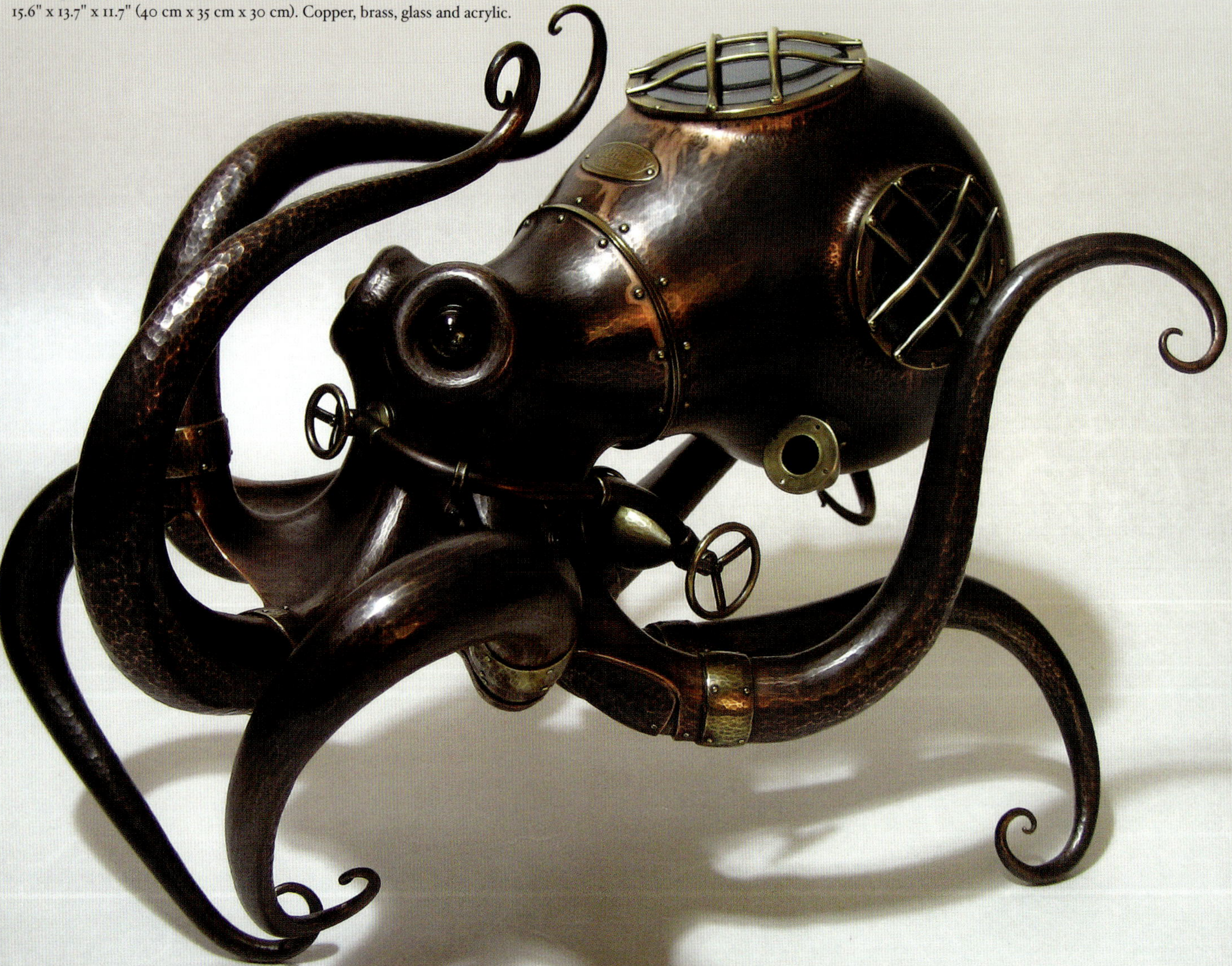

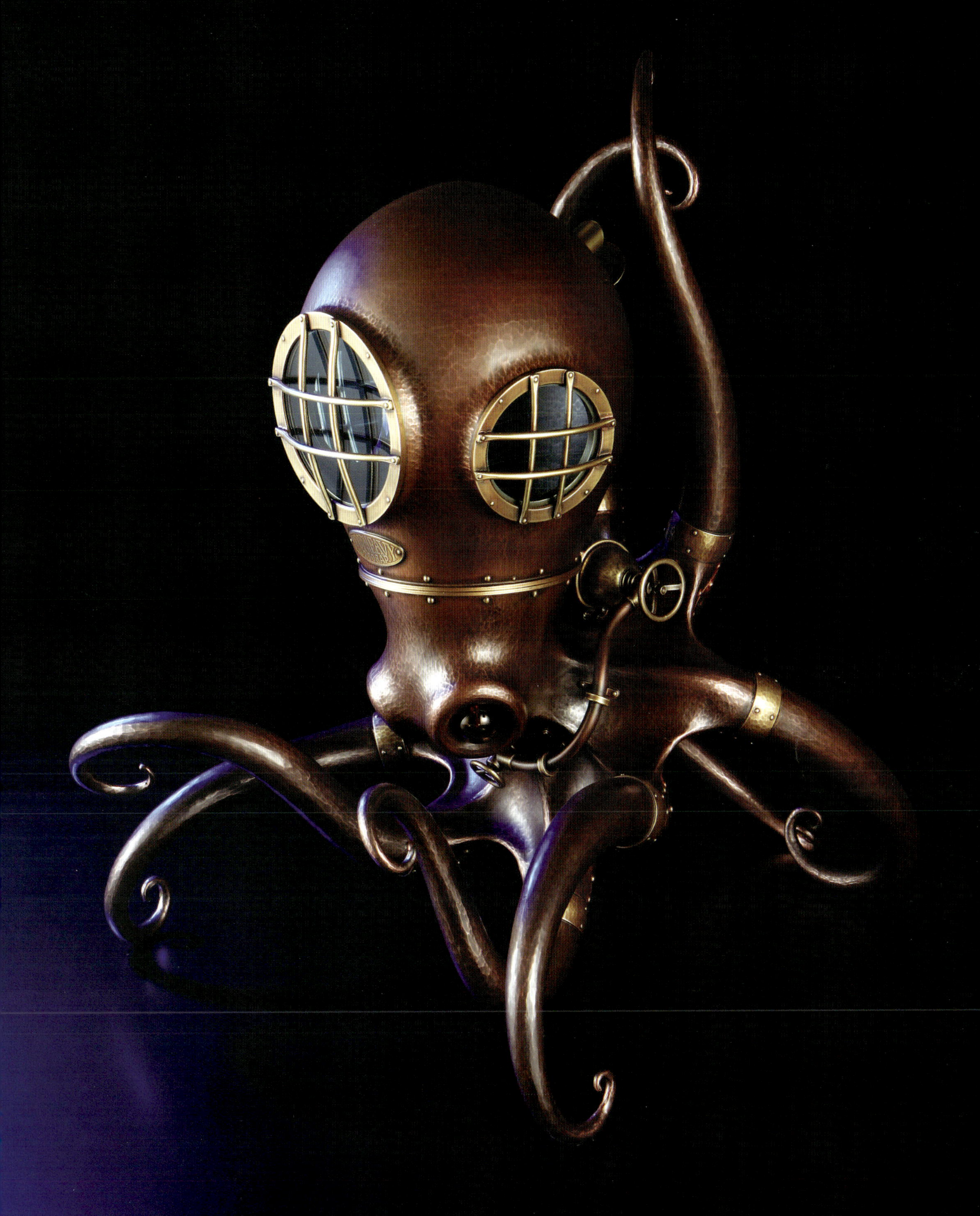

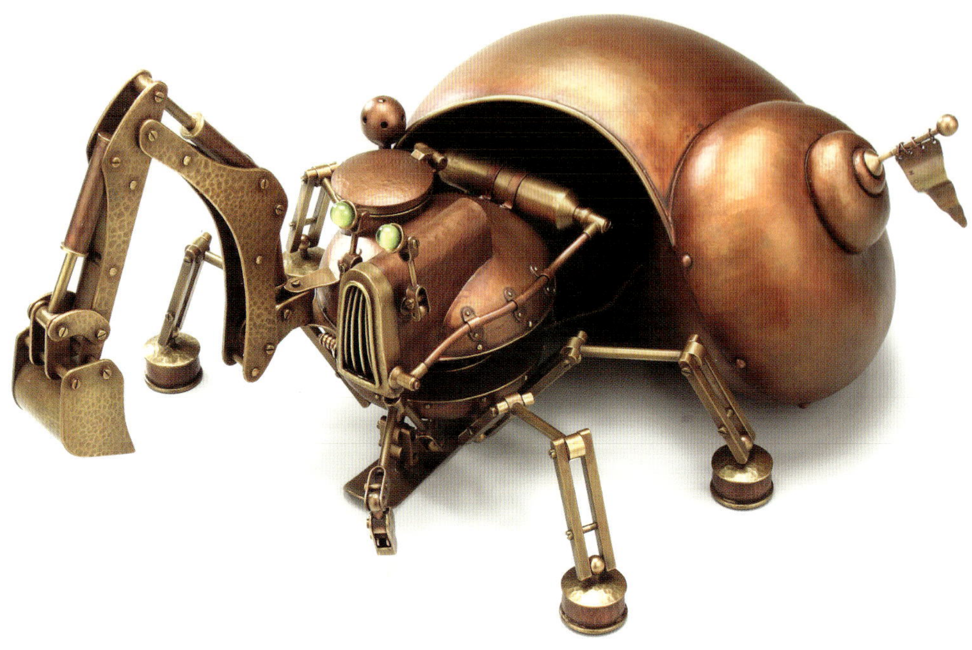

Above: *Yadokari Digger*, 2006. 15.6" x 15.6" x 9.75" (40 cm x 40 cm x 25 cm). Copper, brass and glass.

Below: *Yadokari Bulldozer*, 2006. 15.6" x 15.6" x 9.75" (40 cm x 40 cm x 25 cm). Copper, brass and glass.

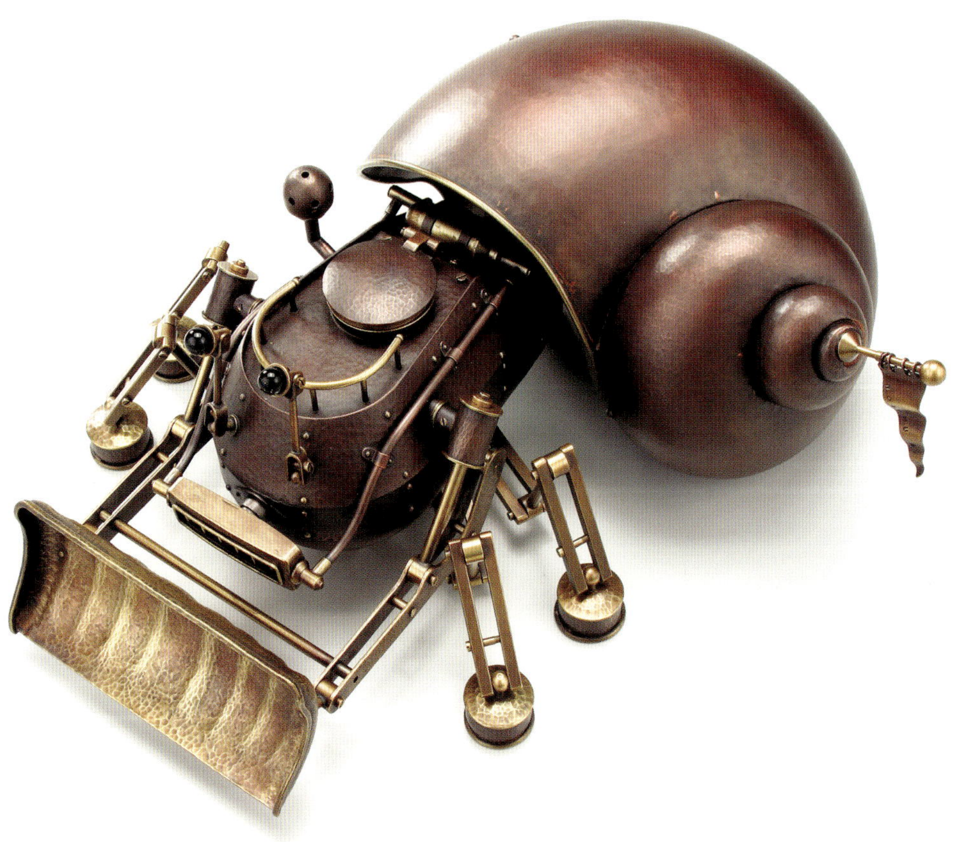

Right and Below: *One Million Leagues Under the Sea*, 2006.
21.5" x 25.4" x 13.7" (55 cm x 65 cm x 35 cm).
Copper, brass, glass and acrylic.

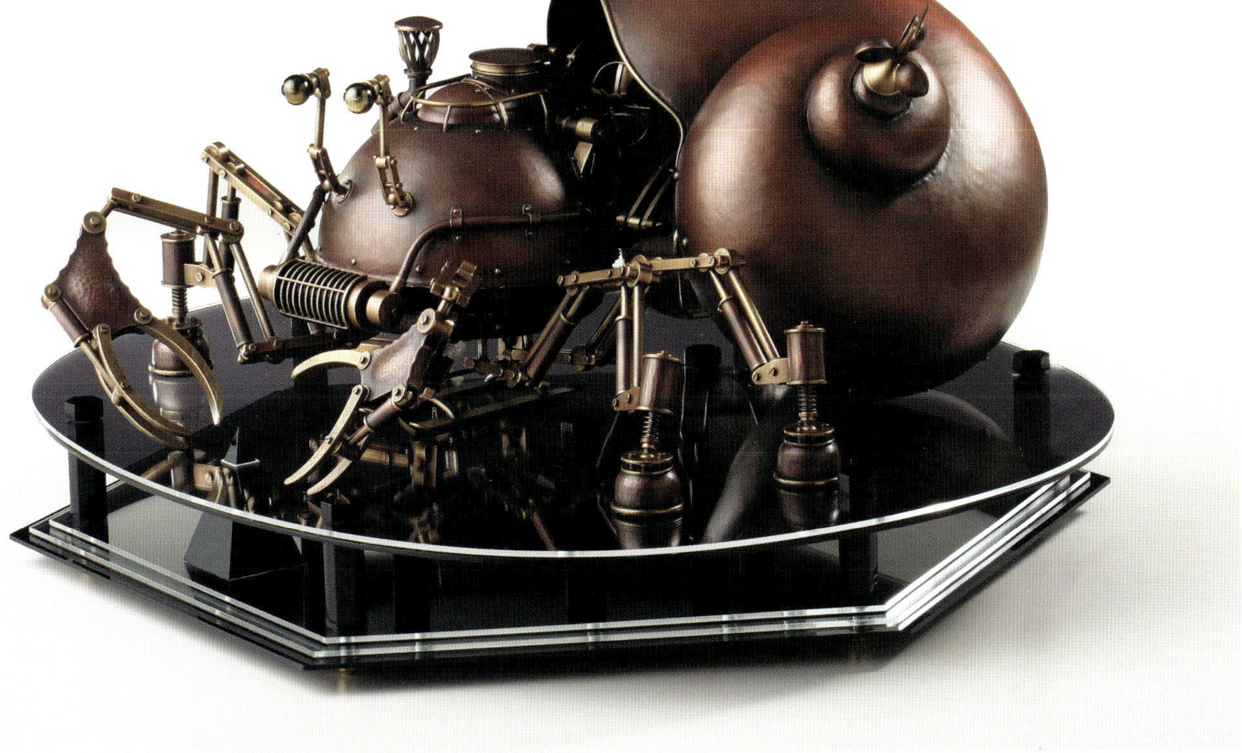

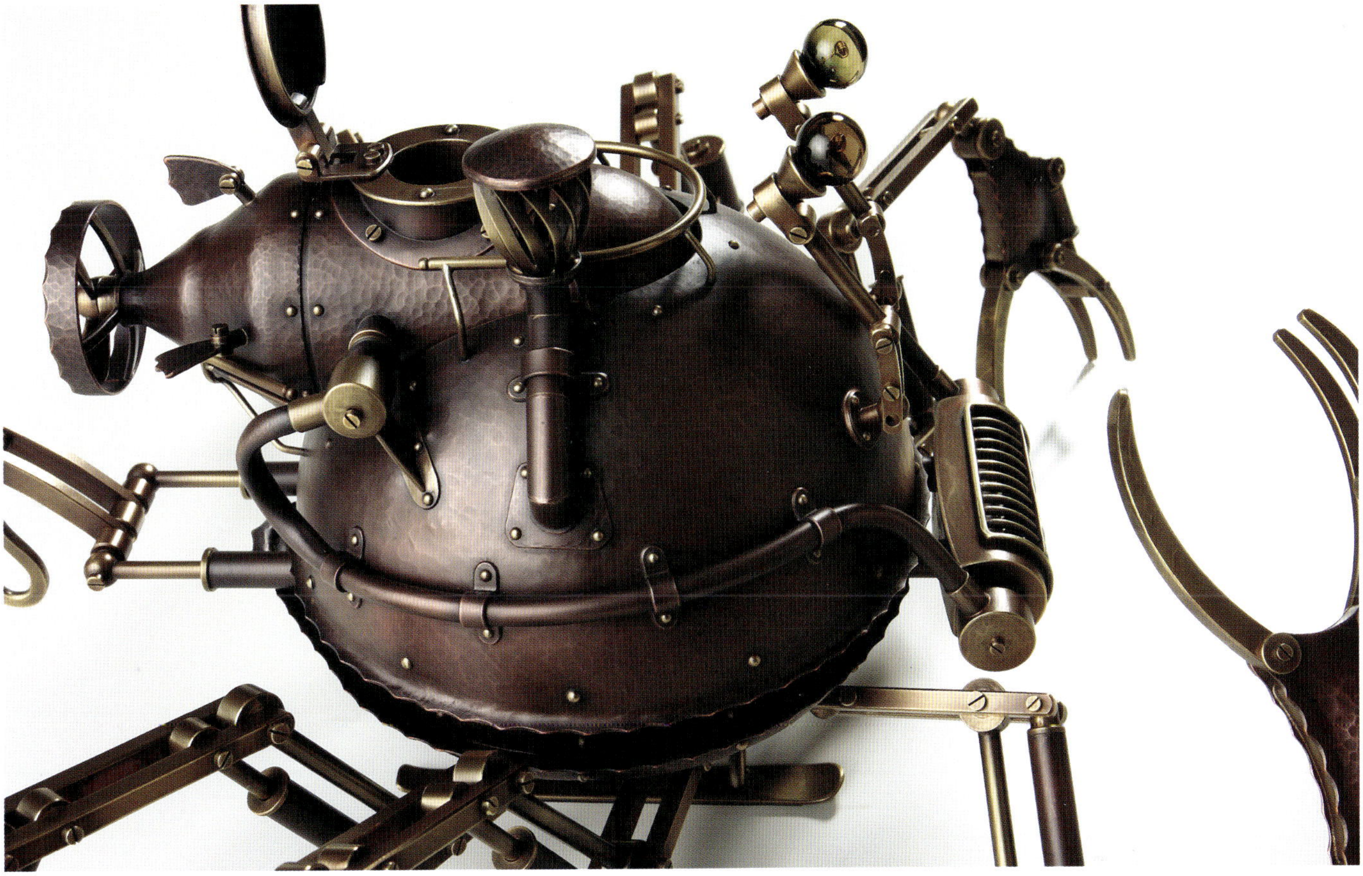

HARUO SUEKICHI

"I had never heard the word 'Steampunk' until some magazine introduced one of my pieces as a Steampunk watch", says Tokyo-based Haruo. As a child he used to read a Reiji Matsumoto comic called *Galaxy Express 999*, but other than that he can't point to any specifically Sci-fi influence. He makes watches because he loves making things – "the plan is there is no plan, my point of departure is looking for the fun in things." He trained at an industrial design school, worked for a while at a printing company, and then turned to his creations full-time, after first selling them at flea markets. Inspired by seeing a master watchmaker at work, Haruo makes everything from scratch, using brass, leather and working with a blowtorch; the only thing he buys in is the movement. "If my watches make people laugh or smile, or help a guy communicate on a date, I've achieved my aim" says Haruo. He now has an international following; in 2010 he was the only Japanese artist featured at the Oxford Steampunk Exhibition.

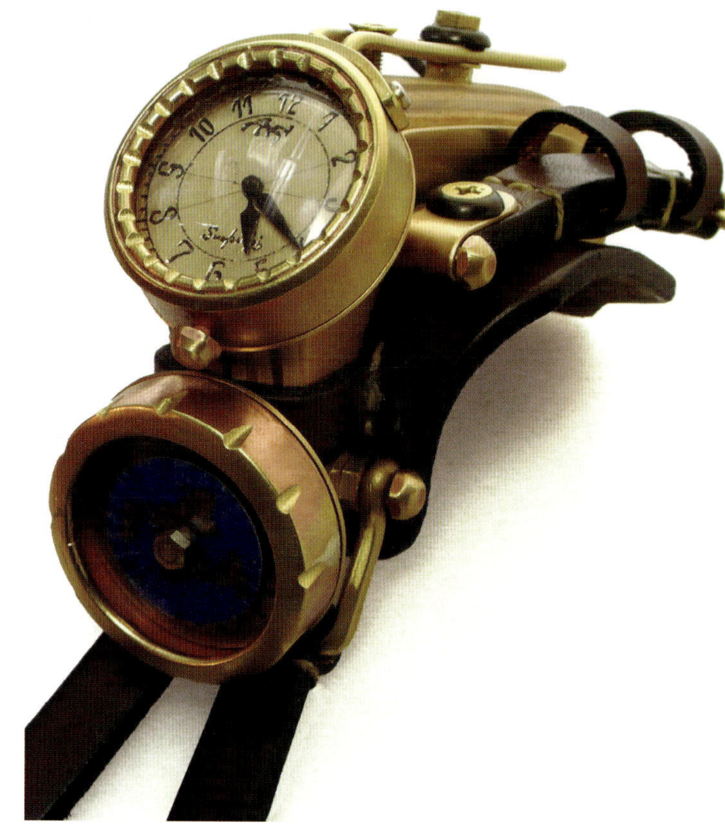

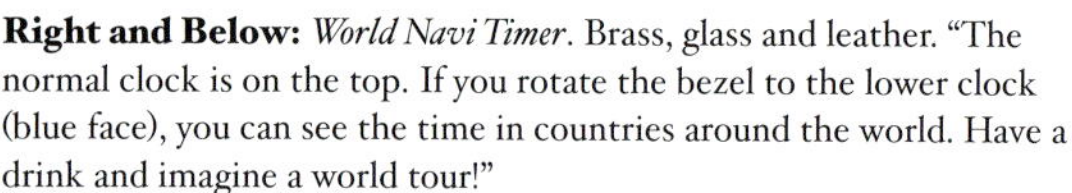

Right and Below: *World Navi Timer*. Brass, glass and leather. "The normal clock is on the top. If you rotate the bezel to the lower clock (blue face), you can see the time in countries around the world. Have a drink and imagine a world tour!"

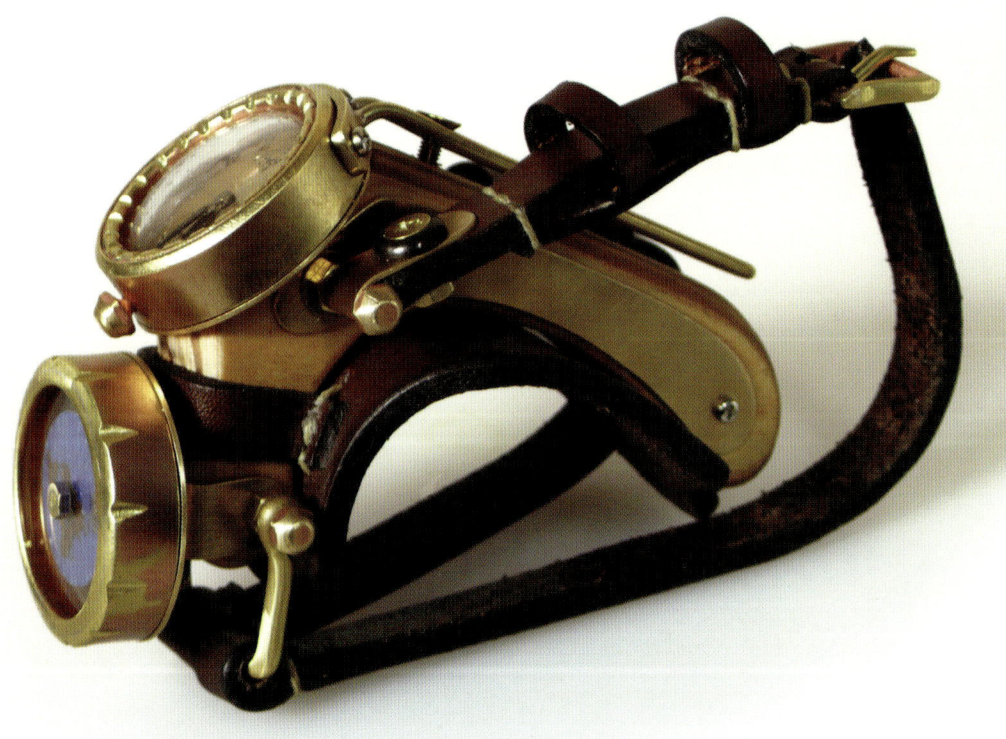

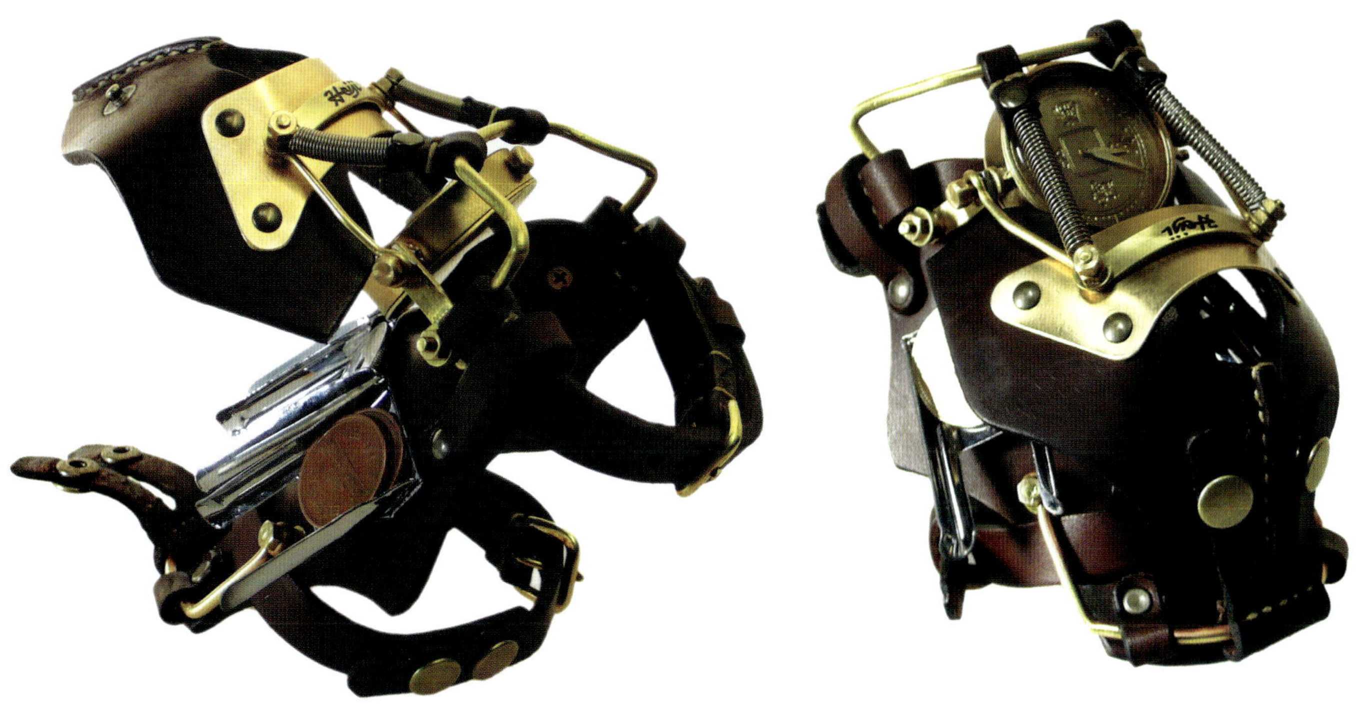

Above and Below: *Heiji*. Brass, leather and glass.
"Zenigata-Heiji were civilian police more than two hundred years ago. I imagined a Heiji when making this watch."

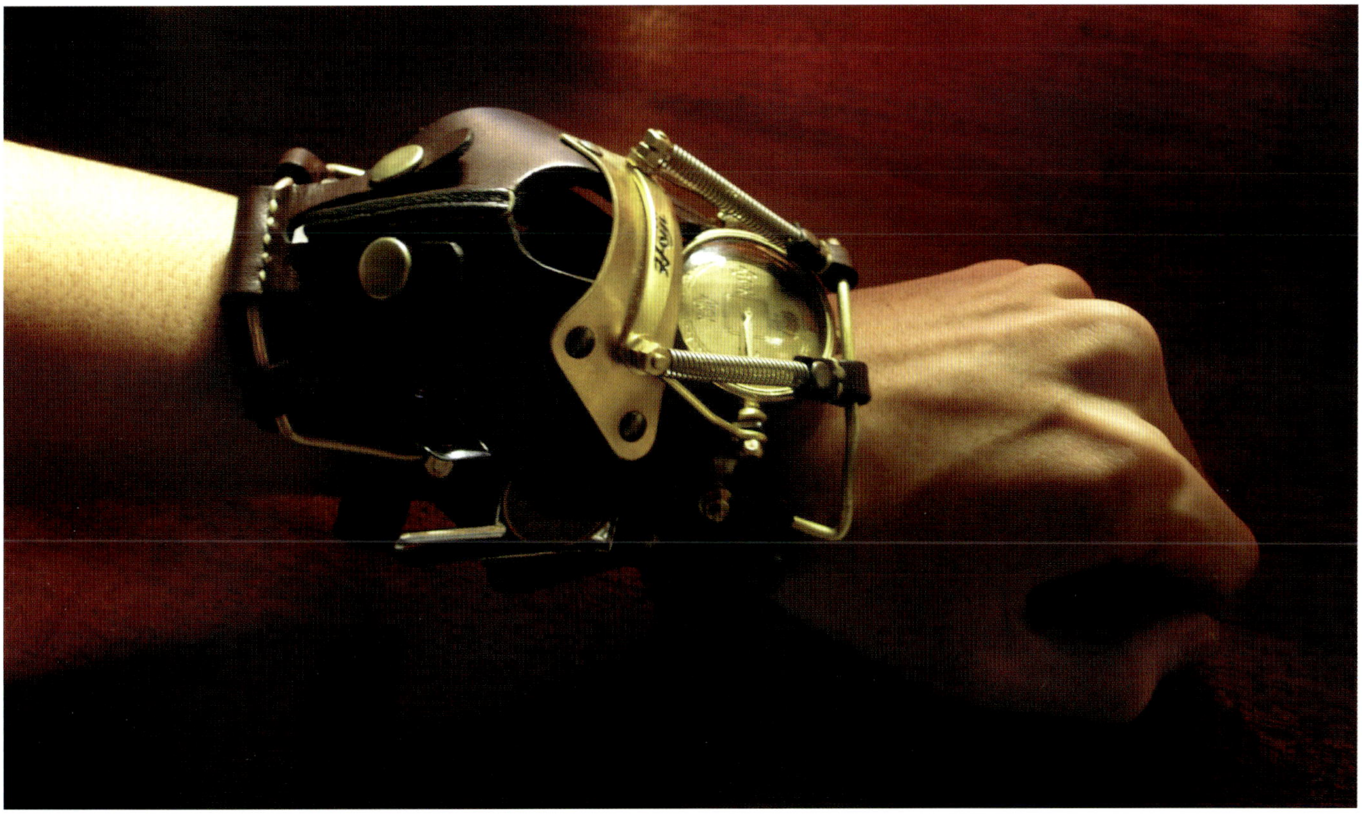

Below: *Toto*. Brass, wood, glass and leather. "Inpired by Toto, Japan's most famous manufacturer of lavatories. The lid mechanism opens in a similar way to a toilet. Japanese toilets are the world's best."

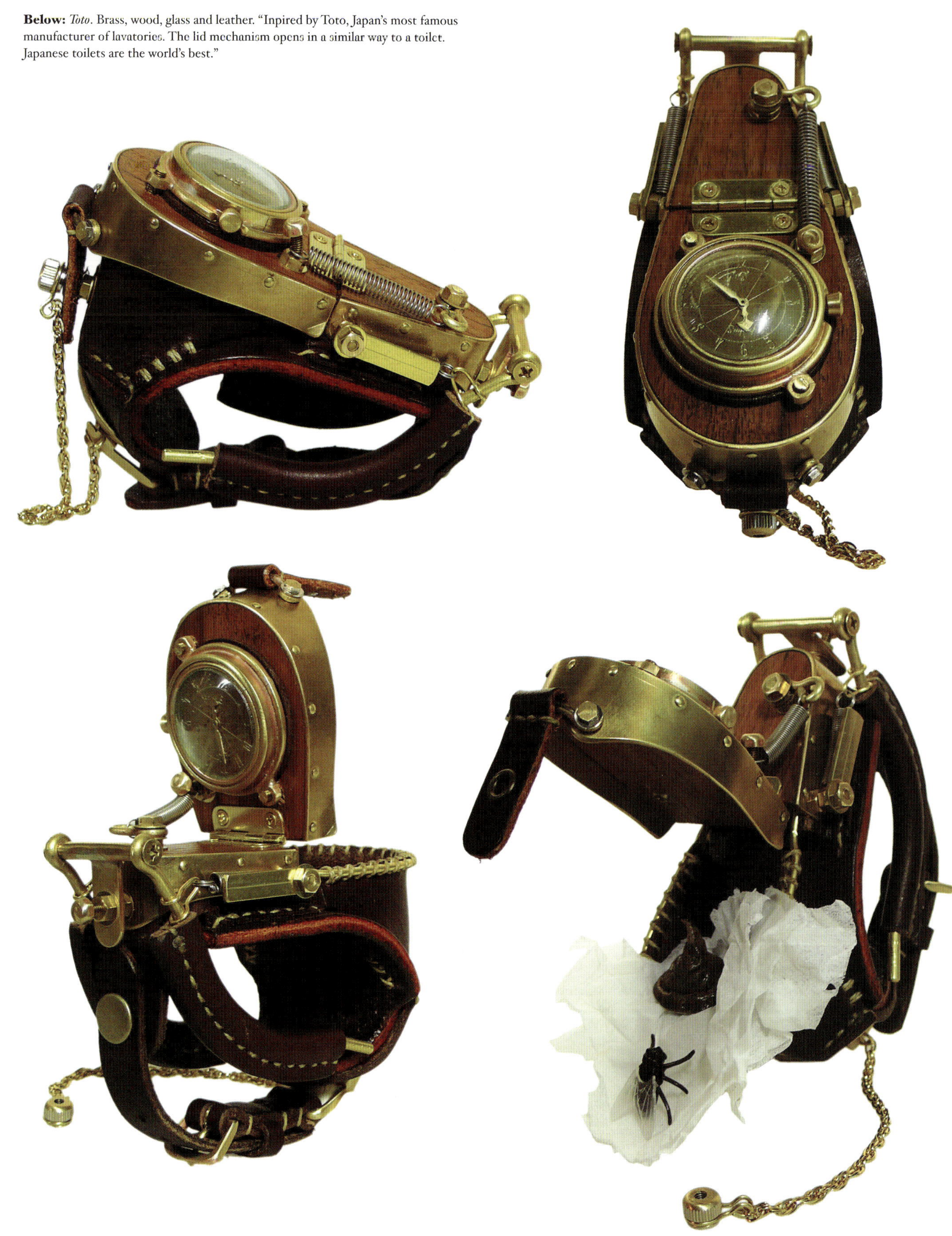

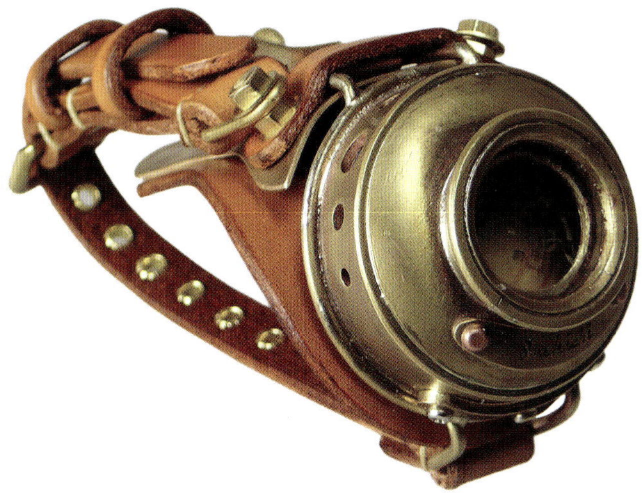

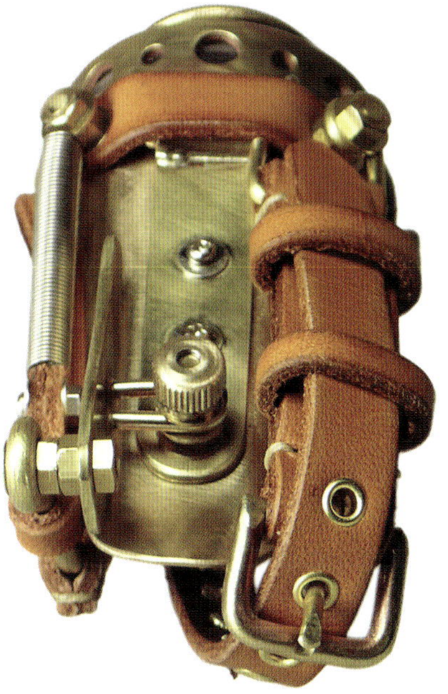

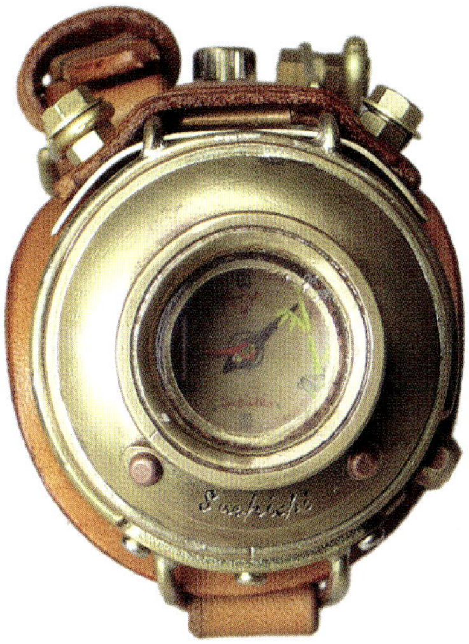

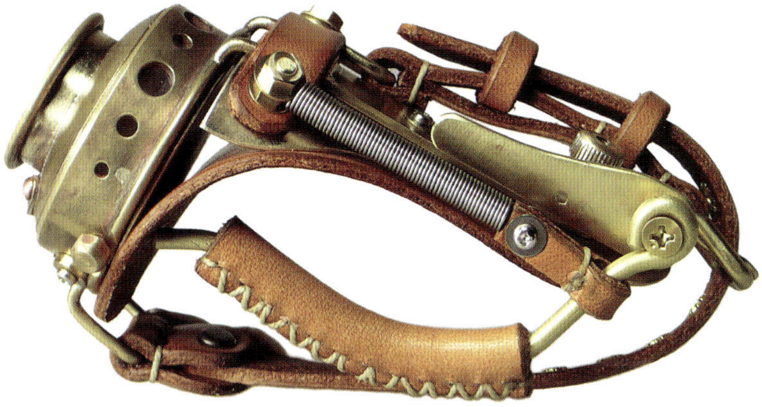

Above and Below: *Peephole*. Brass, leather, steel and glass. "One day, I was drinking in a bar and some foreigners asked me "what is your profession?" I answered, "I am watch-man." Everyone laughed and laughed. So, the theme of this watch is a peephole."

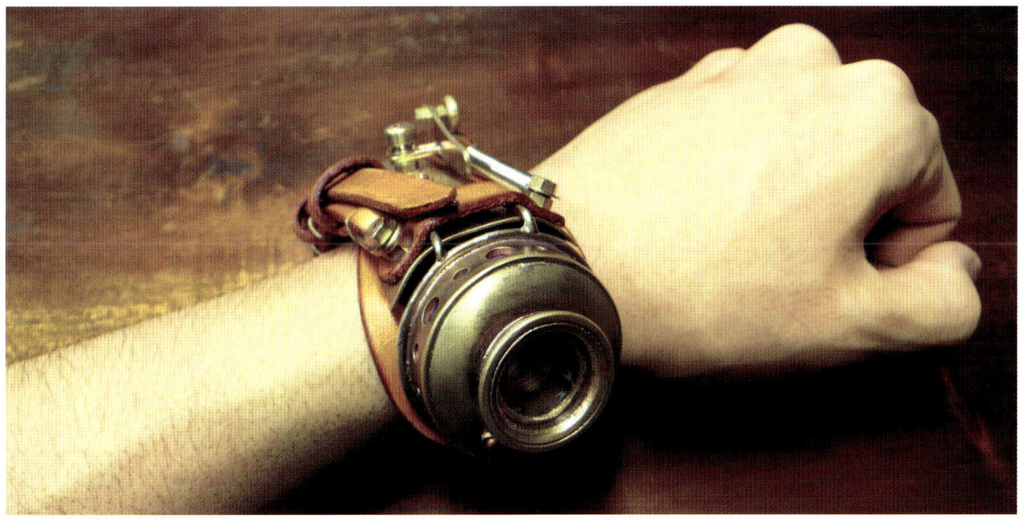

BRIAN POOR

Growing up among the sequoia forests and rugged coast of northern California allowed Brian to spend "many a rainy afternoon tinkering and creating in my father's and grandfather's workshops." At Humboldt State University he studied electronic technology and gained a BA in studio arts, followed by a decade working for the Film and TV industry as a conceptual illustrator and animatronics designer of robots and monsters. His credits include *Mimic*, *Species II*, *Virus* and *A.I.* and he created many creatures for Disney Imagineering. In the meantime Brian was honing his art and developing his theories about art and technology. He has a fascination with robotics. "At a primal level we are hard-wired to respond to other creatures...technology has created a whole new form of being with which we must contend: robots." His art, which uses technology to "breathe life into my creations" is devoted to exploring this relationship. For Brian, this is the extension of a long tradition: "The Greeks used steam and water to move statues, Da Vinci created mechanical animals and European clock makers in the Eighteenth Century delighted in creating automata."

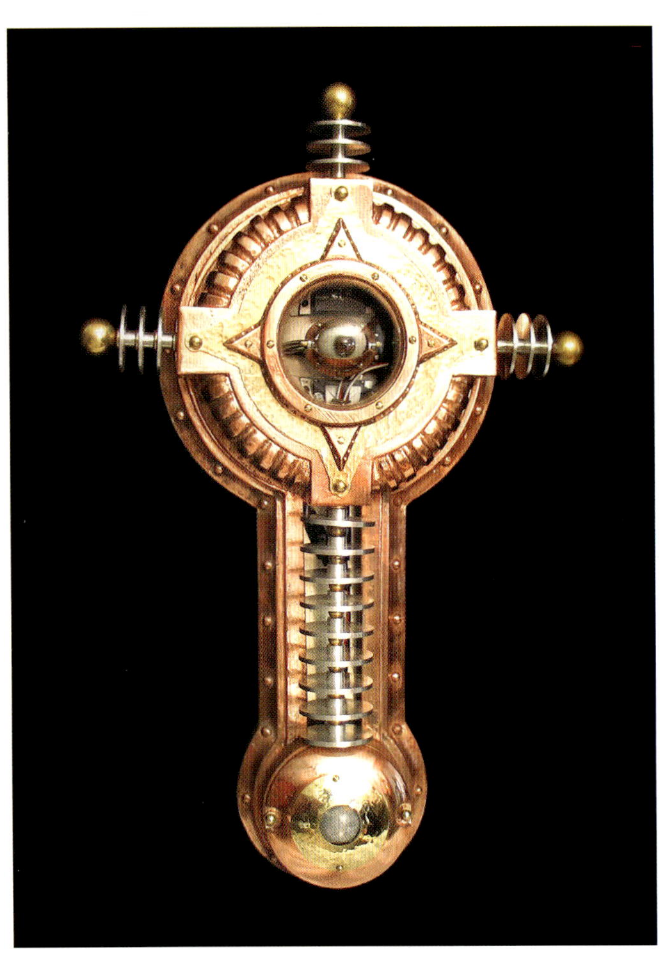

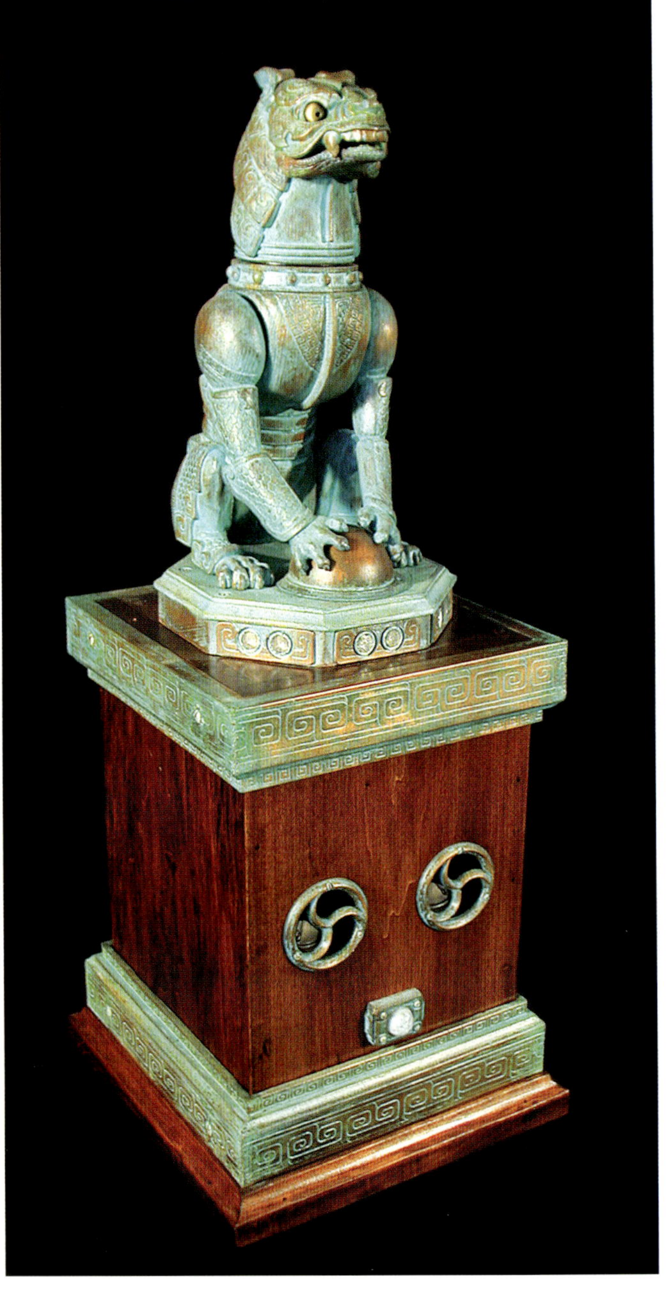

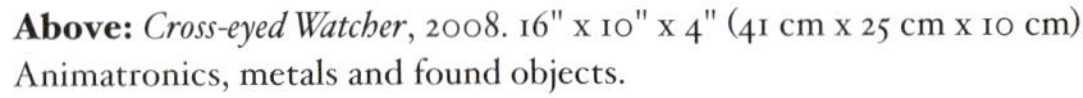

Above: *Cross-eyed Watcher*, 2008. 16" x 10" x 4" (41 cm x 25 cm x 10 cm).
Animatronics, metals and found objects.
Functionality: antique glass eye looks around in response to movement.

Right: *Foo Dog Intercom*, 2002. 33" x 11" x 11" (84 cm x 28 cm x 28 cm).
Animatronics, metals and cast resin.
Functionality: head and eyes track movement, jaw syncs with audio signal.

Far Right Top: *Ocular Bot*, 2007. 12" x 6" x 6" (31 cm x 15 cm x 15 cm).
Animatronics, metal and found objects.
Functionality: Antique glass eye looks around in response to movement.

Far Right: *Aqua Bot*, 2008. 11" x 11" x 9" (28 cm x 28 cm x 23 cm).
Animatronics, metals and found objects.
Functionality: Antique glass eye looks around in response to movement.

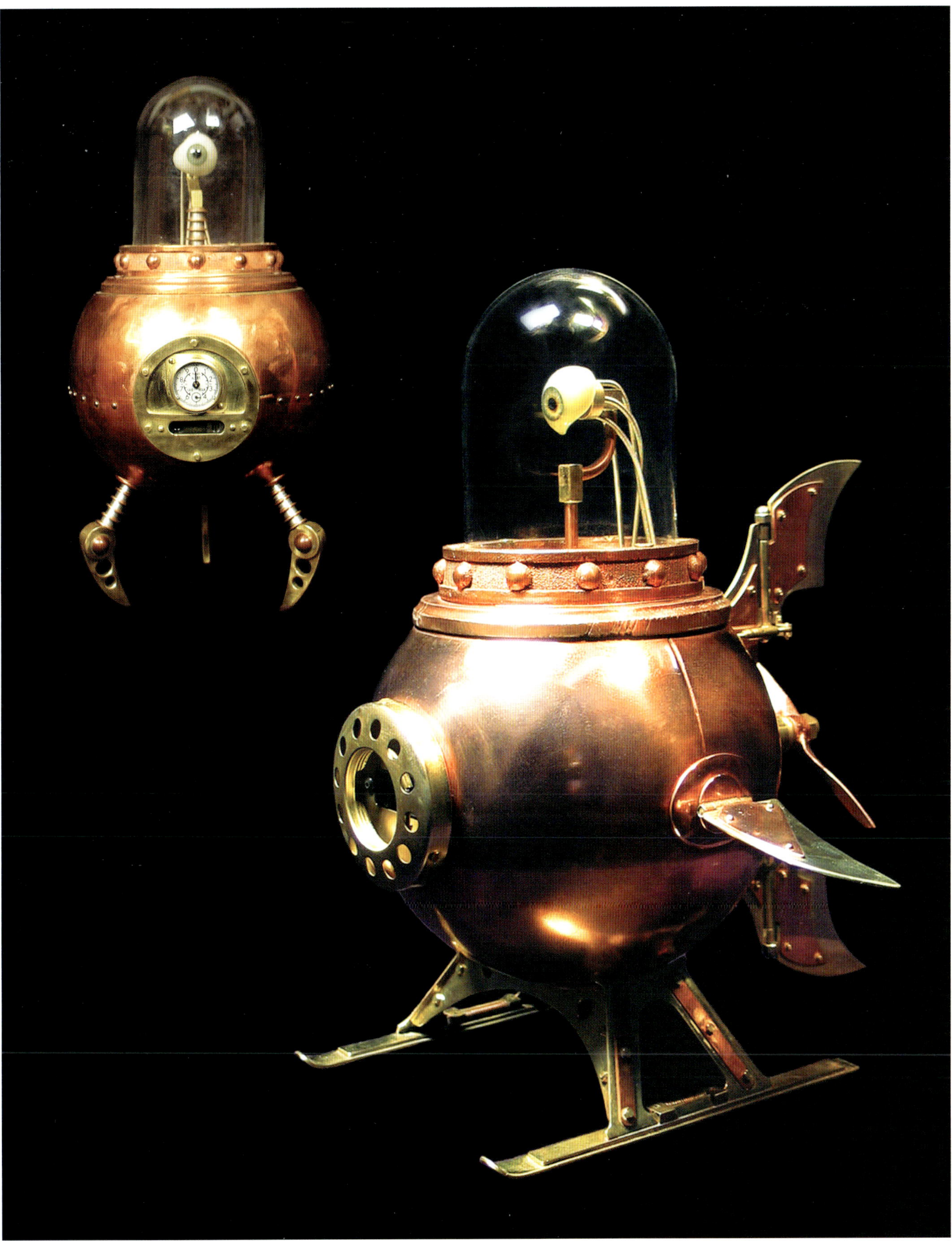

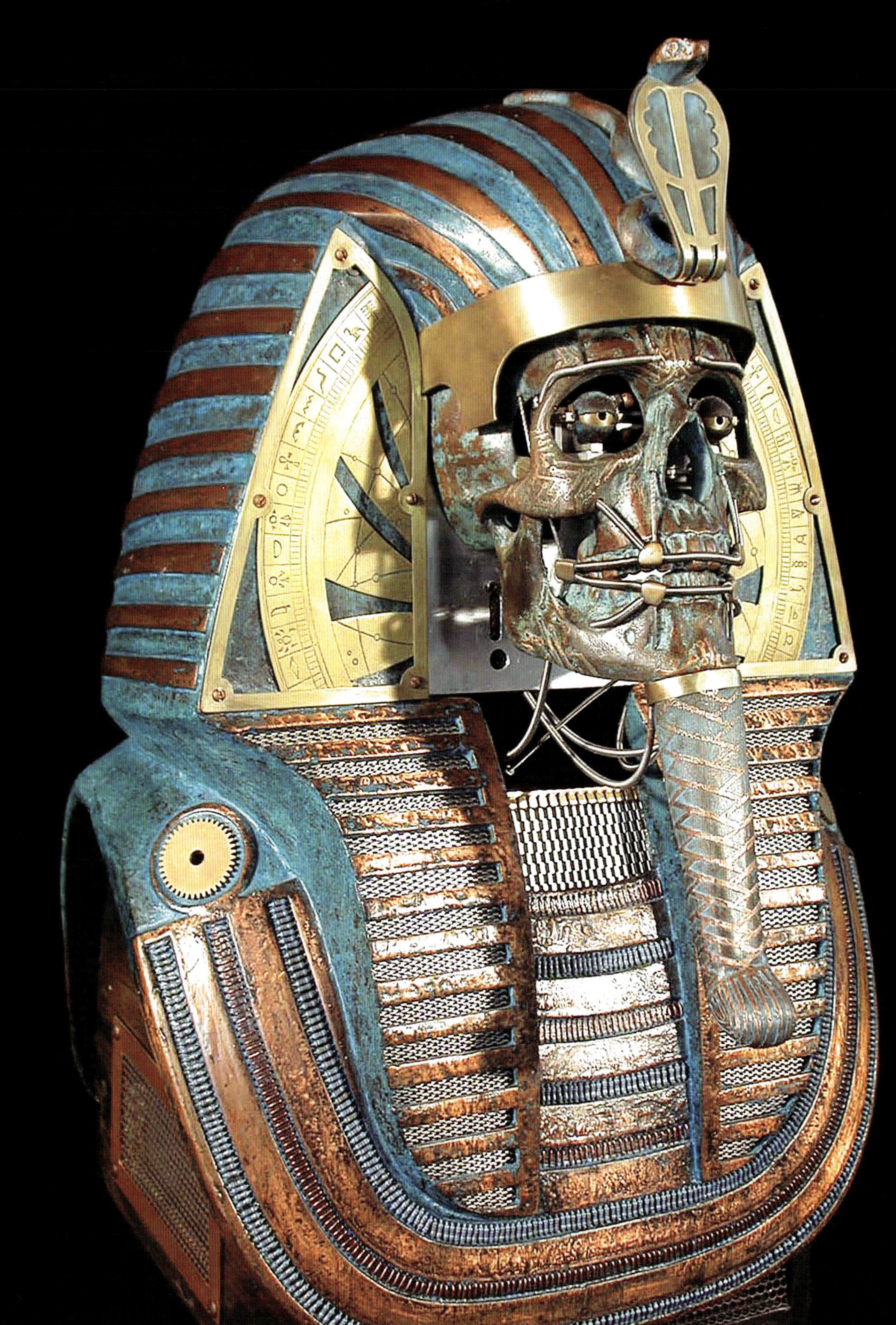

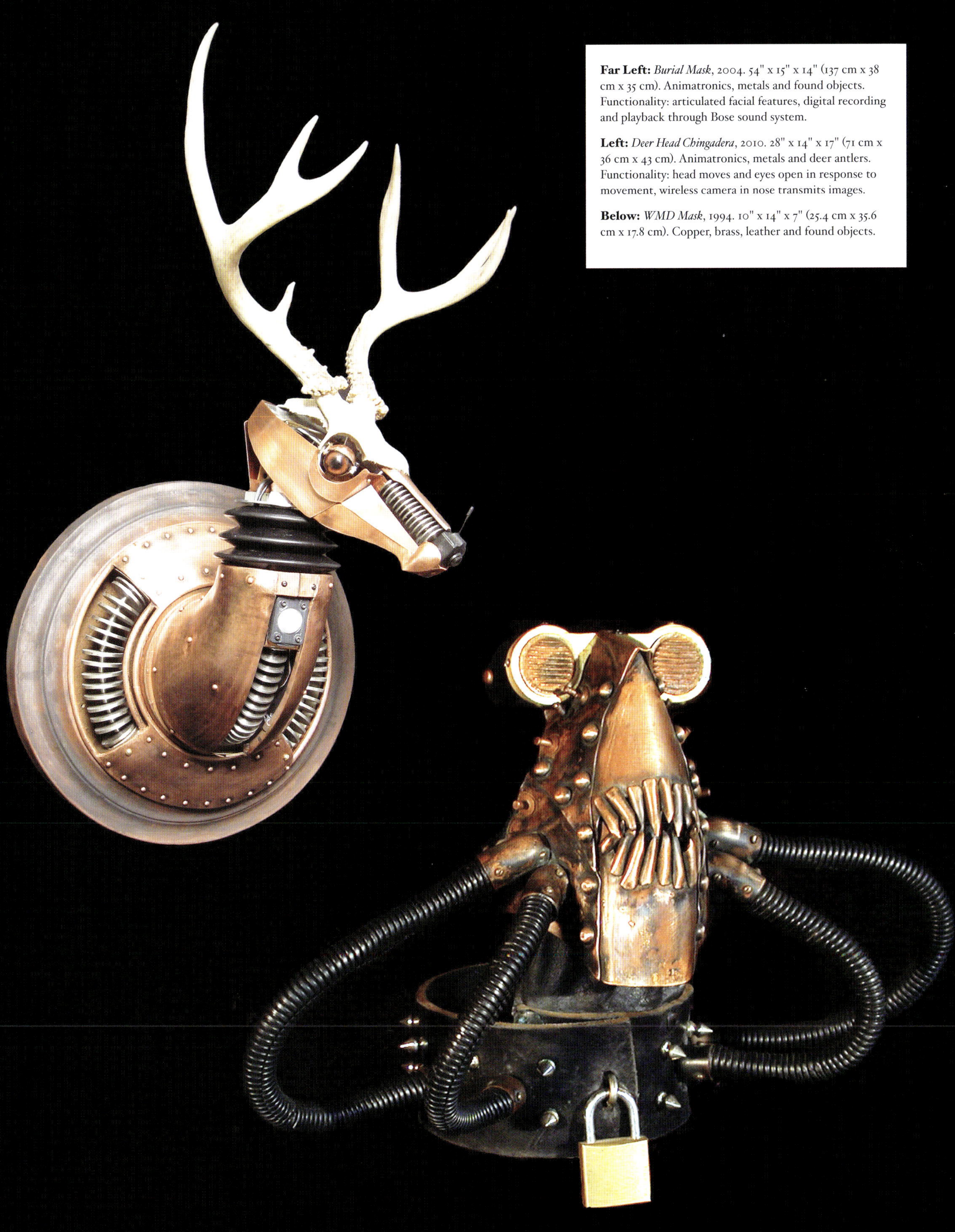

Far Left: *Burial Mask*, 2004. 54" x 15" x 14" (137 cm x 38 cm x 35 cm). Animatronics, metals and found objects. Functionality: articulated facial features, digital recording and playback through Bose sound system.

Left: *Deer Head Chingadera*, 2010. 28" x 14" x 17" (71 cm x 36 cm x 43 cm). Animatronics, metals and deer antlers. Functionality: head moves and eyes open in response to movement, wireless camera in nose transmits images.

Below: *WMD Mask*, 1994. 10" x 14" x 7" (25.4 cm x 35.6 cm x 17.8 cm). Copper, brass, leather and found objects.

DANIEL PROULX

Montreal-based Daniel was always interested in "imaginary fantasy worlds such as Dungeons and Dragons, *The Lord of the Rings* and Science Fiction in general." These remain an inspiration, as well as his fascination with mixing organic and mechanical shapes, and contrasting futuristic with ancient designs. Daniel stumbled on jewellery-making after his partner, Catherine, had been on a ring-making course, and he began creating retro-futuristic designs. He discovered the sub-culture that is Steampunk only when a friend told him he was working in that vein. A lot of press attention followed, allowing Daniel to devote himself to creating jewellery and sculptures full time. He is fearful that the growing fashion for Steampunk will turn it mass-market: "Then it won't be real Steampunk – a mass-produced object can, by definition, never be Steampunk."

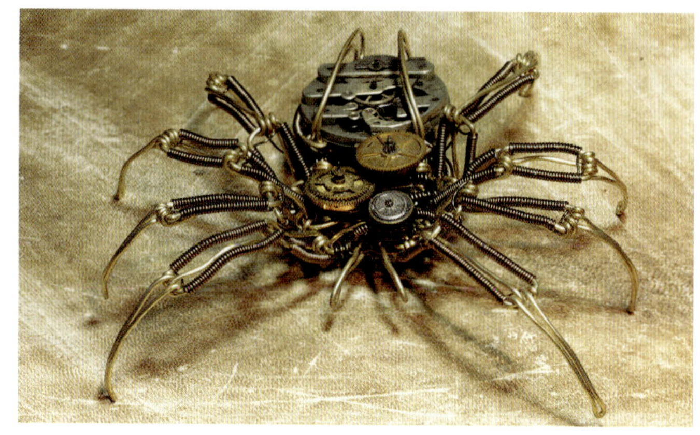

Above: *Spider*. Brass, brass springs and clock parts.

Right Top: *Kabuto Mushi* (Japanese Rhinoceros Beetle). Brass, brass springs, clock parts and glass eye.

Right Below: *Crab Robot*. Brass, springs and clock parts.

Below: *Pseudo-spider Robot*. Brass, brass springs, clock parts and copper 'taxidermy' glass eye.

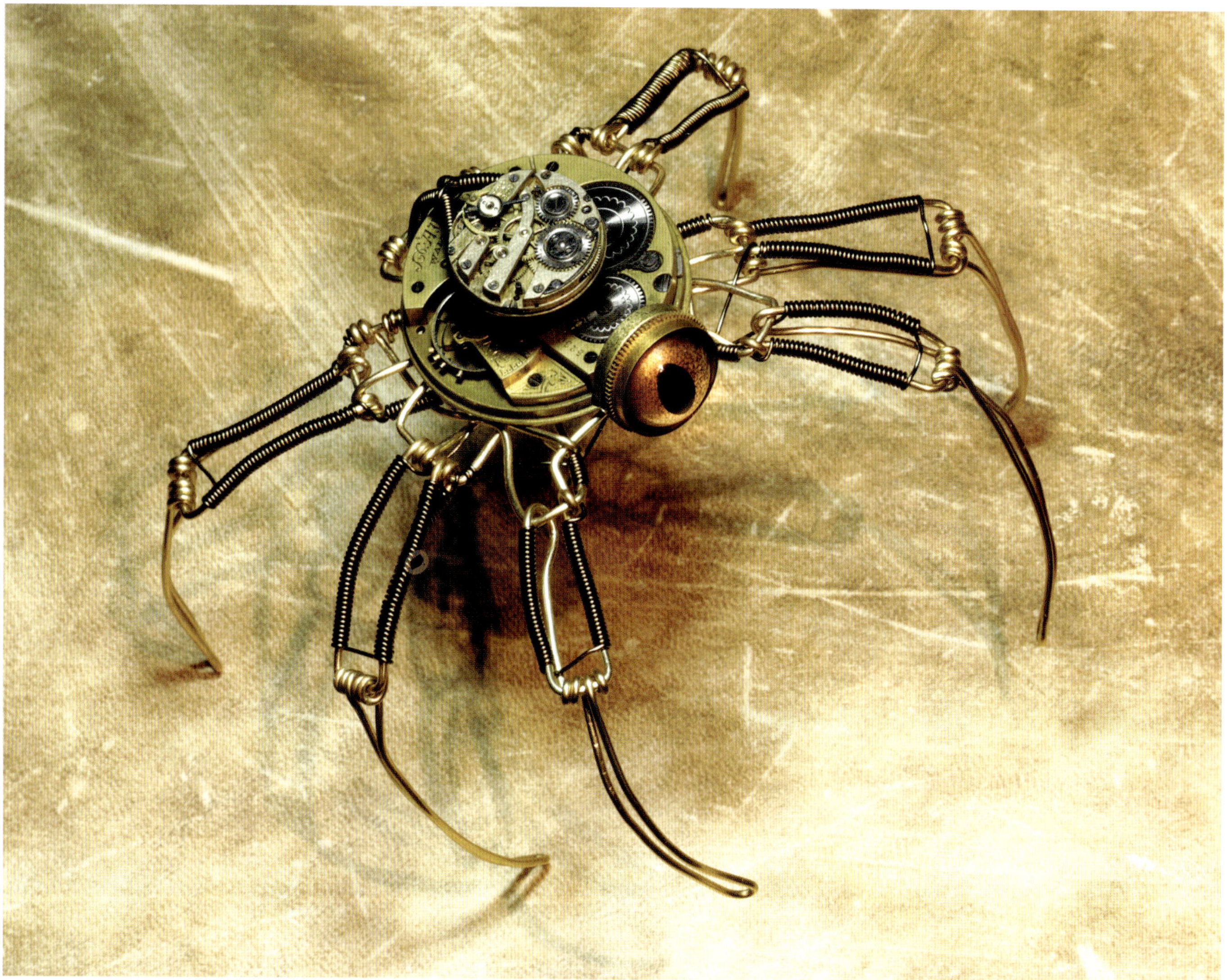

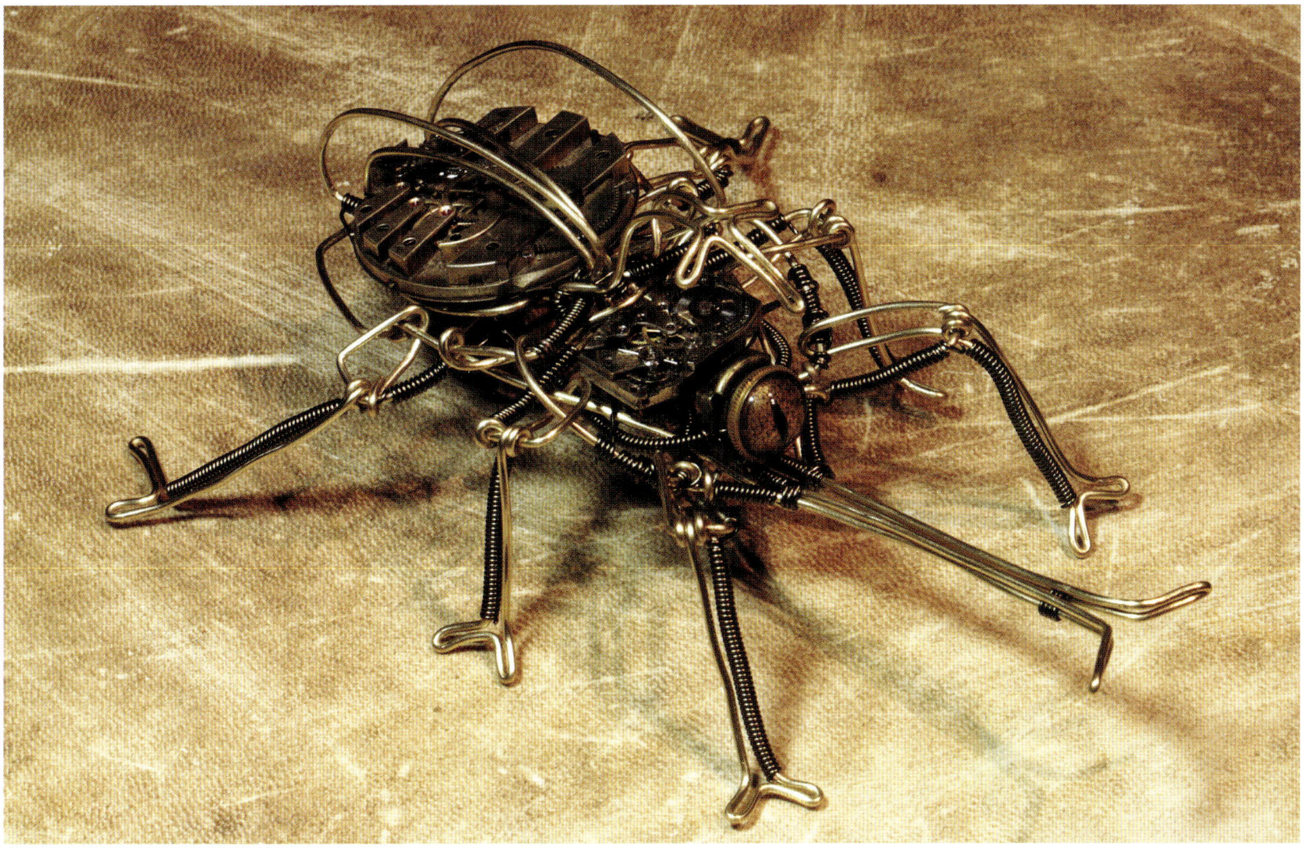

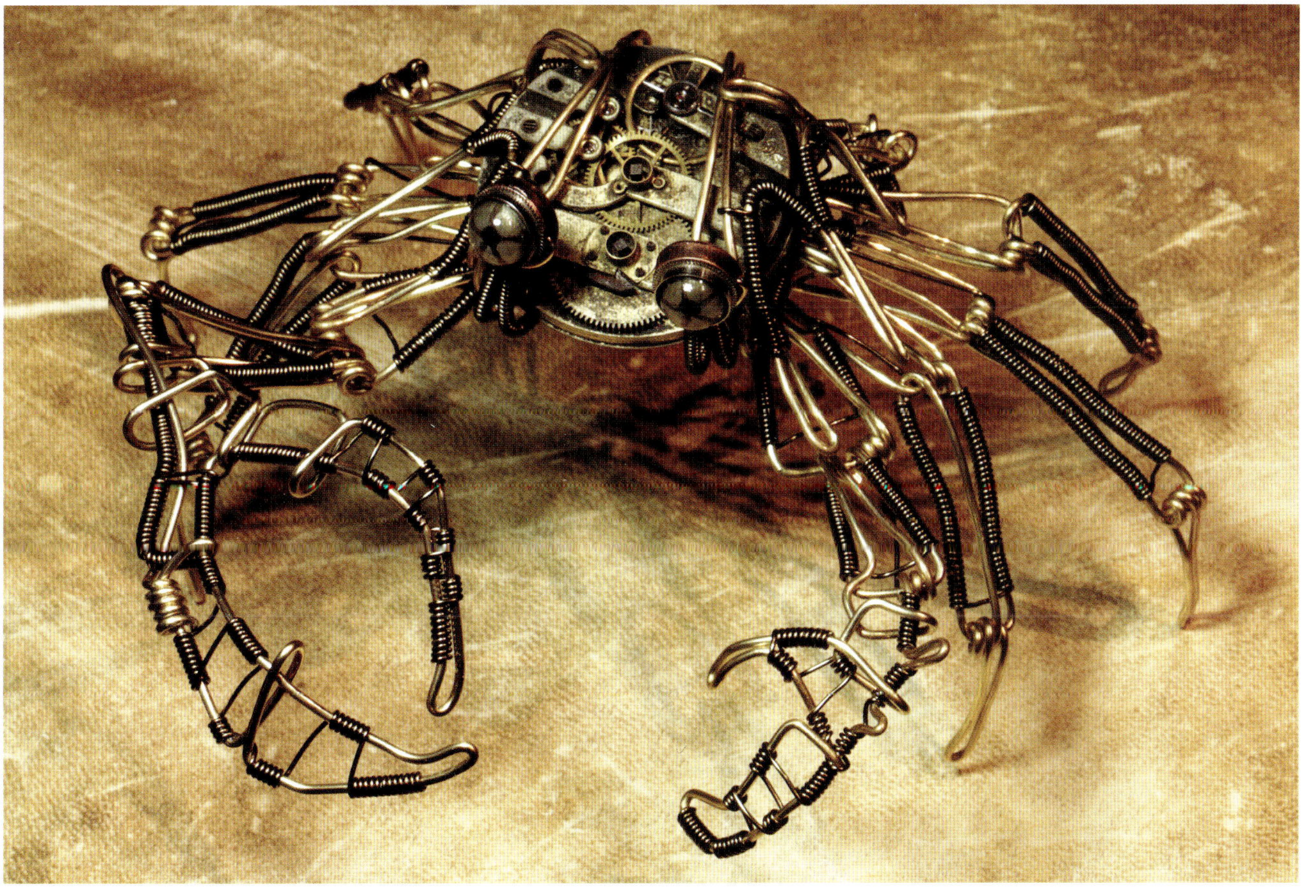

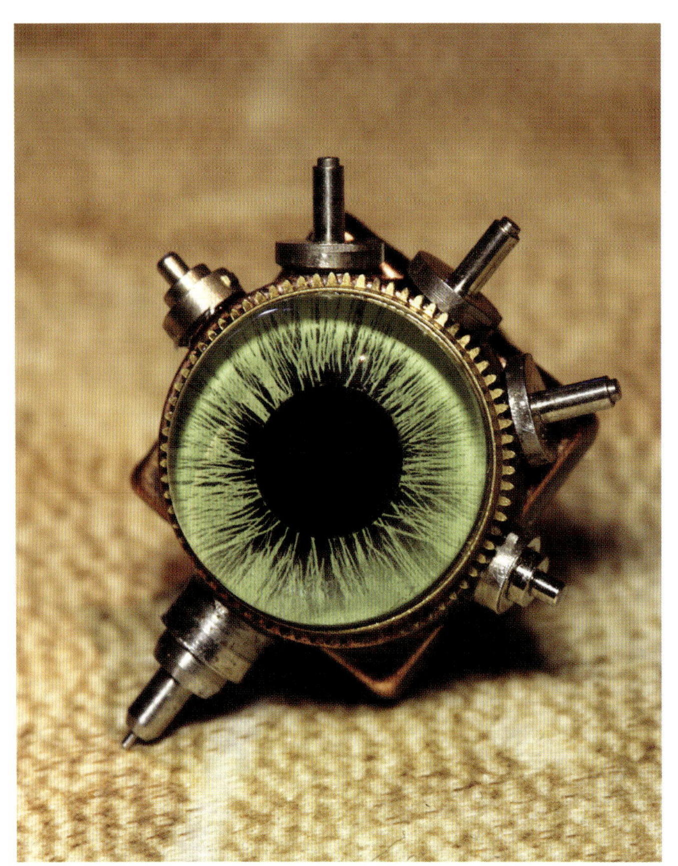

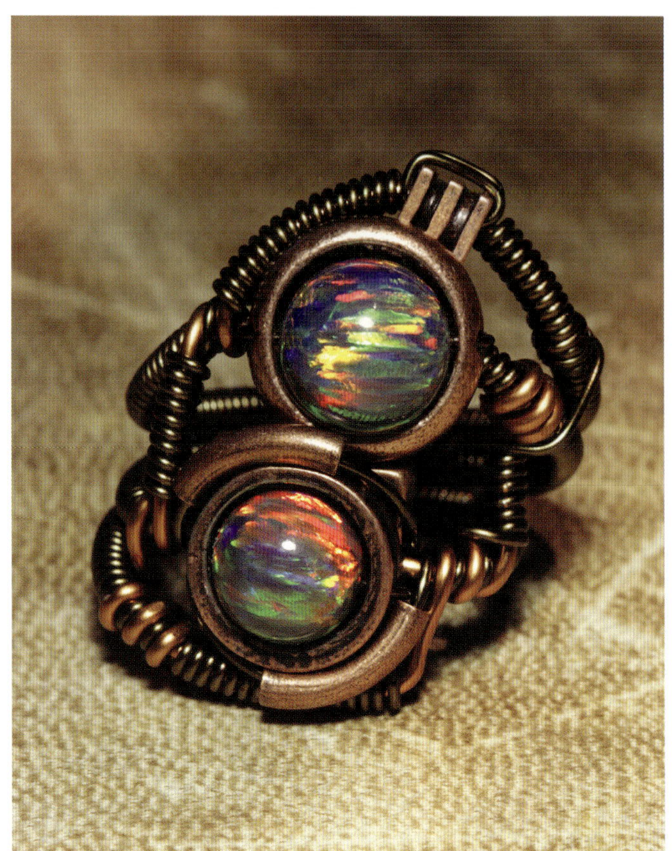

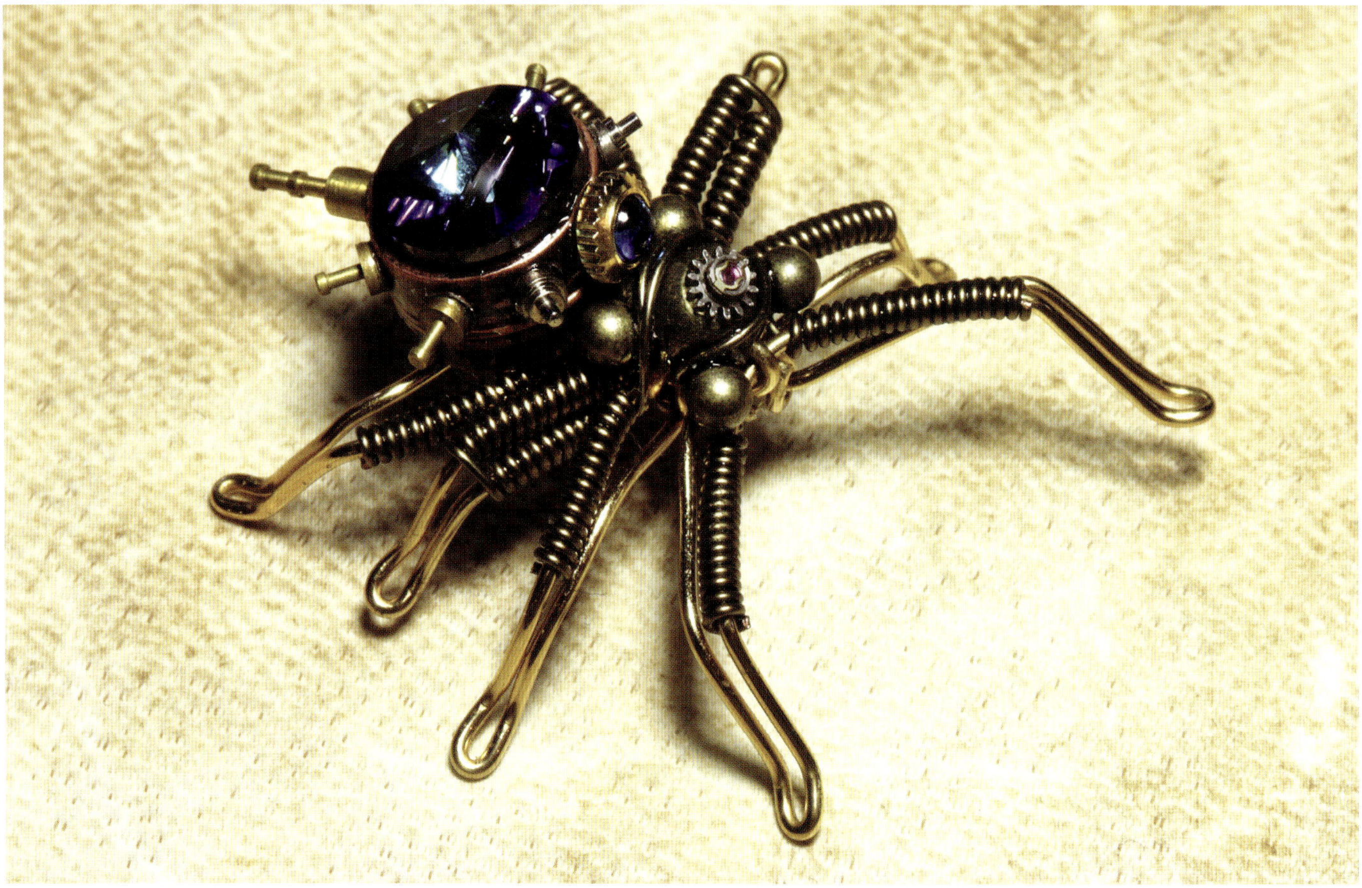

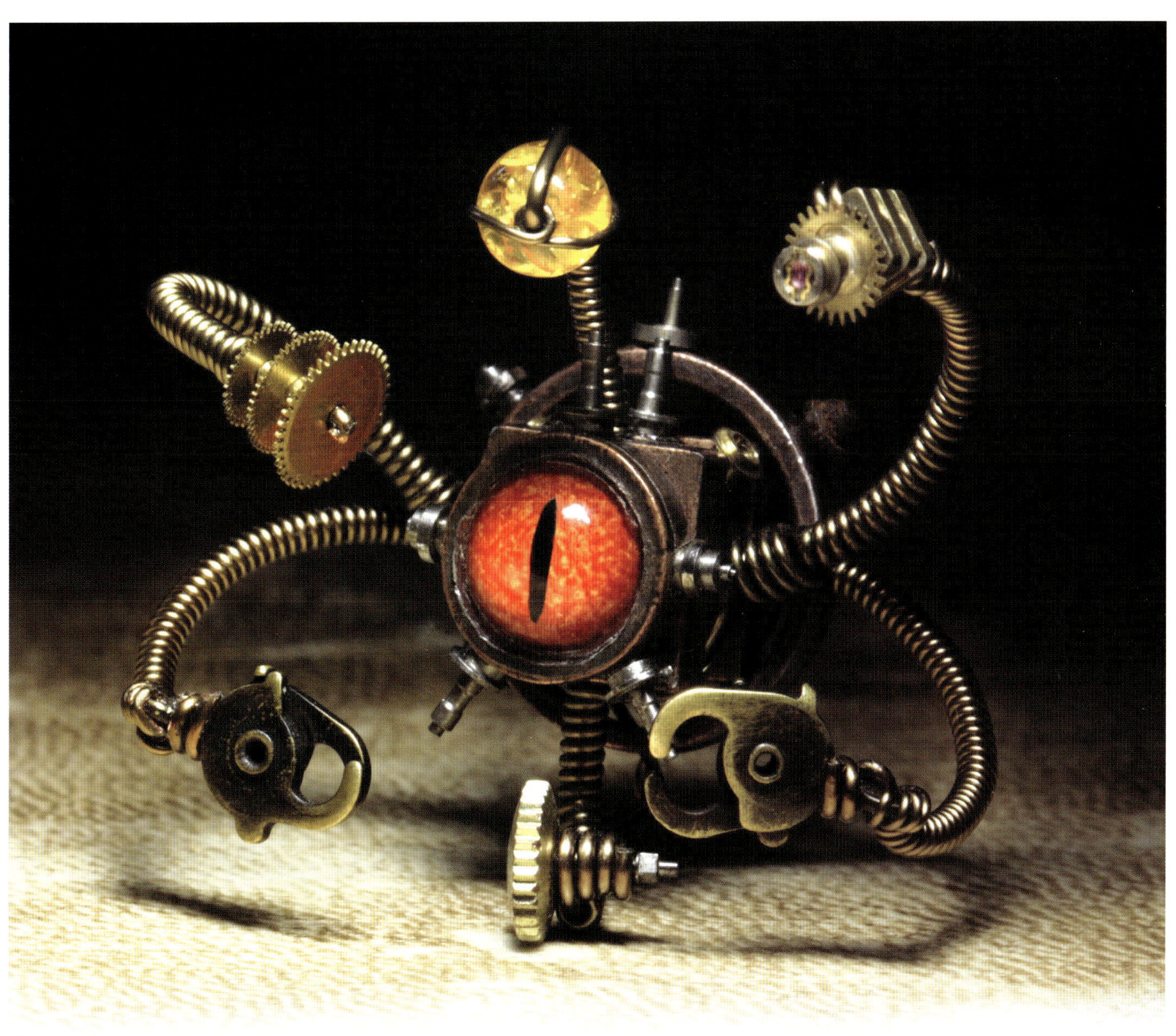

Above: *Beholder Robot*. Brass, clock gears, amber and reptile 'taxidermy' glass eye.

Left, Top Left: *Tie Tack.* Clock parts and green 'taxidermy' glass eye.

Left, Top Right: *Ring.* Brass and laboratory-manufactured opals.

Left, Bottom: *Steampunk Spider Sculpture.* Described as 'The Smallest', 1.5" x 1.4" x 0.8" (4cm x 3.5cm x 2cm). Brass, gears and glass.

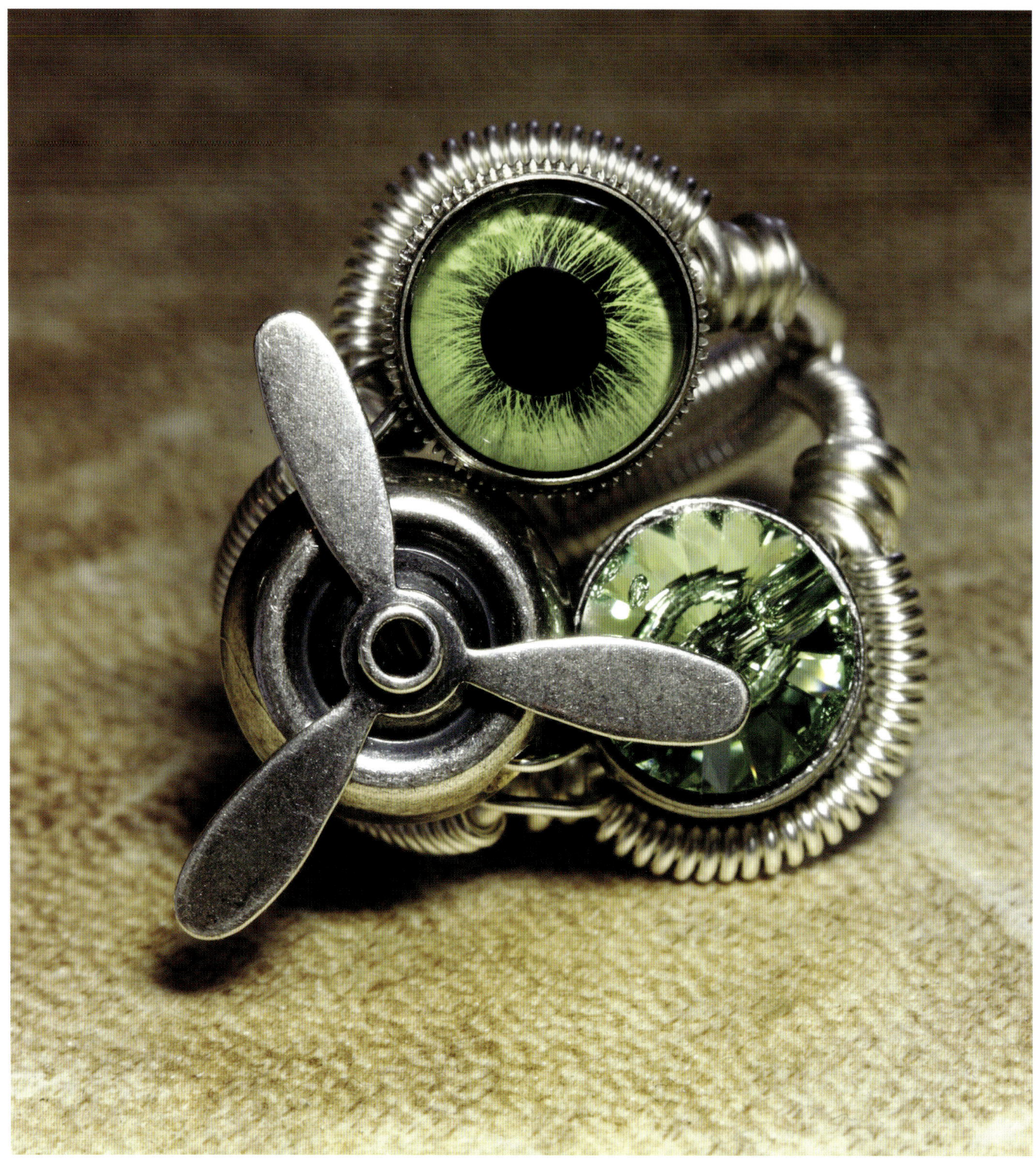

Above: *Airship Pirate Steampunk Ring.* Green 'taxidermy' glass eye, chrysolite Swarovski crystal and propeller.

Right, Top Left: *Steampunk Ring.* Brass and 3 'taxidermy' glass eyes.

Right, Top Right: *Mad Scientist Steampunk Ring.* Antique vintage watch movement, amber and dark green 'taxidermy' glass eye.

Right: *Ring.* Amber with clock parts inlay.

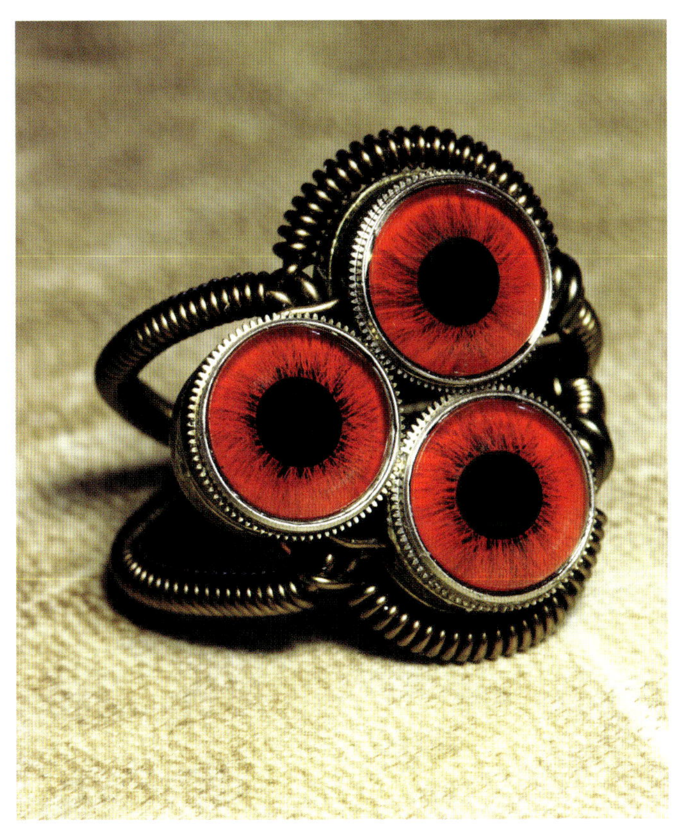

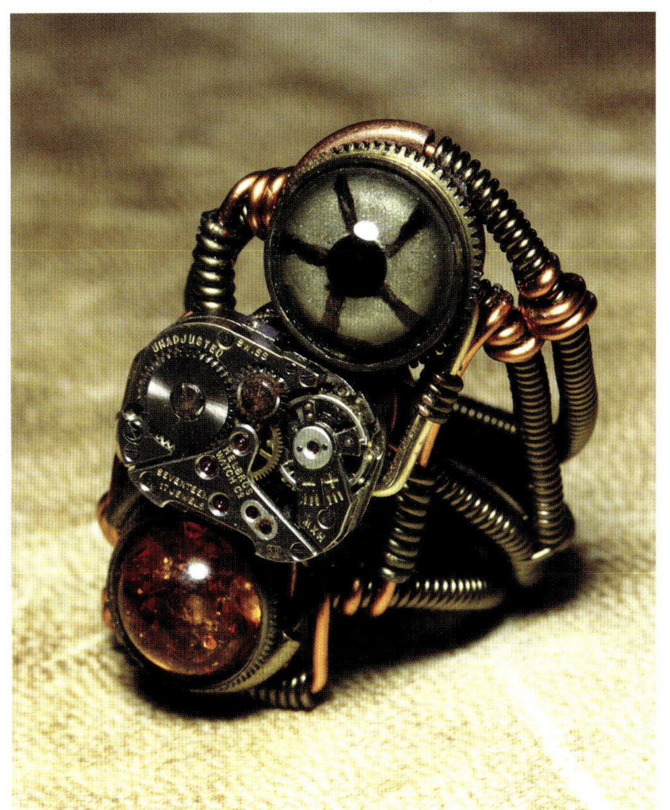
UNADJUSTED
SWISS

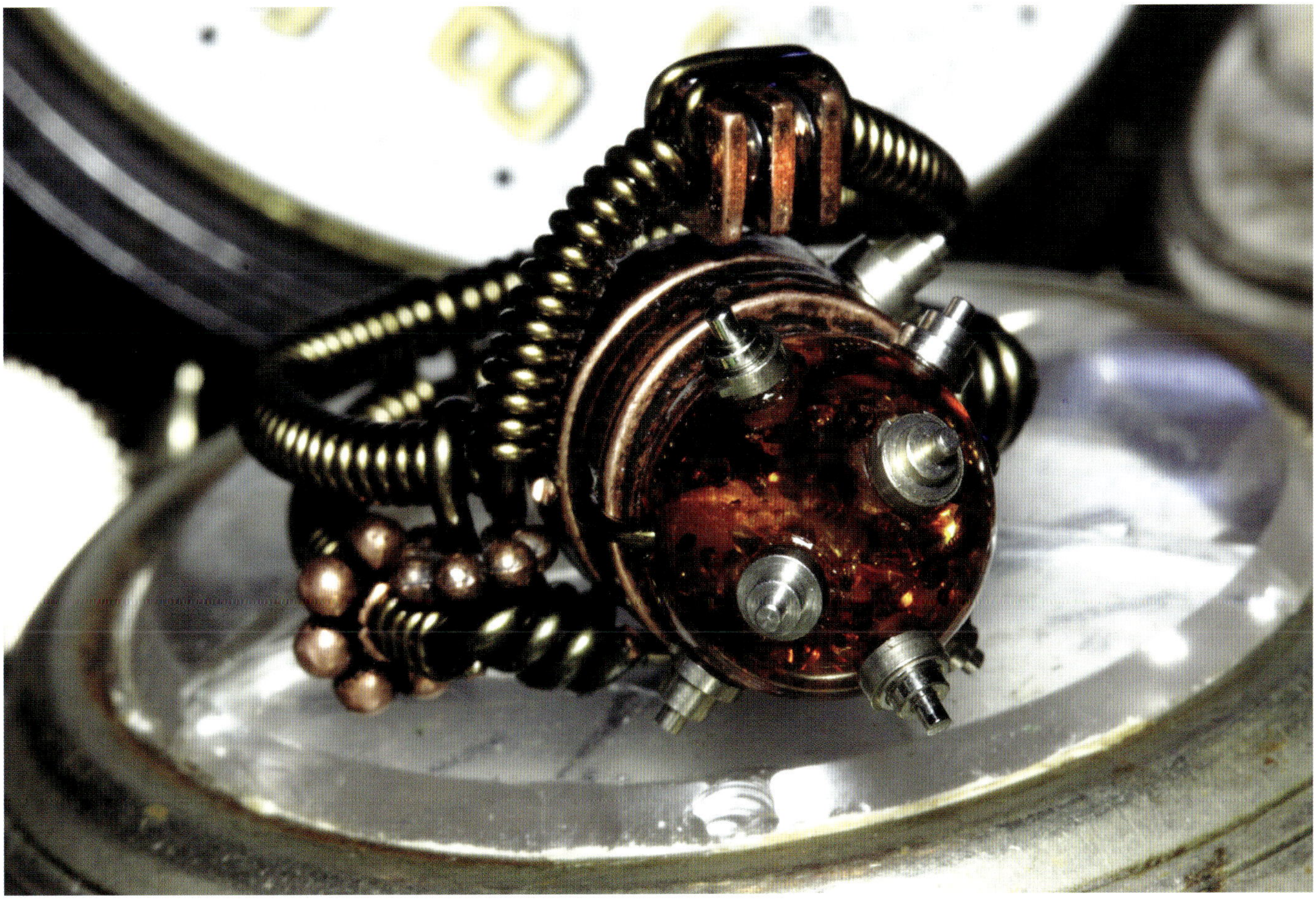

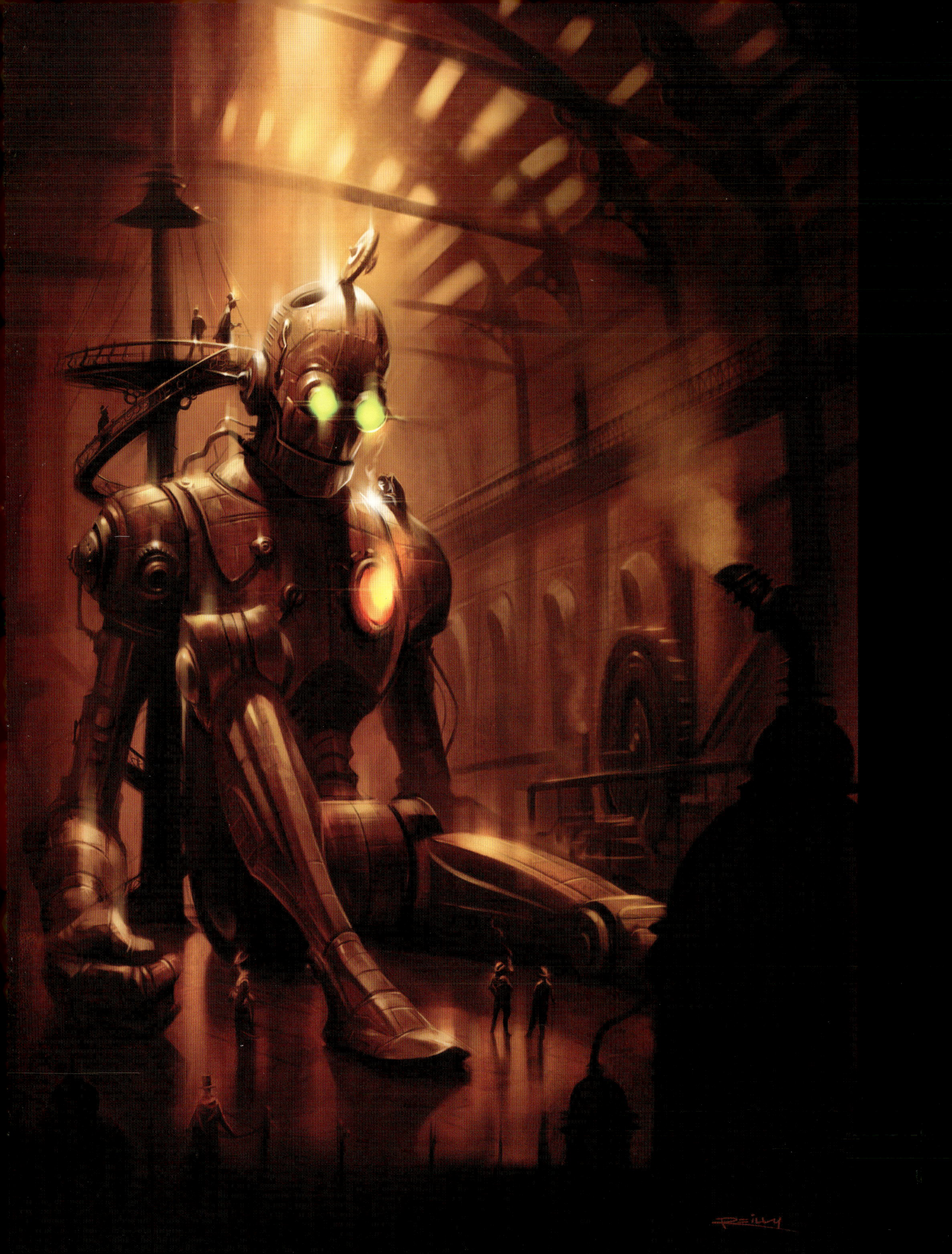
REILLY

FEATURED ARTISTS

Tom Banwell
Penn Valley, CA, USA
www.tombanwell.com

Wayne Martin Belger
Tucson, AZ, USA
www.boyofblue.com

Greg Brotherton
San Diego, CA, USA
www.brotron.com

Frank Buchwald
Berlin, Germany
www.frankbuchwald.de

Chris Conte
Bellmore, NY, USA
www.christopherconte.com

Doktor A.
Yorkshire, UK
www.spookypop.com

Eric Freitas
Royal Oak, MI, USA
www.ericfreitas.com

Dr. Grordbort
Wellington, New Zealand
www.drgrordborts.com

Stéphane Halleux
Belgium
www.stephanehalleux.com

Mike Libby
South Portland, ME, USA
www.insectlabstudio.com

Pierre Matter
Buhl, France
www.pierrematter.com

Kevin Mowrer
Barrington, RI, USA
mowrerart.blogspot.com

Kazuhiko Nakamura
Kawasaki City, Japan
www.mechanicalmirage.com

James Ng
Hong Kong, China
www.jamesngart.com

Sam Van Olffen
Montpellier, France
vanolffen.blogspot.com

Nozomu Shibata
Aichi, Japan
hp.did.ne.jp/hope-craft

Haruo Suekichi
Tokyo, Japan

Brian Poor
Los Angeles, CA, USA
www.brianpoor.com

Daniel Proulx
Montreal, Quebec, Canada
www.danielproulx.blogspot.com

ADDITIONAL ARTISTS

Felix Bennett
www.felixbennett.com

Jeff de Boer
www.jeffdeboer.com

Michael Dashow
www.michaeldashow.com

Brian Despain
www.despainart.com

Guillaume Dubois
www.duboisguillaume.be

Jason Edmiston
www.jasonedmiston.com

Alastair Fell
www.darkrising.co.uk

Paul Guinan
www.bigredhair.com

Marcin Jakubowski
www.balloontree.com

Thomas Kuebler
www.tskuebler.com

Lex Machina
www.lexmachinaphoto.com

Steve Mitchell
www. 57design.co.uk

Richard 'Doc' Nagy
www.datamancer.net

Kate O'Brien
www.kateobriencreative.com

Patrick Reilly
preilly.deviantart.com

Stephen Rothwell
www.darkhousequarter.com

Paul St George
www.paulstgeorge.com

Dennis 'DXTR' Schuster
www.behance.net/dxtrs

Michael Smolyanov
www.solifdesign.blogspot.com

Chad Ward
www.digitalapocalypse.com

Weyers and Borms
www.weyersborms.com

ADDITIONAL PHOTO CREDITS

p.7 Collection Edouard Crevel; p.8 Look and Learn; p.15 Edwin P. Riven Collection; p.17 Getty Images; p.19 Edwin P. Riven Collection; p.20 Science Museum, London; p.21 courtesy of Henry Havelock Esq. ; p.25 Look and Learn; p.29 (top) Peter Harrington Rare Books, Chelsea, London (www.perterharrington.co.uk); p.29 (bottom) Edwin P. Riven Collection; p.34 Getty Images; p37 3D Films/ SBS/ Film Vic/ AFC; p.38 istockphoto; p48 Artichoke Trust (www.artichoke.uk.com); p.52-55 Topher Adam Photography (topheradam.com), models: Kellen Hart and Matthew Molcillo.

ACKNOWLEDGEMENTS

Thanks to Harry Strongman, Julienne Davis, Sannah Wheatley, Julia Cornborough, David Lubich and Kevin Mowrer for all their help with the writing of this book.
Jay Strongman

In addition to all the brilliant artists featured in this book, Korero would particularly like to thank:

Serena Castello-Cortes, Rick Mayston at Getty Images, Laura at Peter Harrington, Nicky Webb at Artichoke, Laurence Heyworth at Look and Learn and Alan Moore, Kevin O'Neill and Mike Mignola.

Left: Patrick Reilly, *Steampunk*, 2007. 10" x 14" (25.4cm x 35.6 cm). Digital artwork.

Overleaf: Brian Despain, *A Vexing Quiet*. 16" x 20" (40.6 cm x 50.8 cm). Oil on wood.

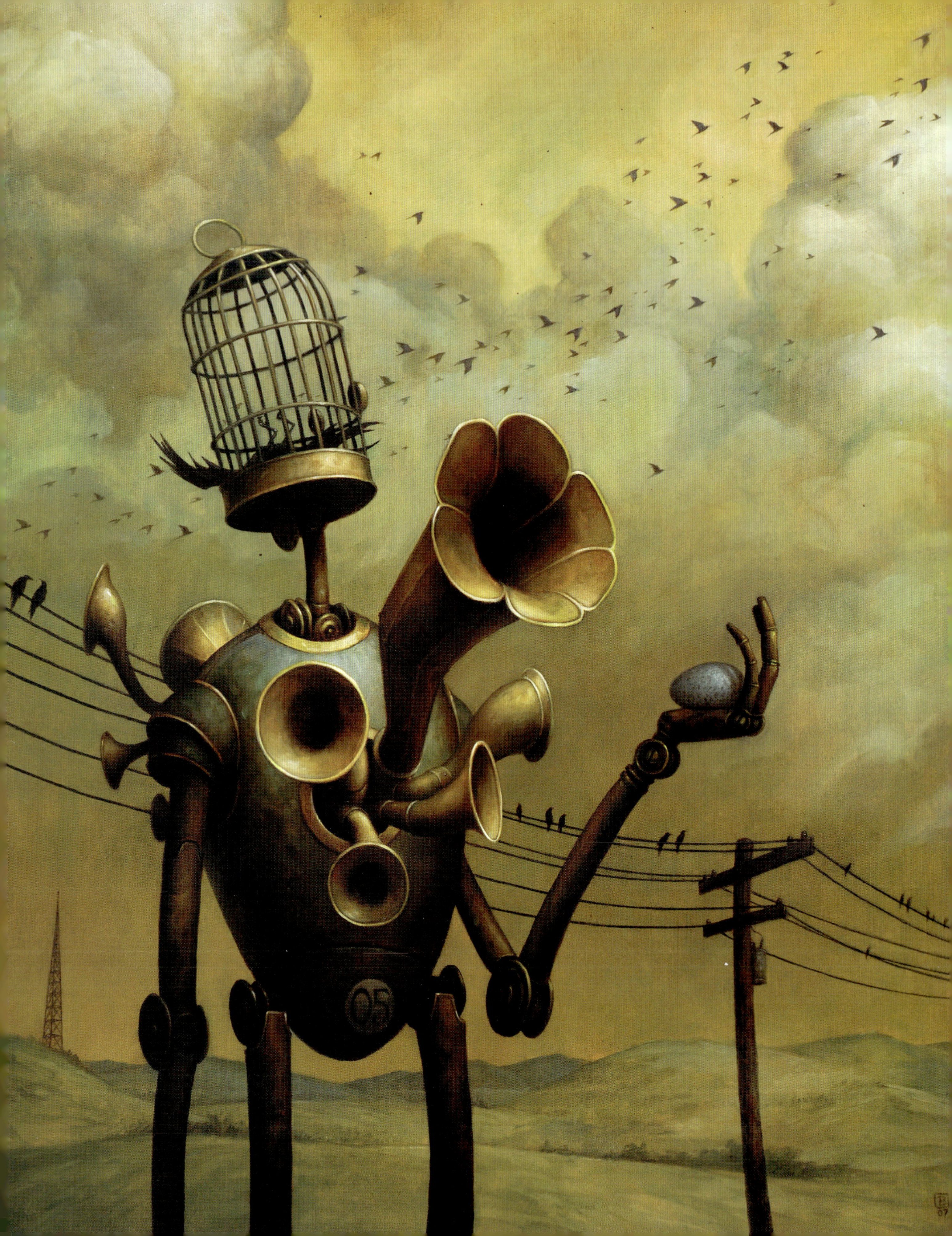
05

ookshop
ing town lights
pop. as laid
2 vols. Thin
6d.
RARY. Shore
6d.
AND MEDI-
FIC LINES.
B.C.) Paper.
eady Jan. 15.
Siemens and
od.
OF THE
upplementary
S IN THE
parative Den-
A DIRIGI-
vised. 5s. 9d.
RACING IN
2s. 6d.
THE AIR-
LIFT AND
grams, 8s. 6d.
SHIFTING
BLES. 8s. 6d.
S OF THE
TURES AT
s.
HOW TO
CONDARY
ERSTORMS.
ENTS AND
5s. 6d.
AND THE
ESORTS OF
MO. 8s. 6d.
AND FUL-
TS. 7s. 6d.
BACTERI-
ATED STAR
attachment,
of heavens,
mps for bin-
2. 2. 0. (In-
With A.B.O.
ALAYAS, 5s.
RAS, 5s.
KIES, 5s.
LS, 5s.
cloth, with
IN MOUN-
READING

MY
o.
mps
ies.
Wells
ONIIC.
ies, Kent

ER
ter
ent
ve!"

ELECTROMECHANICAL

MAN-SERVANT REPLACEMENT

Portable, pulsating and compact with three applicators, very useful and satisfactory for home service. Whirring noise induces a sudden attack of fright in the enemies of Empire. An aid that every women appreciates.

Write today. Accessories and spares available.

Shipping weight about 2 pounds.
Doktor Oppenheimer, Harley Street, London.

No. 5769 £6

AEROPLANE AND DIRIGIBLE GOODS

Remember

We shall always be pleased to see you.

We build and test and guarantee our dirigibles for all purposes. They go up when you please and they do not come down till you please.

You can please yourself, but—you might as well choose a dirigible.

STANDARD DIRIGIBLE CONSTRUCTION CO.
Milwall *and* Buenos Ayres

Remember

Planes are swift—so is Death
Planes are cheap—so is Life

Why does the 'plane builder insist on the safety of his machines?

Methinks the gentleman protests too much.

The Standard Dig Construction Company do not build kites.

They build, equip and guarantee dirigibles.

Standard Dig Construction Co.
Millwall *and* Buenos Ayres

MISCELLANEOUS

A medley of music hall mayhem by
Mr. J. Lydon & his Steam Pistols Orchestra.

Available on Edison tune tubes.
Available in-store at His Master's Voice.

Women's airship fashions by
MADAME JULIENNE
of Paris

Be sartorially correct on those long haul journeys to the outer islands.

31 Rue Cambon, Paris

Remember!

¶ It is now nearly a century since the Plane was to supersede the Dirigible for all purposes.

¶ TO-DAY *none* of the Planet's freight is carried *on plane.*

¶ Less than two per cent. of the Planet's passengers are carried *on plane.*

We design, equip and guarantee Dirigibles for all purposes.

Standard Dig Construction Company
MILLWALL and BUENOS AYRES

SAFETY WEAR FOR AERONAUTS

Flickers! Flickers! Flickers!

High Level Flickers

"He that is down need fear no fall"
Fear not! You will fall lightly as down!

¶ Hansen's air-kits are down in all respects. Tremendous reductions in prices previous to winter stocking. Pure para kit with cellulose seat and shoulder-pads, weighted to balance. Unequalled for all drop-work.

Our trebly resilient heavy kit is the *ne plus ultra* of comfort and safety.

Gas-buoyed, waterproof, hail-proof, non-conducting Flickers with pipe and nozzle fitting all types of generator. Graduated tap on left hip.

Hansen's Flickers Lead the Aerial Flight
197 Oxford Street

The new weighted Flicker with tweed or cheviot surface cannot be distinguished from the ordinary suit till inflated.

Flickers! Flickers! Flickers!

CUTHBERTS

PURVEYOR'S OF THE FINEST RAY-GUNS.

Bring manly wholesome joy to your boy's heart with the best ray gun in the world. Numerous children's sizes available. Tough but Lightweight construction. Lock to stun to avoid accidentally killing something. Gives a boy an air of manliness and power, makes him alert, self-confident and resolute.

Sold by Hardware and Sporting Goods Dealers across the Empire. Ask for our free booklet. Not suitable for girls.

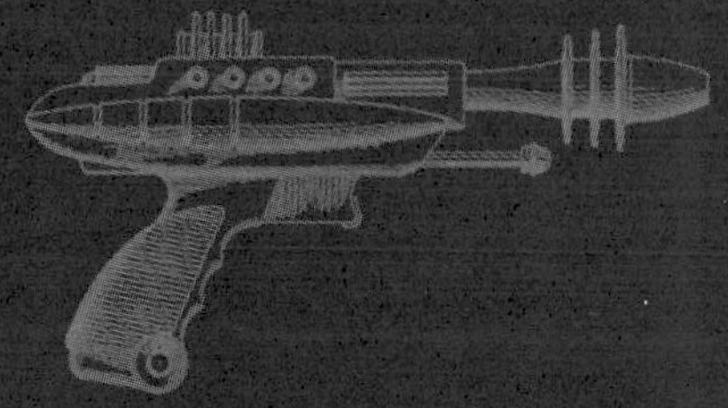

Don de Castell y Cortez,
Salehurst Road, Mafeking
Largest Ray Gun Factory in the known World.

BAT-B

Flint & Man

Southampton

FOR

at the end of Season th

GRISELDA, 65 knt., 42 ft.,
under-rake rudder.
MABELLE, 50 knt., 40 f
Douglas' lock-steering g
IVEMONA, 50 knt., 35 ft.
accelerator), Miller keel

The above are well
Coast as sound, wholeso
with ample cruising acc
carries spare set of H
can be lifted three foot
with ballast-tank swun
not lift clear of water, a
for beginners.
Also, by private trea
(76 winning flags) 13
Davidson double under
season and unstrained.
motor, Radium relays
Bronze breakwater forv
forced forefoot and entr
keel. Triple set of Hofr
mum lifting surface of 5
Tarpon has been lifte
for two miles between to
Our Autumn List of
ready on the 9th January

ACCESSORIES

CHRIST

Hooded Binnacles
recording change of lev

All heights from 50 to
With Aerial Board of C
Foot and Hand Foghor
any club note; with a
from motor
Wireless installations sy
requirements, in nea
hundred mile range

Grapnels, mushroo
winches, hawsers, snap
for lawn, city, and publ
Detachable under-car
Keeled under-cars for
ing-gear, turning car in
the wrist. Invaluable
Head, side, and ridin
20 A.B.C. Standard,
colours and tones of t
A selection of twenty
International night-signa